WITHDRAWN

THE MUNDA
OF CENTRAL INDIA

THE MUNDA
OF CENTRAL INDIA
An Account of their
Social Organization

ROBERT   PARKIN

DELHI
OXFORD UNIVERSITY PRESS
Bombay   Calcutta   Madras
1992

Oxford University Press, Walton Street, Oxford OX2 6DP
New York Toronto
Delhi Bombay Calcutta Madras Karachi
Kuala Lumpur Singapore Hong Kong Tokyo
Nairobi Dar es Salaam
Melbourne Auckland
and associates in
Berlin Ibadan

SBN 0 19 563029 7

Typeset at Bookshelf, New Delhi 110 003
Printed at Rekha Printers Pvt. Ltd., New Delhi 110 020
and Published by S.K. Mookerjee, Oxford University Press
YMCA Library Building, Jai Singh Road, New Delhi 110 001

Contents

Tables

Figures

Preface

The present work is essentially an account of Munda social organization, the first comparative effort of its kind directed specifically at the speakers of this group of related languages, who are located mostly in the eastern areas of peninsular India. This does not mean that it attempts to argue in favour of any sort of linguistic determinism in cultural matters—quite the contrary, for it is clear that the Munda share many if not most of their values with neighbouring low-status groups who speak Indic or Dravidian languages instead. Rather, it is intended as a contribution to thinking on the problem of the relationship between caste and tribe, or better, perhaps, high- and low-status groups in the sub-continent. The controversy here has surrounded the feasibility and desirability of distinguishing such populations from one another rather than subsuming them all under a model of Indian cultural and sociological unity. While no decisive resolution of this controversy is likely to emerge in the forseeable future—and certainly none is offered here—it may help to lay some of the foundations of future work on the question by offering an account of one particular group of populations who have a degree of separate identity through language, if not in other respects, and who include both 'tribes' and 'low castes', to use the standard shorthand definitions. One further justification for focussing particularly on the Munda at the present time is the fact that the Dravidian field has been covered recently by Thomas Trautmann (*Dravidian Kinship*, Cambridge University Press 1981). This the present work may supplement to some degree, for Trautmann found the lack of any consolidated account of Munda kinship a definite handicap when it came to fixing the parameters of his topic. As far as possible the data are left to speak for themselves, and it is mainly in the first and last chapters that the wider arguments are concentrated.

Although much of the research on which the present book is based was originally undertaken in pursuance of a doctoral degree, it excludes the conventional fieldwork, which I was unable to carry out for medical reasons. Instead, it draws on the already published work on the Munda, which, although widely differing in quality, is sufficiently comprehensive to allow a clear idea of the nature of

Munda social organization to emerge (for the most part, it considers only work published during this century). It represents only a part of my doctoral thesis (Oxford, 1984), which was on the kinship of all Austroasiatic speakers (i.e., of the larger language family of which the Munda are just one branch), and at this remote juncture can best be described as a largely forlorn attempt to test the idea of the language family as a unit of sociological comparison. The relevant parts have been almost entirely rethought and rewritten, and an effort made to incorporate research published subsequently.

By way of acknowledgement, I would like to thank first and foremost Dr N.J. Allen, my doctoral supervisor at Oxford, who first inspired my interest in the problems and possibilities posed by the Munda, and allowed and encouraged my own ideas to develop without neglecting to curb my less sustainable propositions; in preparing this work I have been ever mindful of his dictum that 'no description exhausts reality' (1976: 582). I also wish to thank the SSRC (now ESRC) of the United Kingdom for funding the initial research and writing of the thesis in which the present book originated; Prof. Dr Georg Pfeffer, of the Institut für Ethnologie, Freie Universität Berlin, and the Deutscher Akademischer Austauschdienst, for granting me the finance and facilities to produce the final draft and revision of the text; the Director of the Royal Anthropological Institute, London, for permission to reproduce, as Chapter 7, a revised version of an article that originally appeared in *Man*, Vol. 20 (Parkin 1985); the University of Hawaii Press, for permission to reproduce in Chapter 2 and Appendix I material that first appeared in my *Guide to Austroasiatic-speakers and their Languages*; and a small but dedicated group of students in Berlin who, always patiently and sometimes, I hope, with interest, followed the lectures I gave based on that draft and made many valuable points. The following were kind enough to help me with some advice and additional information relating to particular parts of the book: Claudia Gross, Aasha Mundlay, Georg Pfeffer, Hilary Standing, Piers Vitebsky and Norman Zide. Lukas Werth helped with the transfer of the typescript on to disc. Naturally, the willing cooperation of these various individuals and institutions does not make them at all responsible for the contents of the present work.

The translations of passages from works in French are mine; the sole translation from German was kindly checked for me by

Claudia Gross. Kin terms have been abbreviated in many parts of this book (especially Chapters 7, 8 and 9), as follows:

P	parent	G	sibling	C	child	E	spouse
F	father	B	brother	S	son	H	husband
M	mother	Z	sister	D	daughter	W	wife
ms	man-speaking	ws	woman-speaking	ss	same-sex	os	opposite-sex
e	elder	y	younger				

These are also used in combination, e.g., PGC, MBD; the last six refer to the whole formula when in final position, e.g., MBDms.

R.J.P.
Berlin, May 1990.

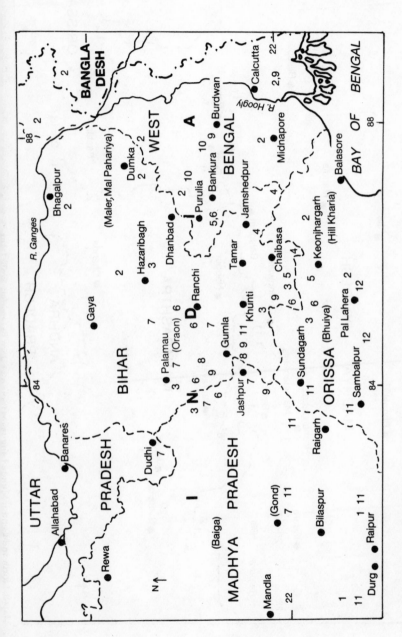

Map A: North and Central Munda Languages (Core Area). Scale 1:4m.

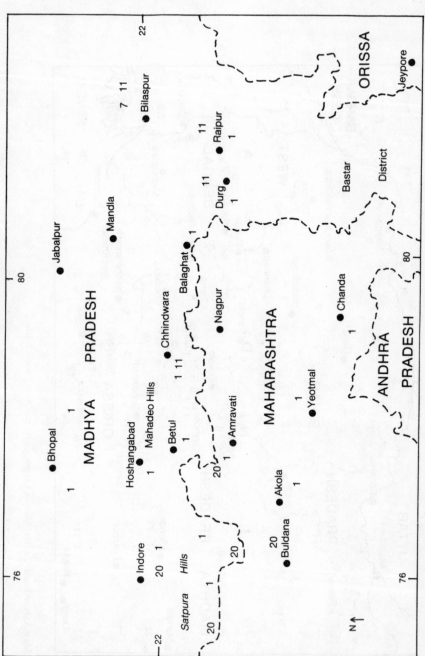

Map B: North and Central Munda Languages (Southwestern Extension) Scale 1:4m

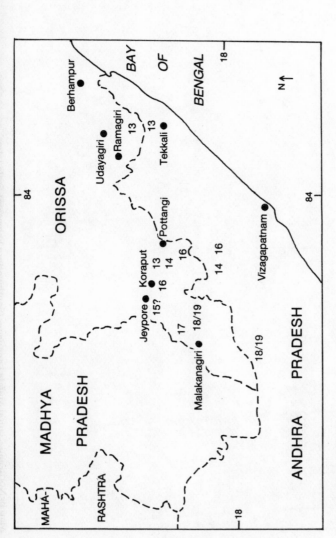

Map C: Koraput Munda Languages. Scale 1:4m.

The following conventions are used on the maps. Lower-case place names denote towns and cities, and occasionally other geographical features. Upper-case names denote states and sea areas. Munda groups are indicated by their entry numbers in Chapter 2. Numbers within chevrons denote lines of latitude and longitude. Lower-case names in parentheses denote major neighbouring non-Munda tribes.

Chapter One
Introduction

1.1 Introducing the Munda

An overwhelming proportion of the population of India speak an Indo-European or Dravidian language, but this by no means exhausts the inventory of languages spoken within the territory of the modern republic. Most of the remainder are either Tibeto-Burman, spoken in the north-east and also further west, in the Himalayan foothills; or Austroasiatic, comprising in India Khasi in Meghalaya and Nicobarese in the Nicobar Islands, as well as the Munda.[1] The present book will concentrate on the Munda speakers, who consist of around six million individuals divided into a number of separate ethnic groups, of which one alone (the Santal) accounts for two-thirds of the total. These populations are located on the Chotanagpur Plateau and its extensions (southern Bihar, northern Orissa, eastern Madhya Pradesh and western Bengal), with others centred on the Koraput district of southern Orissa and the Nimar district of western Madhya Pradesh. Thus in their main area of concentration they cover nearly 1000 km of territory (between Jeypore in Koraput and Dumka in Santal Parganas), though they are very much interspersed with castes and tribes speaking Indo-European and Dravidian languages. Less than one per cent of the population of the Republic of India, they form the most westerly branch of Austroasiatic, whose other languages are found throughout continental Southeast Asia (though also much interspersed with other language groups). Most of the Munda would be regarded conventionally as tribes, though some Munda-speaking groups can be considered low castes.

There are between ten and nineteen Munda languages, depending mainly on whether certain of them are classed as dialects or separate languages. However, this does not affect the discrimination of ethnic groups, of which at least seventeen and possibly nineteen can be identified, and I shall follow the broader version. A complete list of languages and/or dialects is given in Chapter 2, together with details of the ethnic groups that speak them. The list is based in the first instance on those identified by Professor

Norman Zide and his colleagues, who have done a great deal of work on these languages in the last three decades. The main criterion for including particular groups in the present book is their possession of one of these languages; speakers of languages that are not Munda—and that includes Khasi and Nicobarese, despite their relationship with Munda through Austroasiatic—are therefore excluded, as are a number of doubtful cases, also dealt with in Chapter 2.

1.2 The Munda and Scholarship

Like the other major language families present in India (Indo-European, Dravidian, Tibeto-Burman), Munda has affiliations with languages spoken outside the Republic.[2] By the end of the nineteenth century it had become accepted that the Munda languages were distinct both from Dravidian and from any Australian languages.[3] Following preliminary suggestions by E. Kuhn, Konow, Logan, Phayre, etc., the Austrian scholar Pater Wilhelm Schmidt attempted to prove that Munda was connected with the Mon-Khmer languages of Southeast Asia, a grouping he called Austroasiatic (AA) (1906). His work has come to be accepted, thanks largely to more recent studies by Pinnow,[4] but it was for long a matter of controversy.[5] Many found fault with Schmidt's methods, and his internal classification of AA languages has been revised a number of times.[6] A number of alternative connections were proposed in the 1920s and 1930s, most of which were dismissed almost as soon as they were published, if not quietly ignored. These include suggestions of links between Munda and Basque (Edmonston Scott 1920), certain Bantu languages (chiefly on the basis of numerals, Trombetti 1928), Turkish (Koşay 1939), Burushaski (Barbour 1921) and Finno-Ugrian and/or Maori and/or Hungarian, the latter the creation of Wilhelm von Hevesy (e.g. 1930), a Hungarian who also wrote under the pseudonym of F.A. Uxbond (Uxbond 1928; see Schmidt 1935). This theory was widely discussed in the 1930s and early 1940s, for Hevesy had his supporters as well as his detractors, but today it is just another curiosity. There have also been somewhat more plausible attempts, reaching back more than a century, to link Munda with the so-called 'pronominalized' Tibeto-Burman languages of the Himalayas.[7] Some, like Maspero, though sceptical, were at any rate prepared to accept borrowing as an explanation—the two areas are not very remote from one another, after all.[8] But a number of the shared features are found more widely than just these language groups, and the current view is that the explanation lies solely in independent development.[9]

Thus Schmidt's Austroasiatic theory has survived all its rivals and, with modifications, is now established fact, being accepted by most if not quite all the scholars working on these particular languages at the present day, whether Munda or Mon-Khmer. However, Schmidt's further attempt to link AA with Austronesian in an Austric super-family is still treated with scepticism, even though its only serious challenger, Benedict's Austro-Thai theory, which attempts to link Austronesian with Thai instead of AA, has fared little better.[10]

Despite the controversies between Hevesy and Schmidt, the fact that the linguistic evidence suggested an easterly connection for the Munda was quickly exploited to try to show that the Munda themselves had come from that direction. Other sorts of evidence were brought in to support this theory, such as the distribution of youth dormitories, megaliths, swidden cultivation and a particular type of axe-head (the 'shouldered celt').[11] But anthropology has become increasingly sceptical of the models that have resulted from such evidence, in which particular cultures are seen as the result of whole sub-continents being peopled by vast waves of migration from elsewhere. Most of this evidence, after all, concerns items of material culture and economic methods, exceedingly easy to transfer between essentially alien cultures and therefore quite unreliable on their own as a means of identifying and distinguishing particular cultures from one another.

This is no less true of language, even though transfers are likely to be less sudden and to take longer to effect. While the linguistic evidence does point to a connection of some sort with, ultimately, southern China—the favourite location for an Austroasiatic 'homeland'—it is not clear how this can affect the Munda specifically. The period in which any concentration of Austroasiatic speakers was present in this 'homeland' must have been one of much greater linguistic unity than obtains today and one long before the Munda languages became identifiable as a group separate from their AA parent—and this takes us back a very long time. So diverse are the Munda languages themselves that their separation from one another has been placed at 2,500 BP at the latest (Zide and Zide forthcoming), and clearly their separation as a group from Proto-AA must have taken place earlier still. The most we can say is that speakers of languages ancestral to Munda were probably once located to the east of where the latter are now to be found (i.e. in north-east India or perhaps some part of Southeast Asia), and that very probably those that entered peninsular India spoke languages that already constituted a distinct group within AA, whether or not they could be further distinguished from one another.

Thus although the evidence for a linguistic connection between Munda and other AA is now considered incontrovertible, the link is still a very remote one. Typologically, Munda and Mon-Khmer, the two main branches of AA, oppose one another in almost every respect (Donegan and Stampe 1983), the evidence for their connection resting much more on regular phonetic and lexical correspondences than on any similarities in morphology, grammar or syntax. This means that Austroasiatic has greater linguistic diversity than most other Asian language families. In matters of culture and social organization there is not even this degree of connection (Parkin 1984), and we can also be sure that no link is normally recognized by the people themselves. Even the shortest distance between Munda and Mon-Khmer speakers is nearly 500 km (i.e. between Dumka in Santal Parganas and Shillong in Meghalaya, where the Khasi are found), and for most groups it is much greater. Any non-linguistic parallels between these two groups are probably due to similar structural entailments, or similarities brought about by the centuries of cultural influence that Indian civilization has exercised over Southeast Asia as well as in the subcontinent itself. Indeed, many features are also shared by non-AA speakers in these regions, and they cannot be seen as a product of any AA 'survivals'.

The alternative is to postulate a western origin for the Munda, which was Schmidt's own preference, because of the large number of Sanskrit words in Munda (according to him, the Mon-Khmer speakers migrated out of India in an easterly direction). This fits in with the presence of one group, the Korku, far to the west, in Nimar, and isolated from other Munda speakers, and with the Munda's own traditions which tell of their coming from Rohtasgarh and Azamgarh, either side of the Uttar Pradesh-Bihar border, and even from the Punjab.[12] Of course, oral traditions can express a multitude of truths, and there is no guarantee that they correspond to any historical reality. Nonetheless, other scholarship has also given credence to a western origin,[13] much of it depending on references in the Vedas and other early Sanskritic texts to groups with names similar to the Munda (e.g. Kaurava for Korwa, Asura for Asur, Koli for Kol) and to similar comparisons between present-day Munda ethnonyms and place names. Such theories rely on greater continuity than it is possible to prove, and they also fail to take into account the possibilities of coincidence and linguistic convergence. Still, it is possible to reconcile these rival theories, especially given the long period of time that the Munda have been in India. Even if their original entry was from the east, as seems most likely, they may have migrated quite far to the west at first, only to be pushed back and/or assimilated by later invaders, who were perhaps Dravidian as much as Indo-European. And, in being more recent and associated with groups with whom they continue to be in contact, it is these events rather than those associated with their original entry into India that are most likely to have persisted in their oral traditions.

At all events, 'Austroasiatic' is a linguistic classification only, not in any meaningful sense a cultural or sociological, much less a racial one. Yet at one time it was invoked as evidence that the Munda speakers were the most 'primitive' stratum of population in the subcontinent, and even its aborigines. And this in its turn promoted another development: it bolstered the feeling that those groups which had conventionally come to be called 'tribes' could and should be distinguished as such, historically as well as culturally, from the castes that made up the bulk of the population.

To a large extent this distinction was and is a purely administrative one, created by the British in their census reports and perpetuated since by the government of the republic. With it have come certain legal and social benefits for those classed as 'tribes', and this has clearly reacted on the identity of several ethnic groups, as well as ensuring the survival of the term as an administrative and scholarly one in India itself. Many early scholars were influenced by this definition, especially since many were themselves also administrators.

As with the theory of migration, this distinction depended at first mainly on economic and material evidence, of exactly the same kind and with exactly the same limitations, though later other factors were called upon, such as the absence of specialist occupations among the tribes, their relatively greater dependence on agriculture, their readiness to consume meat and alcohol, and the relative absence of 'Hinduism'. Yet neither singly nor in combination can any of these be seen as a marker of tribal identity, partly because none of them are universally found among those groups that most ethnographers would consider to be tribals, partly because none of them can be clearly linked to any particular social and cultural circumstances of the sort that are of most significance in post-Durkheimian anthropology. Moreover, many of these traits can also be found in the world of caste as well as among tribes: there are many purely agricultural castes, for example, and the Rajputs provide as example of a Kshatriya caste well known for their consumption of meat and alcohol. Similarly, the 'non-Hindu' nature of tribal religion is quite problematic, even if Hinduism itself were sufficiently well defined: cross-influence is a perpetual process, and it is rarely clear just where a particular aspect of ritual or cosmology may have originated.

The differences between caste and tribe begin to disappear even more rapidly when we examine the use of cultural symbols to express distance and hierarchy. Many tribes refer to themselves as *jati*, thus inviting the identification of their own society with a caste right at the outset. This receives additional expression in the fact that most tribes are as concerned to maintain a strict rule of endogamy as any caste, more so than their Mon-Khmer affiliates in Southeast Asia.[14] Such a refusal to intermarry is, of course, one marker of caste status; another is the refusal to accept food from inferiors. This applies no less when it comes to tribal identity, though it may sometimes take a surprising form. Some Munda tribes, such as the Santal and Mundari, are militantly anti-Hindu and accordingly will not accept food even from Brahmans,[15] though even while inverting the application of this particular symbolic gesture they are still acknowledging its force and therefore the existence of a common cultural vocabulary. The Sora too, while equally keen to distance themselves from Hindus, are still prepared to use Hindu symbols to express superiority in ritual.[16] Finally, many tribals recognize the existence of the hierarchy associated with caste and its implications for their own status in the eyes of others, even though they may dispute their particular position within it or even reject it entirely as a value for themselves.

Many tribes have, of course, made the transition into the world of caste by winning some sort of recognition as such—usually but not invariably of a very low status—while at any one time others will be seeking to rise in the scale by imposing greater controls over the marriages, diets and other activities of their members (banning communal dances, for instance), and possibly by adopting an artisan specialization. Such attempts often meet with resistance from within the group, with the result that some tribes, like the Kharia, have become divided, much as castes divided into subcastes; and eventually there ceases to be any social connection between them, though they may retain a common language and traditions of a common origin. But nonetheless, it is still not at all easy to determine where the boundary marking the transition should be placed, in view of the many similarities between tribes and low castes, which extend even to social organization—for instance, the payment of brideprice instead of dowry, the acceptability of exchange marriages, and the reciprocity of identical ritual services,[17] all of which violate high-caste ideology.

It is not surprising, therefore, that there was eventually a reaction against the commonly held but ill-thought-out view that tribal and caste societies were essentially different in India. Some of this reaction, however, took a rather polemical turn for one reason or another. The struggle for Indian independence and the shock of partition that accompanied its final success stimulated a political desire to emphasize the unity of India as much as possible as a counter to risks of further secession. A number of Indian anthropologists of the period fell in with this trend, for example, Ghurye, who dismissed the tribes as 'backward Hindus' in a book whose title aptly summed up this view: *The Aborigines—'so-called'—and their Future* (1943). He was soon followed by the French anthropologist Louis Dumont, whose statements, though more sophisticated than Ghurye's and not at all politically grounded, were for other reasons no less polemical.

By way of launching a new journal, *Contributions to Indian Sociology*, Dumont (in co-operation with David Pocock) issued what was in reality a policy statement to the effect that 'India is one', 'most so-called "primitives" [tribes] in India [being] only peoples who have lost contact'.[18] This was initially the result of his dissatisfaction with the older traditions of migration theory and culture history, which led him to reject the standard view of India's 'diversity' as resting on unsound evidence. But also important in his considerations was the fact that the tribes had so far received much more anthropological attention than the castes, who actually made up the vast bulk of India's population. There were some earlier studies of caste, by Bouglé and Hocart on the system in general, and by himself, Aiyappan and Srinivas on specific castes in south India, but nothing compared with the great number of monographs and articles on tribals and other apparently primitive populations in India—a direct consequence of the preoccupations of the culture historians. Dumont proposed to rectify this by calling on Indology and some recent anthropological studies, including some of his own, in order to replace the diffusionist and archaeological approaches of the past. He was, in fact, mostly concerned with Indian society at the present day rather than with historical speculations for which evidence was lacking. Like most structuralists, his attitude to the processes of history is a selective one, neither dismissing them as totally irrelevant to anthropology as the functionalists did, nor relying on them exclusively like the schools of evolutionism and diffusionism that the functionalists sought to replace. For Dumont, while such processes may help us understand how a culture or society has come to assume its present shape, they cannot explain why these same values continue to be of relevance at the present day to those whose lives they order.[19] But Dumont's methods are also revealing, for he was very much a product of the French sociological tradition of Durkheim and Mauss (he had been the latter's student, after all), in which the emphasis was more on the integration of particular societies than on differences between them, and to this he added a structuralist or relational approach. The culmination of the work was, of course, *Homo Hierarchicus* (1966b), in which the polarity between pure and impure became a relational axis integrating the whole society— and this implicitly includes the tribes, even though they receive scarcely a mention in the book.

This dissatisfaction with the then state of anthropological studies relating to India is perfectly understandable, and of course Dumont himself has played the greatest part in rectifying it. But the supposition of a cultural and even social uniformity for the whole subcontinent that this led to was, in his earliest statements, at least, mainly assertion alone—a programmatic statement rather than an argument—and as such open to challenge as polemical rather than proven. This challenge came initially from Bailey (1959) who, writing at the invitation of Dumont and Pocock, made just these points generally and then put forward his own solution to the problem of the tribe in a second article (1961). This was the tribe-caste continuum, best explained in his own words: 'We see tribe and caste not as a dichotomy, but as a line, at different points along which particular societies are to be placed' (1961: 18). However, this solution has not really constituted an advance, and indeed the more cynical might regard it simply as an ingenious way of admitting the difficulties of distinguishing caste and tribe without really seeming to. As Dumont himself immediately realized (1962b), a sliding scale of this sort needs defining criteria just as much as a dichotomy, at least in setting the limits at either end, and in this respect could be said to differ but little from it. Bailey did try to provide such criteria, choosing as an example what he saw as differing relations between the political structure and access to land: tribespeople have direct access to land, whereas members of castes have access only indirectly, through dependence on the locally dominant caste. However, Dumont objected to this purely arbitrary choice of many possible criteria, and he pointed out that even this choice would make most dominant castes, which are usually of fairly or very high status, resemble tribes very closely. One can also add that many Munda only have access to land through a similar dependency (in their case, on a locally dominant agnatic group rather than a caste; see Ch. 4). Bailey was trying to see the tribes as whole societies, in contrast to the castes, each of which was only a part of a society, a point later revived by Godelier and adopted recently by Bouez.[20] However, even this model of the autonomy of tribal society has to face the reality that many tribals are to some extent dependent on Hindu castes, whether ritually or economically or both.

Thanks to its legal status in India, the term 'tribe' has retained rather more scholarly currency there than in Western anthropology, where definitional problems of all sorts are keenly felt and constantly debated, and never blindly accepted for long. Here, it is Dumont's view that has tended to prevail over Bailey's, and the term has become merely what Evans-Pritchard in other contexts used to call a 'portmanteau' word—a sort of shorthand expression with only an approximate meaning, not one implying a rigorous definition. But although Dumont's position may be defensible on that score, it can be still argued that it is not itself a wholly balanced one, that he has 'over-corrected' earlier theories to some extent. In the first place, there are definitional problems not only with the notion of 'tribe' but also with that of 'caste', to which Dumont sought to assimilate it, and with the Hinduism with which the latter is intimately bound up. Secondly, Dumont's model of the sociological unity of India rests on the assumption—implied rather than stated—that it simply consists of the spread of Hindu and caste values throughout its population, at whatever level.[21] However, it is not true that every aspect of social organization in India can be traced simply to the particular values of caste and Hinduism alone, for a number of them clearly have a more global distribution. Later parts of the present book (especially the final chapter) will attempt to demonstrate this, but I will take up each of these points briefly here. It should be pointed out first, however, that such a demonstration does not depend on solving any of these definitional problems, and indeed no attempt will be made to do so here.

It is unfortunate that the mistakes of earlier writers led Dumont to devalue the lessons of history and concentrate almost entirely on the present. It has, of course, proved notoriously difficult to unravel the Hindu from the aboriginal in Indian society, and this has led many to see the attempt as practically impossible, and sometimes as theoretically misconceived. Such views tend to assume Hinduism to be a static, monolithic and all-pervasive force; yet the reality is less stark, and one cannot define it as a body of belief so readily as, say, Islam or Christianity. This is partly because of its own greater tolerance of diversity, and partly because it is more intimately bound up with the society within which it exists—it is less a 'world religion' either in its claims or in reality than either of these or even Buddhism. Moreover, it too has had a history of development. It is much more difficult to fix an origin point for it than it is for the other major religions—it has no charismatic founder—but one can certainly argue that it is an essentially post-Vedic development. This is not to deny the importance of recognizing the Vedas for any Hindu, but Hinduism today has developed quite different values. The rise of the principles of abstinence and vegetarianism, for instance, can be shown to have originated as a tightening of values in reaction to the competition of Buddhism and Jainism and they can be traced with reasonable

certainty to a particular historical period.[22] The doctrines of
karma and reincarnation can also be argued to have a post-Vedic
origin of about the same time (see Ch. 11).

In addition, the spread of these ideas has been uneven across the
sub-continent, coming relatively recently to some areas. At the
extreme, not even Dumont or Ghurye tried to incorporate the
Tibeto-Burman speakers of the north-east into peninsular Indian
society: though clearly 'tribals', they could hardly be considered
'backward Hindus' or 'Hindus who have lost contact'.[23] As
Bouez has pointed out,[24] there are no references to Hinduism in
their culture—no Hindu gods, no Brahmans, no pure-impure—
and thus they can be compared to tribes outside India. Indeed, far
from losing contact, they are encountering it only now in some
cases, and frequently resisting it with insurrection. Yet this is but
the history of Chotanagpur repeating itself some three centuries
later. Before the Mughal rulers began to encroach on the upland
areas in the late eighteenth century there seems to have been
relatively little contact between castes and tribes compared to
today, when they are thoroughly interspersed. Many of the rulers
of this area were of tribal origin, and although they sometimes used
Hindu soldiers and gave land to Brahmans, the massive and dis-
ruptive takeover of tribal land and the imposition of taxation that
impoverished the tribes appear to have been relatively late, associated first with the Hinduization of the ruling Maharajas of
Chotanagpur in the seventeenth century and then with the imposition of British rule from 1770 onwards. Both of these events, but
especially the latter, led to an influx of Hindu officials, landlords
and soldiers which depressed the tribals economically and politically. McDougall (1977) shows that there were two reactions to this
among the indigenous population. One was the creation of strong
tribal identities based on anti-Hindu sentiments, as among Mundari speakers and the Dravidian-speaking Oraon and later the
Santal. The other was Sanskritization, as with the Bhumij and other
groups: many of the present-day agents of Hinduization in the area
have a tribal origin, and some of them, like the Asur or Mahali or
Turi, are Munda-speaking. Thus Hinduization in Chotanagpur is
a historical as well as a social and cultural phenomenon, just like
Hinduism itself, and the polarity between tribe and caste may have
been strengthened by tribal reactions to the process.

Our ability to trace this process, however dimly, itself suggests the presence of social ideologies autonomous from Hinduism and caste among the tribes formerly—otherwise, we would not be able to recognize them as human societies at all. Dumont himself conceded right at the outset that 'the postulate of the unity of India is seriously challenged in the field of kinship' (1957: 18). Here, of course, he was thinking not of the tribes, but of the contrast between caste societies in north and south India, a contrast he later sought to eliminate by trying to show that caste values subsume kinship ones in the north but not in the south (1966c). However, it would seem that this did not really convince even Dumont himself, and he has recently qualified his original programmatic slogan to read 'the India *of caste* is sociologically one' (1983: 106, my emphasis).

The available evidence suggests that most of the tribes of central India, regardless of language (i.e. including Dravidian and even Indo-European as well as Munda), have systems of affinal alliance of the sort known variously as cross-cousin marriage, elementary structures or prescriptive alliance. This is shown especially by their kinship terminologies, but also to a large extent by their patterns of affinal alliance. This cannot itself be used to distinguish tribe from caste at the present day, for south India has very similar kinship systems existing in both caste and tribal groups. What *is* significant, however, is the presence of equally similar systems outside India, e.g. in Southeast Asia, ancient China, Australia, the Amazon Basin and parts of Oceania, some of which bear a very detailed resemblance to what is found is central India (see further, Ch. 11). Most of these areas are sufficiently isolated from one another to rule out any explanations in terms of historical contacts between them, and these similarities can only be the result of more fundamental structural properties common to all. This means that where they occur in the Indian context they represent a fundamentally autonomous social system that owes nothing to the dominant values of caste and Hinduism, even though these may have caused its attenuation in some cases. It is this which ultimately sets a limit to Dumont's attempts to unify India sociologically, and which this book seeks to describe further.

1.3 Munda Ethnography

Since the present book relies completely on the previously published work of others, it seems desirable to say something about previous and current work on the Munda. Only a general review of the major figures will be given here, since a more detailed look at the literature on each group appears in the next chapter. A fuller bibliography is given at the end of the book, but in the main this only covers works actually referred to in the text, which are mainly on kinship. Elizabeth von Fürer-Haimendorf's bibliographies (1958, 1964, 1970, 1976) should be consulted for works up to about 1970, and there is also Troisi's bibliography on the Santal (1976). On language, there is Zide's review of work up to the late 1960s (1969), and Huffman's recent bibliography on Southeast Asian languages (1986) includes Munda. Little published before 1900 has been taken into account in the present book, but much of the data used is still old, and while I have attempted to take into account the relative age of sources when discussing discrepancies between them, use of the ethnographic present must be assumed very frequently.

The pioneer proper of Munda ethnography is undoubtedly Sarat Chandra Roy (1871–1942), an Indian barrister who defended tribals in the courts and became interested in them and their culture generally. His first work (1912), mainly a history of Mundari speakers but also covering other tribes, led to more ethnographical monographs on the Birhor (1925) and Kharia (1937, with his son), with two others on the Dravidian-speaking Oraon (1915, 1928) and one on the Indo-European-speaking Hill Bhuiya of north-west Orissa (1935a). His other monument is *Man in India*, which he founded in Ranchi in 1921 as a general anthropological journal for all India, and though it has never really covered the caste society and at periods has almost been taken over by human biologists, it has always had many articles on the Munda. Roy was soon followed by Dhirendra Nath Majumdar (1903–1960), who wrote much on the Ho (especially 1950) and to a lesser extent the Korwa, as well as a general but now completely outmoded textbook on the anthropology of India (originally published in 1944 but much expanded in subsequent editions; see Majumdar 1961). He too founded a journal, *Eastern Anthropologist*, also of significance in this field and rather less parochial than *Man in India*. The work of both authors naturally enough reflects the standard anthropological preoccupations and interpretations of their time, but on the whole it is the work of Roy, the non-professional, which has lasted the better: Majumdar, although Professor of Anthropology at the University of Lucknow, was often unreliable even with raw data, and he tends to assume too readily a connection between race and culture.

Many of the early ethnographers were administrators, a fact reflected in the encyclopaedia-like gazetteers many of them produced.[25] Others were missionaries, a trend which has continued. Special mention should be made of Hoffmann's massive *Encyclopaedia Mundarica* (1930 *et seq.*), whose publication was due to be completed only in 1979, despite Hoffmann himself having died over fifty years previously, in 1928.[26] Similarly extensive in scope and scale is Bodding's five-volume *A Santal Dictionary* (1932–6). Verrier Elwin (1902–66) also came to India with the intention of being a missionary, but he soon gave up this idea in order to absorb himself in tribal life, not excluding marriage (see Elwin 1940). He published a massive amount in journals and books, with major monographs and articles on the Sora (1955), Remo (1950) and Juang (1948) among Munda groups as well as ones on the Dravidian-speaking Muria (1947) and Maria (1943) and Indo-European-speaking Baiga (1939) and Agaria (1942). In addition, there were collections of folktales and other general works, each covering a range of different tribes in middle India. He became an associate of Gandhi through his sympathy with the independence movement, a sympathy which led in the short term to his exclusion from India for a time by the British authorities, and in the long term to a series of pamphlets and other works outlining particular policies for tribal areas, though none are directed specifically at the Munda. His interest in psychology sometimes influenced him unduly in accounting for sociological phenomena (especially in *Bondo Highlander*, 1950), and his study of the Sora led him to the extraordinary conclusion that they lacked social organization.[27] But though like Roy a non-professional he had enough anthropological knowledge to make most of his work of continuing value if used with care. It is also far more readable than the average anthropological monograph, if at times immensely, even excessively detailed.[28] The other great European figure among the ethnographers of tribal India, Christoph von Fürer-Haimendorf, has been concerned more with the north-east and the Gond than with the Munda, but he has two articles to his credit (1943a, 1943b) on the Remo and Gadaba, and the Munda are covered in a number of his more general works (e.g. 1945a, 1950).

Since independence, many more Indian anthropologists have carried out fieldwork among different Munda tribes and published the results, much of it under the auspices of the Anthropological Survey of India. Most of the names concerned appear regularly in the text, but it is worth pointing out here that they include a handful of writers who are themselves Munda (e.g. M. and S. Topno, R.O. Dhan and P.N. Hansda). Much of this work is pedestrian and theoretically old-fashioned, often based on data collected on short tours from the home base in a contact language (Hindi, Oriya, Bengali etc.) rather than the tribal language. Nonetheless, with sufficient circumspection it can still be used as raw data, and for some groups it is all we have.

For work on the Munda that is more in tune with the preoccupations and perceptions of modern anthropology, one must generally turn to European and American writers. From America have come Martin Orans, who worked among the Santal steel-workers at the Tata plant at Jamshedpur (1965), and later George Somers, who studied village Santal (1977). More or less contemporary with Orans was Charles McDougal, who worked among the Juang in the early 1960s and published a couple of articles on them (1963b, 1964). His thesis (1963a) has also been published in microfiche and should be regarded as a major piece of work on the Munda, the more so as it is theoretically completely unprejudiced and leaves the ethnography to speak for itself. Subsequently Nepal has claimed his interests (including running a mountaineering and trekking shop). In England there are Hilary Standing on Mundari speakers (1976, 1981) and Piers Vitebsky on the Sora (1980, 1982, forthcoming), while Michael Yorke, as well as having assisted in the work of Fürer-Haimendorf on the Gond, has filmed the Ho. France is represented by the husband-and-wife team of Serge Bouez on the Santal and Ho and Marine Carrin-Bouez on the Santal. Both have recently brought out monographs (1985 and 1986 respectively) as well as several articles. There is also one article by Elizabeth Chaussin on the Sora (1978), though she subsequently seems to have left the field. Finally, in Germany Georg Pfeffer of the Free University of Berlin has produced a number of comparative and monographic studies of middle Indian tribes of all language groups, Dravidian and Indo-European as well as Munda (especially 1982a, 1983).

This may seem like an impressive list, but in reality it is disappointing because of the outmoded or indifferent quality of much of the published work and the fact that much of the most promising material is not widely available, some of it remaining hidden in the relative obscurity of university departments as theses difficult of access. There is still absolutely no ethnography on one or two Munda groups (Karmali, Juray) and very little indeed on others (Turi, Kora, Gorum), while that on the remainder often needs considerable updating. In fact, Munda linguistics has been much better served than Munda ethnography in recent years. This is principally due to the massive amount of work undertaken over the last three decades by Norman Zide and his colleagues and students at the University of Chicago, though studies have also been carried out independently of this group, most notably by Hans-Jürgen Pinnow at the Free University of Berlin. As a result, the external relationships and internal structure of the Munda languages are now better established, and much more knowledge is available on them individually.

As for comparative work, there are quite a number of studies on Indian tribes generally, Indo-European and Dravidian as well as Munda, and Karvé's Kinship Organization in India (1965) includes some of the Munda along with other groups of eastern India in the final chapter. However, there are no previous comparative ethnographic studies devoted specifically to the Munda apart from Mukhopadhyay's The Austrics of India (1975)—a run-of-the-mill and sketchy piece of work devoted to religious traditions—and two early articles by the present author, both of which were in press for some time and now need considerable revision (1986a; 1988b). Karvé's 1968–9 article has only two pages of text on the Munda, though the tables of kin terms compensate for this to some extent. Bhattacharya's article on Munda kin terms (1970) contains very little anthropology and consists mainly of etymological lists. I have attempted to rectify this myself in a more recent article (1985), which has been considerably revised and rewritten as Chapter 7 of the present work. Zide has promised a series of papers devoted to the linguistic reconstruction of Munda kin terms, the first of which is due to appear shortly (Zide and Zide forthcoming).

Chapter Two
Munda Tribes and Castes

The term Munda is of Sanskritic origin and appears to represent a root meaning 'substantial, wealthy'; later it came to mean 'head' and from this 'headman', still its meaning in a number of North Munda languages. Less favoured is Przyluski's view, that it represents an alternative root (*munda* 'shaven') present in Indo-European but of Austroasiatic origin. Tedesco refuted this suggestion, arguing that this too is of Indo-European origin and that it is the Santali forms cited by Przyluski that are the loans.[1] British administrators first applied the word to one particular tribe of Munda speakers (3, below) in the early nineteenth century, and it has since become established not only in administration but also in scholarship and even in the tribe itself to an increasing extent. Subsequently, its use was extended to become also the normal scholarly designation for the whole group of related languages and those who speak them. However, this double meaning is liable to lead to confusion, especially in a comparative work like the present. Accordingly, I shall restrict use of 'Munda' to the whole group of related tribes and languages only, and instead use 'Mundari' for the single tribe *and* its language, though conventionally this is restricted in meaning to the latter.[2]

Many Munda groups, especially the North Munda, are also designated Kol by their neighbours, but this is regarded as insulting by the people to whom it is applied,[3] even though it may in fact be a corruption of *hor* etc.,[4] a North Munda cognate meaning 'man' and much preferred by these groups themselves. Kol, sometimes Kolarian, entered the language of scholarship at an early date, but this usage is now old-fashioned and in view of its pejorative connotations is best avoided.

Figure 1[5] shows the internal structure of this sub-family. As can be seen, there are two major divisions, North Munda and South Munda, of which the latter is generally considered to be the more conservative. Each division is itself divided into two: North Munda into Korku and Kherwarian, and South Munda into Central Munda and Koraput Munda. Further proto-languages appear in Koraput Munda before we reach the level of existing languages.[6]

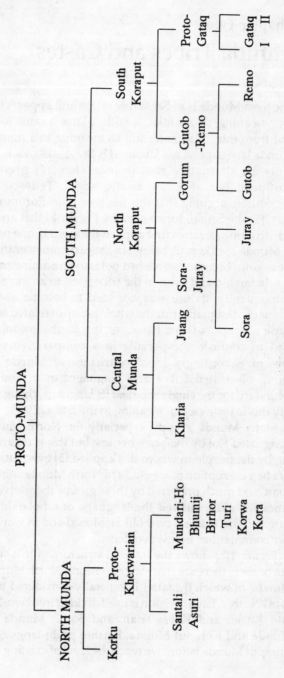

Figure 1. The Munda Languages

Many of the above designations are also the 'real' ethnonyms, that is, those used by each group for its own members rather than those given to them by neighbours or administrators or other outsiders. Variant and alternative names will be given in the survey that follows, but thereafter only the designations in Figure 1 will be used, with these exceptions: Gadaba will be used instead of Gutob, the name of the language only; Kora will be preferred to Koda (following conventional usage); and no distinction will be made between the two groups of Gataq, since at present this is only of proven significance linguistically, not ethnographically.[7] A number of these or similar names, especially Bhumij, Kharia, Asur, Turi, Korwa, Savara or Saora (Sora) and Gadaba, are used of groups speaking Dravidian or Indic languages[8] as well as Munda speakers. These too are mentioned in the present chapter for clarification but will be disregarded thereafter (but see Appendix II). Population figures have been arrived at by taking into consideration Stampe's figures (1965, 1966) and those of the 1961 and 1971 Censuses of India, but inevitably they must be regarded as approximate (the 1981 Census had not produced any ethnically or linguistically based figures at the time of writing). The literature I cite at the end of each entry mainly covers those items that have been useful in the preparation of the present book and does not specifically attempt to be comprehensive as regards matters falling outside its concerns.

A North Munda Branch

A (i) Korku Sub-Branch

1. Korku
The Korku are geographically isolated from other Munda groups, being found mainly in southwest Madhya Pradesh, some 500 miles to the west; they are, in fact the most westerly Munda- or Austroasiatic-speaking group. They are said to have become isolated in this way by the same northern expansion of Dravidian-speaking Kui, Gond and Kurukh that, it is claimed, drove the other Munda tribes eastward and northward about five or six hundred years ago.[9] But despite their isolation their language is still recognizably close to Kherwarian. Its roughly 200,000 speakers live in the Mahadeo and Satpura ranges, in the districts of Berar, Nimar, Betul, Hoshangabad and Chhindwara; there are also some in In-

dore, Dewas and Bhopal, in the Vindhya range; in Mandla, in the Maikal Hills; in Sahore, Raisen, Nargingpur, Balaghat, Durg and Raipur districts, Madhya Pradesh; and in the Amravati, Akola, Wardha, Yeotmal and Chanda districts of Maharashtra.[10] Sahay derives the ethnonym from *kodaku* 'young man'; more probably it consists of *kor* 'man'—a term which has cognates in other North Munda languages—plus the plural suffix *-ku*.[11] Ali and Fuchs distinguish two endogamous groups, the Raj or Deshi (land-owners) and the Potharia, presumably labourers and/or tenants. There are also four 'sub-castes', named Muasi, Bawasi or Bawaraia, Ruma and Baidoya (also Bondoya, Bondhi, Bhovadaya, Bhopa, Bopchi); these are territorial groups and are endogamous accord-ing to Fuchs—certainly the Muasi are of higher status than the Ruma. They are found respectively in the Mahadeo and Satpura ranges; in Betul; in Amravati and Nimar districts; and in the Jaitgarh area of Wardha district; the last-named number only a few hundred. According to Stampe, 'Muasi, which is not a separate language or dialect but merely an alias, is to be included in Korku; on the other hand Koraku [or Kodaku], also called Korku, spoken in district Surguja of Madhya Pradesh, is a separate language apparently akin to Korwa [q.v. 7].' The 14,768 speakers of 'Korku' enumerated for the Surguja district in the 1961 Census are in reality Kodaku.[12]

The ethnography on the Korku in English consists of Fuchs' recent monograph (1988) plus some articles and information in general books (e.g. Chattopadhyay 1946, Pandye 1962, Ali 1973, Fuchs 1966). In German, Hermanns' three-volume work on this area (1966) has a long section, mainly on Korku religious ideas and ritual.

A (ii) Kherwarian Sub-Branch

According to Santal traditions, Kherwarian is the name of the people from which most of the Munda tribes stem.[13] It actually refers to certain North Munda origin myths in which a *kher* or goose plays an important part. It occasionally appears as an ethnonym (e.g. in the 1961 Census, where 647 'Kherwari' are enumerated, pp. clxxx ff.), but it does not clearly designate any identifiable group and should not be used as such. There is no longer a Kherwarian language, but the name is used by linguists to designate the proto-language from which all the North Munda languages apart from

Korku have evolved, as well as the sub-branch formed by these languages (see Fig. 1). Speaking of this sub-branch, Stampe says: 'their degree of mutual intelligibility...is so high as to qualify many of them as dialects, rather than distinct languages.' This excludes Santali, however, which is not mutually intelligible with the other dialects, though it is linked to them by Karmali and Mahali according to Leuva, by Asur and Turi according to Grierson, or possibly by Birhor (discussed below, 6).[14]

2. Santal

The Santal are by far the largest Munda tribe and one of the largest in India.[15] They number about four million and thus outnumber all the remaining Munda-speaking groups together by about two to one. They, like other Munda, may once have occupied parts of the Gangetic plain, having been pushed into Chotanagpur subsequently by Hindu expansion; but their history before the mid-eighteenth century is obscure. Following the famine of 1770, which decimated the local Hindu population, they moved into the Raj-mahal Hills under the double impetus of overpopulation in Chotanagpur and East India Company policy. This area was eventually to be reserved for them as the Santal Parganas, first as a part of Bengal but later transferred to Bihar. Between 1838 and 1851 its population rose from 3,000 to 82,000, and today some 85% of its population are Santal—88% if the closely related Mahali and Karmali are included. They have a strong tribal identity, marked by hostility to Hindus, advancement of the Santali language and traditional culture, and political activity through the Jharkhand Party for, *inter alia*, a specifically tribal province.[16]

According to tradition, there was a taboo on crossing to the south bank of the river Damodar in northern Bankura, but today Santal are found throughout this district and further south, in Midnapore and northern Balasore.[17] Other concentrations in and around Chotanagpur include Birbhum, Bhagalpur, Monghyr, Hazaribagh and Manbhum. They form about 50% of the population of Mayurbhanj, and there are about 7,000 next door in Keonjhar.[18] This certainly does not exhaust their distribution, however. According to Gautam they can be found in Bihar, Bengal, Orissa, Assam, Meghalaya, Tripura, southeast Nepal, northwest Bangladesh and southern Bhutan, and yet others are reported in Manipur and the Andaman Islands. This expansion seems to have originated with the second Santal rebellion of 1855–6, whereafter many Santal crossed the Ganges into northern Bengal and the Assam tea estates. Those in Nepal seem to have crossed into Morang in the late 1920s, following the abolition of slavery there. These are clearly the same as the semi-nomadic Satar mentioned by Bista; the eight clan names he cites are certainly Santal, as is *majhi*, their name for 'headman', and he also says that their language is unique to the area, though he gives no idea of its affiliations.[19]

There are two closely related variants of standard Santali, spoken respectively in the north (Bhagalpur, Monghyr, Santal Parganas, Birbhum, Bankura, Hazaribagh, Manbhum) and south (Midnapore, Balasore) of the central area. There are two further dialects, Mahali and Karmali, each associated with an endogamous sub-tribe rather than any particular area.[20] The Mahali seem to be an outcasted group of Santali and Mundari whose traditional occupations as palanquin-bearers, basket-makers and drummers are regarded as degrading by the Santal proper; they are themselves divided into at least five endogamous sections. Found throughout the central Santal area, they are said to have come from the west. According to the 1901 Census they were to be found mainly in Chotanagpur, Santal Parganas and Orissa, but there were 28,233 in West Bengal in 1961 and 47,247 in 1971. In this state many speak Bengali, but Munda-speaking Mahali live in Jalpaiguri, Midnapore, 24 Parganas, Malda, West Dinajpur, Burdwan etc., and formerly, at least, Birbhum. There may also be some in Ranchi and Manbhum, and the name also appears as one of a number of alternatives for a Mundari sub-group (q.v. 3). Some barber castes in Berar (Madhya Pradesh) are also called Mahali, but these are almost certainly a separate group entirely. Nor are they to be confused with the Dravidian-speaking Maler or Mal Pahariya of Santal Parganas.[21]

The Karmali are traditionally ironsmiths and are found in Manbhum, Hazaribagh and Santal Parganas. They too may be partly Mundari in origin: their headmen, for instance, are known by the Mundari word *munda*, not the Santali term *manjhi*.[22] Indeed, it is possible that in myth or in fact both groups originated in intermarriage between Santal and Mundari, contrary to the normal rule of tribal endogamy, and that this is the main reason for their separation. They may not be the only low castes to speak a Santali dialect (see end of chapter). Many Santal speak Hindi, Bengali or Oriya in addition to Santali.[23]

Early writers derived Santal from 'Samanta' or 'Saont', the latter being the name of a village. The Santal themselves derive it from another toponym, Silda, in Midnapore District, where they were once concentrated. However, because Hindus use it for them, 'they show dislike of the term "Santal"', greatly prefer *hor hopon* or 'the sons of man', and generally call themselves *hor* ('man').[24] However, this is shared by other Munda groups, and 'Santal' will be used here to avoid confusion.[25] One other ethnonym is Manjhi, a word also used for 'village headman'.[26] Another is Kherwal, a reference to the origin myth in which the first Santal were hatched from two eggs of a *kher* or goose.[27]

In view of their numbers the Santal have received a great deal of scholarly attention, with monographs by Biswas, Bouez, Carrin-Bouez, Culshaw, Datta-Majumdar, Gausdal, Gautam, Kochar, Mukherjea, Orans, Somers and Troisi, and numerous articles; there are also Bodding's collections of folk tales etc. and his five-volume dictionary, which is more of an encyclopaedia and contains much ethnographic information. Indeed, so great has been the ethnographic attention devoted to them that they have come to warrant their own substantial bibliography (Troisi 1976). Sengupta and the team of Chakraborty and Kundu have dealt with the Mahali, but the Karmali still await their ethnographer. Orans (1955) and Banerjee (1981) have concentrated on Santal industrial workers. Zide's research group have not paid much attention to their language except in comparative work, perhaps because so much had been done by earlier writers (especially Bodding and Campbell).

3. Munda

The present-day meanings and possible etymologies of the word 'Munda' have already been discussed, as have the reasons for preferring the word 'Mundari' (strictly the designation of the language) when this tribe alone is mentioned and for reserving 'Munda' for the whole group of languages and tribes in the present work. Even among the Munda themselves Indic Munda is beginning to replace Mundari Horo.[28]

With a population of maybe 750,000, the Mundari are the second largest Munda tribe. They live mostly in eastern, southern and south-western Ranchi as well as in Singhbhum, Manbhum,

Hazaribagh, Palamau and parts of northern Orissa and northern Madhya Pradesh. Roy says that 'it is Azimgarh that forms the starting point for their historical traditions', and many hundred years ago they are reputed to have been settled here and in Ghazipur and also further south-west, in Rewa and Bundelkhand. Subsequently they migrated, eventually reaching Chotanagpur, where they have remained. Since the beginning of the eighteenth century they have had to face competition for land from the Dravidian-speaking Oraon as well as from Hindu immigrants, though today the two tribes have much in common. Many Oraon around Ranchi have adopted Mundari, and some local low castes are also Mundari speakers. Like the Santal the Mundari have a strong tribal and anti-Hindu identity and have equally been in-volved in rebellion (especially the Birsa Munda rebellion over land and access to the forest in 1895–1900). There are some Christian Munda.[29]

According to Stampe, Mundari has four dialects: Hasada, spoken in the Khunti-Tamar-Chaibassa triangle in southern Ranchi; Naguri, spoken in northern and western Chotanagpur; Latar, spoken in the east, in Tamar Pargana, and much influenced by Bengali; and Keraq, spoken in the Ranchi area, but much in-fluenced by Hindi and Kurukh. Most other authorities give only the first two, these being the 'purest'. Hasada, though leaning towards Ho, has some prestige as the purest of all, Naguri being closer to Santali and more influenced by Hindi and Sadani, the Indo-European-based lingua franca of the area, which many Naguri speakers understand. The Hasada-speaking area is 'the area considered, subjectively, to be the pure Munda country.'[30] There are also two endogamous divisions, the Kompat or 'true' Munda, which also includes the closely related Ho (4, below); and the Tamaria or Khangar (also known as Mahali Munda, Marang Munda or Patar Munda). The latter are the 'elder brothers' of the former but inferior in status; they were rejected because the brother from whom they are mythically descended inadvertently ate the umbilical cord (i.e. the leavings) of his younger brother.[31] This group are presumably to be identified with the Latar dialect of Tamar Pargana (see above).

The name of Sarat Chandra Roy is especially associated with the Munda, the subject of his first monograph (1912), and there is also the massive *Encyclopaedia Mundarica* of Hoffmann, which should now at last be completely published. Later work includes Choudhury's 1977 monograph and two lavishly produced volumes by Japanese scholars (Sugiyama 1969, Yamada 1970).[32] An East German anthropologist, Icke-Schwalbe, has produced a number of Marxist-oriented studies comparing the Munda with their Oraon neighbours in terms of ethnic identity, social organization and economy (especially 1983b, but also 1979, 1983a, 1988). At least two Munda have themselves produced work (M. Topno 1955; S. Topno 1970), and Singh has published on the Birsa Munda rebellion (especially 1983). Hilary Standing worked among the Munda in the 1970s for a doctoral thesis and has one article on them (1981), both she and Exem (1982) having worked principally on their religion.

4. Ho

There are over 400,000 Ho in Singhbhum, of which roughly half live in Kolhan and the rest in the Seraikella and Dhalbhum areas. They are an offshoot of the Mundari and are regarded as 'little' Munda, and as their 'younger brothers'. Their language seems to have derived from the Hasada dialect of Mundari and is fairly homogenous throughout; it is mutually intelligible with Mundari. They were formerly found further north in Chotanagpur and migrated from there before the appearance of the Oraon in the area towards AD 1700. In migrating, they displaced the Bhumij rulers of Singhbhum; they also rebelled against the British in the 1830s, their militancy earning them the name of Larka or 'fighting' Kol. Ho is the regular cognate of Mundari *horo* and like it means 'man'. The pejorative alternative, Kol, is, of course, present in 'Kolhan'. Some Ho are Christian.[33]

D.N. Majumdar published a number of articles and two monographs (1937 and 1950) on the Ho, though the latter is really an expanded version of the former and incorporates much of its actual text. Earlier there is Chatterjee and Das (1927) and later Chattopadhyay (1964) and Dhan (1961), the last-named being herself a Ho. Bouez has devoted half of his recent monograph (1985) to them, this being the best analysis of their social structure so far.

5. Bhumij

The Bhumij are a disparate group that has come under varying degrees of Hindu influence. Their name consists of the Sanskrit root *bhumi* 'land', which together with *-aj* means 'one born of the soil'. They are probably to be regarded as distinct from the Bhuiya or 'children of the soil', who at least in northern Orissa speak an Indic language or dialect.[34] 'Bhumij' itself is so widely applied, to castes as well as to tribals, that it must often refer to groups that have never been connected. The most Hinduized have long lived in Gangpur, southern Manbhum and Dhalbhum, many being wealthy and claiming Kshatriya descent, and most speaking Bengali; a lesser number are found in the northern districts of Bihar. Other, apparently less Hinduized Bhumij are found in Orissa, specifically in Mayurbhanj and around Jeypore in Koraput, in both of which areas they speak Oriya. Yet others occur in Singhbhum, Assam and West Bengal, especially Midnapore and Hooghly, and in the Surguja, Jashpur and Korea districts of Madhya Pradesh. According to Elwin, the Chhattisgarhi-speaking Baiga of Madhya Pradesh may be another offshoot.[35]

Thus many so-called Bhumij speak only Hindi or Bengali or Oriya, though those in Bihar are mostly bilingual, using Bhumij only at home and with fellow tribespeople. In fact, only about a third actually speak the Munda language that has been given that name. They are found mainly in northern Orissa, Singhbhum and Purulia, but not in Manbhum, where they all speak only Bengali.[36] The Hinduized Bhumij hold themselves aloof in all respects from their lower status neighbours, and in Orissa there are said to be a number of ranked and endogamous territorial and occupational groups: those in Koraput, for instance, are divided between Bada and Sano. Many of the lower status Bhumij have been campaigning in recent years to have themselves legally recognized as a tribe, a trend opposed to the Sanskritization of other Bhumij.[37]

Because of this confusion we cannot be very sure exactly how many Bhumij there really are: the 101,000 of the 1951 Census had grown to 142,000 by 1961 and shrunk back to 51,000 by 1971. For a similar reason, it is not always clear whether particular items of literature deal with tribal or more Hinduized Bhumij, but those dealt with by Roy (1935a) and Das (1931a) seem to be largely the latter. Roy's group were Oriya speakers but Das's seem to have spoken Bhumij judging from their kinship terminology (1931a: Appendix II). Ray Chowdhury (1929) and Sahu (1942, 1943) seem to have dealt with more tribal groups, though these are not necessarily Bhumij speakers and Ray Chowdhury's apparently spoke

Oriya. Sinha has published a number of works on Bhumij Sanskritization and acculturation (1957, 1958b, 1962, 1966), but there is no recent ethnography.

6. Birhor

The Birhor language is close to Mundari but contains some Santali vocabulary, a fact which has led some writers to regard it as a dialect of the latter, but they are opposed by others who prefer to emphasize the link with Mundari.[38] They refer to themselves as the Mundaris' 'younger brothers', though the latter despise them as 'scavengers'. Many know Sadani, and in Singhbhum and Ranchi this is rapidly replacing Birhori, especially among the younger generation. Their name means 'men (hor) of the forest (bir)', but in Orissa they are known as Mandiki or Mankar Khia Kot, a reference to their eating of monkeys.[39].

In Bihar, they are found in southern Hazaribagh, southern Palamau, northern and northeast Ranchi, and Singhbhum. Those in the former two regions apparently have no contact with those in Ranchi, who alone were dealt with by Roy in his monograph of 1925. There are about 100 in Purulia, but no others in West Bengal. There is much disparity in census data. Sen, following the 1951 Census, says that most in Palamau and Ranchi speak Birjhia, an Asur dialect (8, below), and that there were only 37 Birhori speakers, mostly in Hazaribagh. Stampe's figure of 600, apparently based on the 1961 Census figure of 590, must refer only to those in Singhbhum and Ranchi, since this census actually gives a grand total of 3346, including 1233 in Hazaribagh and nearly as many again in the rest of Chotanagpur, plus some in Madhya Pradesh and Orissa. Bouez says there are only 1000 at most.[40] Not doubt their nomadic habits make any assessment difficult.

Traditionally hunter-gatherers and rope-makers, the Birhor are probably still nomadic in Orissa and Madhya Pradesh, where they are known as Mankiria and Birhul respectively, but those in Bihar and West Bengal are more settled, an increasing trend. They do not appear to have any endogamous sections: the distinction they make between Raonsa and Magahia seems to amount merely to a distinction in traditions of geographical origins and in the minutiae of ritual observance, and it is not identifiable with the other, Uthlu-Thania or nomadic-settled dichotomy.[41]

Roy's monograph (1925) is still the main contribution on this group, though there have been numerous articles, especially by D.P. Sinha and Chakraborty; there is also the recent book by Adhikary (1984). They have found their way into the comparative literature on hunting-and-gathering groups worldwide in work by Vidyarthi (1960) and Williams (1968), and Martel, a French anthropologist, has done work on them more recently (1979). Williams' article is particularly insightful and thorough on their social organization, despite its brevity and the fact that he himself is a physical anthropologist by training. Their wandering habits and 'primitive' way of life have led some to suggest that they represent a stratum of the Indian population even older than other Munda, having at some time abandoned a previous language and become Munda speakers. However, this is very speculative: they are not the only hunter-gatherers—a way of life probably pursued by many other Munda groups until quite recently—and they do not really differ markedly in any cultural sense from other Munda.

7. Korwa

The Korwa seem to have been confined originally to Hazaribagh and Palamau, from where they migrated to Surguja, the Jashpur district of Raigarh, and Bilaspur in 1911. From Palamau and Surguja some moved to the Dudhi district of Mirzapur in Uttar Pradesh, and it is mainly these who are dealt with by Bhandari (1963) and Majumdar (1944). The 1961 Census records yet others in Maharashtra. The Kodaku (alternatively Koraku, Korku) are a Korwa sub-group found mostly in Surguja, where they outnumber other Korwa, and in Palamau and neighbouring areas; they should not be confused with the Korku (1, above). There is no intermarriage between the Kodaku and other Korwa.[42]

Stampe says that Jashpur has the main concentration of Korwa speakers, but he gives a population figure of only 16,000. Both this and Leuva's figure of 17,000 Korwa speakers seem too low in view of the figure of over 19,000 Korwa and Kodaku in Surguja alone given by Rizbi and that of 21,000 Korwa, mostly in Palamau, given by Vidyarthi, though these figures may include some Korwa who no longer speak the Munda language. The 1971 Census gives 18,717, mostly in Palamau, and about 20,000 Kodaku, three-quarters of them in Surguja. Although basically Kherwarian, the Korwa language has some affinities with Kharia, but it is yielding to Sadani and Chhattisgarhi and there are now few monolingual Korwa speakers. As far as the Kodaku are concerned the men speak Hindi and/or Kurukh as well as Kodaku, but the women speak only the latter, a familiar enough situation in multilingual contexts.[43]

The popular etymology derives their ethnonym from *kodwa*, a word apparently referring to their swidden cultivation, and said to be preferable to Korwa, but more likely the first element, *kor-*, is a cognate of Mundari, Santali, etc., *hor* 'man', to which the Indic nominalizing suffix *-wa* has been added.[44] There is basic division, involving endogamy and no commensality, between the sedentary, plains-dwelling, agricultural Dehari (also Dih, Danr) and the nomadic, hill-dwelling, food-gathering and basket-making Pahari or Benwari. In Jashpur, at least, there is also a linguistic distinction: the Plains Korwa speak the Indic-based lingua franca, Sadani, the Hill Korwa a Munda dialect called Singli or Ernga locally, presumably the Korwa of Zide etc.[45]

Majumdar's early work on the Korwa (1930, 1932, 1944) is very unsophisticated and often misleading, but there are recent monographs by Sandhwar (1978) and Deogaonkar (1986). Also to be noted are the articles of Rizbi (1977), Bhandari (1963) and Srivastava and Verma (1967). Singh (1977a, 1977b) and Singh and Danda (1986) write on the Kodaku, who are regarded as a separate tribe by the latter.

8. Asur

Asur speakers live mainly on the Neterhat plateau in southern Palamau and northern Ranchi and around Gumla, further south. These also know Sadani, while other Asur, mostly Agaria in Rewa and other north-eastern parts of Madhya Pradesh and in Mirzapur, Uttar Pradesh, speak what Elwin calls 'a corrupt Hindi'. Those in the last-mentioned area are recent immigrants.[46] The Asur are often claimed to be the descendants of the Asura of the Vedas, hence the Sanskrit etymologies 'powerful people' and 'non-Aryan' that have been offered. The whole question is discussed by Roy and Leuva but there is clearly no established direct link.[47]

There are a number of internal divisions. Roy gives the Soika or Agaria, who are almost entirely ironsmelters; the Birjhia, ironsmelters and bamboo-workers; and the Jait, Hinduized ironsmelters and agriculturalists. The name of the second of these is glossed as 'fish of the forest [*bir*]' by Bhattacharyya. Leuva confirms the first two but gives the Bir ('forest') Asur as the third, whom it is hard to equate with the Jait; they are nonetheless of higher status than the Birjhia, who are also known as Soenka or Agaria. Roy mentions a number of other divisions, but he does not indicate whether or not they are endogamous. Like the Birhor the Birjhia and Agaria are divided into settled (Thania) and nomadic (Uthlu) groups: the Thania Birjhia are divided further, into consumers and non-consumers of beef (Rarh versus Dudh) and into users and non-users of vermilion as a mark of marriage (Sindhuraha versus Telia).[48]

The 7,000 Asur were thus traditionally ironsmelters, though they have had to give up this occupation because government forest laws prevent them from obtaining the necessary charcoal. They are now purely agriculturalists, except that the Birjhia have taken up basket-making. These occupations have made many Asur resemble low castes, the most Hinduized being around Jobhipat. There are a very few Christian Asur.[49]

Jain (1958) and Leuva (1963) have provided the main studies of the Asur proper, while Bhattacharyya (1953a) and Das Gupta (1978) deal with the Birjhia. Elwin's monograph on the Agaria (1942) deals at least in part and perhaps entirely with Indic-rather than Munda-speaking groups. Leuva's group are Munda speakers, even though the kinship terminology he records is completely Indic lexically. He speculates that they have acquired a Munda language secondarily through contact with the Mundari, who are important customers.[50]

9. *Turi*

The word Turi refers to artisan groups in many parts of India but the 1500 Munda speakers we are concerned with are found in Burdwan and 24 Parganas (West Bengal), Palamau, Ranchi and Singhbhum (Bihar) and Raigarh and Chhattisgarh (Madhya Pradesh). They have been described as 'a Hinduized offshoot of the Munda' and are divided into four 'sub-castes'. They have a traditional occupation, basket-making, though some serve as *pahan* or priests in many multi-caste, multi-tribe villages in Chotanagpur.[51] They have thus acquired some of the characteristics of a low caste and, with it, a lower status than the Mundari, Santal or Kharia.[52] Some speak only Sadani or Hindi and these tend to be classed as Dombo. In talking about their origin, however, they associate themselves with the Munda.[53] Apart from one very short article (Rosner 1956) and occasional passing references to them elsewhere, there are no studies on the Turi, and they will receive little mention in the rest of this book.

10. Kora or Koda

Numbering altogether 31,000 in the 1961 Census, only about 1 per cent of the Kora of West Bengal (mostly in Burdwan and Bankura) actually speak a Munda language. The rest speak Bengali, while those in eastern Ranchi, Manbhum and Madhya Pradesh are said to be Kurukh-speaking and virtually identical with the Oraon.[54] They are not mentioned by Stampe and are mostly disregarded by Zide etc., but from the little ethnography relating to them they do not appear to differ markedly from other Munda tribes (they should not be confused with the Dravidian tribe called Koda found in the Nilgiri Hills in Tamil Nadu). Their name may refer to their traditional occupation of digging the soil, or else it is cognate with *hor* etc. and thus means 'man'. In some parts they are known as Kisan or 'cultivators', though many are said to be nomadic. Datta gives Mudi, perhaps a variant of Munda, as another ethnonym.[55] Apart from the article by Ghosh (1966), there are only passing references to them elsewhere. They will not feature much in the present work, partly because of this lack of data, but also because of uncertainty of the Munda status of particular groups of Kora mentioned in the literature.

B   South Munda Branch

B (i) Central Munda Sub-Branch

There are just two languages in this sub-branch, Kharia and Juang, Together, they are intermediate between Kherwarian and Koraput Munda, though rather closer to the latter than the former (see Fig. 1).

11. Kharia

Fifty years ago, groups called Kharia were to be found mostly in Chotanagpur and adjoining regions, but there were others in Assam and parts of West Bengal (where they had become very Hinduized), in Surguja, as far west as Chhindwara, and as far south as Kalahandi in Orissa; whether these were all Munda speakers or some Indic speakers is not clear. Vidyarthi and Upadhyay give the most up-to-date information, saying they are found in Durg, Raipur, Raigarh, Bilaspur and Chhindwara (Madhya Pradesh), Mayurbhanj, Sambalpur and Sundargarh (Orissa), Bankura and Jalpaiguri (West Bengal) and Chotanagpur, especially in Santal Parganas but also in Singhbhum (Bihar). Most sources mention three main Kharia sub-divisions, the Pahari, Erenga or Hill Kharia or Kheria; the Dhelki Kharia; and the Dudh Kharia. Their degree of Hinduization increases roughly in that order. The Hill Kharia are found mainly in the hills of Mayurbhanj and in Singhbhum, Dhalbhum, Manbhum, Bankura and Midnapore, and the Dhelki mainly in Jashpur, northwest Gangpur and Sundagarh; 'the Dudh Kharias far outnumber the Dhelki Kharias and the Pahari Kharias together' and are found mainly to their east and south, in southern Ranchi, Gangpur and western Sambalpur (virtually all the Kharia of Ranchi and Gangpur are Dudh Kharia).[56]

The Dudh and Dhelki Kharia claim to have come from Rotasgarh, the Dhelki having migrated first, whence their name ('Seng Dhelki', literally 'he who came first'). In myth, they separated from the Dudh in Ranchi for accepting food from the Mundari. *Dudh* is from Indic 'milk', probably a reference to their relatively greater ceremonial purity, for the Dhelki eat beef, the Dudh do not. Roy and Roy assumed that the Hill Kharia had also migrated from elsewhere though they claim to be indigenous to Mayurbhanj. However, it seems that the name Kharia has come to be applied to a number of totally separate groups.[57] The indigenous version tends to be confirmed by the attitude of the Hill Kharia studied by Hari Mohan (1961), for they did not recognize the other divisions set out by Roy and Roy. Certainly they have no contact with the other two groups and differ from them greatly in culture. They speak Oriya or a Bengali dialect called Kharia Thar, and not the Munda language known as Kharia.[58] Roy and Roy imply that they once spoke Kharia, but this seems to depend too much merely on the name, and we are probably safe in regarding them as a totally separate group. The other two groups do speak Kharia and, what is more, recognize each other as Kharia. 'Many Dudh Kharias agree in saying that the Dhelki Kharias are known as "Bar or Barka Kharias" and themselves as the "Chhotka Kharias" because the former are the descendants of the elder brother and the latter of the younger brother.'[59]

There are some 160,000 speakers of the Kharia language according to Stampe, and over 190,000 were recorded in the 1971 Census. It is spoken chiefly in Ranchi, Gangpur and Jashpur and to a lesser extent in Madhya Pradesh (an area broadly coinciding with the distribution of the Dudh and Dhelki Kharia). Some also know Oriya, Bengali, Hindi or Sadri according to area.[60] The word Kharia may conceivably be derived from Khaidya, which is an ethnonym used by the Hill Kharia perhaps meaning 'man'. However, it has also been connected with Mundari, Santali etc. *hor* 'man', even though this root is absent from the Kharia language itself.[61] Bhowmik suggests that it may be from Proto-Munda *kher* 'bird', perhaps a reference to an origin myth (cf. the Santal, 2, above) or to the fact that some Kharia hunt birds and sell their meat. Less favoured is the derivation from *khar-khar* or 'palanquin'.[62] About half the Dudh Kharia and a lesser proportion of the Dhelki Kharia are Christian, a higher proportion than in any other Munda tribe.[63]

There are a fair number of studies available on the Kharia, especially Chatterjee's early short article (1931), the two-volume work of Roy and Roy (1937) and the more recent monograph of Vidyarthi and Upadhyay (1980). The latter are dismissive of Das's monograph (1931b), which was the result of only ten days' fieldwork (with the Hill Kharia, in Singhbhum and Dhalbhum).[64] However, they are less critical than Hari Mohan (1961) of the work of Roy and his son.

12. Juang
The Juang are found in Keonjhar, Dhenkanal and Pal Lahera in Orissa and number some 17,000.[65] Keonjhar is supposed to be their original home, and traditional Juang culture is to be found mainly there; the Juang of Dhenkanal are more Hinduized. Those in the former area are known as *thaniya* or 'original dwellers',[66] those elsewhere being *bhagudiya* or 'those who have fled'; there is no intermarriage or commensality between the two groups, for the latter consider themselves superior.[67] They nonetheless share Keonjhar with the Oriya-speaking but otherwise quite similar Hill Bhuiya, who have the northwest part of the district, the Juang being to their south. These are both hilly areas, the plains to the east being occupied by Oriya. It is the northern part of the Juang area that is the oldest area of settlement and which was dealt with by Mc-

Dougal in his thesis (1963a). They consider the village of Gonasika to be their place of origin.[68]

Etymologically Juang simply means 'man', but the word is now only the ethnonym, Oriya loans being used for 'man' (*vir*). The Oriya name for the Juang is Patua or 'leaf', their traditional dress consisting of little else apart from ornaments, and they are also known as Patua Savara, a name which is liable to lead to confusion with the Sora (13, below).[69] Some Juang in Pal Lahera are basket-makers; possibly these and certainly other Juang in Dhenkanal show signs of wishing to convert themselves into a caste with, for example, restrictions on divorce, but most Juang are clearly tribals. There are apparently no monolingual Juang, the tribal language being spoken at home and generally amongst themselves, while Oriya is used in schools, markets, with officials etc. Two Juang dialects can be identified, that of Keonjhar-Pal Lahera and that of Dhenkanal.[70]

There is a traditional connection with the neighbouring Hill Bhuiya, the Juang being their 'younger brothers', but no commensality or intermarriage, since the Bhuiya regard them as inferior and untouchable and are also locally dominant. The link is expressed in myths in which the two groups are descended either from two brothers, one of whom ate beef and thereafter became a Juang, or else from two sisters, one of whom took to wearing leaves, thus becoming a Juang. Especially in Keonjhar, they are a very inward-looking group and have little contact with the Oriya and other local groups, but even they regard the Domb and Pano, local low castes, as inferior.[71]

The Juang are comparatively well served in the literature, the main work consisting of McDougal's excellent thesis (1963a) and articles (especially 1964; also 1963b) and Elwin's 'Notes' (1948), which are long enough for a short book. However, the latter differ quite drastically from McDougal's work on the same area (Keonjhar), and Elwin found his group very difficult to work with. Earlier work was done by Bose (1928, 1929), and more recent work by Patnaik (1964) and Rout (1962, 1969–70), McDougal's field assistant. Parkin 1990 uses Juang material in a comparative article on kinship in general in India.

B (ii) Koraput Munda Sub-Branch

B (ii) (a) North Koraput

13. *Sora*

Sora is preferred by Zide's group as the spelling of the ethnonym, which also appears as Saora, Sabara, Savara: Elwin gives a complete list of variants.[72] Some authorities think that they may once have been one of the most important and powerful tribes in northeast India. In about AD 500 a tribe called Savara is said to have overthrown and expelled the Cheros, then in control of Bihar, and presumably to have replaced them as the local rulers.[73] However, the word is used very loosely and over a wide area, being another of those misleading general designations for a number of different groups which we have already encountered and which need to be used with care. Today, groups of this or a very similar name are to be found in Singhbhum, Ranchi, Hazaribagh, Bundelkhand and northern Madhya Pradesh. The Malto-speaking Mal Pahariya or Maher of the Rajmahal Hills call themselves Sauria, but as they speak a Dravidian language they are not to be included here. The Lodhas of Midnapore claim descent from a branch of the ancient Savaras, while yet others of the name occur in Manbhum and Raipur, and some Juang (12, above) are known as 'Patua (Leaf) Savara'.[74] According to Majumdar the Savaras' original homes were in Uttar Pradesh and Madhya Pradesh, but this must be based on the confusion of names rather than on any hard evidence.[75]

In fact, none of these groups are of relevance to the present book. The Sora with whom we are concerned are to be found further south, in the Pottasingi taluk of eastern Koraput and the Serango and Ramagiri-Udayagiri taluks of southwest Ganjam, where there are over 200,000 speakers of the tribal language. There are also some near Tekkali in northern Andhra Pradesh, but most of those further south now speak Telugu. Those of the former group who live on the plains have generally become more Hinduized than the 'pure' Sora of the hills, some to the extent of adopting Oriya as their mother tongue. They tend to be bilingual, unlike those in the hills (except to some extent the younger generation).[76]

The most typical Hill Sora, called Patua or 'leaf' Sora by Hindus, are found around Gumma and Serango in Ganjam and around Pottasingi in Koraput.[77] Elwin and Sitapati mention three social strata, *gamang*, *buyya* and *parja*, the first two being of equal status and intermarrying, the third being inferior and only able to give, not receive, women from the other two. The very name *parja* clearly indicates dependency. *Gamang* means literally 'great man' and is thus also used for 'headman'.[78] There are also a number of named Sora sub-groups, some occupational, some denoting Plains rather than Hill Sora. The Hill Sora are predominantly called Lamba Lanjhia by the Oriya and are divided by Elwin into Jati ('real'; from *jat* 'caste'), Arsi ('monkey', though the connection in this context is obscure) and Jedu (Sora for 'wild' according to Elwin). Vitebsky, however, regards these and the names of the Plains Sora (see below) as characterizations 'used for pride or abuse' rather than as classes. In addition, there are some minority and Sora-speaking 'occupational' groups whose occupations, though without economic value today, are referred to in some rituals. There is a tendency for these groups to be endogamous, but except for *buyya* (priestly) families the rule is not a strict one. The Kampu Sora are Telugu speakers of the plains; the Sudda or Sarda, Based (= 'salt', i.e. coastal) and Bimma Sora are Plains Sora rapidly becoming assimilated, though some still spoke Sora thirty years ago. Subbarayan associates the name Kapu (= Kampu?) with Sora *ryot* or tenants.[79]

The earliest work in the present century on the Sora was carried out by S.N. Roy (1927) and Sitapati (see references), son of Ramamurti, whose grammar and dictionary (1931, 1938) were published in the same period. Elwin's massive monograph (1955), chiefly on religion, was the subject of two review articles, one by Dumont (1959), the other by the Africanist Victor Turner (1967), which is largely guesswork, owing to the gaps left by Elwin. Subsequent publications include Chaussin's 1978 article (she has apparently since left the field). Piers Vitebsky has done fieldwork with the group in recent years and has published some articles (1980, forthcoming), and his thesis (1982) is to be published as a book. Two other doctoral theses appeared on the Sora in the 1970s, one in France (Petit 1974), the other in India (Suryanarayana 1977).

14. Gorum

The Gorum, whose language is closely related to Sora, number 'less than 10,000' according to Stampe (the 1961 Census gives only 767 speakers and they are not mentioned at all in the 1971 Census). They are found chiefly in the Nandapur and Pottangi taluks of

Koraput, but like the Gataq, Remo etc. they are often classed locally as Poroja. The language may also be spoken in Vishakapatnam, but at least some know Oriya. They are called Parenga by the Oriya, a designation which has entered the academic literature, though in reality it may be one of two endogamous sections—the other being Kholei—into which they are divided; it is sometimes used also of the non-Munda-speaking Poya Gadaba of the Salur area.[80] They are also called Gadaba colloquially, a usage which entered the *Linguistic Survey of India*, but these are in reality distinct (see 16, below). The only ethnography consists of a handful of articles (Satpathy 1963–4b, Choudhury 1963–4, Pattanayak 1968), and they will appear only infrequently in the rest of this work.

15. *Juray*

A.R.K. Zide identifies Juray as a sister language of Sora and Gorum, apparently spoken in Koraput.[81] Nothing is known about those who speak it, for there is absolutely no ethnography, and this is thereafter the first and last time we shall meet them.

B (ii) (b) South Koraput

16. *Gadaba*

The Gadaba live in Kalahandi, Koraput, Vishakapatnam and Bastar. They should not be confused with the Dravidian-speaking Ollar of the same area, who were frequently called Gadaba or Gadba in the older literature until Bhattacharya pointed out the difference in the 1950s.[82] However, there are many other subgroups, and it is not always clear which speaks which language. The Boro or Moro (also Bodo, Bada 'big'[83]) Gadaba, not to be confused with the Bondo or Remo (q.v. 17), are Munda speakers.[84] The Sano or 'little' Gadaba, by contrast, are Ollar speakers or, around Jeypore, Oriya speakers. According to one source they are known as Parenga Gadaba, though 'Parenga' is the Oriya for a completely separate tribe (14). Both groups appear to be endogamous.[85] Another group are the Kathera or Mudli of Andhra Pradesh, Munda speakers, but with Telugu as a second language; they may or may not be the same as the Katuria mentioned by S.N. Roy as a division of the Plains Sora. Like the Bodo they claim a higher status than other Gadaba and are also endogamous.[86] Less is known about the affiliations of groups called Kaleyi (but cf. the Kholei, a sub-group of the Gorum, q.v. 14) or

Katini or Kapu (but cf. the Sora, 13), the latter perhaps meaning
'plainsmen'. However, in Andhra Pradesh both the Kapu and the
Kathera 'claim to be Bodos and Ollaros migrated from the hills', so
presumably they consist of both Dravidian and Munda speakers;
and since the Kathera speak Munda, the Kapu may well be Ollar.
Also to be excluded are the Poya Gadaba of the Salur area, who
speak Ollar.[87] The designation Gadaba is clearly a wide and
indiscriminate one. In addition to the Ollar and Gadaba proper,
Zide writes of 'distinct Munda and Indo-Aryan groups of Koraput
who have been, or still are, so called', and he remarks that the
'Gadaba' of Vishakapatnam mentioned in the *Linguistic Survey of
India* are in reality Gorum (14, above). Fürer-Haimendorf says that
the Boro Gadaba call the Remo (17, below) the San or 'little'
Gadaba, though these are a Dravidian group according to other
authorities (see above). His confusion may be because the Gadaba
regard both groups as well as the Gorum (14) as their 'younger
brothers'.[88]

Thus the 47,000 or so speakers of the Munda language, called
Gutob, seem to consist chiefly of the Bodo and Kathera Gadaba,
though Stampe admits that even this figure may include some
Ollar. They are found in the Nandapur, Semiliguda, Machkund
and Pottangi taluks of Koraput and in Andhra Pradesh. As well as
Gutob, all Gadaba also know Desia, the Oriya dialect of southern
Koraput district and the name the tribes of Koraput give to themselves and to the Dombo and other local low castes that have dwelt
in the area for a long time (this dialect is used between different
ethnic groups in the area). The Munda language is closely related
to that of the Remo (q.v., 17).[89]

There are several etymologies for Gadaba in the literature:
Telugu etc. *gedda, gadda,* or Oriya *gad* 'river' plus *-ba, -va* 'belonging
to'; Tamil *kadava,* from *kadu* 'ear' (because of their large earrings);
Sanskrit *kadvada* 'speaking indistinctly', also 'vile, contemptible';
or Sanskrit *gatvara* 'palanquin-bearer', their traditional occupation.[90] According to Sahu they call themselves Kadami, according to Burrow and Bhattacharya Gutob, though the latter is strictly
the name of the language and has been found to mean nothing to
them as an ethnonym. The river Godavari plays a part in their
account of their origins, to the effect that they should not go there
for fear of dying, but it is not clear whether in fact their name
derives from it.[91]

The little ethnography on them is scattered in articles old and recent, much of it by Indian anthropologists, though Fürer-Haimendorf (1943b, 1945b, 1950), Izikowitz (n.d.) and Pfeffer (especially 1984a, ms., but also his general writings) have all worked and published on them. The article of Thusu and Jha (1972) concerns Ollar speakers. It is unclear which groups are covered by Subba Rao (1965) or Somasundarum (1949).

17. Remo
The Remo live chiefly in the Jeypore Hills in Koraput, west of the Machkund river in southern Mathili and northeast Malkangiri taluks, centred on the village of Mundlipada. Others further east are more under Gadaba influence, though this does not prevent intermarriage. A third group live in the plains, but are more Hinduized than either of the others and intermarry with them increasingly rarely. There are about 2,500 speakers of Remo, a language that has borrowed heavily from Gutob in vocabulary but is typologically closer to Gataq. Most also know Oriya, and there are few monoglots.[92]

Remo is the ethnonym, Bonda being Oriya. Only the former will be used in this work, though it means 'man' not only in Remo itself, but also in Gutob (remol) and Gataq. Other designations include Bondo, Bondo Poroja and Nanga Poroja.[93] Despite the popularization of the pronunciation 'Bondo' through Elwin's monograph (1950), Bonda is a more accurate transcription.[94]

Elwin's study is still the chief work, one which reflects his parallel interest in psychology; its data on social organization should be read in conjunction with Fernandez's later critique (1969). There are also relevant articles by Fürer-Haimendorf (1943a, 1943b) and G.N. Das (1956a).

18/19. Gataq
The Gataq live between the Remo to their north and the Dravidian-speaking Reddi to their south, i.e. in the hill country on either side of the Sileru river, towards Malkangiri, along about twenty miles of the Machkund river between the Duduma Falls and the Kondakamberu, and in East Godavari district, Andhra Pradesh. Like many other groups in the area they are known locally as Poroja or 'subject'. The Oriya call them Dideyi (also Didei, Dire), but their ethnonym is Gataq, the regular cognate of Gutob.[95] They are also said to call themselves Gutare or 'people'.[96]

There are today 2–3,000 speakers of Gataq, but most also speak Oriya.[97] It is possible that there are in fact two Gataq languages (hence the double number for this group), namely Riverside-Hill Gataq and Plains Gataq, which are as different from each other as Gutob and Remo. They form a pair in opposition to Gutob-Remo, the two pairs themselves being co-ordinate within South Koraput (see Fig. 1). Virtually nothing was available on the Gataq until the appearance of a monograph in 1970 by Guha *et al*. Fürer-Haimendorf seems to regard them as in some sense 'pre-Munda',[98] but as with the Birhor (6), this must remain conjecture.

C   *Nihal Branch*

20. *Nihal*

There is one further group to be taken into account, namely the Nihal,[99] who call themselves Kalto.[100] Their language is spoken by perhaps 1200 in the border areas of Madhya Pradesh and Maharashtra. 'Symbiosis' is a favourite word used to describe their relationship with the Korku (1), with whom they live and work closely, though in a position of subordination. The difficulties surrounding the classification of Nihal have yet to be resolved, especially since 'earlier investigators attempting to learn the language were, apparently, deliberately rebuffed or misled'. According to Kuiper, between sixty and seventy per cent of its vocabulary has been borrowed, 36% from Korku, 9% from Kurukh and other Dravidian, and about 25% from Indic, mostly Marathi and the Nimari dialect of Hindi. However, 'about 24% of the Nahali vocabulary has no correspondence whatever in India.' Pinnow has suggested that although this element may not be Munda it may be Austroasiatic, while Mundlay, who has done linguistic fieldwork with this group, does seem to regard their language as Munda, though only remotely connected. Zide, on the other hand, is much more doubtful of its Munda status. He has advanced the alternative view that this isolated body of vocabulary is simply a thieves' argot—plausible, in view of the Nihals' reputation for robbery and dacoity—and whatever its origin does eventually prove to be, the language does indeed seem to play such a role.[101] Because of the uncertainty surrounding their status as a Munda group, it has been decided not to incorporate the little ethnographic information on them (mainly in de Candolle 1961) into the body of this work.

However, in the academic division of labour their language has become the responsibility of Munda scholarship, and accordingly it has been felt desirable to give a précis of their social organization and other data in Appendix I.

Other Possible Munda Groups

It is probably now less likely than it once seemed that yet other Munda languages remain to be discovered, for example, in the remoter parts of Orissa.[102] But there are many other groups that have occasionally been claimed to be Munda, often in a racial rather than a linguistic or cultural sense. They include the Chero, landowners of Palamau and other parts of Bihar and West Bengal; the Lohar or Lohra, traditionally weavers of Ranchi; the Jadua Patua and Gorait (the latter is really a standard term for village watchmen and messengers); and the Lodha, an 'ex-criminal' tribe of Midnapore who claim descent from the ancient Savara (see the Sora, above, 13). All these are said to speak Santali or Mundari as well as an Indic language and are perhaps tribals who have only become identified with these castes in the past few generations.[103] However, sometimes a Munda language may have been adopted by a non-Munda-speaking group. According to the *LSI*, 'the Kurukhs [i.e. Oraon] in the neighbourhood of the town of Ranchi have adopted Mundari as their home tongue.' Chatterji speculates that the Koli of Rajasthan and Kandesh (northern Maharashtra) may once have been Munda speakers, but he is clearly relying on the similarity of name alone. The 'Kol' studied by Griffiths are clearly Indic speakers, of Rewa and Jabalpur in Madhya Pradesh, and he is careful to distinguish them from the Munda. The Kisan of Jashpur have also been linked with the Munda.[104] The Bhil have been the target of such speculation too,[105] despite the fact that there is no evidence that they have ever spoken anything other than the Indic language they speak at present. None of the above will feature in the present work.

Chapter Three
Economy, Property and Family

3.1 Land and Economic Activity

Today, most Munda tribes live by cultivation of some sort, much of it swiddening (shifting or slash-and-burn cultivation). There is also much irrigated cultivation, especially in the more Hinduized groups. Some groups have alternative or additional occupations: some are semi-nomadic hunters and gathers, while others have acquired a specialist occupation, often as part of an attempt to enter the caste system.

The clearing of swiddens is generally a co-operative activity undertaken by the locally dominant agnatic group and/or village (the two are often identified; see sect. 5.2 (ii)), usually the recognized owner of the swiddens. However, each family is normally allocated particular strips or plots and thus carries out most other agricultural operations alone. It will enjoy the usufruct of the land while it continues to cultivate it or until the next distribution, but the land itself will always revert to the village and/or wider descent group in default of direct patrilineal heirs. Redistribution is normally carried out by the village headman or family heads and is often a ritual as much as an economic matter. The clan normally wants to retain its swidden land, which therefore should not be alienated to other clans, though this rule may be breached in some cases.[1]

Irrigated land is more likely to be owned outright by a particular family, due to its permanence and to the extra labour involved in building terraces and irrigation ditches—generally a result of individual or family initiative rather than a communal enterprise. Fruit trees are also regarded as private property, particularly if they have been planted deliberately, but otherwise the products of the forest are, as far as the tribals themselves are concerned, open to all (today, of course, access to the forest is very much restricted by the government's forest laws). The village may control other economic activities, as well as swiddening. Among the Juang, for instance, it controls hunting for large game, though small game is a purely individual affair, and gathering a matter for each family separately.

Similarly, it is the *mati* (shamans) and *naya* (priest) who have control over the communal monkey hunts of the Birhor (in which the foreleg of the animal goes to the family which owns the hunting net).[2]

Of the hunting and gathering groups, the Birhor are the best known, though they are not the only ones to live mainly in this fashion. Traditionally, they group themselves into bands or *tanda*, gathering the fruits of the forest, hunting monkeys, hare and other game, and collecting fibre from which they make ropes, which are traded. Bands vary in size according to hunting possibilities. 'There is some resentment towards a band which moves outside its traditional area and encroaches closely on another band' and much more resentment towards the Santal annual hunt, but there is little the Birhor can do about either.[3] It is likely that they always used to spend at least a part of the year more or less in one place, and in the last few decades their wandering has become increasingly restricted. Even in 1925 Roy observed that some had become permanently settled, and in 1960 Vidyarthi noted that even the remainder were migrating shorter distances for shorter periods of time.[4] This is partly the result of a deliberate government policy to encourage permanent settlement, and increasingly severe forest laws have also restricted their traditional activities, though some have become sedentary on their own initiative. Thus a distinction has grown up between the settled Birhor (Jaghi or Thania) and those who still migrate (Uthlu or Bhuliya), though there does not appear to be a corresponding social distance between them, and they still intermarry. Despite having become sedentary they continue to hunt when possible, and indeed they have generally not made a success of cultivation but have to obtain the cereals that are the basis of their diet from local markets in exchange for the forest products they collect. They have increasingly become vegetarian, however, thanks to Hindu influence.[5]

The Birjhia and Agaria Asur are also divided between Thania and Uthlu, the former clearly being to some extent Hinduized, though whether they maintain any social distance from the latter is not clear. A similar distinction, and one which does involve such social distance, occurs among the Korwa, where some of the settled group (called Diha or Dehari) are Sadani rather than Korwa speakers (e.g. in Jashpur). By contrast, the Hill Korwa, known as Pahari or Benwari, are gatherers and basket-makers, selling their work in the local markets, and the closely related Kodaku live by collecting forest produce or working as agricultural labourers. Some of this hunting and gathering activity is 'regressive', for although the government has tried to restrict it through the forest laws, it has also tried to discourage swidden cultivation in favour of irrigated cultivation and has not always received the response intended.[6] Even the cultivating Munda exploit the forests to some extent, and formerly hunting and gathering may have been more widespread among all these tribes. When the Oraon encountered the Mundari in Chotanagpur the latter were still jungle hunters, and it may have been the former who introduced swiddening, as they certainly introduced the plough, into the area in the sixteenth century. But however it was introduced to the Mundari, swiddening remained their pattern of agriculture until the nineteenth century, when wet-rice methods were introduced as well.[7] Today, it has become increasingly difficult to rely on the forests as an economic resource, not only because of the government's forest laws but also because of their own depletion; even fairly remote areas like Koraput are now largely deforested. Among the Santal there is now virtually no gathering, and hunting has become merely a sport. Hunting has also disappeared from Mundari life.[8]

Some Munda groups have taken up a specialist occupation or craft, which in some cases can clearly be associated with attempts to gain entry into the caste system. However, in others the motive appears to be purely economic: it is doubtful whether the Birhor tradition of rope-making can be connected with attempts to rise in status, for instance.[9] More significant in this respect may be the artisan speciality of the Asur, who were traditionally iron-workers, though today they are primarily cultivators or else basket-makers; the Karmali, supposedly an outcasted group of Santal, are also iron-workers.[10] Some other groups are basket-makers, like the Gataq, the Juang of Pal Lahera, some Korwa (see above) and the Mahali, another Santal outcaste group; the latter are also bamboo-workers, palanquin-bearers and drummers. All these occupations are regarded as degrading not only by the upper castes but also by the Santal, one possible reason for the exclusion of the Mahali and Karmali from them.[11] The Kora's traditional occupation is as earth-workers, diggers of ditches, etc. The Kharia were supposedly palanquin-bearers, though this interpretation may in fact reflect a false etymology for their name.[12] The Gadaba also have this tradition (see Ch. 2). The more consciously anti-Hindu tribes like the Santal and Mundari tend to despise all artisans and disdain such work themselves, partly because of the influence of Hindu values over them, partly through contempt for those tribals with any pretensions to caste status, however low, and the frequent recognition, even by local high castes, of the higher status of tribes over low castes.[13] There do not seem to be any such occupations among the Koraput Munda. Choudhury gives a whole list for the Sora, but this may have a mythological rather than an economic basis, like similar lists of Santal clans. Most of these specialist groups practise cultivation also, though it seems that even a change in the pattern of agriculture can be prompted by considerations of status. According to Bose: 'In the villages of Dhenkanal and Keonjhar where the Juangs have given up shifting cultivation and taken to the plough, there has arisen a new and rather superficial kind of demand for being regarded by others as one of the peasant castes.'[14]

Many tribals have also entered the modern Indian economy, for which there is considerable scope in Chotanagpur, now a heavily industrialized region often called 'India's Ruhr'. Many Santal in particular work in the steel plants and coal mines of the area, usually in low-grade jobs. They live in the *bustees* that are located just outside most industrial cities such as Jamshedpur but return to their villages on important occasions such as marriages, etc. Usually, they prefer to remain non-unionized rather than join the recognized trade unions, which they regard as Hindu-dominated and ineffectual. Although most Ho are agriculturists, some are also miners and yet others (as with many tribes) work as day-labourers for local Hindu landowners.[15] Other tribals work in the tea plantations of the north-east, something of a traditional escape for those involved in domestic difficulties at home.[16] Finally, even agricultural groups may find it more profitable to market the food they grow instead of consuming it themselves: Izikowitz reports that some Gadaba trade most of the rice they grow and live on finger millet instead.[17]

3.2 The Domestic Environment

Membership in all the agnatic descent groups and families of the Munda is acquired in the first place by birth for both males and females, i.e. through patrilineal descent. Generally, there is a rite of incorporation at or soon after birth, often connected with the name-giving ceremony. The Santal *janam chatiar* rite is an example: 'it admits the child into the sib of its father, and thereby gives it the status of a *hor*, i.e., a human being; and it individualizes a child by giving it a name.' Similar are the ear-boring rites found in the Kharia and other groups.[18] But while male children almost invariably continue in membership until death, female children may or may not. In some groups women join their husband's descent group on marriage.[19] In the case of the Ho a married woman remains a member of her husband's *kili* even after death and so her remains are buried in his clan's burial ground or *sasan*.[20] Although, according to most sources, this is also true of the Mundari (unless the woman is divorced), Choudhury maintains that 'the adoption of the husband's clan by a woman is temporary, valid only for the duration of her marital life.' At all events, she is buried in a section of the ossuary apart from HF, HFB, HeB and other senior affines, and her birth in another clan limits her participation in the ritual of her husband's family.[21] Among the Birhor and probably elsewhere, married women observe their husband's, not their natal totemic taboos.[22]

A Juang woman is incorporated into her husband's descent group, which must perform her death ritual, even if as a widow she goes to live elsewhere. Apart from death, 'only formal divorce can terminate this obligation'. Rights over the woman are transferred by the payment of the brideprice, and she may be transferred to another agnate if widowed.[23] Similarly among the Kharia, a married woman may enter the cattle shed of her husband but not those of her father or brother or other close agnates, and she may not cook for her natal family or enter their kitchen. Here, as elsewhere, she will join her husband and his ancestors after death, not her own agnatic ancestors.[24] Marriage is also the only alternative to birth for acceptance into Remo agnatic units, and this only for women, of course: the *guppasing* rite is performed to incorporate her into her husband's *kuda, bonso* and *tsoro* group (see sect. 4.2). So complete is this incorporation that she can remarry into her natal village if widowed, even though at the time of her first marriage this would have constituted a most serious offence.[25]

Such a transfer of membership is not invariable, however. For a Sora woman it is not certain until after her death and the rituals which accompany it. Korku and Kodaku women remain in their own clans.[26] A Santal woman does not fully join her husband's descent group. The vermilion mark applied at marriage signifies her acceptance by her husband's clan and qualifies her to help him with the domestic ritual, but not for the assumption of jural, ritual or inheritance rights. These she retains in her natal clan, to which she will return if widowed or divorced, and she retains also her natal clan name. While her flesh and bone pass after marriage to her husband's family, her 'blood of the ear', which signifies agnation, must stay with her natal family. Only she, no other female, may enter the *bhitar* or domestic shrine; not even a married daughter may do so, for fear she may harm her husband's family through continuing to deal with her natal spirits.[27] In general, however, there is a tendency for an agnatic group to try and retain the women it has acquired in marriage even after they become widowed by remarrying them to another agnate—typically to the younger brother of her husband, though this is not invariable (see sect. 6.5 for a full account). As far as males are concerned, the only exceptions to patrilineal descent as a qualification for the membership of agnatic groups are *ghar-jawae* marriage and adoption, both being designed to circumvent the lack of a male heir (see below, sect. 3.3). Among the Santal, children should always be born in their father's, not their mother's home, though conversely the Remo have 'no objection to the child being born in the house of the girl's parents'.[28]

The patrilineal bias of family organization is a constant factor among the Munda, but there is less consistency in either size or composition. The literature tends to give the impression of a general trend away from joint or extended families and towards nuclear ones everywhere, and this is often presented as being the outcome of modern economic changes. However, this need not be the case, and Parry has warned against assuming too readily the prevalence of either. Large families are always breaking up through internal quarrels or the deaths of the senior members around whom they were formed, and new ones are always coming into being as individual sons or whole sets of brothers marry and have children.[29] Thus there need not be a contradiction between the statement of Orans, that among the Santal 'the extended family in the traditional village seldom survives the marriage of all its sons', and Chakraborty's finding of a ratio of 55:45 between extended families and nuclear families in one of his areas of research, also among the Santal.[30]

The Santal *orak* ('house') will always consist of either a nuclear family or a group of agnatic kinsmen of two or three generations, who control 'patrilineal landholding and the worship of the *khunt* [sub-clan] deity'; it may also contain some affinal relatives (e.g. WG, WM, WZC, DHM, Z, ZC), but they have no jural rights within it.[31] Among the Kharia, 'married brothers generally manage to live in a joint family but separate after the death of the father.' Among the Birhor, on the other hand, sons may continue the *tanda* after the death of their father, though they may also join new ones. For the Juang the extended family is the ideal but the nuclear family the norm, because tensions between brothers prevent them from cooperating for more than a few years after their father's death. The Juang themselves make no nomenclatural distinction between these two types, all families ideally being extended ones called *inya* (lit. 'house, family'). More Hinduized groups often have larger families resembling the classic Hindu joint family, as do the Christian Kharia. Only in the case of the Mundari is a clear distinction between the nuclear family (*hor-hopon*) and the extended family (*orako* or *ora-enko*) recorded in the literature.[32]

Residence is usually virilocal or neolocal, though in the former case this may mean the village or hamlet of the husband's father rather than his actual homestead.[33] There are some circumstances, generally rare and / or temporary, which give rise to uxorilocal residence, namely *ghar-jawae* marriage (see sect. 3.3), marriage by brideservice, and short symbolic periods of uxorilocal residence immediately following the wedding (see sect. 6.4). Some Juang reside in the village of a ZH,[34] perhaps because one of the preferences for marriage is with a classificatory eZHyZ (see sect. 8.4). There are some reports of there being no clear rule of residence. This may be the case especially in a nomadic group like the Birhor, where a man may join the *tanda* of his wife's father, especially to avoid paying brideprice, which is quite heavy in terms of the Birhor's income. Even here, though, residence is normally virilocal.[35] *Contra* Turner's similar reading of Elwin's data on the Sora, Chaussin reports virilocal residence as normal here too.[36]

3.3 Inheritance

Apart from irrigated fields, the family home and fruit trees, most personal property is movable and inheritable. Inheritance is basically patrilineal and usually occurs strictly speaking on the partition of the family rather than on the death of the father, though obviously these two events often coincide. Thus it may take place before the father's death, or conversely the sons may continue to cooperate for a time thereafter.

Property is generally divided equally between the sons, except that the eldest son may receive more, even if a minor. Among the Mundari he receives the main living hut and the cattle byre, as well as his share of the land, and among the Santal double the amount that the other sons receive. The Juang only allow him more if an equal division of movable property (e.g. livestock) proves impossible, but the home goes to the eldest son still living there. Among the Birhor the shares of each son are ideally graded according to their respective ages, though this must frequently be hard to carry out, especially with such little property involved.[37] This favouring of the elder brother reflects the fact that he normally succeeds to his father's position as head of the family and thus becomes the latter's representative in the village council, as well as assuming control over its activities and interests and jural problems: he may, for instance, have to find the brideprices of his younger brothers and the expenses of his sisters' weddings. Sometimes he may succeed to this role prior to his father's death: for example, a Juang may become head of the family when his father is widowed, this reflecting the explicitly non-sexual, non-jural, but ritual status of elders. Moreover, in those tribes that practice cremation it is often his duty (as among Hindus) to light his father's funeral pyre, though this may be undertaken by some other relative, for example a brother or ZS among the Gadaba, or the youngest son among the Birhor.[38]

This not the only possible regime of inheritance. Among the Korwa and Korku, only those sons who have remained at home may inherit: the sons who have married and moved away receive nothing.[39] The situation is similar for the Sora, but inheritance is fully by ultimogeniture, the youngest son remaining at home to look after his parents. Ultimogeniture is also the norm for the Santal in Keonjhar, and for the Mundari as far as the house is concerned.[40] Among the Gataq both eldest and youngest sons may receive extra. Sometimes rights to inheritance are limited to those who have contributed to the funeral expenses of their parents, as with the Ho, where the inheritance goes in equal shares to the sons who contributed to the *pathalgiri* ceremony (installation of stones for the dead).[41] In value terms inheritances must often be very small, due to the poverty of many of these groups. However, it will generally include access and use rights to land, even where swidden land is deemed to belong to the village or agnatic group in the wider sense: i.e. the usufruct is itself inherited patrilineally.

There is often some inheritance by women, despite the preponderance of patrilineal rights. Ornaments, female clothing and some other movables devolve matrilineally,[42] while unmarried girls in all tribes have a right to their maintenance until marriage and to their wedding expenses.[43] There is no female inheritance among the Juang, however, a woman's property simply being left at the cremation site.[44] Statements to the effect that daughters or wives may inherit land and other normally agnatic property in default of sons probably refer merely to temporary provisions (see below).

Generally, 'land is conceived of as belonging to the clan', and in most tribes it can never devolve permanently to women because they marry out of it. Korwa women, for example, can only alienate their own personal property, not land or the house. In default of sons, therefore, land generally goes to the nearest male agnates: for example, among the Santal to the deceased's brothers or classificatory brothers in equal parts, and with brother's children preferred to sister's children among junior kin. Among the Gataq too, 'if a man dies leaving a daughter but no son his property goes to his brother.'[45] This may not happen immediately, however. For one thing, widows and daughters may be allowed the usufruct of the land during their lifetimes or until (and if) they marry. Secondly, there is also the custom, standard though not necessarily common in most Munda tribes (and occurring also in Hindu society), of adopting one's daughter's husband as an heir. He may have to work for his prospective father-in-law for a period of years in order to earn his right to inherit, in which case the brideprice is normally waived,[46] and henceforward he lives uxorilocally: but he inherits the land as an intermediary, for he cannot alienate it to his natal clan, and indeed some of it may revert to the agnatic group of his wife's father immediately.[47] His portion is inherited by his own son, as it would be normally: but the latter is usually counted a member of his mother's, not his father's clan (see Figure 2).

A

Figure 2. *Inheritance in* ghar-jawae *marriage*

A is the *ghar-jawae*. The arrows show inheritance remaining in the same agnatic line in the long term.

Among the Santal, the children enter the clan and sub-clan of the DH, who cannot change his natal clan and indeed retains his inheritance rights in it and his natal *bonga* or spirits. It is hard to see how the children can inherit from their mother's father in this particular case, but they are at any rate named after the wife's, not the husband's relatives (cf. Ch. 10).[48]

The Santal call this particular arrangement *ghar-jawae bapla* or 'house son-in-law marriage', the first phrase of which is Indo-European, one which has cognates in most other Munda languages (*bapla* is Santali). Troisi distinguishes this permanent arrangement from temporary marriage by service in place of paying brideprice (see sect. 6.4), which he calls by the slightly different name of *ghardi-jawae* marriage, but Mukerji denies that the Santal make this distinction, which appears to have originated with Skefsrud.[49] It is possible that in some cases a bargain is made between a sonless father and a poor youth unable to pay a brideprice, to the effect that the latter should marry the former's daughter in return for living uxorilocally in a low-prestige marriage and enjoying the usufruct of his father-in-law's land.

Among the Mundari, the adoption of a son-in-law is rarer than the adoption of some agnate, especially a paternal parallel cousin, brother's son or agnatic grandnephew, who can inherit the land without it leaving the clan.[50] The same is true of the Juang, where McDougal recorded only one case of DH adoption out of a total of 318 marriages.[51] Step-children are occasionally adopted, but they cannot always inherit.[52] The adoption of non-agnates is generally disliked as a threat to immediate patrilineal rights in land, though it is often necessary so that the agnatic group may retain it in the long term. Adoptees may be completely incorporated into their adopter's agnatic group if this is different from their natal one: Santal adoptees can marry into their natal clan, for instance. Other strategies for obtaining a legitimate male heir are junior levirate and polygyny (see sect. 6.5). In default of all near agnates, land is supposed to revert to the village community in most cases, which in practice often means the locally dominant agnatic group. However, according to Dhan, the Ho will let it go to a daughter or maternal kinsman or affine in such a case (to MBS or FZS rather than to MB or FZ).[53]

Chapter Four
The Organization of Descent

4.1 Introduction

Descent theory, and more particularly the image of descent groups as corporate groups controlling most aspects of individual lives, held a dominant position in British social anthropology for many decades, in relation not only to Africa, for which the theory was originally worked out, but also to other ethnographic areas. However, in the 1950s these other areas began producing data casting doubt on the relevance of the model outside Africa—a reaction eventually culminating in it being dismissed for Africa itself.[1] Ethnographers on the Munda have always been prepared to set limits to the relevance of African models in their own work, as have anthropologists interested in other parts of India. In the main, they have limited themselves to minimizing the corporate structure of descent groups and emphasizing instead their exogamy and their significance for the regulation of marriage. Certainly genealogical knowledge is limited and genealogical memory shallow; at its widest extent agnatic relationship is a matter of having the same totem rather than of traceable hereditary links. However, while it is true that higher-order segments are mainly instruments of exogamy, at a local level agnatic groups may also be of importance through their immediate control of economic resources and political power.

4.2 The Structure of Descent

All Munda have patrilineal, exogamous descent groups of maximal extent which the literature generally describes as clans. Apart from those of the Sora, most are also totemic. However, the regularity with which this fundamental institution occurs is not repeated exactly either in the ways these clans are grouped together and opposed to one another at a higher level, nor in how they are internally subdivided. In a general sense there is a distinction to be made between the Koraput Munda and those further north; we start with the latter.

Among the North Munda and the Kharia the maximal units, which following the convention I shall call clans, usually have the generic name of *kili, khili* (Kharia, Ho, Mundari, Bhumij, Asur), *kuri* (Korwa) or *kul* (Korku), the last two of which seem to be from the Indic root *kula*.[2] The most probable derivation of *khili* is Indic *kila*—'stake, peg', a meaning it retains in Santali, though here it is restricted to certain sub-clans only.[3] The clans of the Santal are called *paris*.[4] The more Hinduized sections of some tribes (Kharia, Mundari, Bhumij, Asur and Turi) use the common North Indian term *gotra*, as do some Korwa, Korku and Birhor.[5] The Santal, Korku of Melghat and Mahali have borrowed *jati*(Korku *jadho*) in this sense, but there is no evidence that it means 'caste' in any of these cases.[6] The Juang designation is *bok*, which is clearly related to *boko* 'younger brother'.[7]

Santal

Virtually all traditional accounts of Santal clans state that there were originally twelve, of which only eleven survive.[8] The twelfth clan, Bedea, is generally said by ethnographers to have died out. In reality, informants may include it only to lend a certain mythological completeness to the structure—the number 'twelve' is frequently important in myth and ritual.[9] It does exist as something like a separate entity in other contexts, namely as the designation of a separate tribal group in the 1961 Census[10] and as the name of a *khut* or sub-clan of the Soren clan.[11] In some areas, only nine of the eleven that are said to exist are actually encountered. Orans could only find nine in the southern part of the Santal area, a fact confirmed more recently by Bouez, and Somers could find no more even in Santal Parganas.[12]

The totemic names are the usual designations and are the means by which the members of different clans are identified from one another; today they are also used as surnames. All the clans except Hansdak have a mythical territory, fort and occupational specialization associated with them.[13] The occupations too are mythological, and although they remind one of the caste system and may have indeed been inspired by it to some extent, considerations of purity and impurity seem to be absent. There is also a distinction between the first seven clans—those that are mythologically descended from the incestuous marriages of the first seven sons and seven daughters of Pilcu Haram and Pilcu

Budhi, the primordial couple—and the remaining five, descended from 'those who came later'. There is some asymmetry of status between these two groups, entailing avoidance of intermarriage. While the occupations attributed to each clan remain constant, the choice of which are the top seven clans and the order in which they are placed tend to vary from informant to informant; indeed, to a large extent this depends on which clan the informant himself belongs to, this usually being placed at or very near the top. Gausdal accorded a priority to the Hansdak, which in a general sense is plausible: its origin myth is also that of the Santal generally, its name means 'goose', from whose egg the first humans were born, and it clearly represents the main line of descent, which derives from the eldest of the original seven brothers and seven sisters; the Murmu, as priests, also have a generally high status.[14] But although most writers follow Gausdal here, one of Bouez's informants placed Hansdak third and his own clan, Soren, first. Another placed Kisku first, his own clan Murmu second, and Hansdak last (i.e. seventh), and omitted Soren from the list of seven altogether. Moreover, he and yet another informant included Baske in the seven senior clans (this clan is placed eighth and therefore among the 'late-comers' by Gausdal) and omitted Murmu, one of the 'senior' clans according to Gausdal, altogether. This may be a quirk of Keonjhar, where Bouez worked, for next door in Mayurbhanj the order given by Gausdal is said by Carrin-Bouez to be 'the most current', Hansdak and Murmu being superior to the rest. Besra and Core are everywhere accorded a low status, and so mostly is Baske, every though its function is to cook and provide food for the kings.[15]

There are bars to intermarriage between some pairs of clans, e.g. Kisku and Marndi, Kisku and Hembrom, Tudu and Besra, and Hansdak and Murmu. In Mayurbhanj, Kisku, Hembrom and Marndi form a group of rather inferior status to the rest (i.e. in this area not only Hansdak and Murmu, but also Soren, Tudu, Baske and Besra are 'good' clans), but although this influences alliances to some extent, 'one must emphasize that this does not involve the formation of either exogamous or endogamous moieties'. Many writers deny that these distinctions indicate hypergamy: 'distinctions between clans are mythical rather than real'. According to Kochar they are due to 'traditional rivalries' rather than any 'inherent social inferiority of any of the clans in question', and Somers says that they are not observed in practice and that there is no hypergamy between clans. However, Bouez clearly disagrees and sees hypergamy as a fundamental though partial aspect of Santal alliance (see sect. 8.4), status differences between clans being enshrined in the origin myth. Bouez's view applies, of course, only to Keonjhar, but further north too, Gautam reports 'marriage preferences associated with a ranking order of the clans'.[16]

With at most eleven clans for a population of about four million, Santal clans are necessarily widely dispersed, and localized only mythically. Bouez attributes this to the displacement of the Santal and their loss of land in recent centuries, necessitating their identification with occupations and totems as well as simply localities.[17] Such circumstances must completely rule out the possibility of actual agnatic links being traceable throughout a *paris*.

Santal *paris* have internal divisions known generally in the literature as *khut*, a term which Bodding derives from Hindi *khut* 'part, side', while Gautam glosses it as 'pole, line'; it is usually translated as 'sub-clan'. This generic name is apparently rare or unknown in the south of the Santal area, though from Bouez's description and his awareness that the term occurs elsewhere, it is evident that the concept itself exists there.[18] As with the clans there are traditionally twelve, but many more occur in reality, most of which are only found in a few *paris*.[19] Some, however, are found in all, and these seem to have a special significance. Those called Nij (from Oriya *nijjor* 'real, authentic') have priority as the central, original branch of the clan, and accordingly are sometimes identified by the *paris* name only. Second in rank are the Bitol (from Hindi *bitlaha* 'expulsion'), said to have been rejected by the Nij for some ritual fault or accident; the opposition between them is one of pure versus impure according to Bouez.[20] Other branches that are considered collateral in relation to the Nij are the Manjhi Khil and the Naeke Khil,[21] supposedly descended respectively from two brothers, of whom the elder had been village headman and the younger village priest; consequently, the headman is senior to the priest here (but cf. the Mundari, below), a fact which is enshrined in myth. Finally, those called Sada (Hindi *sada* 'simple, clean, white') are distinguished from the others by not using *sindur* (vermilion) in ritual. This may or may not denote inferiority to other *khut*: one of Bouez's informants, a Naeke, said that it did, while another, a Manjhi and therefore of higher status than the Naeke, said it did not—possibly, suggests Bouez, because the Naeke, representing the priestly function, was more particular in such matters. It may reflect *clan* status, however, since there are said to be only six clans that use *sindur*. Gausdal gives a sixth *khut*, Gar, as common to all *paris*; it is not exactly clear what sociological significance this has, but the designation is clearly a reference to the mythical fortress of the clan.[22]

The actual segmentation of clans, and not simply their division into parts, is recognized in myth, and sub-clans recognize their relationship through the parent clan, even if unable to trace the actual links. This sense of identity is so strong that Santal sub-clans, unlike those of the Ho, can never become separate exogamous clans in their own right.[23] Bouez leaves little doubt that at least the Bitol, Manjhi and Naeke sub-clans are 'defined as collaterals of the founding branch, Nij', and internally too they are agnatically defined, though also associated with clusters of between ten and fifteen villages. He also considers that they have mainly a ritual function and little or nothing to do with marriage:

> Sub-clan names play no role in the regulation of marriage, and the sub-clans do not even constitute exogamous units that are more strict than the clan. Nor do there exist between sub-clans any privileged relationships such that the same sub-clans of different clans show a tendency to intermarry and thus assume a caste-like endogamy; for a Santal, sub-clan hierarchy is only of significance within his own clan.[24]

Orans disagrees with this in part, for he calls the sub-clan 'the exogamous unit par excellence', marriage within which is much more serious than marriage within the clan. This is also suggested by Carrin-Bouez, who says that in Mayurbhanj there is some intra-clan marriage in the Hansdak and Murmu clans, though the sub-clans must be different. This seems to be due to the fact that these two clans are demographically the largest, as well as among the highest—most would say *the* highest—in status.[25] Clearly, however, the sub-clans are not endogamous, and Orans stresses the exogamy of each of the three principal units he identifies—clan, sub-clan and lineage.[26]

In fact, most authorities agree with Bouez in seeing the sub-clan as mainly a ritual unit, though Gautam adds that it is also important in inheritance. There is much secrecy over *khut* names and ritual. The name of the sub-clan divinity is known only to the eldest male of the sub-clan, who passes it on to his eldest son at the approach of death. The ritual itself is performed in secret, and by males of the agnatic group only, who are called *kond*—women and daughters' husbands are excluded and should not even know the place of assembly.[27] Thus the sub-clan has a strongly agnatic character, which means that it should be avoided in marriage, though the secrecy of its name prevents it from being the main vehicle for forging actual alliances. Bouez regards this ritual as vital for *khut* identity: being widely dispersed, identification with a particular cemetery (cf. Ho and Mundari) is less feasible here, and indeed there is none.[28] Nonetheless, the image of ancestry is associated with land locally, descent being 'closely connected with the dead ancestors—the original reclaimers of the land'. *Khut* ritual is carried out both at the *bhitar* (domestic altar) and in the fields. By contrast, *paris* ritual concerns the tribal *bonga* or spirits and is devoid of secrecy.[29]

Three ethnographers also report 'lineages' among the Santal, although they do not appear to have much sociological significance. According to Somers, 'the *bos* appears to have the prime function of determining inheritability [and succession] beyond the household in the absence of a male heir', and it rarely extends beyond second-cousin range. It 'cannot be labelled a "corporate group"' but appears to refer to something like a 'blood line'. Somers is the only ethnographer to report it, but the term has also been noted by lexicographers. Campbell glosses it as 'children, descendants, race, stock, family', Bodding as 'descendants, family lineage (generally agnate), race (animals)'. Most of these translations seem to have a general sense, perhaps not covering actual descent groups. According to Orans, on the other hand, 'the local lineage is a group of patrilineal kinsmen, living within a few miles of one another, periodically worshipping as a unit, and gathering together on such occasions as marriages and funerals'. This description resembles that which Bouez and others have given for the sub-clan and also that of Somers for what he calls sub-clans, though he gives them the name *gutia*.[30] Bodding regards this (from Hindi *gotiya*) as a term designating a sub-clan of inferior status to one's own within the clan, a distinction apparently of significance at clan rituals. Bodding also makes two other distinctions, which seem to refer respectively to the members of a sub-clan (*dahgi*) and of a clan (*gusti,* from Hindi *goshthi*), rather than to the actual units.[31] Kochar says that these too are rather loose conceptions. He claims that lineages are unrecognized among the Santal, though he goes on to define and find some significance for them nonetheless, and even identifies the deities known as *abge bonga* with them.[32]

Thus it would appear that the Santal descent system is organized first into exogamous, totemic *paris,* whose primary significance is in the regulation of marriage and whose members are perhaps known as *gusti,* and at a lower order the *khut,* with a mainly ritual significance and whose members are known as *dahgi.* The *bos,* if it means anything at all sociologically, is perhaps simply those nearer agnates with whom one mostly interacts and who have priority in inheritance rights in default of a direct heir of one of their members. At the widest possible level, all Santal regard themselves as agnatically related to one another, as reflected in the origin myth.[33]

The closely related Mahali have at least thirteen clans, called *jati,* ten of whose names they share with the Santal *paris;* they are not ranked in relation to one another. They are also divided into sub-clans, which are exogamous, like the clans of which they appear to be segments.[34]

Mundari

Mundari clans, called *kili,* are also patrilineal, exogamic and totemic, but there are many more than among the Santal, despite the fact that the latter are four or five times as numerous as a tribe. Roy gives a list of the 'original' ones, which, he says, number twenty-one, although at least as many again appear elsewhere in his book. Each is traditionally descended from a common ancestor and has a totemic designation.[35] Yamada says that 'the functions of the clan are mainly confined to the marriage regulation', though occasionally endogamy occurs through ignorance of clan names or premarital affairs; such relations constitute *mago* (incest), but they are generally ignored unless the girl becomes pregnant.[36] Standing stresses that it is only *kili* members who have 'full "ancestral" rights to land', each village being associated with just one clan.

However, it seems to be the *khut*, into which the *kili* are divided, that have the greatest economic significance at the operational level.[37] 'Within the clan, land is held by coparceners of local lineages *(khut)*....' There have to be at least two of these to each village (and therefore clan), one (the 'elder') representing the village priest, the other (the 'younger') the village headman; they are called respectively *pahan khut* and *munda khut*. Thus as with the Santal there is a status distinction expressed through the idiom of relative age, though the polarity is reversed. In Naguri villages there is usually also a *mahto khut*, descended traditionally from the third son of the village founder who, again according to tradition, furnished the *munda*'s assistant, though today there is no such post.[38]

The *khut* may at one time have been revenue units, but this was presumably an imposition by local administrations and one growing out of their former importance as land-holding units. According to Sugiyama, 'any member of this group has a potential right of inheritance with belongs to other members', but this can only be relevant in the rarest of circumstances, since Standing says that 'the inheritance unit is...considerably smaller than the *khut*'—in fact confined to the *khewat* or smaller revenue units which have been established during this century and rarely exceed six agnatically related households.[39] There is some economic co-operation within the *khut*, such as the loaning of labour and money, the sharing of produce, and contributions towards brideprice, but it does not have any political role, such as help in a feud. It is localized, with the eldest male as its leader. It is also a ritual unit, with the exclusive use of a joint burial ground or *sasan* within the village and joint attendance at the rites of passage of its members, in which sense it seems to be the outer limit: the dead join *khut*, not *kili* ancestors, and members of different *khut* of the same clan do not attend each others' rites of passage, save for weddings in some villages.[40] Thus the Mundari *khut* has both ritual and economic significance, in contrast to the identically named unit among the Santal, which seems to be a ritual unit only, though again the ritual is a male preserve with the exception of the oldest female in the family.[41] There also seem to be fewer *khut* names and consequently a rather more regular pattern of clan division. The *khut* are clearly agnatically defined and as such are bound by the rules of clan exogamy. This means that members of the two *khut* of a single clan cannot marry, but members of two *khut* of different clans may, whether or not they share the same *khut* name.[42]

Ho

Ho clans are, like those of the Mundari, called *kili*, of which there are over a hundred; their names are often used as surnames today. Most villages are associated with just one *kili* or *kili* segment, either in fact or by tradition, but there are many multi-clan villages. Each clan has its own *sasan*, which together with locality are more important as indicators of agnatic identity than among the Santal. *Kili* genealogy is normally untraceable and exogamy is therefore important, but occasional intra-*kili* marriages are tolerated if the partners do not live in the same village or share the same *sasan* or ossuary: sexual relations between those linked to the same cemetery through agnatic links constitute incest. Totems are not very common as *kili* designations.[43]

Each clan is divided into sub-clans, the respective members of which occupy different hamlets *(basti)* within the village. Sub-clans originate as clan segments, and it may take three generations before they are completely separate and mutually exogamous. Segmentation increases the pool of potential spouses in cases where the segments have become separate clans. It is the eldest line that preserves and perpetuates the original name: until complete separation, the segments are identified by prefixes attached to this name, and thereafter these alone are used. However, since the same prefixes are used for sub-clans belonging to different clans there is no guarantee that they indicate the same clan when used alone. Thus the ability to trace genealogical links is both more feasible and more important here in deciding matters of affiliation and marriageability than it is at *kili* level. There are some status differences between sub-clans of the same clan, though, as in the case of Santal clans, their positions in the hierarchy vary according to informant. There are also patrilineages, five to six generations deep, called *haga* or *bhayad* (both of which mean 'brother'), whose members share a burial ground and also contribute to the brideprices of their members, provide some political support, and attend each others' rituals. It is not clear whether or not these are the same as Bouez's sub-clan, especially since he does not give any generic name for the latter, though the descriptions bear some similarities.[44]

Korwa

The generic names given by the Korwa to their descent groups vary according to region. At the apex are the usual exogamous, totemic clans, called *kuri* in Surguja and *gotara* in Palamau. Of the former there are said to be only four (Samat, Hansda, Mundi and Ediga), which are not hierarchized. Each clan is represented on the village council, and its members tend to cluster in hamlets within the village. Their chief significance is the regulation of marriage, but they also have some ritual unity in mutual attendance at members' rites of passage and family festivals, especially funerals. There is a degree of economic co-operation on such occasions and in times of need. In Palamau, by contrast, it would seem that it is the 'lineages', called *khili-bans*, which are the ritual units (for *khili*, see above; *bans* is clearly from Indic *vamsha;* see n. 51, below). These are also exogamous and are presumably segments of the *gotara*. They are named after localities, with which they seem to be associated, and they form a ritual unit at rites of passage, etc.: at ancestor veneration rites (which only men carry out) each *khili-bans* eats together, and apart from the others. This seems to be significant for an individual's identity with a particular *khili-bans*: 'Khili means a man who can eat the same head (sacrificed goat or pig or chicken) and bans means same stem.' In Surguja there are also patrilineages, called *bhaiyar* (from Indic 'brother'), whose internal genealogical relationships are known, but their significance is not clear.[45] The Kodaku sub-group have a similar structure to that of the Korwa of Palamau, namely of clans called *goti*, whose co-members are *gotia* (presumably from Hindi *gotiya;* cf. *gutia,* given by Somers for the Santal sub-clans), and unnamed lineages (called *pahuna*?), which are significant only at mourning rites. There are no preferences for particular *goti* in marriage, for they are all of equal status.[46]

Birhor

As a hunting-and-gathering group, the Birhor are organized into semi-nomadic bands called *tanda,* but it is unclear how far these are unilineal. Roy denies that the *tanda* are in any sense either unilineal or exogamous and says that each consists of at least two or three clans, which persistently intermarry (he also tends to use the term in the sense of 'settlement'). More recent writers tend to disagree.

Sinha is the most unequivocal, saying that: 'A Tanda constitutes a minimal patrilineage comprising five to eight nuclear families and on...average...thirty persons'; three generations deep, it is self-sufficient economically, relying on other *tanda* only for marriage partners and communal hunting. Martel and Williams probably come nearest the truth in suggesting that the *tanda* normally has a core of patrilineal kinsmen and is therefore exogamous. However, its membership is very fluid, and it may also contain affines and collateral relatives, though some are temporarily attached rather than full members. Sometimes two or more descent groups will come together in one *tanda* (this approaches Roy's interpretation): in a sample of twenty-five *tanda*, Williams found that thirteen consisted of just one patrilineage, eight of two, three of three, and one of four. In opposition to Sinha, Roy, Malhotra, Adhikary, and apparently Chakraborty all regard the *gotra* system, of patrilineal, exogamous, totemic clans, as entirely separate and as cross-cutting the *tanda* system. There are apparently twelve clans traditionally, as with the Santal, but in reality there are many more names: Malhotra adds a further ten to Roy's original list of thirty-seven.[47]

Other North Munda

All the other North Munda tribes have patrilineal, exogamous and totemic maximal descent groups similar to the Mundari *kili* and Santal *paris*, but their numbers vary and sometimes (e.g. Asur, Turi) there seem to be no further levels of segmentation down to the level of the family, or at least these are not recorded. The same seems to be true of the Korku, though there is certainly evidence here of the division of clans *per se* into new exogamous units. Some of their clans (Totae, Tota, Sakom, Busum) have a low status and rarely intermarry with the rest, though in theory they could do so. Similar evidence of segmentation of clans, some being able to intermarry while others retain a sense of common origin and are therefore barred to one another, comes from the Bhumij, though in parts of Orissa they were said sixty years ago to lack clans altogether. Bhumij clans are not localized themselves, but their sub-clans are affiliated to different ossuaries, and they therefore probably have some ritual significance at funerals (cf. Ho and Mundari).[48]

Juang

Juang clans are called *bok*, from the kin term for 'younger brother'. Each *bok* has a single totem, which is associated with the clan founder in the origin myth. In Dhenkanal, villages tend to be multi-clan, though each clan has its own hamlet and headman. In Keonjhar, the Juang area for which we have most information, each village is generally associated with a single clan, but some clans occur in more than one village, which are usually contiguous. Villages are therefore ideally associated with agnatic groups and the only non-agnates present should be in-marrying spouses, though some affinal and matrilaterally related families may nonetheless be resident too. The presence of such families is usually temporary, but even if permanent they 'are not absorbed into the local descent group by means of genealogical fiction'. McDougal also says:

> The Juang conceptualize the village in terms of ideal structure; ties of co-residence are phrased in the idiom of agnatic kinship.[...] The village is always a corporate unit; unless the male members of a clan form a local descent group at only one village, they never constitute a corporate group. The clan *per se* is not an economic, ritual, or political unit. It is the village, the localized co-residential unit, which is critical.

Thus although the clan is not a corporate unit, the localized, co-residential segment is—and conceptually this is virtually equivalent to the village.

There are eighteen clans in Keonjhar, with two, at most three, levels of segmentation. The *kutumali* (an Oriya word) is the minimal, unnamed segment of four to five agnatically related families. It has some ritual and economic unity through mutual food exchange; through its ritual elder or *kamando,* usually its oldest male member, especially at life-crisis rites; as the preferential unit of inheritance in default of direct male heirs (B, BS, FB); and as the main contributor to brideprice—more than other families in the village, even if agnatically related. It also tends to form a residential cluster within the village. 'Large' *kutumali* are also identified sometimes, but these have little significance (*kutumali* alone will hereafter refer to the minimal segment unless otherwise stated). At the village level there are still larger units, which McDougal, presumably following Leach, calls 'local descent groups' (LDGs), there being thirty-eight in Keonjhar, the same as the number of villages. For the largest of these units genealogical ties are assumed but not demonstrable, and in fact genealogical connections cannot normally be traced beyond the immediate group of two or three agnatically linked families—certainly never beyond the *kutumali*. Genealogical memory is limited to three or four generations at most, often to just two, and all these units have a 'low degree of solidarity', with 'no balanced opposition' between the various segments of the sort that Evans-Pritchard detected among the Nuer. There is little or no co-operation among agnatic LDGs, especially if in different villages: 'other structural principles, especially generation, override these vertical cleavages in most social situations'.[49]

Kharia

As with the Santal, the clans of the Dhelki and Dudh Kharia are hierarchically ranked, there being twenty-four among the latter and thirty-one among the former at the present day. However, as with the Mundari this is far more than the number of clans supposed to have been the original ones, namely eight among the Dhelki and nine among the Dudh. Among at least the former, the two lowest ranking clans, Mail or Kilo (= Tiger? cf. Gadaba, below) and Topno, cannot give food to the rest, while the highest status ones here are Muru (= Santal Murmu?), followed by Samad. A similar situation occurs among the Dudh, the three clans that are superior in status here being Dunglung, Kulu and Samad or Kerketa, also conceptualized as King, Queen and Barber respectively. It is not clear how this hierarchy affects actual alliances. Soren occurs as a clan name in both sections, and Hansda among the Dhelki (cf. the Santal).[50]

Gataq

The Gataq have clans or *kuda*, a name perhaps associated with *kula* etc. Beneath them are the *biria* or lineages, in which office devolves in some cases and which have the ultimate control over land distribution and initial control over marriage, brideprice, divorce, etc. The *kuda* are grouped into wider units called *bonso* or *gta*,[51] and it is these, not the *kuda*, which are identified by totems. There are five *bonso*, named as follows (with the number of clans in each *bonso* in brackets following): Nkoo or Tiger (8); Mala or Cobra (12); Gbe or Bear (4); Mosali or Crocodile (1); and Goi or Tortoise (1). According to Guha *et al.* these five totem groups are further collected into two moieties which are exogamous and divide Gataq society into discrete intermarrying groups: one's own is called *nairamoan* ('group of brothers'), while that into which one marries is called *moita* ('group of friends').[52] Mohapatra gives them the names Ghia and Nta, which sound like specific labels rather than descriptive and relative ones, though we do not know which applies to which *bonso* or moiety. Guha *et al.*'s 'moieties' are discrete and do not overlap, but the grouping of *bonso* and *kuda* into them is unequal: one moiety consists of just the eight clans of the Nkoo totem, while the other four totems, which total eighteen clans, form the other, Mala being predominant. However, while this may be the picture, it is more likely, on areal grounds especially, that there are no sociocentric moieties here and that *nairamoan* and *moita* are simply categories that are ego- or at any rate *bonso*-centric. The distinction between agnate and affine is fundamental for all Munda tribes, but it is doubtful that it ever amounts to a true dual organization. Guha *et al.*'s interpretation is perhaps in reality that perceived by members of the Nkoo *bonso* only, for the 'moiety' consisting of this single *bonso* would naturally be *nairamoan*, and it is evident that all the other *bonso* are, from its point of view, *moita*. Although we cannot at present be certain, it is very likely that the classification would be applied differently if the perspective were switched to another *bonso* (e.g. Mala), i.e. its members would be *nairamoan* to one another, all the others—but including Nkoo, and therefore a different set from above—being *moita*. This interpretation is reinforced by the fact that the two single-clan *bonso*, though both *moita* to Nkoo, may and do intermarry (though Mala and Gbe are said to be barred to them).

Each *bonso* is exogamous, but the situation concerning the *kuda* is less clear. Fürer-Haimendorf says that they are not necessarily exogamous, 'for branches of the same kuda may belong to different bonso and the two units of bonso and kuda can thus be compared to intersecting circles.' However, Guha and his colleagues, whose account is more recent and based on longer periods of fieldwork, insist on the exogamy of the *kuda*, and they also found that only one of the twenty-six *kuda* names they recorded occurred in more than one *bonso*.[53]

Remo

The *bonso/kuda* distinction again occurs here, though in this case neither are totally exogamous, whereas the village is very strictly exogamous. According to Fürer-Haimendorf:

> the Bondo's system of phratries (*bonso*) and clans (*kuda*) is akin to that of the Gadabas, but marriage within the *bonso* or *kuda* is permissible and the only strictly exogamous unit is the village community.

> Each village with its sub-settlements forms an exogamous unit. Although the Bondos are divided into phratries (*bonso*) each bearing the name of an animal such as 'tiger' or 'cobra', and into numerous clans (*kuda*), the village is the only unit decisive in the regulation of marriage relationships. Marriage within the clan, while not frequent, is permissible, and the rules of phratry exogamy are violated with impunity, but sex-relations between members of the same village, men and women who partake of the same sacrificial food (*tsoro*), is considered a most heinous offence.

Tsoro food 'is rigidly restricted to members of the same village.' Withholding it is the sanction against breaches of village exogamy; the only exception allowed stems from the fact that women enter their husband's *tsoro* group on marriage and thus may remarry into their natal villages if widowed or divorced.[54]

The division into *kuda* seemed to Elwin to be a fairly recent development, resulting from the impact of 'civilization', which for the Remo meant, in his view, the Hindu but low-caste Domb. The *kuda* names, of which he gives nine (mythologically there are seven, as with the Santal and Birhor), were those of village officials or outside tribes—one (Jigri) claimed descent from a Gadaba—and some seemed to him to be the result of borrowing from neighboring peoples. He also speculated that they were traditionally associated exclusively with just one village but had later become spread throughout the Remo area in different villages. In many villages the different *kuda* were found in separate hamlets, and they always had separate memorial menhirs. Elwin did not consider them to be as significant as the *bonso* system, which he regarded as older than either the village or the *kuda*. This was partly because he thought the *bonso* had genuinely Remo names, unlike the *kuda*, whose names were undoubtedly Indic—even those named after villages, whose Remo names were used only rarely. He found that there were two major *bonso*, Ontal or Cobra and Killo or Tiger; but the former being far larger, *bonso* exogamous rules were perforce broken in nearly half of all marriages. These two in particular seemed to him to be fundamentally Remo because of their names, though they are in fact Desia. Although other *bonso* names existed, they appeared to be the product of intermarriage with other tribes such as the Gataq (Bear and Monkey; but cf. note 52), Gutob (Bear, Fish, Sun, Monkey) and Gorum (Monkey, Vulture, Sun, Tiger, Cobra).[55]

Elwin seems to have placed too much importance on the 'borrowing' of parts of the system, whereas in all probability only the names have been borrowed (so many Munda designations for significant concepts have been taken from Indic languages that this cannot be seen as of any great significance in itself). Indeed, some twenty years later Fernandez was to find that even the Ontal and Killo *bonso* now had other names, also Indic (Nang and Bag), as did the other two *boish* (= Elwin's *bonso*) he came across, namely Git (Eagle or Falcon) and Balu (Bear). He emphasized especially that there were four *bonso*, not just two, as Elwin wanted to suggest. Another difference between Fernandez and earlier writers concerns the interaction of *bonso* and *kuda*: while Elwin and Fürer-Haimendorf maintained that the two systems were cross-cutting—according to Elwin all but one *kuda* were found in both his 'original' *bonso*—Fernandez maintained that each *kuda* was found in only one *bonso*, and he therefore suggested that they were really *bonso* segments (i.e. sub-clans or lineages: he agreed with Elwin that there were nine *kuda*). However, his own interpretation is much influenced by Murdock's standard definitions of descent groups—so much so that these sometimes seem to have been imposed on the data rather than vice versa. It is equally possible, as with the Gataq, that the *kuda* are simply grouped into *bonso* rather than being segments of them, even if each is unique to a *bonso* as Fernandez claims. He goes on to suggest that the *tsoro* group may in fact be a lineage, and this does indeed seem to have a patrilineal core: according to Fürer-Haimendorf, 'even long residence does not admit a man to the ritual fellowship of a village with which he has no hereditary ties', though affines and maternal kin may be admitted after 'the performance of an elaborate ritual' and women become members by marriage into it (see above). Fürer-Haimendorf criticised Elwin for stressing the *bonso* too much and the village too little. However, Elwin did state that while the *bonso* marriage rules were kept in about a half to two-thirds of his sample, the *kuda* rules were kept in about five-sixths of them, and the rule of village exogamy in virtually all cases.[56]

Gadaba

The published data on the Gadaba descent system is very confused, with little or no agreement among the various writers. Fürer-Haimendorf says that there are a number of exogamous *kuda* with non-totemic names and that these are grouped into *bonso*, which he translates as 'phratry' and which have totemic names (of which he gives as examples Tiger, Snake and Bear). According to him they are not strictly exogamous, and there are normally at least two to each village. Elwin's brief note talked of Tiger, Cobra, Bear, Fish, Sun and Monkey *bonso*. Chandra Sekhar, whose list refers to both Ollar and Bodo (i.e. Dravidian- and Munda-speakers), identifies Parrot in place of Fish and Bear but otherwise agrees with Elwin. It now appears more clearly, however, that there are four *bonso*, definable as totemic groups: Kora (Sun), Golleri (Monkey), Killo (Tiger) and Onthal (snake) (these are Desia names, the Gutob ones being respectively Gili, Gusha, Druka and Bulebu). *Contra* Fürer-Haimendorf, they are exogamous and not grouped in any dual organization. The Snake and Tiger *bonso* are ranked senior to Sun and Monkey, with Snake senior to Tiger, but wives may be taken from any that is not one's own.[57]

The *kuda* are four in number and named after offices indicating status rather than actual administration, namely *boronaik, munduli, sisa* and *kirsani*. These names are also used as surnames. The first two belong to the secular sphere, the last two to the sacred, and they can also be divided crosswise, between elder and younger (certainly the first two, though attribution of status to the second two is not clear). Each village is divided by *kuda* both sociologically and spatially, each *kuda* occupying a separate quarter of the village; ideally all four *kuda* should be present (whence the term *chari jono* or four men for the village council, supposedly one from each quarter), though sometimes there are less. Since the *kuda* are to be found in more than one village the two units of *bonso* and *kuda* may be seen as cross-cutting globally, though within the village the latter appear as segments of the former; in reality, the *bonso* are only characterized by their exogamy, being categories rather than groups, while the *kuda* of a single village are the nearest the Gadaba have to corporate groups. Both *kuda* and *bonso* are defined as patrilineally related, at least within the village, though not necessarily to identically named groups outside it. Each *kuda* quarter is divided further into unnamed sub-units consisting of a household or a number of households. It is the quarters (i.e. village *kuda*) or their sub-units that are the operational units in alliances outside the village, the whole village (excluding resident low castes) forming an exogamous community through the sharing of the same ritual food (Desia *tsoru*, Gutob *goyang*; cf. Remo, above). The *kuda* of a single village also owe each other ritual services and are the basic units in marriage and death ritual. Each village is dominated by the leader of one *kuda*; these *naiko* or chiefs consider themselves *morolog* (Gutob; Desia *borolog*, both literally 'big man'), their status depending primarily on their influence as individuals.[58]

Gorum

Satpathy mentions patrilineal, exogamous clans here, and Pfeffer has confirmed the presence of eight exogamous phratries (*bonso*?) with totemic names (Tiger, Cobra, Sun, Monkey, Vulture, Bear, Cow, Fish), which he calls a standard pattern for this region among all language groups and low castes as well as tribes.[59] Data are badly needed, however, on all aspects of this tribe's social organization.

Sora

The Sora have appeared exceptional to most writers in that they have no totemic, exogamous 'clans' but only the *birinda*, a unit claiming descent from a common male ancestor which Elwin and Chowdhury describe as an 'extended family', Chaussin as 'the principle kinship unit in Sora society', and Vitebsky as 'agnatic kin-groups'. In other words, the maximal patrilineal descent groups of the Sora have no totemic designations, each being named instead after a village officer if the post devolves within it, or otherwise after its oldest male member, so in this sense they

resemble the *kuda* of other Koraput Munda. Each *birinda* is generally confined to one village, giving the latter a tradition of common
descent.[60] The three most significant social groupings seem to be:
(i) the household (*singbirinda*), united by landownership and ancestor cults; (ii) the *birinda*, exogamous, united ritually and through
association with a particular hamlet of houses grouped together
(*longlong*); and (iii) the village community, consisting of several
birinda and divided into hamlets but united politically and ritually;
branches of a *birinda* are called *tega*.[61] Each ego distinguishes his
own *tega* within his *birinda* as his *tap-rungkun*, a ritual group which
holds certain fields in common and comprises 'those who eat the
same rice, my rice-brothers'. This appears to reflect once again the
ritual importance of food. This unit also has some ritual unity in
respect of agricultural rites, with its own altar. Cremation and the
erection of memorial stones are, however, the responsibility of the
birinda, each of which has its own cremation ground and menhirs.[62]

Thus the maximal descent groups of the North and Central Munda
tribes are totemic, patrilineal, exogamous clans variously designated *kili, kuri, paris, gotra* or *bok*. Most are divided in segmentary
fashion, the segments being called *khut* in some cases but having
no generic name in others. These segments are generally regarded
as lineages or sub-clans by ethnographers and have local or office
names (if any), not totemic ones. Being clan segments, they are
necessarily exogamous, but their significance is more likely to be
ritual or economic (especially in matters of inheritance) than concerned with the regulation of marriage (a matter mostly left to the
clan). Among most Koraput Munda there is a quite different system (the Sora differ yet again). Here the *kuda* seem to be the main
units that are ordered primarily by descent, for they are patrilineal
and in some cases divided into segments (e.g. the Gataq *biria;*
possibly the Remo *tsoro* group). However, they have local or office
names, not totemic ones, and are not everywhere clearly exogamous (e.g. among the Remo and Gataq). In all four groups
(Gataq, Gadaba, Remo, Gorum) they are grouped into *bonso*, which
are totemic but again not always clearly exogamous (at least, not
among the Remo). The links between *bonso* and *kuda* do not appear
to be conceived as consisting of genealogical links, let alone as
being traceable, but membership of such groups appears at least to
be defined agnatically—cf. the distinction between 'brothers' and
'friends', or agnates and affines, general in these societies (sect. 8.2).

In all tribes the tendency is to identify the higher-order descent groups with totems, the lower-order ones with local or office names, probably because the greater size and geographical extent of the former precludes or inhibits any local identity (the Santal are the most striking example of this, the Ho a partial exception). The higher the level of segmentation the less likely it is that actual genealogical links will be traceable—hence the greater importance of myth as an expression of putative ancestry at the clan level when compared with actual rituals in which all the members of a lineage or sub-clan are present or represented.

4.3   Interpreting the Structure

(i) Ritual or Genealogy?

Although agnation is the idiom structuring descent groups at all levels, right up to the moieties of the Gataq, the ability to trace actual genealogical ties is often minimal. According to Elwin,

> The Bondos do not normally think in genealogical terms and their memories are bad; it was, in the main, only exceptional men who could remember their family tree for even three generations.

McDougal tells a similar story of the Juang:

> because of a general inability to trace collateral linkages in the grandparental or previous generations, the membership of the unit cannot normally be demonstrated genealogically. When two males of the same descent group classify each other as brothers, their children automatically class one another as siblings. The children may not be aware of the genealogical relationship between their fathers; the system does not depend on their ability to trace such a link.[63]

Thus not even at the level of the local descent group or village is much attempt made to memorize, let alone record, genealogical links. Other, more ritual expressions of agnation are in fact preferred at all levels.

For instance, totems are clearly more significant than genealogies in establishing agnatic relationships across the whole society. Totemic designations serve as emblems distinguishing individual clans or *bonso* from one another, and an early question when marriages are being considered is likely to be a comparison of the totems of those getting married, which, given clan exogamy, should always be different. Totems also signal the association of each descent group with the object represented by the totemic name, and these are mostly naturally occurring objects, usually animate. However, the Korku have virtually no animal totems but instead many connected with the plant world, especially in respect of cultivation. Fuchs associated this with the recent adoption of permanent cultivation by the Korku and claimed that their totemic system was therefore also recent, but Ferriera found the predominance of plant totems to be characteristic of this area, especially Maharashtra, and not only of the Korku. Ferriera claims that the Juang too have mainly plants as totems, but a scrutiny of the lists given by Elwin reveals a number of names referring to animals and to villages too. We can also discount Roy and Roy's claim that totemic clans are missing from the Juang of Keonjhar in view of McDougal's specific mention of them there.[64]

The totem object is generally protected in the sense that members of that particular clan are forbidden to kill, eat or otherwise harm it. This is not true of the Korku, presumably because of the predominance of plant totems there. Among the Ho too, Majumdar claims that 'most totems are not items of food and there exist few dietary restrictions', though here totems are not very common anyway for the large number of clans that exist.[65] Totem objects also feature in clan origin myths. Some of these mention the clan's descent from its totem (Juang, Santal, Kharia, Agaria Asur), while others stress the autonomy of clan and totem, only members of the former being descended from a common human, if mythical ancestor, although the totem may have played some part in the ancestor's fortunes and/or the clan's origin (Birhor, Ho, Mundari, Kharia, Santal, Mahali, Juang). There is no worship of the totem object and no rites designed to increase its number and thus the size of the clan, although the reverse belief is frequently held, namely that any serious decrease in the species will threaten the existence of the clan (hence the taboo on harming it). However, some reverence and respect may be shown to the totem in the form of salutations or averting one's gaze from it (Asur, Birhor, Kharia), and there must generally be a sense of common identity with it.

These and other taboos and observances are, of course, clan-specific: the observances in relation to any particular totem object are only applicable to those individuals grouped under it, not to members of any other clan.

Lineage unity is marked in a variety of ways, some ritual, some economic. Many have already been noted: partaking of the same food (Korwa, Sora; Remo, Gadaba *tsoro*); attendance at members' rites of passage and specific lineage rituals (Santal, Mundari, Bhumij, Ho, Korwa); possession of a common burial ground (Mundari, Bhumij, Ho) or memorial stones (Gadaba); control over land or other economic co-operation (Mundari, Gataq, Korwa, Ho); or any combination of these. A common mark of agnation is the 'blood of the ear': one's ears must be pierced before marriage, cremation, or acceptance into one's natal descent group in many tribes.[66]

(ii) Corporate Groups or Alliance Units?

Maximal agnatic units (clans, *bonso*, moieties) are clearly more concerned with the regulation of marriage than with anything else, though their effectiveness is often incomplete. This may be due to the relative ignorance of clan names, even of one's own in some cases.[67] In other cases clans may simply be large but few in number, and status considerations may also be significant (see the Santal, sect. 4.2). Of course, the exogamy of lower-order segments is normally governed by that of the maximal units, and in any case exogamic rules tend to become more rigorous the nearer one approaches recognized agnatic ties. Only rarely are marriages reported to occur *within* any agnatically defined unit (e.g. Remo and Gataq *kuda*, Santal clans, one Gataq moiety). These cases all seem to reflect the breakdown or absence of an explicit rule of exogamy rather than any positive requirement for endogamy, and many of the reports concerned are anyway contradictory or in some other way suspect. In this particular context it is only the tribe or sub-tribe as a whole that can be compared with the castes of the majority Indian society, not any of the agnatically conceived and normally exogamous units into which it is divided.

The relevance of maximal agnatic units for the regulation of marriage is reflected in a number of other circumstances. As will be argued in sect. 5.3, the multi-village federations of many Munda tribes, which are above all concerned with breaches of marriage regulations (especially incest and marriage outside the tribe), in reality seem to be clan assemblies, whether in fact, in origin or in tradition. Secondly, there is the distinction most tribes make between those clans and, where appropriate, *bonso* and moieties, from whom one can take a wife and those from whom one cannot—the latter mostly being defined agnatically (see sect. 8.2). Certainly these maximal descent units do not appear to be corporate groups in the classic Africanist sense: Korku clans, for instance, have no common property, no traditions of mutual help, no headmen. Orans remarks of the Santal clan that it 'does not exist as a corporate unit' but 'serves as a reference point establishing kinship relations among all Santal', especially in respect of marriage, and this is true of the Munda generally.[68]

However, at a lower level most Munda tribes identify the village and its swidden land with a particular local group of agnates (see below, sect. 5.2 ii), characteristically a lineage or an even smaller unit, and village residents who do not belong to it usually have less rights to land or none at all. The locally dominant agnatic group generally consists, in myth or reality, of the descendants of those who founded the village, and it is typically its eldest male, usually also the village headman, who controls access to land and redistributes it when necessary (see sects. 3.1, 5.2). Thus most Munda villages distinguish between original settlers and latecomers, or rather between their respective descendants, though the exact significance of this varies from tribe to tribe. This has nothing to do with the ritual status of clans throughout the tribe: one clan will be dominant in one village, another in another.

Among the Mundari, for instance, the descendants of the original settlers are known as *khuntkatti* settlers or 'lineage settlers'.[69] Following the foundation of the village, maternal kin, affines and members of specialist artisan castes—the latter usually non-tribal—would join the original nucleus through marriage or invitation and be given land. The affines of the original settlers and their (the affines') descendants, or *kuar*, were eventually assimilated to the *khuntkattidar* even in the *sasan* or burial ground. However, later affines and their descendants, classed as *raiti* or tenants, were and are dependent politically and for land on the dominant clan, which owns the land (having originally cleared it) and monopolizes village offices. Unlike resident low castes the *raiti* are not excluded from speaking in village meetings, though they tend to have poorer quality land, and many work as labourers instead of farming. If a *raiti* family moves from the village or dies out the land reverts to the control of the dominant clan. The distinction between *khuntkattidar* and *raiti* is perpetuated beyond death, a separate part of the *sasan* being used by the latter, or often the *sasan* of a separate village where their clan is the dominant one.[70]

Whether the story of how this distinction came about is actual or mythical is not very clear, especially since there is little documentary evidence concerning such matters. There is some evidence that British legislation made the distinction between *khuntkattidar* and *raiti* more significant than hitherto.[71] Nonetheless, what is significant is that these traditions validate the position of the dominant clan and are the basis of their particular claims to land, which is normally owned by and perpetually inherited through the founding clan of the village. This does not mean that other residents do not have access to such land, but they have use rights only for the most part, and if they die out or abandon the land it reverts to the direct control of the dominant clan, without whose consent it cannot be alienated.

This system of access to land for all residents alongside retention of ownership in just some has come under pressure from outside, especially in the last two centuries, during which time Hindu landlords and local officials entered many Mundari areas with the support of the British. The progressive Hinduization of local Mundari chieftains had already led to grants of Mundari land being made to Brahmans and Hindu soldiers, who were imposed on the Mundari as landlords. At first, it seems to have been possible for the tribes to open up new areas of land, but by the late nineteenth century these were becoming scarce. For a number of reasons, therefore, many Mundari had lost land altogether or had become dependent for access to it on local Hindu landlords, a situation which contributed to the Birsa Munda rebellion of 1895–1900 and to other uprisings. This in turn led to the Chotanagpur Tenancy Act of 1908, which confirmed the position of the *khuntkatti* families as the most privileged tenants and indeed increased their rights to some extent. It did not do as much for the *raiti*, and indeed it may be at this stage that the distinction between the two became crucial in terms of access to land.[72]

In Ho areas this imbalance has not occurred, for the descendants of the village founders (*mura* or *khuntkattidar*) and incoming *porja* enjoy essentially the same access and use rights. Even here, though, land ultimately belongs to the former alone and cannot be alienated. Ho lands have generally been freer from outside pressure and more under the control of the village panch than in some other cases: the British introduced reforms here much earlier than among the Mundari, restoring Ho lands and abolishing taxes after the Ho rebellion of 1831–2.[73] A similar situation occurs among the Juang and Kharia, except that in Kharia villages non-Kharia artisans have no access to village land.[74] The founding lineage also controls village land among the Santal, and on the same basis. For instance, in the village in Midnapore where Saha worked six clans were represented, though the members of only one (Soren) claimed to be descendants of the original settlers. Although all resident Santal can work village land for themselves if there is sufficient, frequently there is not, and many become share-croppers or day-labourers for Hindu neighbours instead. Like the Mundari, the Santal suffered much dislocation and dispossession of land in the nineteenth century, and British reforms came later to both areas than to those of the Ho.[75]

There is a similar distinction in Sora society between the dominant group of residents (*gamang* and *buyya*), apparently agnatically defined—they provide the village officers—and the lower status, dependent *ryoti* or *poroja*. It is not clear exactly what rights in land, if any, the latter enjoy, though Elwin says that they 'are generally poor'. The headman's *birinda* has more wealth and status than those of other villagers, and marriage between the two groups is hypergamous, to the extent it takes place at all.[76] Lineages ultimately control land distribution among the Gataq, and Gadaba villages are usually dominated by a single agnatic group, which is distinguished from the affinal ones that are also present, but it is not clear how this affects control over land.[77]

Chapter Five
Village and Territory

5.1 Introduction

Ethnographers on the Munda not only agree that descent groups are not to be seen as corporate groups, they also tend to limit their significance as political bodies or instruments of economic control. Thus the village or *hini* is the most important political unit of the Gataq and is virtually self-sufficient economically. Although there are affinal and consanguineal links between villages, these do not overshadow or compete with the autonomy and self-sufficiency of the village *vis-à-vis* its neighbours. In Dhenkanal most Juang villages are multi-clan, but although each clan has its own hamlet and headman, village unity soon appears in any dispute with another village; and even in Keonjhar, where most villages are associated with just one clan, agnatic relations produce less solidarity than the men's house that is the ritual centre of each Juang village. According to McDougal, 'Juang villages are economically self-sufficient, ritually self-contained, and politically autonomous', needing the outside world only to provide them with spouses (since villages are usually dominated by a single clan); the kinship system, by contrast, does not produce marked solidarity in Juang society. Among the Sora, too, a 'high degree of political autonomy [is] enjoyed by the most important residential unit, the village', village rather than *birinda* names being used in mutual salutations. Here, there is village-wide cooperation in large-scale agricultural tasks such as rice transplantation and harvesting, and in the associated ritual. Most commentators on the Santal also stress the importance of village unity over kin ties, and Standing makes a similar comment in relation to the Mundari: 'All men of the same generation in the village are considered to be "brothers" regardless of clan. The village thus has a moral unity which cross-cuts genealogical connections.'[1]

Choudhury, however, contradicts this view of a paramount village unity in saying that, among the Mundari, 'a man has a greater obligation to his clan than to his village if the latter is not a uniclan village', and presumably just as much if it is.[2] Indeed, there generally exists an agnatic core at the heart of most villages, and the significance of this should not be minimized, however limited exact genealogical knowledge might be. While village unity may be expressed in some contexts, it can be argued that ultimately this depends on the assimilation of other residents in the village to the dominant clan rather than to any concept of the village as a territorial or administrative unit. The latter is an outsider's view but not necessarily the indigenous one. In fact, many of the political and economic institutions of the Munda prove to be basically agnatic in composition and recruitment, despite the greater fluidity with which many ethnographers seek to endow them. McDougal admits this even while expressing a view of the village as autonomous, since the one respect in which it—like the descent group—is not self-sufficient is in obtaining women to marry. This is also made evident through traditions in which the village is seen as the creation of the members of a single clan which continues to dominate it politically, economically and ritually, despite the presence of in-comers within it today. As we have seen (sect. 4.3 ii), these traditions support the claims to land of particular agnatic groups and they also validate their dominance generally, especially regarding control over village offices. However, this dominance is localized, i.e. specific to particular villages or groups of villages: in other areas other clans will be the important ones, so that no overall asymmetry of status arises as a result (though it may be present for other reasons—see the Santal in sect. 4.2).

5.2 *The Village*

(i) Assemblies and Officials

All the settled Munda groups have a similar village constitution with, at the minimum, a council, headman and priest. To a large extent this uniformity must be the result of the influence and requirements of the wider society and its jural arrangements, and not necessarily just in the modern period. The councils are rarely directly comparable with caste panchayats, for it is not often that the rules and prohibitions of caste are an issue.

Although the village councils are generally referred to as panchayats by most writers, this is not necessarily the indigenous name. The Santali term *kulhi durup* means literally 'sitting in the village street' and seems to refer to the actual meeting of the village assembly, itself called *more hor*, literally 'five persons' (cf. Hindi *panchayat*), though usually many more attend. The meeting-place is the *manjhi-than*, a sacred grove dedicated to the spirits of past headmen, as its name suggests (see below).[3] Mundari *hatu panch* literally means 'village panch', like the term *grampanchayat* (though the latter is a government-sponsored assembly for a whole group of villages that is found all over India, and not just in these areas—see sect. 5.3). The Juang *baro bhayki* means literally 'twelve brothers' and meets in the men's house or *majang*, the ritual focus of the village, for judicial cases are heard there. The Gadaba assembly is called *chari jono*, literally 'four men', one from each agnatically defined *kuda* or quarter within the village.[4]

The traditional assemblies generally consisted of at least the village officials and the male heads of households, but whether others may attend, speak or vote varies from tribe to tribe. Residents belonging to clans other than that which is dominant in the village and even co-residents of different ethnic affiliations may participate in discussions of common interest, but they do not usually take part when matters of concern only to the dominant clan are being considered.[5] The matters these assemblies are concerned with may be ritual (infringement of custom, such as incest or avoidance rules or endogamous or totemic restrictions, and also the readmission of offenders after expiation, though the village federations may have charge of these matters—see sect. 5.3), criminal (theft, assault, etc.), marital (adultery, divorce, desertion, approval of marriages taking place within the village), economic (the distribution of land, the siting of a new well, inheritance disputes etc.), confirmation and removal of village officers, and the handling of external relations (assessment of tax liabilities, problems arising from new legal requirements, etc.): 'strong emphasis is put on the concept of consensus'.[6] An important traditional sanction was *bitlaha* or the exclusion of offenders from the village until expiation was made. This was an often violent demonstration of hostility against the offending person, involving the destruction of his house and its contents, accompanied by singing, drumming, naked dancing, defecation in the house, etc.; it is now illegal and has anyway become increasingly unpopular in some groups. Among the Juang it is in a formal sense the penalty of the village federation rather than the village itself (see sect. 5.3). Fines are another sanction, though in the past, when money was even scarcer than it is today, feast-giving must have been even more common; it is still often required, especially as a means of expiation to the whole village allowing the offender's readmission into it. Sandhwar mentions corporal punishment among the Korwa, but this is not noted elsewhere. Panches are characteristically not at all formal but very loosely organized, *ad hoc* affairs. Some are losing their attractiveness as a means of solving disputes: Sengupta reports that the Mahali are turning increasingly to the police instead. Nonetheless, these assemblies are still of importance in most villages as regards *tribal* custom, and unlike the officially established *grampanchayats* they rarely have any official thrust upon them today.[7]

The number and type of village offices also varies from tribe to tribe, but there are generally at least a headman, a ritual specialist and a number of assistants. The headman is frequently called *naik* in the southern part of the Munda area, while in the north the terms *munda* (Mundari, Ho, Karmali, Kharia) and *manjhi* (Santal, Mahali) are prominent, alongside *mahto, pradhan* etc. Sometimes the different titles depend on the area or on tribal sub-divisions. It cannot really be said that the post is elective, for although the incumbent normally has to be confirmed by the assembly, the obvious candidate is usually the eldest son of the previous incumbent, and sometimes this is actually enjoined as the rule. However, the eldest son need not be the chosen successor; if he is felt to be unsuitable for some reason another son may be picked, and in default of all sons the office will usually go to a close agnate in a collateral line. The period of office is not generally limited, the incumbent serving for life or until removed by death and illness or by the panch (for misconduct, incompetence etc.).

Another constraint on automatic succession has been the attitude of the agents of the central or state government, for village headmen have frequently been burdened with official powers as police officers, tax collectors etc.; formerly, for instance, the appointment of the Santal *manjhi* had to be confirmed by local government officials (ethnographers disagree as to exactly which) as well as by the heads of families in his village.[8] This can place the headman in an equivocal position, torn between the conflicting demands of government and villagers; normally, however, he is at one with the latter, who support him in their turn as a form of protection against the interference of outsiders in general and officialdom in particular.[9] There is no reported tendency to chose a non-entity as headman as a means of blunting official interference, as is occasionally reported from elsewhere, though the headman may sometimes have less power and influence than the priest or some other official: e.g. the Kodaku *mukhia* deals theoretically only with outsiders and has less influence than his assistant, the *jati pradhan*, especially within the village.[10]

In addition to the duties imposed upon him by outside authorities, the headman convenes the village panch when necessary and represents its authority on a day-to-day basis. Like the panch he has some responsibility for ensuring that the rules of alliance and kinship (e.g. avoidance relationships) are properly kept, and his permission must be obtained before any marriage can take place within the village. This applies especially, perhaps, to *ghar-jawae* marriages, which affect patrilineal rights, and he is also concerned in respect of inheritance disputes generally. Sometimes he may allot land for cultivation and he may have a minor ritual role, for example, in agricultural rites, weddings etc. He may be something of an opinion-former or political leader, but he is rarely if ever comparable to the Big Men of Papua New Guinea, though the Gadaba are something of an exception. Among the Juang, political influence depends more on oratory on particular occasions than on office or a particular following and need not go with the headmanship. Similarly, Mundari 'village headmen carry out routine administrative functions but rarely play an active mobilizing or political role.'[11]

The headman is usually aided by deputies, messengers (often called *gorait*), village watchmen etc. The latter two categories are often non-tribal: e.g. the *bariko*, messengers and village watchmen in Koraput, are usually Domb, and in Korku villages most watchmen or *kotwar* are Nihal, especially in Melghat.[12] Most of these posts seem to be more or less hereditary, but some are elective, at least in principle,[13] and others appointed: e.g. the Santal *gorait* is chosen by the headman for three years and can be dismissed by him, though he is usually in the same clan and may act as his deputy.[14] These are probably all posts that the tribals recognize, whatever their origin, but others, such as the *tehsildar* or village accountant and the *patil* or tax collector, have clearly been created by outside governments alone.

There are two main sorts of ritual specialists among the Munda. First there is the village priest, called *sisa, pahan, dihuri, baiga* etc., whose main role is the performance of those rituals that are directed at maintaining or re-establishing the correct social order, whether in 'individual' life-crisis rites (which, though focused on individuals, are really matters for the whole community) or in explicitly collective rites (agricultural, yearly renewal etc.). Among the Juang there are two, the *dihuri* being concerned with village rituals, the *bhuitar* with personal ones. Like the headmanship, the priesthood normally devolves hereditarily in the male line, with the same provisions as to suitability. There are also some outright exceptions. In Keonjhar, the Santal village priest is normally chosen by divinities during possession, while in the same area the Juang *bhuitar* and *ordhan/podhan* are always respectively the first and second senior members of the ritual elders or *kamando* [15]

The second sort of ritual specialist are normally regarded as 'shamans' by ethnographers and locally are called *ojha, guniar, mati, dissari* etc.; these are diviners (of illness, the fate of the dead, possible reincarnations etc.), witch-finders and communicators generally with the other world and its powers.[16] As Elwin says, 'the Sisa is for routine, the Dissari for emergency', and this division between the ordered, auspicious ritual world and the disordered, inauspicious one is reflected in the essentially unofficial status of the shamans: for example, whereas Santal priests and their assistants are ex-officio members of the village panch, shamans are not.[17] Characteristically they 'emerge' by demonstrating their powers rather than being appointed or elected or succeeding their predecessors hereditarily.[18] Nor is this an exclusively male preserve, like the other posts: while most Remo shamans are men, many Sora ones are women. However, although opposed, the two posts are complementary, and both may be involved on certain ritual occasions, as in the communal monkey hunts of the Birhor. Occasionally, one individual regularly holds both positions (e.g. the Kodaku), but even here the two posts are regarded as essentially separate.[19]

Both priests and shamans have their assistants, some of whom have particular tasks: e.g. it is the Santal *kudam naeke*, literally 'priest at the back of the house' or 'field', who performs the sacrifices to the main deity, Sing Bonga, and to the local deities. The Kodaku *baiga* propitiates, his assistant or *alwa* divines.[20] Often, priests and shamans are from a separate group, particularly in a multi-ethnic village, where they serve all the groups resident there. Thus the Korwa shaman need not be a member of the tribe, and their priest or *baiga* was formerly usually a Chero, though today he is more likely to be a Korwa.[21] The Turi, as well as being basket-makers, also serve as priests (*pahan*) in many parts of Chotanagpur. The Birjhia Asur have their own priest or *dehari*, but the neighbouring Baiga serve all the castes and tribes in the area in certain contexts.[22]

The Santal have one other official, the *jog-manjhi*, who is appointed by the *manjhi*, though not all ethnographers agree on his significance. Most call him a 'censor of morals', with the task of preventing incestuous and otherwise improper marriages, though Kochar explicitly dismisses this interpretation and calls him a 'director of marriage ceremonies', also saying that he collects evidence on behalf of the headman concerning cases brought before the village panch. Gautam probably comes nearest to the truth in saying that he has 'responsibility for the avoidance of any village scandal resulting from conflicts, illicit sexual relations, breaches of exogamy' etc. Carrin-Bouez incorporates the basic versions of these two authors in saying that he 'is essentially responsible for the conduct of the young people and...organizes the main village festivals'. He is aided by his wife in controlling the girls of the village and has certain other duties, namely finding a suitable father for illegitimate children and collecting contributions for purchasing sacrificial animals. Mostly, however, it seems that he represents the villagers' interests in maintaining the rules relating to marriage, which involves not only the prevention of incest, which all other writers apart from Kochar stress, but also the maintenance of tribal endogamy, the performance of correct ritual at weddings, etc.[23] Possibly the absence of village dormitories among the Santal, with their control over the behaviour of the young, has something to do with his presence here, though he is not unique in the Munda world: the Korwa have the *lotadar*, who also presides over the panch and may be more effectively the headman than the *mukhia*, described by Gupta as 'only a tutelary head'. Another post with a mainly ritual role is the *pargana* of the Mahali, 'whose main ritual function is now the ceremonial immersion of the bones of the dead'.[24]

Such are the basic 'office-holders' of the typical Munda village at the present day. But it is possible to exaggerate the element of pure office-holding in the traditional system, for this has undoubtedly been strengthened and formalized by modern governments (who in this context include the Mughals as well as the British and the modern republic). The Sora *gamang* or headman, for instance, derived much of his authority in political and judicial matters and as a tax collector from the Raja of Jeypore, but today he is little more than a figurehead with only minor judicial powers.[25] This outside interference has led some writers to question the existence of the headmanship in the traditional system, and some have sought to merge it with the priesthood.[26] In some cases this is unquestionable. The Juang, for example, have the *podhan* as the chief village officer, formerly the village's representative to the State of Keonjhar. But it is his ritual role that is more important to the Juang: it is he who performs sacrifices for the *bhuitar* or priest, for instance. Indeed, he is not necessarily even the *de facto* leader of the village, but simply a figurehead and contact with outside authorities.[27]

However, we cannot really dismiss holders of such titles as *munda* and *manjhi* as simply modern creations. Formerly, although they may not have had the police and tax powers they are endowed with today, they must at least have had a role as day-to-day decision-makers and convenors of the panch in difficult cases, and their ritual functions, though less weighty than those of the priest, must also have existed (the powers of the priest have probably been more constant). Above all, the existence of two posts, not one, is indigenously recognized and well established, even where, as sometimes happens, the same individual comes to hold both.[28] In most cases the relationship between the two is an agnatic one, since hereditary and patrilineal succession to the major offices ensures that they normally remain in the dominant agnatic group of the village, which is traditionally the founding one. Among the Mundari, for example, the priestly and headman lineages of any one village are said to be related as elder brother and younger brother, though they are both affiliated to the same clan; in Naguri areas there is a third lineage, that of the *mahto* or assistant headman, traditionally descended from the third son of the village founder, though the post itself has now lapsed (see sect. 4.2). There is a similar situation among the Bhumij and Ho. The Juang *podhan* is junior to the *bhuitar* but senior to all other villagers. Often the priest has a greater influence than the headman, as with the Kodaku *baiga*.[29] At least in Keonjhar the Santal reverse this pattern and it is the headman who is senior, but the division of the village that this suggests is more 'empirical and diverse' that among the Mundari. Here, however, the two posts are likely to be associated with different clans, the priest being traditionally but not necessarily a Murmu, the headman a Hansdak or a member of the founding clan of the village. This is even more the case with the closely related Mahali, the headman and priest both being Mandi, the *gorait* (messenger) a Besra, the *paranik* (assistant headman) a Kanti or Baske, and the *pargana* (see above) a Murmu.[30]

Very often these office titles give their names to descent or status groups, especially in Koraput, where the *kuda* (and Sora *birinda*) may have such names instead of the names of villages. The monopolizing of village offices by certain clans in some tribes tends to create, or perhaps more correctly is the expression of, an oligarchy within the village, e.g. among the Santal, where those in possession of village posts are supported by local government officials, or among the Sora, where officials and their families also maintain a distance from the 'dependent' or 'subject' *poroja* or *ryot*, partly through hypergamy.[31] As a body, village officials may also have a ritual status in respect of ordinary villagers: among the Juang they may wear their hair and beard long and should not attend funerals.[32] Sometimes their dominance may mark them off from other lineages of the same clan. However, as well as being generally supported by the villagers themselves in order to block outside interference (see above), their power is to some degree tempered by the myth of a common relationship for all villagers, by the need to consult with and answer to the panch, by their removability for misconduct or incompetence, and sometimes by a tradition of allowing access to land to all within the village, regardless of descent-group affiliation (though not necessarily on equal terms; see sect. 4.2).

(ii) Village and Descent Group

The typical Munda village has other foci for its identity, at once topographical and ritual. One of these is the *sasan* or bone burial ground, usually a final depository for funerary remains following cremation. All villagers may be buried there, though often the distinction in life between 'original settlers' and 'newcomers', i.e.

between members of the dominant clan and members of other clans, is perpetuated in the *sasan*.[33] Then there is the sacred grove called *sarna* (Mundari), *jaher, jahira* (Ho, Santal) etc., the seat of the spirits that are associated with the village and protect it, and the megalithic platforms, especially in Koraput, which are also dedicated to village spirits (e.g. the Remo *sindibor*).[34] There is also the *akhra* or dancing ground in some groups (Mundari, Santal, Birjhia Asur, Ho, Kharia), which is not maintained by the nomadic Birhor, though they do have the *sasan*.[35] Finally there is the youth dormitory, which exists in many parts of the Munda area as, in part, a matchmaking institution for the unmarried of the village, and as such it creates and maintains contacts with other villages; however, it is not universal, and in particular it does not occur among the Santal, the largest tribe (see sect. 6.2).[36]

The unity of the village is also expressed partly in terms of a marriage rule, namely the maintenance of village exogamy. This rule is consonant with the tradition that villages were once uniclan, and it is still required or considered highly desirable, even though many villages are now multi-clan and can therefore tolerate village endogamy.[37] Among the Juang this identity between agnatic group and village is stressed also in the circumstance that it is the village rather than individual families who arrange marriages by capture (the most common form) and who receive the bulk of the brideprice and other marriage payments. In many tribes (e.g. the Kharia) there is a requirement for all families within the village, whatever their actual totemic affiliation, to take part in all the rituals performed within it.[38]

However, certain other considerations tend to support Choudhury (above, sect. 5.1) against other writers in questioning the view that it is really the village that is the focus of identity rather than the main agnatic group within it. Yamada explicitly says that the '"*hatu*" or... village is, of course, a geographical concept, but actually it always includes the meaning of *hatu-renko*, i.e., the people of a village who are members of [the] *khuntkattidar* of the village'. Similarly, Majumdar indicates that in most rituals, *hatu* and *killi* are interchangeable.[39] The very concept of the village as a place of permanent settlement may be relatively modern. Although in Koraput most Gadaba and Remo villages seem to be several hundred years old, settlement may be quite recent in some areas. Martel dates the founding of many Santal villages at as recently as the 1920s, and Bouez associates permanent settlement with irrigated cultivation, which seems to have come relatively late to these areas.[40] The village is certainly of little significance for those groups that are still nomadic today, such as the Birhor, where the *tanda* is more important, and more Munda tribes may once have followed a similar way of life. This applies almost as much to shifting cultivation, which may involve movements of settlements as well as fields, and persistent illness may also cause a village site to be shifted, though usually within a limited area.[41] In such cases the ossuary may be the real focus of territorial identity, for this, of course, will remain in one place. (Even the Birhor have such ossuaries,[42] though the Santal do not.) However, we have seen that it may segregate the agnatic group of the village from its non-agnates, just as there is usually segregation in terms of access to land and the inheritance of land-use rights for the villagers in life (see Ch. 3 and sect. 4.3 ii). The redistribution of the land itself may be under the control of the village headman, who is typically head of its dominant clan also. All these facts reflect the dominance of one agnatic group within the village, and sometimes village unity is explicitly associated with clan unity. Among the Ho, where many villages are uniclan anyway, this is expressed through ritual unity at weddings, funerals, annual rites etc. Another example is the Juang, for whom ideally the only non-agnates present in a village should be in-marrying spouses.

Although the village, not the clan, is the true corporate unit, other non-agnates who may be present (affinal and matrilaterally related families) 'are not absorbed into the local descent group by means of genealogical fiction', even though 'the Juang conceptualize the village in terms of ideal structure [and] ties of co-residence are phrased in the idiom of agnatic kinship'. [43] The Remo village also seems to be conceived as a group of agnates, for the only exception to birth within it as a qualification for membership is the in-marriage of women:

> every village is a ritual unit whose members partake of the same sacrificial food and do not intermarry; new settlers are not automatically accepted into the unit, but remain for ceremonial

purposes and with regard to 'the marriage regulation members of their paternal village.

...even long residence does not admit a man to the ritual fellowship of a village with which he has no hereditary ties.

This fellowship is strongly agnatic and is expressed through the *tsoro* libation, the main megalithic platform or *sindibor*, the periodic sealing-off of the village from the outside world for the performance of ritual, and the girl's dormitory, through its 'open invitation to youths of other villages and the taboo on the local boys—who are, of course, classed as agnates. Accordingly, the requirement of village exogamy is very strong here. The Gadaba also appear to have ritual food defining agnation, called *tsoru* or *charu* in Desia (Gutob *goyang*).[44]

There may be segregation in other respects too. In multi-clan villages the dependent, incoming clans often have their own assemblies. In the multi-clan Juang villages of Dhenkanal each clan has its own hamlet and headman. Each Mundari *khut* also has its *tola* or hamlet, and what ethnographers call the *tola* headman and panch must therefore be in reality a *khut* headman and panch. However, this must apply only to villages with a *raiyati* or dependent (i.e. multi-clan) population, for 'in a village with a predominant [single] clan population the village council becomes coextensive with the clan council.' Ho, Remo, Gadaba and Sora descent groups also seem to be localized into hamlets where there is more than one descent group to the village, and those of the Ho have separate panches.[45] In such cases, the 'village' panch is in reality that of the dominant clan, or, to put it the other way round, it is only that of the dominant clan that is used to discuss village-wide matters generally. Such clan councils are called *bhayari* (from Indic 'brother') or *kutumayat* (cf. *kutum*, sect. 8.2) by the Korwa and meet mainly at funerals, though they also deal with breaches of relationship taboos (see sect. 9.1). The latter term also occurs with the Birjhia Asur, indicating the presence of something similar there. At a lower level too, there may be recognized elders, as in Gataq *biria* or lineages, where the eldest and second eldest males (respectively *mnanang* and *dhanang*) dominant affairs.[46]

In all these circumstances, the identity of the village focuses on its principal agnates through either the exclusion of other residents or through their assimilation. From the indigenous point of view this concentration on a particular agnatic group may be a truer representation of the situation than the conventional but basically ethnocentric picture of the Munda village as primarily a territorial unit (not only as an administrative one—most writers recognize ritual forms of identity also). In some cases, Munda words may have been translated too readily as 'village' in the latter sense. Such is the conventional gloss of Mundari *hatu*, for instance, but this word really conveys more the sense of 'domestic, civilized', in contrast to *bir* 'forest, wild'.[47]

5.3 Village Federations

The villages of specific tribes are very often grouped into federations, though this does not apply to all of them: we have no information on the Turi, Korku or any of the Koraput Munda apart from the Sora, while the Mahali and Kodaku definitely lack them, as do the nomadic Birhor.[48] These federations also have councils, often called *parha* or *pirh*, and headmen, frequently drawn from the most powerful and influential of the village headmen in the area. In some cases the significance of these supra-village groupings has been nullified by regional governments, while in others they continue to co-exist alongside official administrative arrangements, but the Juang federations certainly have an indigenous origin,[49] and indeed this generally seems to be the case. Those of the Mundari, called *parha*, are said to have originated as groups of twelve or so villages, formed soon after the initial settlements in Chotanagpur. Each had its own panch and *manki* (headman), elected by the *munda* of the area, and the link between the component villages seems to have been the fact that the dominant clan in each was the same. Later, under the local Hindu Raja, the *parha* were supplemented by the similar *patti*, an administrative and taxation unit (from Hindi *pati* 'lease'). Initially, this was introduced together with the Hindu landlords and just superimposed on the traditional system, and thus it coincided with it—the only changes were one of official name from *parha* to *patti* (similarly, the *manki* clans were redesignated *bhuinhar*) and the appointment of the *manki* by the Raja instead of his election (the *manki* was now also a tax collector). Nonetheless, in the older areas of settlement in the north and west the term *parha* eventually seems to have ousted *patti*, for it is *parha* that is found in the Naguri dialect spoken there. Further south, however, in the newer areas of settlement around Khunti, the two arrangements eventually ceased to coincide, the divisions no longer being identified exclusively with particular clans, and *patti*, having entered the local Hasada dialect, became the dominant term. According to some authorities there is therefore no inter-village organization of the traditional sort in Hasada-speaking areas today. However, Yamada stresses the survival of the *parha* in both Hasada and Naguri areas as a basically uniclan organization named after the particular clan each is associated with. For him, the only difference is that those in the former area tend to contain some affinal groups and no longer hold the *pagu sendera* or spring ritual hunt like the Naguri *parha*.[50]

The *parha* panch is traditionally higher in authority than the *hatu* or village panch in regulating ritual matters and tribal custom generally, especially that concerning incest and marriage outside the tribe, and it includes non-clan members and even non-Mundari in its jurisdiction.[51] The *parha* have some significance as the unit of political organization through the Jharkhand Party, attendance being confined to the Mundari and debate mostly to the locally dominant clan. Administratively, however, their place has been taken by the modern government *grampanchayat* (see below).[52]

The Bhumij federations too once had administrative importance. Formerly, villages in groups of about twelve, also called *parha*, were placed under a *manki* or *parha raja*. The *parha* were further grouped into *taraf*, under a *sarkar*, and the collectivity of *taraf* constituted the State of Barabhum, under its Raja. Here too, *parha* were most probably once 'definable in terms of clan organization'. They still existed earlier in this century under a non-hereditary *pradhan*, who appears to have been a headman and rent-collector, possibly for the landlords of the area rather than the government.[53] Ho villages are also grouped into federations, called *pir*, of which there are seventy-three in Kolhan (they are absent from Seraikella); each is under a *manki* and consists of between five and thirty villages. They too are clan-based, their constituent villages having the same dominant clan. The system was eventually taken over by outside rulers, and the village headman remained subject to the authority of the *manki* or *pirh* headman, both now being nominated by the government (formerly the Raja) to act in a quasi-official capacity as rent- and tax-collectors;

they were to some extent subject to the control of the *pirh* panch, presumably in matters affecting tribal custom, not taxation. Today, the *manki* is losing his official powers to the *grampanchayat*, and it is the *munda* or village headman who decides those cases for which the penalty is expulsion.[54]

In Keonjhar, villages were grouped into *pirh* under the State of Keonjhar, four of them being mainly Juang in composition, though these do not coincide with clan areas. They appear to have had an indigenous origin but are still recognized by the modern government, even though the *grampanchayat* system exists alongside them. Each is under a *sardar*, who is the intermediary between *pirh* and government. He is elected by the inhabitants of the former but responsible to the latter, the post itself having been created by the State. From the Juang point of view, the post should ideally be hereditary in the male line and in the same village, a member of another village being chosen only if the obvious candidate is too young or otherwise unsuitable or is unwilling to take up the post. However, the *sardar* has little actual power today, though his office involves some responsibility and prestige and hence it generally devolves on someone already influential in the *pirh*. More important for the Juang themselves is the *pirh* council. This consists of representatives of all villages in the *pirh* and claims jurisdiction over sexual offences in particular, though it also deals with 'threats to group solidarity'; the *sardar* himself is not necessarily involved. In relation to the former, the *pirh* council deals with cases of incest or *bogodung* and those involving illicit relations between members of opposite generation sets (see sect. 9.1), which are considered almost as serious; mere adultery, however, is dealt with by the village. Difficult cases and those involving more than one village are also covered by the *pirh* (inter-village conflict arises especially through boundary disputes or in the course of the ritual drumming contests that are held between affinally related villages). Exclusion from the community is the ultimate sanction in respect of serious breaches of marriage rules, and it would seem that only the *pirh* can formally expel individuals, though in practice each village can presumably find ways of ejecting troublemakers. In Dhenkanal, the *pirh* are being increasingly modelled on caste councils and indeed these are now called *jati sabha* (literally, 'caste assembly').[55]

The Santal federations are known as *pargana* (*bangla* according to Troisi) and as such they have given their name to that district in eastern Bihar where the Santal are particularly concentrated. They may have been founded originally by Moslem rulers, who certainly gave them their name. Each is under a *parganait* (*pargana* according to Bouez and Carrin-Bouez), who is surrounded by many of the symbols of royalty and whose assistant, the *kharji*, appointed by himself, transmits his instructions to the *desmanjhi* or local assistants.[56] Before independence in 1947, the *parganait* were appointed by the local *zamindar* or landowner and acted as revenue collectors. The British recognized the *pargana* panches in 1856 and the *parganait* themselves were made sub-inspectors of police, though this post was abolished in 1950. Today they are either elected by the *manjhi* and elders of their area (in Mayurbhanj and Santal Parganas) or succeed hereditarily (in Keonjhar), though officially they are still government appointees with some police powers and control over local *manjhi*.[57] The *pargana* assemblies themselves have seldom met since the 1930s, a decline due not only to the competition of the official government *grampanchayat* but also to the influx of non-Santal into the area and the increasing autonomy of the village. Today they are just *ad hoc* bodies and are mainly concerned with difficult cases relating to tribal custom and the readmission of offenders into the tribe, but the *parganait* themselves have acquired more influence since the lapse of the *lo bir sendra* or tribal council.[58] As in other tribes these cases concern breaches of the rules of tribal endogamy and clan exogamy, the fulfillment of economic and other obligations concerning marriage, and the legitimacy of children.[59] The sanctions against breaches of such rules are excommunication (*bitlaha*) and the destruction of the offender's home and family shrine, though readmission may be possible for a fine in cases of incest, especially between classificatory relatives between whom no genealogical connection is known (the rite of exclusion makes reference to the origin myth). It is the *parganait* who decides cases involving the possibility of expulsion, and he also fines the headman of the village concerned. They are apparently not uniclan bodies.[60]

The Kharia *doklo* or *jati mahasabha* or *parha* or *kutumb sabha* consists of all village headmen under an *adhikari* voted afresh for each meeting (therefore he is presumably a presiding officer rather than a headman as such). These are multi-clan bodies, as is indicated by the term *kutumb sabha*, a reference to intermarriage here (see sect. 8.2). They meet every two years to discuss difficult cases and lay down tribal custom, especially that involving the regulation of marriage, though it seems to be very much an informal, *ad hoc* affair among the Dhelki Kharia: 'there must be present both *bhayads* [i.e. agnates] and relatives by marriage...so that villages belonging to different and related clans may take part in the deliberations.' As elsewhere, it is today losing powers to the *grampanchayat*.[61] Similar are the Sora assembly and the Korwa *pargana* panch, though in the latter case there is disagreement as to whether there is any *pargana* headman. Sometimes, such associations have only an economic basis today: among the Gataq, contiguous villages tend to join together to exploit a tract of land in common, open only to residents (Gataq and non-Gataq alike), these units often being a continuation of the old revenue units of the Maharaja of Jeypore.[62]

Thus although federation headmen were given increased powers in the past as a consequence of the federations having been taken over by earlier regional governments, today they are losing these powers to the modern *grampanchayat* and government officials. The *grampanchayat* system was set up all over India by the newly independent government in 1947 as a democratic body, which in this part of India characteristically represents groups of eight to ten villages and over 1,000 inhabitants drawn from all ethnic groups, both tribals and castes. Roughly intermediate in size between the village and federation panches, they are headed by a democratically elected *mukhia* and are units of revenue collection as well as of democratic government. They are further grouped into *halka* under a *halka* officer (always a 'Diku' or non-tribal, partly the successor of the Sub-Divisional Officer of pre-Independence days) and his tribal assistant, the *karmchari*. It was 1956 before they became operative in Mundari areas. They do not conflict here with the *hatu* or village panch, for the two deal with separate issues, but among the Sora the *grampanchayat* has removed most even of the village headman's powers.[63] It is frequently unpopular with tribals, for a number of reasons. First, it is an invasion of unwelcome Hindu influence; secondly, it is inter-ethnic; thirdly, it is an overtly secular and political body which takes little or no account of the kinship network that pervades traditional institutions; and finally, its rules are frequently disliked, especially its insistence on periodic changes of personnel in place of the traditional life tenure of office and hereditary succession to it.[64] Indeed, it is sometimes not properly understood: some of the Korwa that have sat on it have been known to retain their position after their formal tenure has elapsed, through unfamiliarity with the modern rules.[65]

The recent contraction of the powers of the older, traditional federations may seem dramatic, but it is possible that it simply represents a return to the state of affairs that existed before any outside interference was imposed. They have lost only the administrative powers with which they had been burdened as a result of this interference, and they continue to be valued in most tribes as the final regulators of tribal custom and arbiters of serious disputes. Perhaps the main preoccupation of tribal justice is to ensure that a properly constituted kinship universe is maintained through correct marriages, and this is ultimately of more importance than even inheritance disputes or public-order offences. This is especially so as regards marriage outside the tribe and breaches of exogamous rules, the most serious of all offences to most tribals, and where they exist it is the village federations that are ultimately concerned with them. This in itself suggests that they have an indigenous origin, since regional and national governments are less likely to concern themselves with such matters as maintaining tribal endogamy, while cases of incest, in so far as they are of modern government concern at all, are more likely to be dealt with in the courts than in the more political *grampanchayats*. It also suggests that many of these multi-village councils are probably to be regarded fundamentally as clan councils, in view of the fact that clan boundaries are also exogamous ones. It is true that the existence of clan councils is often denied by ethnographers—Roy, for instance, considered the Mundari federations to have been mainly defensive in origin,[66] and there are certainly exceptions (e.g. the Juang, Dudh Kharia and Santal). However, in a number of cases the link between component villages is explicitly stated to be their association with different segments of the same totemic group, at least traditionally (e.g. the Ho, Mundari and Bhumij). Thus as with the village itself, the village federation may sometimes have an agnatically conceived focus, though at this level the connection is provided by association with a common totem rather than any traceable or putative links.

5.4 *The Tribe*

Two Munda tribes were organized into states in Chotanagpur up to the coming of the British. One of these was the Ho/Mundari kingdom of Chotanagpur, said to have been founded some time between the sixth and tenth century and lasting as a political entity until 1839. Its Maharaja was originally elected from among the federation headmen. The kingdom fell more and more under Hindu influence as a result of Mughal expansion into the area in the seventeenth century, the now Hinduized Maharaja bringing in many Hindu officials, soldiers and landlords; this influx increased between the start of British rule in 1770 and about 1810. The Bhumij also had states, especially in Barabhum, upon which they have based their claims to Kshatriya status. Later, the Raja of Chotanagpur replaced the tribal chiefs with Hindu officials or *kayastha*, which together with the loss of land to local Hindus contributed to the Hinduization of many tribals.[67]

A few groups also have or once had tribal assemblies. The only meeting of all Santal is traditionally the *lo bir* (*sendra*) or 'annual hunt (in the burnt forest)' (a clear reference to swidden cultivation), a democratic body presided over by the *dihri* and usually held near the river Damodar.[68] Any male Santal can attend this meeting, which has 'the supremely important function of reviewing usage and of asserting and extending the ancestral law [and is] the only authority entitled to impose sanctions against misbehaving manjhis and parganaits', with powers of excommunication.[69] Singh says that the whole arrangement is now defunct, partly because of the decline in hunting following the imposition of restrictive forest laws, but Troisi says that it still exists.[70] There is, or was, a similar meeting of all Birhor *tanda* called *disum sendra*, and the Remo also have an annual hunt. The Gataq too supposedly had a tribal assembly, attended by most village officers and presided over by the *mlehsanasi*, the headman of one of the larger villages, but if it ever existed in more than myth it is now defunct. Finally, although the Mundari do not seem to have had anything similar, they are today united in the 22 Parha Mahasabha or Society of 22 *parha*, an advisory rather than jural body which meets at Tapkarra, ten miles west of Khunti.[71]

Otherwise, there is no institutional expression of tribal unity among the Munda. Such unity may depend instead on an origin myth in which all the members of the tribe are descended from the primordial couple (e.g. the Santal myth; see sect. 4.2). Equally important is the rule of tribal endogamy, violations of which may be regarded more seriously even than marriage within the clan.[72] There is some intermarriage across tribal lines nonetheless, especially involving the Mundari, namely between Mundari and Bhumij in the border areas of Ranchi, especially in Patkum Pargana, between Kharia women and Mundari men (their issue being known as Munda Kharia), but never vice versa, and occasionally between Ho and Mundari. Intermarriage of Mundari with Santal or Ho is generally discouraged, though accepted in the latter case in view of the firmer tradition of a common origin. Mundari intermarriage with the Dravidian-speaking Oraon 'is common and arouses little comment in practice'.[73] Kisan men sometimes marry Kodaku women. The Gadaba regard themselves as superior to the Gorum and will only accept brides from them if the latter undergo a purificatory rite first. The Birhor allow their women to marry occasionally with outsiders from whom they would be willing to accept food. Even though they cease to be Birhor, men and women who marry into the tribe can usually become Birhor if admitted ritually. Such marriages are disapproved of, but there is no brideprice to pay.[74] The Mahali (and possibly the Karmali) are today endogamous as a whole, even in relation to the Santal proper, of whom they are offshoots, though whether in myth or in fact their very separation from the Santal may have originated in marriage outside the tribe, probably with Mundari. The exceptional keenness of the Santal to maintain tribal endogamy is probably partly due to their intense desire to preserve their identity and unity *vis-à-vis* the outside world in general and Hindus in particular. According to Gautam, 'no outsider can be recruited into the Santal community either by marriage alliance or by adoption', though Chattopadhyay reports the occurrence of occasional intermarriage between Ho and Santal, and Bouez between Santal men and Kurmi girls. The Kurmi are a local caste that is superior to and the 'elder brothers' of the Santal, so here hypergamy is inverted.[75] One factor in the breach of the rules of tribal endogamy is that under modern conditions more and more tribals are working away from home for long periods of time. Majumdar stresses this particularly in relation to the Ho, where although a wife taken from outside the tribe has to observe certain ceremonial restrictions and occupy a hut apart from her husband, the consequences of her acceptance in marriage can be circumvented by a sacrifice and communal feast.[76]

Many of these restrictions may just be due to the claims of particular tribals to a higher status in caste terms, as with the refusal of the Kui-speaking Jatapu to intermarry with their Sora neighbours.[77] Sometimes, though, this can take a surprising and novel turn. The Mundari, for instance, a tribe with a well-developed sense of identity, allow no commensality or marriage with either artisans or high-status Hindu castes on pain of excommunication.[78] This shows neatly how the Mundari have adopted one of the cultural symbols of the upper-caste society to mark their distance from it.[79] Ho who marry or accept food from a 'Diku' or Hindu are also subject to expulsion from the tribe.[80] Similarly, the *naeke* and *godet* (priests and messengers) of the Santal are also ritual barbers today, having replaced (so it is said) the Hindu specialists that were used formerly. Such statements are a consequence of the Santals' resistance to Hinduization and of their desire to distance themselves as a tribe from Hindu society. 'Uplift' here means not claiming affiliation with a particular caste or *varna* by special ritual observances and the adoption of a particular occupation as, say, the Asur or Turi or Mahali have done, but trying to remove outside criticism of the society by reforming it—banning communal dancing, for instance, or discouraging the consumption of alcohol. Even the city Santal distance themselves from Hindus, knowing that their assimilation as a caste would only would give them a lower status.[81] Another example are the Kharia who, 'in order to improve [their] social position, subvert the high social position of the Brahmans', with myths concerning the latters' theft of the sacred thread from them.[82] However, the general superiority claimed by tribes over low castes also tends to be admitted by higher castes in this area.[83] Thus the Gataq may marry into neighbouring tribes but not into an untouchable caste, which, like commensality with such a caste, is subject to expulsion from the tribe.[84] Similarly, the Hill Juang regard themselves as superior to the more Hinduized Juang of the plains.[85]

However, some of these restrictions have gone much further and have led to the splitting up of what were once unified tribes. In fact, most Munda tribes are divided into endogamous sections which are well on their way to complete *de facto* separation, and indeed some have achieved it, such as the Mahali and Karmali, both of Santal origin, and the Dudh and Dhelki Kharia (see Ch. 2 for details). This separation is expressed most cogently through the prevention of intermarriage, for commensality may survive division under certain circumstances, and common origins are often recognized.

Thus at all three levels of Munda territorial organization—tribe, federation and village—kinship appears to be a truer expression of identity than any explicitly political or territorial idiom. The village is typically dominated by the members of a single agnatic group united through land and ritual, that which supposedly founded it and with which it is associated in most contexts, despite the presence of incomers. The same is true of many of the territorially more extensive village federations, in which hereditary links are more likely to be obscure or unrecognized. Here, totemic affiliation becomes the emblem of association, and the regulation of marriage is more significant than land or ritual. At the tribal level such connections become even more tenuous, so that explicitly there is little but the bare recognition of a common identity, perhaps enshrined in myth; but tribal unity is also maintained through refusal of intermarriage and, in some cases, of commensality with outsiders. However, this very refusal can also come to signal the division of particular tribes and their ultimate separation into what are recognized as discrete ethnic groups. It is noteworthy too that the assemblies are at each level mainly interested in matters relating to the maintenance of a proper kinship universe, and any more political or fiscal powers they may exercise are likely to have been imposed upon them by outside authorities. What is significant is that in the modern era they have been left with the former set of powers while progressively losing the latter to the official *gram-panchayat* or government servants.

Chapter Six
Marriage

6.1 Marriage and the Individual

Among the Munda, although naming and birth rites give the individual some social status, it is above all marriage that makes one a full adult tribal member. Leuva talks about 'the shame of remaining unwed', and according to Roy and Roy 'it is only after marriage that a Kharia is considered to be a full-fledged member of the tribe'.[1] Similarly, 'it is not until he is married that a Birhor is considered to be become a full member of his clan', and it is only marriage that makes a Korwa a full adult, giving males the right to sit in the panch.[2] '...men and women who are unwed are regarded by the Hos as socially less effective members of the community',[3] and among the Korku it is marriage which enables one's *jiv* (soul substance) to return to Bhagwan.[4] In these respects marriage seems to be more important than any specific puberty or initiation rite, which is often absent altogether.[5] There are exceptions, such as the Santal *caco chatiar* rite, necessary for marriage, inheritance and cremation and usually performed between the ages of four and twelve (male children only), but even so the unmarried state is regarded as a disgrace or as something to be pitied.[6] While certain other rites, such as the frequently occurring ear-boring ceremonies carried out soon after birth (see sects. 3.2, 4.3), may incorporate a child into the agnatic group, they are still not enough to give him full tribal status as an adult later on. This lack of status may affect divorcees and widow(er)s too to a lesser extent. Mundari divorcees, like unmarried children, are called *dangra/i* and return to the youth dormitory. The same is true of Juang widows, and of both categories among the Remo.[7] Asur men living in concubinage without being properly married are regarded as bachelors.[8]

Despite the importance of marriage, couples do live together without ceremony, often for financial reasons, as among the Ho, where brideprice payments are particularly high. Elsewhere, expectations may be stricter. Pregnancy may lead to immediate pressure to marry, and the Asur and Korku expect couples to be married before their children may marry.[9] Attitudes towards pre-marital relations as such are often quite relaxed, but many groups do expect fidelity after marriage: the Kodaku regard it seriously enough to impose fines on male offenders, and for the Juang extra-marital affairs can only be incestuous or adulterous, never legitimate—their discovery generally leads to community pressure to marry.[10]

Marriage, especially one's first, generally involves the whole village. Sometimes this includes the collection and distribution of the brideprice, and in the Juang case also the ritualized 'marriage by capture' that is a part of all weddings. Often the panch must be consulted as to the desirability of a particular match, especially one involving the most prestigious form of marriage ceremony, and its members have to be included in the feasting; they may even set the brideprice and conduct the negotiations, as among the Gataq. Finally, the village headman's permission is generally required before any marriage may take place within his village, in order to ensure that the correct rules are being followed.[11] Once again, we see the preoccupation of apparently village authorities with matters to do primarily with kinship, in this case correct marriages (see sect. 5.2).

One generally marries in one's teens or early twenties, and there is little child marriage except in some of the more Hinduized groups, e.g. some Juang and Kharia, and the Bhumij of Chotanagpur, but not of Orissa.[12] Ethnographers sometimes report an increase in child marriages, sometimes a decrease,[13] though usually without adequate statistics to support their claims. The norm concerning the respective ages of bride and groom varies from tribe to tribe, Remo brides especially being older.[14] Pfeffer associates those cases where it is the brides who are older with the attribution of seniority to females in parts of Koraput.[15] Among the Juang and elsewhere there is a tendency for a group of same-sex siblings to marry in age order.[16] This reflects the status of elder siblings, especially an elder brother, who is the bearer of the family's descent line and in many ways assimilated to one's father, but it also corresponds with actual marriage preferences in some cases (see sect. 8.4).

6.2 Spouse Selection and the Dormitory Institution

By their very nature, of course, child marriages have to be arranged by the parents or whoever else has jural authority. Such pre-arrangement is not necessarily incompatible with adult marriage, however. Among the Juang, 'the principals to a marriage ordinarily have no say in the selection of their spouse', 'it being understood that the principals almost never arrange their own marriage', and it is one's father or elder brother who makes the arrangements, often in consultation with other near agnates. Among the Turi also, 'the choice of a bride is the wish of the parents'.[17] These constraints on individual choice may reflect considerations of wealth and status in the more acculturated groups, but other possible reasons suggest themselves, especially the existence of positive marriage rules, a general feature of Munda social organization (see sect. 8.4). However, not even this would limit choice completely, since the prescribed category would normally contain a number of individuals, not just one, and parental arrangements can sometimes be upset by the wishes of those actually being married.[18] But although ethnographers often write as though the matter were left entirely to the individual, parental and even village sanction will ultimately be required if the marriage is to be recognized, partly because parents and other relatives help provide the brideprice and other expenses, and partly because they will wish to ensure that the match conforms with exogamic, endogamic and preferential rules.

Any marriage not conforming to the rules is unlikely to survive unless the couple leave the village to live elsewhere, and difficulties may also be placed in the way of marriages that are disliked for reasons of wealth, personality etc. Mostly, the initial proposal comes from the youth's side rather than the girl's, and this may be virtually mandatory in some cases.[19] In any second marriage there are none of these family constraints as far as men are concerned, in the sense that it is they themselves, rather than their parents, who will be responsible for the observance of the proper rules. However, women may have less freedom in such a situation, because at the end of their first marriages they either revert to the control of their natal group (i.e. their brothers and fathers, if still alive) or else remain in those of their husbands, perhaps through remarriage to a younger brother of their husband or some other agnate (see sect. 6.5).

Many ethnographers have seen the village dormitories which many Munda have as one means of finding spouses, since they are the focus of inter-village visits by groups of young people. In some cases the dormitory may also be a men's house similar to those found in Southeast Asia and Papua New Guinea,[20] but there is one sense in which none of the Munda dormitories resemble the most famous example in this area, the *ghotul* of the Dravidian-speaking Muria Gond to the west. Elwin compares this with the Remo *ingersin* or youth's house by saying that '*ghotul* relationships should never lead to marriage; *ingersin* relationships should never lead to anything else'. Here, in fact, there are two dormitories, that for the girls being called *selani dingo*, and Fürer-Haimendorf indicates that this is the more important:

> To the Bondo [Remo] who must find his mates in other villages, the friendships made in the *selani dingo* are the only conceivable avenue to marriage and any breakdown in the dormitory system would be tantamount to a revolution in his social life: indeed it is probable that in the place of mutual attraction, family interests and considerations of wealth would become the decisive factors in the conclusion of marriage.[21]

However, while there *is* a rough correlation between the existence of the dormitories and a lack of explicit parental interference, the former are not the only means of spouse selection because of the importance of previous alliances and preferential rules, and they may have little to do with actual courting. Among the Juang, for instance, spouse selection is entirely out of the hands of either of the principals and firmly in those of the youth's father and even village. Nonetheless, it is the mutual dancing visits between villages, which are closely associated with the dormitories, that provide the main opportunity for capturing girls from other villages as brides for one's own, this being a standard means of spouse selection here. Here and among the Gataq it is the girls of marriageable villages who visit the youth's villages,[22] but in most groups it seems to be the other way round.[23] The main rationale for the dormitories in fact seems to be the requirement for boys to sleep apart from their parents and sisters from the age of ten at the latest, this being linked to the prevention of incest.[24] A similar rule may apply to girls also, hence the separate dormitories for them in some tribes. For instance, Juang boys sleep in the *majang* or men's house from the age of about ten, and girls in a widow's house or occasionally in a special building of their own. The *majang* is especially connected with the unmarried and otherwise sexually inactive, and widowers also sleep there. The Gataq and Mundari also have separate dormitories for males and females, those of the former being called respectively *ingiridoa* and *selandoa*.[25] Sometimes there are no special dormitory buildings for either or both sexes, the house of an elderly couple or widow being used instead.[26] The largest tribe, the Santal, have no dormitories, only communal dancing, as do the closely related Mahali. They are not present among the Korwa or Sora nor probably the Korku either, in view of their general absence in that part of India.[27]

In fact, there is some evidence that they have been declining throughout the Munda area. They are reported to have existed among the Birhor in the early 1920s and the Ho in the 1930s (though only in areas adjoining Munda territory), but Sachchidananda could find no trace of them in either tribe in the 1950s. The Bhumij have them only in Orissa. Even in 1937 those of the Kharia were described as 'an effete institution which has long lost its utility and is fast decaying', a situation confirmed by Sachchidananda twenty years later.[28] Their decline may be due in part to the influence of Hindu and Christian moral codes which are opposed to the 'promiscuity' with which they are often, if exaggeratedly, associated, but sometimes they have been deliberately established by missionaries for the unmarried young among their converts as a way of acquiring greater influence over them. Elwin suggests an increasing tendency towards marriage within the village as another cause, but this is just as likely to be a symptom of their decline.[29] Altogether, their importance in spouse selection may have been exaggerated, and we must recognize that many of the activities associated with them—dancing, for instance—may take place without them. Their complete absence from the Santal, the largest and most dispersed Munda tribe, is noteworthy. There is, in fact, no evidence that this tribe has ever had them, even though the standard assumption among ethnographers is simply that they have died out here.

6.3 Prestations in Marriage

A brideprice is universally required, but its significance and the exact conditions under which the obligation is fulfilled.vary from tribe to tribe. Thus McDougal says that among the Juang 'the

payment of brideprice results in the transfer of rights and obligations over the person of the bride, not only to her husband's family,
but to the LDG [local descent group] collectively'. Similarly, among
the Mundari it confers full status on the marriage and full inheritance rights for the children born of it.[30] Among the Asur it
is described by Leuva as 'only symbolic of the utility of a woman',
'a token for the stabilization of the marriage',[31] and for the Santal
in Keonjhar it remains 'more a sign of adherence to a traditional
norm than a true economic prestation'.[32] Although it can be a
heavy burden in some tribes, this is rarely insuperable, especially
since the whole village may be involved in its collection. A youth
can usually expect considerable help from his family or kin group,
though marriage without the consent of the parents may leave the
groom with the sole responsibility for paying it.[33]

Thus brideprice does not have the economic importance it is
conventionally credited with in Africa, where men are often unable
to marry until a brideprice has been received for their sisters.[34]
However, Majumdar reckoned that the Ho had to find an exceptionally high brideprice, possibly beyond the reach of not only the
groom himself but also his family and even village, in which case
he would be faced with accepting a lower-status form of marriage
than he would wish, or cohabiting without ceremony, or even
remaining celibate or contracting an intra-clan marriage through
inability to pay it. The Korku brideprice was also said to be high in
terms of the local economy in the 1940s, though some could be paid
by service (i.e. the groom works for a period for his future father-
in-law).[35] In theory, this is not to be confused with *ghar-jawae*
marriage (see sect. 3.3), for in the present case residence will
eventually become virilocal, i.e. when the brideservice has been
completed; in practice, however, the two may be combined. Standing suggests that labour, not brideprice, was formerly the recognized means of obtaining a bride for the poor and *raiyati* among
the Mundari. Today, however, both seem to be very rare among
Munda groups, and the latter is certainly much less usual than
among Mon-Khmer groups in Southeast Asia.[36]

As we shall see (next section), the level of brideprice depends to
a large extent on the circumstances surrounding the betrothal and
on the status of the marriage ceremony itself: the more elaborate
and prestigious the ceremony the higher the brideprice. If one
undertakes a second marriage the brideprice will almost always be

less or waived altogether, as it is in the case of *ghar-jawae* marriage. It is generally given to specific close relatives of the bride, and in a specific form: typically the male relatives receive money and/or cattle while the female relatives, and sometimes the male, receive cloth. Those most directly involved are the bride's parents, but both her own and her parents' siblings, especially her MB and FZ, may receive a share, and also her grandparents and even the village as a whole or, perhaps more accurately in some cases, the agnatic core within it. Among the Juang it is the village-cum-local descent group which is the affinal exchange unit and which therefore receives the bulk of the brideprice and other marriage prestations, though the girl's father will, of course, also have a share.[37]

A sufficiently high brideprice may call for a return prestation in the form of a feast for the groom's party. Among the Santal, 'The bride's maternal grandmother is made to "pay" for her cloth' in rice, turmeric and cheroots. In Keonjhar, the return prestation is called *jautuk* and is roughly equivalent to the brideprice itself. It must never consist of money but usually comprises livestock, food or jewels, one each of the first going to the groom's father and younger brother. Such return prestations hardly constitute dowries, despite the fact that *jautuk* has this meaning when used by local Hindus. Brideprice is still the main prestation, even where marriage expenses generally (e.g. for feasting) are shared, and there are no unreciprocated inducements for wife-takers to enter into alliances with families of slightly lower status, as occurs in the high-status ideology of alliance.[38] However, there may be true dowries among some of the more Hinduized groups, such as the Bhumij of Manbhum. Majumdar thought that dowry occurred among the Korwa as a means of attracting young men to sparsely populated areas, but later writers do not even mention it; it may in fact simply have been an instance of marriage by service (see above).[39] The brideprice-dowry distinction cannot be used to distinguish caste from tribe, of course: many groups that would be considered low castes also have brideprice as the major prestation at marriage.

6.4 Forms of Marriage

Seven principal forms of marriage are identifiable among Munda groups, namely regular, exchange, elopement, capture and intrusion marriages, widow remarriage and *ghar-jawae* marriage, though not all of these are universally found (or reported) while yet others are recorded for one or two tribes alone. I shall discuss the relative status of these forms and the occasions in which each of them usually take place, but not in any detail the actual ritual involved.

What we may call the 'regular' form of marriage[40] is universally the most prestigious, expensive and elaborate, though not necessarily the most common (marriage by capture is more common among the Juang and Remo, for example). It involves negotiation by the parents of the principals, the first approach characteristically coming from the youth's side.[41] The negotiations are usually carried out through an intermediary such as the Mahali *raibar* or *dutamdar*, Santal *barhul* or *mebarik*, Dhelki Kharia *agua*, Gataq *jorakaria* or Juang *komandiria* (strictly the representative of the groom's family).[42] He may be a relative of the youth and his family, e.g. his FB, MB or eZH among the Mahali, or a relative of both families (e.g. the Korwa). Among the Ho, however, he should be unrelated to either family, to ensure impartiality. Among the Santal he is often the *godet* or village messenger, among the Kodaku the *baiga*.[43] Also involved are the taking of omens,[44] the payment of brideprice, and a number of days' ceremony at the house of the bride, before she is brought to her husband's home. Here, most of the ritual events are repeated, save for the application of the bride's marriage mark with vermilion. This is usually carried out only at the groom's home, if at all (and some tribal sections do without it, e.g. the Santal; see sect. 4.2). Where it is used, however, it marks the wife's incorporation into her husband's agnatic group and qualifies her to help with his domestic ritual. Generally, this repetition of ritual events means that they are not expressions of inequality between alliance groups.[45] The Gataq have a symbolic period of uxorilocal residence immediately after marriage, the newly married couple spending fifteen days with the husband's parents and then seven with the wife's before returning to live permanently in the household or village of the former.[46]

The regular form is broadly similar to the Hindu ceremony: Roy and Roy describe it as 'the Kharia's tribal custom of "marriage by purchase" overlaid with features borrowed from Hindus'. In some groups there is a distinct and even more elaborate form called 'Diku' or 'Hindu'. Speaking of the Santal, Orans draws a distinction between these two by saying that the application of vermilion to the bride's forehead takes place at *her* home in the Hindu form but at the groom's in the less elaborate form, and she is initially married to a tree in the former. The Santal of Bengal are rather more Hinduized than those further west, and accordingly such forms are more prevalent there.[47] Generally the regular form is preferred, especially for a first marriage, but its relative expense may make it impractical or at least lead to a reduction in the full ceremony.[48] Sometimes the bride may simply gather her belongings and go to the groom's house, where the union in cemented with a brief, simple ceremony (possibly including the vermilion mark). Little or no brideprice is paid, but at least there is something of the aura and status of a regular marriage.[49]

Brideprice can often be evaded altogether by exchanging daughters (or sisters) with another family, an arrangement often regarded in a poor light but sometimes as a necessary evil, especially among such a tribe as the Ho, for whom the brideprice is ordinarily extremely heavy. This arrangement, called *sata palta* by the Korku, *golainti* by the Santal (in Santal Parganas), *goloant* by the Birjhia Asur and *goltaia* by the Korwa, is considered a random and minor one by ethnographers on the Munda, and as one which often takes place between families who are previously unrelated, but it seems to be a universal option for them.[50] The prejudice against exchange marriages clearly comes from the high-status society, but the strong dislike of reciprocity that is the basis of this prejudice conflicts with the ideology of symmetric exchange that is indicated in kinship terminology and which actually prevails (between wider alliance groups than the family) in most groups, though not all (the Asur and Mahali, for example; see Chs. 7 and 8).

Circumventing parental arrangements as well as poverty emerge as the standard justifications for the next three types of marriage. Often a couple will simply elope and go into hiding for a few days, after which any objection to their marrying is understandably withdrawn, provided this does not conflict with the usual rules of endogamy and exogamy.[51] A brideprice may be paid in such circumstances, or postponed until the birth of the first child. Among the Santal the brideprice is higher than normal, and both of the offending couple's sets of parents must feast the village.[52] Such marriages are often said to be quite popular in certain groups,[53] but such statements are rarely based on adequate statistics and sometimes on little more than a vague impression gained by the ethnographer. They may occasionally occur with a married woman, in which case the second husband is himself responsible for the brideprice.[54]

Often no doubt virtually indistinguishable from the foregoing, marriage by capture occurs ostensibly when a youth has reason to believe that the girl he desires would resist any other, more regular approach; she may be a member of a higher-status group, her parents' consent therefore being virtually impossible to obtain. However, in practice the girl herself may well be a party to the ruse, especially if she expects opposition, for whatever reason, from her own parents. The routine is for the youth, usually with some friends, to waylay the girl in some fairly remote spot and 'claim' her by 'forcibly' marking her forehead with vermilion.[55] The marking is in itself a decisive action to take, for it removes her status as an unmarried girl, and if she or her parents insist on her marrying elsewhere she must first be divorced and then remarried in a ceremony of, like all second marriages, inferior status. In most tribes the girl's family are likely to take the youth's action as an insult and are in principle entitled to seek revenge by thrashing him or looting his parents' home and even village and taking other actions likely to cause hostilities. Hence the youth's family must pay compensation, not only in the form of a higher brideprice, but also with a feast to the elders of one or both villages, for their authority too has been insulted, and they may have had to act as mediators in the quarrel to limit its consequences; but there seems to be no exclusion from the village as a punishment.[56] (Here again, we see village authorities being very much involved in sorting out a dispute over marriage.) The risk of hostility keeps its use to a minimum in most groups, and it is not found at all in some.[57] It is a rarity among the Asur, as is elopement marriage, owing to the greater ease of parental consent and the presence of village dormitories according to Leuva. It is common and relatively acceptable among the Ho, where it is said that 'a nominal brideprice is paid if and when demanded', avoidance of the very high brideprice perhaps being one of the motives for it here. Bouez states that 25% of Santal marriages in Keonjhar take place in this form, and among the Gataq they are considered more stable than those in the more expensive and prestigious negotiated form.[58] For the Juang, this is the most common form of marriage and is called *digar kania* (Oriya 'to drag the bride'), and it applies to the groom as well as the bride, for in this group he is no more aware of the arrangements being made on his behalf than the girl. These events usually take place during the mutual inter-village dancing visits, the agnatic group of the host village seizing both partners and celebrating their marriage immediately: sometimes a girl is taken on another occasion (market, fetching water, etc.), but never in her own village. Her family are expected to accept the alliance even if they dislike the idea, and indeed they are presented with a *fait accompli* because of the speed with which the ceremony follows. Marriage by capture is cheaper than the formal type of marriage, since although there is a brideprice there is less feasting, but a mock capture is a feature even of the formal marriage ceremony which some families employ. Similarly among the Remo, marriage by capture (*guboi*) is staged as a part of all but the most prestigious form of ceremony or *sebung*, which, since it involves the hacking to pieces of a buffalo, is quite expensive and therefore rare.[59]

Females also have a special recognized means of imposing their wishes on events. A woman or girl may simply enter a youth's home and stay there, resisting all the consequent provocation and insult from his family which is designed to get her to leave, until at last they relent and accept her. Once she has made her intentions known—e.g. by helping with the housework—she cannot forcibly be evicted, and she may have a reason if the youth is refusing to marry her after having had sexual relations with her. Alternatively the whole affair may have been pre-arranged between them, perhaps in order to overcome resistance in the other quarter, and hence resistance by the youth and his family is nominal. Since the girl's parents are vicariously responsible for embarrassing or insulting the youth's family they have no right to a brideprice, although this is often paid to avoid future bad feeling, especially in faked incidents of the kind. Conversely, they may have their right to it restored if the youth shows a more than token resistance, since the girl's action is binding on them both. It is, generally speaking, the rarest form of marriage, but one used especially by widows and divorcees. Alternatively, a woman faced with a definite breach of promise might enlist the aid of the headman to bring about her marriage by persuasion and mediation.[60]

The last of these two main types of marriage are discussed elsewhere, namely *ghar jawae* marriage (in sect. 3.3) and widow remarriage (in sect. 6.5). There is some marriage by service as a substitute for paying brideprice and with much less ceremony, as among the Korku (where it is called *lemjena*) and Korwa. Often, this is confused with or co-exists with *ghar-jawae* marriage.[61]

The Birhor and Santal have a special form—perhaps just a special name—for polygynous marriages, called *hirum, hirom* (literally 'co-wife'). This was also reported among the Ho earlier this century, but it is not mentioned elsewhere.[62] The Birhor and Santal also have *kirin-jawae bapla* (literally 'bought-husband marriage'), but this term is applied to quite different situations in each of the two tribes. Among the Santal it is the acquisition of a husband for a pregnant girl, whose lover cannot (e.g. if he belongs to a different tribe or the same clan as the girl) or will not marry her. He must, however, compensate the *kirin-jawae* in cattle and / or money. The latter is often the girl's elder sister's husband, to whom she becomes, of course, a second wife, but the children involved cannot inherit from him. Both fathers of the offending couple are fined on pain of the expulsion of the couple from the village, but there is not the same fall in status for the families involved that there would be in Hindu society. For the Birhor this form of marriage is a type of marriage by service, but without the adoption of a daughter's husband as heir; it is simply the repayment of a loan from the bride's father enabling the groom to pay his marriage expenses, the couple living uxorilocally until the loan is repaid. Both cases have the common element that the girl's father pays someone to marry his daughter, but this is because of her pregnancy by another man in one case and because of the youth's poverty in the other.[63]

Two further types of marriage are recorded for the Santal alone. The first is simply the marriage of a pregnant girl, but without the complication mentioned above, and therefore presumably to the father of the child; the second is a simple celebration before the village headman.[64] According to Bouez, the Santal of Mayurbhanj only recognize four types of marriage altogether. Marriage by purchase (*diku bapla*) and marriage by capture (*hor bapla*) at first sight appear to be respectively Hindu and tribal forms, though both are provided for in Manu (in reality as the marriages of low- and high-status groups respectively). The other two are 'bought-husband marriage' and *ghar-jawae* marriage. The Santal of Bengal are increasingly using just the Hindu form, but Orans noted a decrease in high-status marriages and an increase in simple cohabitation among Santal *bustee* workers when compared with village Santal, because despite their higher income there was a reluctance to spend money on traditional ceremonies. With Santal city-workers, however, who are more Hinduized, preparedness to undertake high-status marriages, regardless of cost, reappears.[65]

Elwin mentions a Juang marriage ceremony called *paitu* but gives no further details.[66] This same tribe also distinguish *wadi kania* (literally, 'child marriages'), which are even more elaborate and prestigious than the negotiated form, and *mona moni* (literally, 'to be of one mind') or 'love marriages', where the principals themselves make the choice. The same term is given to pre-marital affairs generally, discovery of which generally leads to marriage, but in all contexts *mona moni* occurs very rarely: only 2% of McDougal's sample were 'love marriages'. Mahali *raja khusi* or 'marriages by mutual consent' may be similar.[67] Even cohabitation without ceremony may have a special name, for example *napam bapla* or 'agreed marriage' among the Santal and *idi me* among the Bir Asur.[68]

But whatever the form—however elaborate or simple, expensive or cheap—a certain ritual minimum is frequently required. Hermanns identifies the following among the Korku:

1. Bathing and clothing the couple and rubbing in *haldi*; 2. handing over the bride to the bridegroom; 3. their common reciprocal, ritual feeding; 4. recognition of the marriage by the community, and through it, admission of the bride within it; 5. recognition of the marriage and admission of the bride into the clan by the ancestors through the couple's offerings to them.

Beck mentions the tuition of bride and groom in their duties by the Kharia.[69]

6.5 The Dissolution and Repetition of Marriage

Only the Turi and Asur, apart from the Birjhia sub-group, do not allow divorce.[70] The Birjhia, who alone of the Asur are said to allow widow remarriage also,[71] may be less subject to Hindu influence than other Asur, who are low castes rather than tribes. Divorce does occur among other Munda, however, and for the most part is straightforward and unrestricted for both men and women. Among the Mundari it is said to be frequent, but its incidence may be less in other tribes: Elwin computed a rate of 5% of marriages for the Remo in 1950 and of only 2% for the Juang in 1948, though McDougal's figures for the latter of fifteen years later, in Keonjhar, indicated a rate of 10%.[72] As elsewhere, such statistics can hardly be regarded as more than a rough guide. It is usually the headman and panch that decide divorce petitions.[73] Among the Santal, 'as marriage is a contract that involves two villages, representatives of both villages are summoned to sanction the divorce', the village of the culpable party being feasted.[74] The recognized grounds for divorce are given variously as adultery, taking a concubine, barrenness or impotence, neglect of duties or failure to support one's family, ill-treatment, refusal to cohabit, theft, witchcraft or disease, but not all may apply in all tribes: among the Juang, for instance, desertion is grounds for divorcing a woman, but not her barrenness, adultery or witchcraft, since the husband's group is itself responsible for her both jurally and ritually.[75] In most groups, the husband can usually claim compensation in cases of his wife's adultery or desertion or where the divorce has been initiated by her, either from her family, in the form of the return of the brideprice, or from any subsequent husband, in the form of a second brideprice. However, if a petition of his own is found to be unjustified he may have to forego compensation or even pay some himself to his wife. Again, the panch and elders decide the amount and also the custody of the children.[76] Rout and Elwin tell just such a story of the Juang, though McDougal says that no compensation is paid in the infrequent cases of adultery that do occur here: instead, both the adulterer and the woman's husband are fined, the former slightly more than the latter, who is penalized for his negligence in letting his wife behave in such a way. Here, divorce is not possible after the birth of a child, though separation still takes place often. Indeed, in this group, most 'divorces' are said to be separations, for they do not involve the husband's group in loss of rights over the woman, since she cannot remarry without their consent.[77] Divorce is usually symbolized by the public tearing in half of a mango leaf and indeed is called *sakem orec* or 'tearing of the leaves' by the Santal.[78] For the Gataq a simple declaration and symbolic payment by the husband is sufficient, and sometimes the woman is simply handed back to her family. Among the Santal, according to Culshaw, 'a wife cannot divorce her husband', running away being her only remedy, though Troisi indicates that she can obtain a divorce for neglect or if her husband takes a second wife against her wishes. According to Bouez, only the husband can obtain a divorce in practice, though in principle it is open to both, and the situation is very similar for the Gataq. Conversely, Elwin says that most Sora divorces are initiated by women, and his further statement that divorce is 'simple, but emphatically disapproved' can be applied generally to all Munda.[79]

In all Munda groups, divorcees, widows and widowers may all remarry with little if any restriction. However, it is always believed that a woman will join her first, not any subsequent husband after death, he being the one who removed her status as an unmarried girl, by giving her her vermilion mark.[80] Thus for a woman, subsequent marriages have a lower status than the first, and the ceremony for the remarriage of widows and divorcees is usually less elaborate and commands a lower brideprice. This is not true of the second marriages of men, but a widower generally has to pay a higher brideprice for an unmarried girl than for a widow, and thus often both partners will be undergoing a second marriage. Majumdar claimed that Korwa widows commanded a higher brideprice than a previously unmarried girl, possibly, he implied, because the former are more experienced in home and field, though Sandhwar gives another, perhaps more plausible reason: 'For a widow a higher brideprice is to be paid, because to marry a widow is thought to be a discredit which is compensated by paying more money'. Childlessness may also increase a widow's value in terms of brideprice.[81].

Widow marriages are generally a separate form with a separate name, for example Ho, Mahali *sanga*, perhaps connected with Ho *sanya*, Mundari, Korwa *sagai*, Santal *sanga* and Korku *pato*; except the latter, these also refer to divorcee remarriage.[82] Among the Santal, although widowers may remarry in order to obtain domestic help, 'most of the women who contract a second marriage have been divorced: although there is no bar to widow remarriage, widows do not often remarry again'. The Juang of Keonjhar distinguish marriage to a widow (*burha kania*) from marriage to a separated or divorced woman (*daki kania*). McDougal's data on such marriages 'indicate that widowers marry unmarried girls and women who have been married previously with about equal frequency. However, separated or divorced males exhibit a greater tendency to marry unmarried girls; rarely does a man who has not been married previously marry a widow.' Here, widowers usually marry in order to retain the status of married men and thus delay the transition to ritual elder. Kharia female divorcees may only remarry after their former husbands have received compensation. Gataq widows may remarry a year after their husband's death—sooner if they remarry into their late husband's clan. Remarriage of widows and divorcees is rare among the Birhor, at least in Palamau. However, with the Remo 'widow remarriage is approved, and indeed generally required.' Although in some tribes a woman joins her husband's descent group on marriage, elsewhere this need not completely remove her membership of her natal group (see sect. 3.2), and often she must avoid the latter in any subsequent marriage.[83]

Most common, however, is the remarriage of a widow to her husband's younger brother, a practice which is normally designated 'junior levirate' in the literature. Indeed, so expected may this be that the kin term for father's younger brother is very often applied to step-father also (see Ch. 7). Among the Juang, for instance, ego may inherit the whole of an elder brother's property, including his wife: he pays no brideprice in doing this, for his local descent group have already paid for this same woman, and there is only a simple rite. It is more a preference, however, and if he cannot or will not marry her, his agnates in the same village, then clan mates generally, and finally anyone not *kutumb* or tabooed to her may do so, after the lapse of a month from her husband's death. Indeed, one's own elder brother's wife is taken less frequently than a classificatory one (see below). The widow herself might wish to stay in her late husband's village, for otherwise she loses all rights to land and maintenance. She should not remarry into a village or local descent group that is *bondhu* to that of her husband, but this does happen in practice nonetheless. Her own consent and that of her deceased husband's local descent group are also necessary for her remarriage. Because women marry earlier than men there are more widows than widowers, so many of them do not marry again. The main consideration seems to be the retention and maintenance of the main heir of the agnatic group and bearer of its descent line, i.e. the eldest brother's eldest son. Among the Santal, for instance, ego usually adopts his elder brother's children, even if his widow marries elsewhere (as frequently happens here), since the eldest son of ego's elder brother is the bearer of the family's descent line; thus the woman can only take her children with her, temporarily, if they are still unweaned. Among the Mahali too, the custom is sometimes restricted to ego's maintenance of his elder brother's wife and children. Mukherjea expresses it differently: 'to keep the family property intact', part of this property being the woman and her children themselves. Indeed, although the fate of the children after widowhood or divorce depends partly on their age and sex, there is generally an overriding concern to ensure the continuity of the husband's family wherever the woman remarries. The only exception to this general rule is the Korwa (including Kodaku), where women and children are looked after by any subsequent husband.[84]

Junior levirate does not seem to be especially marked ceremonially and it may sometimes have been taken for simple cohabitation by ethnographers. Indeed, a woman's husband's younger brother can expect sexual access to his elder brother's wife in many groups even while his elder brother is still alive, though the Juang would regard this as adultery. As a form of remarriage it is regarded so much as a matter of course that in some cases there is a financial penalty incurred for not observing it: for example, among the Sora compensation must be paid to a woman's former affines if she marries elsewhere. Although the younger brother does not pay a brideprice, if the woman should marry outside the family her new husband may have to pay one, which often goes not to her natal family, but to that into which she was first married. Conversely, it may be rare in some groups: among the Santal, for example, it 'is not favoured [since] the wife of one's elder brother is honoured as one's mother.' It appeared in only five per cent of Juang marriages in Elwin's sample. In some cases, dislike of it may be a reflection of high-status disapproval of widow remarriage generally (e.g. the Mahali).[85]

The specification 'husband's younger brother' should be treated here as a classificatory, not a strictly genealogical one, since other genealogical categories are sometimes reported in this context. For instance, HFBS is reported to be a substitute for HyB among the Ho if the latter is already married; among the Juang the widow of a classificatory PF, structurally equivalent to an 'elder brother' here (see sect. 8.4 i), is more usually taken; and among the Korku a male cousin may be involved.[86] Similarly, the Sora allow FyBW as a substitute for eBW, even though of the +1 level (see also sect. 8.1). According to Sitapati, 'unions with elder brother's wife and father's younger brother's wife...are considered adulterous but not incestuous, because custom sanctions...marriage with them when they become widows', and he continues:'in cases of widow remarriage, the widows are generally older than their second husband'.[87] The Remo are an exception in having the senior, not junior levirate—i.e. it is one's *younger* brother's wife, elsewhere tabooed entirely as any sort of sexual partner, whom one inherits. This, called *guising gui,* is also virtually compulsory: 'when a widow remarries [elsewhere] the brideprice is paid to the deceased husband's elder brother; a son cannot claim it.' Elwin finds an explanation for this unique phenomenon in the fact that women are often considerably older than their husbands, so that HeB and yBW will often be of about the same age.[88] However, this age pattern is found in other Munda tribes (see sect. 6.1), all of whom strongly taboo any relationship of familiarity, let alone marriage, between HeB and yBW (see sects. 8.3, 9.1). Other possible reasons are the seniority given to females in parts of Koraput[89] and the deliberate reversal of a high-status institution in order to create a marker of non-Hindu identity. An elder brother's widow cannot be inherited by a man who is already married to her younger sister (i.e. if two brothers had married two sisters in order of seniority), because of the taboo on marrying one's wife's elder sister.[90]

As already noted, the term 'junior levirate' is standard in the literature on the Munda and has accordingly been retained here, but not without certain misgivings. The above description recalls the classical *niyoga,* which was generally condemned by Manu except for girls whose betrothed had died before marriage, and who therefore had to accept relations with his younger brother in order to raise a child to his name. This enabled the agnatic line to be continued and can be regarded as a true levirate.[91] The Munda ethnography never mentions this particular point and emphasizes instead the care of widow and children and the preservation of both within the family to ensure a proper heir. Continuation of the patriline is thus the most important factor in both institutions, but whereas the *niyoga* envisages a specific but rarely occurring need to provide an heir through procreation, in the Munda ethnography such an heir is usually deemed to exist already (though he may be a minor). Alternatively, this difference of interpretation may mean that these lower status groups are less familiar with the rationale behind the *niyoga,* or that it is less significant for them. Conversely, ethnographers may not have perceived any difference, since the same group of agnates is involved whichever interpretation is chosen. Today, many high-status groups dislike the *niyoga,* for it is, of course, a version of widow remarriage, but this seems to affect the Munda less.

Levirate should also be distinguished from polyandry of the Himalayan kind, with which Munda ethnographers sometimes confuse it. While they may superficially seem similar, junior levirate is mainly of significance only after the elder brother's death—a serial and subordinate marriage for a specific purpose. As we have seen, it is generally believed that a woman joins her first husband on death, regardless of any subsequent marriage; and despite the possibility of sexual relations with the younger brother even in the elder brother's lifetime, the woman is actually married to the latter only. In polyandry, by contrast, the emphasis is on the simultaneous and more or less equivalent marriage of a group of brothers to one woman as a standard form.[92]

Junior levirate, as well as of necessity being a type of widow remarriage, may also involve polygyny, if the husband's younger brother is already married. Polygyny in general may, however, take other forms and come about through other motives. Among the Munda, the commonest reason by far is the barrenness of one's first wife,[93] though this sometimes leads to divorce instead. Polygyny is also attributed by ethnographers to the fact that wives are sometimes older than their husbands (the Remo), to the taboo on sexual intercourse for two or three years after the birth of a child (the Ho), or simply to relative wealth and status (Ho and Juang).[94] The commonest form of polygyny is the junior sororate, in which a man takes his wife's younger sister as a second wife. Unlike many instances of widow inheritance, this is in no way mandatory and indeed seems to be altogether less important and less common. For example, among the Juang there is no automatic claim on one's wife's younger sister and one must pay the standard brideprice; and in fact most widowers take their second wife from a different local descent group and different village.[95] Though it represented ten per cent of Elwin's sample of Juang marriages—a quite high figure—McDougal found it to be 'exceedingly rare' here.

The Kodaku do not have it and the Mahali dislike it (here a reflection of Hindu influence) and have no particular ceremony for it, but the Mundari still regard it highly enough to celebrate it in the regular *arandi* ceremony. Among the Birjhia Asur a brideprice is paid only if WyZ has not previously been married.[96]

As with husband's younger brother (above), the specification 'wife's younger sister' is to be taken as a classificatory one: sometimes another wife's relative may be married polygynously, such as WZD, WMBD or some other referent of ego's level or the level below him among the Mahali. Other examples are WBD among the Santal and WeBD among the Ho, and the occasional examples reported of marriages to a mother's sister (e.g. MyZ among the Santali) are perhaps to be regarded in the same light.[97] Marriage to WyZ will obviously not involve polygyny in those cases where ego's first wife has died. Among the Gataq sororal polygyny is not allowed, and marriage to two sisters can only take place consecutively. Among the Kodaku it is not allowed where one's WyZ is the widow of a fellow clan member.[98] One's wife's *elder* sister is completely banned as a marriage or sexual partner among the Munda.

In some groups, other categories may be preferred as second wives, though generally avoided in first marriages. Among the Juang these are classificatory PM and CD and (though less desirable) SSW, any second wife usually being from a different descent group than the first. Sengupta's statistics for Mahali marriages indicate that second marriages occur more frequently with classificatory cousins and sibling's children than with actual EyssG.[99]

Non-sororal polygyny seems to be even rarer. McDougal recorded only six cases of polygyny out of his sample of 331 Juang marriages. Elwin noted a rate of two per cent for the Juang in 1948 and one of seven per cent for the Remo in 1950. In some cases all polygyny is disapproved, though still permitted, as with the Kharia and Kodaku; 'it is not regarded enthusiastically by Bondo [Remo] society' either. The Santal value monogamy for the high brideprice and status it confers and only accept polygyny in cases of barrenness, though the inheritance rights of the children are not affected. Christian influence may lead to its total prohibition. Only the Sora, Bhumij of Koraput and formerly the Ho are said to practice it at all commonly, though this may reflect the different ideas different ethnographers have of what constitutes frequency.[100]

'In all cases of second marriage, the consent of the first wife in the presence of the village panchayat or council is essential.' The first wife has precedence over any subsequent wife except in the case of junior levirate, where ego's eBW retains her precedence over ego's own first wife even after her marriage to ego; this reflects her precedence among the wives of the same fraternal group generally.[101] A man seldom has more than two wives concurrently, though Elwin recorded some exceptions among the Sora, and McDougal was told of instances of Juang men having three wives, though he did not come across any himself. Among the Korku it depends on (and signifies) a man's wealth, since a separate *gonom* or brideprice must be paid for each wife.[102]

6.6 *The Significance of Marriage*

For the individual, marriage is important for personal status and acceptance by the group. For the immediate family, on the other hand, marriage is the chief means of obtaining a male heir. Brides are 'purchased', though the transaction is symbolic rather than truly economic. Once a family obtains a woman through marriage, it will normally try to retain her if she becomes a widow by marrying her to another agnate—typically a husband's younger brother. This ensures the maintenance of the principal carrier of the descent line through this agnate's care of widow and child(ren) and may even continue to produce heirs for the agnatic group, though it is not entirely clear exactly to whom this heir would be attributed—deceased elder or living younger brother. Other means of ensuring an heir in the failure of one's first marriage to produce one include polygyny (especially to one's wife's younger sister) and *ghar-jawae* marriage, in which a daughter's husband stands in place of a son in order to continue the descent line in the person of his own son. Obtaining an heir is also important among upper-caste groups in north India, of course, but here an equally important concern of marriage is the acquisition of merit through the unreciprocated gift of a virgin and other prestations to a family of higher status. This is of no significance among the Munda, nor generally among lower-status groups—low castes as well as tribes—in this area, and even among high-status groups it is by no means universal.[103]

For the society as a whole, marriage is linked to tribal identity in relation to the outside world, through the rule of tribal endogamy. It is also linked to the demarcation of its main internal divisions, whether these are conceived as patrilineal descent groups or some other agnatically defined groups, through their exogamy in relation to one another, though at the same time it is an important means of linking these divisions on a society-wide basis. It remains to examine more exactly how and to what extent descent and marriage interact in affinal alliance between these divisions and/or their segments, for this provides the structure of the whole society, a matter in which individuals and families are no less involved than wider units. First, however, we should examine kinship terminology, the linguistic and categorical expression of this structure.

Chapter Seven
Kinship Terminology

7.1 *Introduction*

Munda kinship terminologies really fall into neither of the two large groups into which terminologies on the Indian subcontinent are conventionally divided. They have a number of symmetric prescriptive features, which to a large extent draws them into line with the Dravidian terminologies of the south—terminologies which have given their name to the type of kin classification otherwise known as bifurcate merging or symmetric prescriptive. They are closer to these than to the terminologies of north India (the other group mentioned above), but there are still a number of differences. It could be argued that they are simply transitional between north and south, and there is indeed a sense in which this is true. But their internal coherence, and the fact that the sixteen Munda terminologies we have in relatively complete form are remarkably consistent from one to another, in structure if not lexically, suggests the presence of particular features worthy of separate analysis. It will be convenient to utilize the threefold division of the Munda languages into North, Central and South Munda at the more detailed stages of the analysis (see also Figure 3a as a guide to what follows). No attempt will be made to cover all the terms that have been recorded by anthropologists and linguists, for the chapter is concerned above all with the semantic pattern of the terminologies rather than the terms in isolation. However, every attempt has been made to preserve accuracy in dealing with the linguistic aspects.[1]

There are many Indic and, in KM, Dravidian loans in these terminologies, which can often be put down to the bilingualism of so many Munda and thus dismissed for present purposes. Some loans, however, have a truly semantic role, since there are no Munda equivalents for them. This suggests that they have been introduced to effect changes in the patterns of these terminologies, probably from a 'purer' symmetric prescriptive type.[2] The same is true of another phenomenon, namely internal Munda innova-

	//		X	
	male	female	male	female
+2	FF MMB	MM FFZ	MF FMB	FM MFZ
+1	F FB	FZ MBW EM	MB FZH EF	M MZ
0	Ego; B PssGS EGE/EGEG/GEGE/ osCEP	(Ego) Z PssGD	PosGC (H) EG/GE/GEG/ssCEP	PosGD W
-1	S BS (DH) EZS	D BD (SW) EZD	ZS DH (S) EBS	ZD SW (D) EBD
-2	SS (DS)	SD (DD)	DS (SS)	DD (SD)

Figure 3a. *Idealized symmetric prescriptive terminology*

Assuming patrilineal descent. The perspective is that of a male ego, but designata in brackets are those viewed by a female ego, where these differ.

tions produced by affixation, compounding, and extension of semantic range.

There is almost complete generational separation, and the terminologies can be seen to fall into two sets of alternate generations to a certain degree, one including ego's level (+2, -2, 0, even +4 and -4 in some cases), the other focused on those adjacent to it (+1, -1, +3, -3). I will deal with each set in turn, starting with the former, and with ego's level.

7.2 Ego's and Alternating Levels

It is not easy to reduce the terms for siblings to a morphological pattern common to all Munda groups. There are three similar roots starting with virtually identical morphemes. *Boko*, typically yG in NM and Ju, may be connected lexically with KM *buyang* Bms and GRG *bulon* Zws. It is probably distinct from Sora *uba* yG, and certainly from KM *bobo, bobre* (*pace* my earlier article, 1985: 712), which is linked with KM, NM *bare*, from **bohre* Bws (ZZ 2, 4–5, 16; Vi). Apparently different again is **bau*, **bao*> Ho, Mu *bau* eB (elsewhere usually EeB, eZH etc.; ZZ 14–15; see further below). Three other terms have a fairly wide distribution, namely *aji* (eZ, in Ju, Sa, Mu, Ho, Kw); *dada* (eB in NM, Kh); and *misera* (Sa), *misi* (Mu, B) or *mes* (Kw), Z. The first looks Indic, since it appears in Bihari, Marathi, Hi, etc. (but as PM except in Hi, where it is eZ), but ZZ (15) appear to regard it as Munda; the second may be Indic, but the third is certainly Munda. Sa *misera* is given either as Z or as Zms, *boko* being either yG or ssG, while Ho *misi* is yZws, with *undi* as yBms (recorded as yB only in Mu). This is not the only evidence of relative-sex sibling terms, for in Mu there is *haga* as ssG, and **bohre* (above) also has this sort of reference. KM may provide examples of a transitional stage between classifications based on relative sex and those based on absolute sex (of referent). Gm has four separate sibling terms (divided as Bws, Bms, Zms, Zws, thus indicating absolute sex of both ego and alter), one of which (*tonan* Zms) appears as Z (ws and ms) in Sora, Gq and Gb. Remo offers a hint of another possibility, namely *boqre* (<**bohre*) as Gws (i.e. indicating absolute sex of speaker, not of referent), although unfortunately there is no mention of a corresponding term for Gms. In Sora there are different sets of terms for true and classificatory G, some showing relative age, some relative sex (Vi).

The splitting up of sibling terms by age relative to ego is a more usual, indeed an almost universal feature in Munda. There is a general tendency to confine independent Munda terms to yG, using a number of innovations for eG. Sa has favoured especially the semantic extension of other Munda terms (especially those for EG; see below), to both eG and, as synonyms, to yG. Mu and its dialects have opted for the creation of compounds and Ku for grammatical affixation, and there are a number of Indic loans, especially in NM. Juang has a Munda (?) independent term for eB (*ka*), but otherwise only KM has such terms throughout this area, usually four in number, many of which have already received mention. This part of the terminology is very confused and possibly in a state of flux, but there is clear evidence of both relative-sex and relative-age structuring. The former—really the cross-parallel distinction of this area of the terminology—is likely to be more fundamental systemically (and perhaps also older) than the latter. The main sibling terms are listed below:

(a) Relative-sex terms
    i. Mu *haga* ssG
    ii. **bohre* Bws
    iii. KM *tonan* etc. Z (ms in Gm)
    iv. KM *buyang* etc. Gos (see **boko*, below)
(b) Relative-age terms
    i. Ho, Mu *bau* eB (affinal elsewhere)
    ii. NM, Kh *dada* eB
    iii. NM, Ju *aji* eZ
    iv. **boko* yG; perhaps connected with KM *buyang*, etc., Gos
    v. Sora *uba* yG
    vi. *misi* yZ

There is a tendency to equate cousins with siblings; otherwise, one generally finds loans of Indic sibling terms or Dravidian cousin terms, or Munda compounds.Independent terms for any PGC category are very few, possibly loans, and confined to KM. In Sora, Gq and R, FZC and MBC are assimilated to one another in symmetric prescriptive fashion with *marenger (u)*, Sora *marongger*. *Maronsel* is applied in Sora to female cross cousins, but both terms also have a wider meaning here, covering MZC and also cross cousins of the two descending generations, but not FBC etc., equated with siblings.[3] *Marenger* may be Dravidian, though it is absent from Trautmann.[4] Gb has *agom, agoi* for male and female cross cousins respectively, these possibly being ss terms only. Here too, therefore, there are some separate cross-cousin terms. Pfeffer reports *giking* as PosGS, *dada* being eB, though *miming* conflates PosGD, eZ and MM. In Gm, similarly, there is a distinction between *dada, bai* PosGC, classificatory sibling, and *ana, abe* 'true sibling', though the former seems Munda. Ju equates cross cousins with siblings but nonetheless distinguishes MBC from FZC, the former being 'eG', the latter 'yG',[5] the only expression of asymmetry between these kin types anywhere in Munda. Also to be noted are Gq *nang* (FBC) and Gb *mena* (FZC; according to Bch 86 it is uncertain whether the latter is AA, Indic or Dravidian).

Categories in the EG/GE fields are also split according to sex and to the age of one's own or one's spouse's sibling relative to oneself, and therefore eight different categories result. yBW and yZH often share terms with SW and DH, but the equivalence between EeG and EP now seems less concrete than it did formerly (cf. Parkin 1985: 710, 713). yZH is *ara* in most NM (not Sa or Ku, which use the standard NM term for eZH, see below, nor Kodaku, with *dulhakin;* there are only Indic loans in Bh). It is *aram* in CM, to which are probably connected Gb *arion* and R *arju*, and possibly Gq *rujua*, Gm *ranya*, Sora *ream*. Similarly, yBW is *kimin* in NM, CM, R and Gq, with possible cognate terms in Sora *kaon* and perhaps Gm *konun* (ZZ are cautious on this point, p.11); the Gb term is *iyong*.

eZH is *tenya* in NM, a term also applied, with suffixes, to its reciprocal WyG in Mu and Ho and WyB in Ku. In KM and Ju there is a separate series, Sora *baon* (Vi; Sora also has *kaku* here; cf. eBW below), Ju *bau*, Gb, R, Gq *(u)mbang;* perhaps also R, Gb *imbing* (eBW), some reflexes of which appear as eB (ZZ 14–15; see above). In Sora it is also EeB, HyB, in Kh EeB, and in Ku eZH, WeB, WyZ (the latter as *baongjei*), and it appears in prefixed combination with *honjar* etc. (EF) as EeB in Kher (not Asur), and suffixed in combination with *kunyar* (a cognate) in Sora. Remo apparently has a direct equivalent between EeB and EF under another possible cognate, *nkui*.

Juang has completely separate terms for EeB, namely *bokar* (HeB) and *sango* (WeB). The Ju for WyB is *inibo*, the last element of which is more probably from *boko* than from *bau* etc. (ZZ 14–15). The first element, *ini-*, can 'tentatively' be connected with terms for EyG (ZZ 6, 13–15), which elsewhere are *erel, ilil* in some KM (Vi *aliboi, eriboi*, EyZ; *erisej* EyB; R, Gq *girin* may be connected, but this is not certain), *erwel(in), iril-kora/-kuri* in Sa (all as EyG), and *iriul (-kora/-kuri)* in Mu, Ho, B (as HyG), Kw, Ku *(ilur)* (as HyB). WyG in Mu and Ho, and WyB in Ku are *tenya* (otherwise eZH, its reciprocal; see above), but in Kw, Bh and Asur most sibling-in-law terms are Indic.

Apart from Ju *inibo*, CM is quite anomalous here. Kh has *boker* (EyG), *boksel* (EyZ), both derivations of *boko*, which exceptionally in Kh has lost its sibling reference and become an affinal term, probably relatively recently according to Zide (1958: 15). Ju also has *boko(ger)* as HyB, together with *kundaisen* (HyZ) and *salirae* (WyZ), the latter perhaps from Indic *sari* (WyZ; cf. some other WG terms in Kh).

Contrary to my earlier suggestions (Parkin 1985: 714), the series represented by *hili* and *iriul* etc. are most probably separate (ZZ ibid. and personal communication). *Hili* is regularly eBW in Kher, though in Kw (including Kodaku) it is also HyZ, a reciprocal category. In KM there are different terms, namely Sora *kake* (Vi also has *buni(boi)*), Gm *akan*, probably connected, and R, Gb *imbing*, Gq *mbang*, perhaps yet another cognate set. The final category to be considered in this field is EeZ, comparable to EeB in NM, in the sense that the root for EM (*hanar* etc.) is prefixed by *aji-/jiji-* (eZ in isolation). The Sa form of this root, *hanhar*, is reduced to *-hnar*, giving *ajhnar* (ZZ 15). The Ju form, *ajikar*, is formed directly on the non-affinal term, unlike in Kher. The EM root is used in Sora with the suffix *-boi* for EeZ (<*bau*?), but in the Gm the full cognate *kinarbi* is used for both EeZ and EM; this language also has *bibi* for EeZ (also eZ). In R and Gq also, there is equivalence between EM and EeZ (cf. EeB, above). The Kh term for HeB in *nana*, possibly Indic, and also eZ, while for WeZ it is *boksel* (also EyZ) or Indic *sali*. This terminological connection between EeG and EP categories becomes a full equivalence of terms in the reciprocal, junior part of the terminology (q.v. below).[6] These terms are summarized below:

   i. *ara* etc. yZH
  ii. *kimin* etc. yBW
 iii. NM *tenya* eZH (and WyG in some languages)
 iv. KM, Ju *bau, *bao* eZH (eB in some NM)
  v. *kuli* (Kher *hili*) eBW (not KM)
 vi. *erwel* EyG
vii. *bau-, *bao-* + *-kankar* (EF); EeB (suffixed in Sora;
      sometimes as EP in other KM)
viii. *aji-* etc. + *-kinkar* (EM); EeZ (suffixed in Sora;
      sometimes as EP in other KM; Ju *ajikar*)

    Usually, EGE = G, though sometimes these categories are assimilated to EeG ones, as partly in Sora, R and Sa, or to GE ones (examples in Ho, Sora, Sa, Asur, Mu, Kh, Ku), and even to EM in Ho. Indic loans are also present. Sa also uses compounds, and like Mu has an independent term for HBW (*nata*), as do R, Gq, Kh (*donkui*), Ho (*tangain, jataing*) and Asur (*jatea*). *Donkui* may be connected with R *nkui* (see above). Ho *unding kui* yZ. There is also Ho *erakin* HZH. Though not one of the usual signatures of a symmetric prescriptive terminology, the equation EGE = G is certainly compatible with a symmetric rather than an asymmetric scheme, for in the latter only EssGE would be equated with siblings. One of the few EGEG categories to be recorded (Kw *bahin* HZHZ) shows that these too are, as expected, 'sibling' terms.

GEG terms are few and poorly recorded but have a particular interest, since there is much evidence that the categories they stand for are preferred spouses, especially in NM and CM groups (see sects. 8.4, 8.5). There is evidence also of relative-sex structuring. *Yar*, for instance, is GEBms in Kw and Mu and is presumably also represented by Asur *earin*, BWyB. On the other hand *goi* and *sangat*, the latter of which is Indic, largely seem to be os terms. The former is GEZms in Mu, possibly GEGos, though Sachchidananda (1979: 348) gives it also as BWZws and GEB (ws?). He also gives *guiram* as an apparently general term for GEG, and this is found in Sa as eBWZ. Kw *goi* is BWZ (ms?), eZHyB (ws), which are prescribed categories, and the similar term *jai* is ZHZms. In Sa, *sangat* stands for the prescribed category eGEyGos, though in Mu it is given by Sachchidananda as another general GEG term. The presumably related *sangi* is glossed as ZHB and BWZ in Asur. *Iyar* and *goi* are also recorded in Kh with apparently similar glosses, though the data are not very clear. In Korwa (including Kodaku) they also cover GEGE and EGEG categories, which one would expect to be assimilated to G: *goi* is ZHZ, HZHZ, *yar* is BWB, ZHeB, ZHZH. In Sa, *iril* (also EyG) is an alternative to *sangat* as ZHG. In KM, there are no recorded independent terms for GEG categories, but cognates of *goi* appear in other contexts, namely *guising gui*, the Remo term for the senior levirate (see sect. 6.5), and possibly Sora *gai*, 'a term of address to a male, with wide idiomatic use; equality always implied' (Vi). There are no distinctions between ZHG and BWG except in Kw. Of these terms, only *goi* and *sangat* seem to specify marriage choice, i.e. eGEyGos (see sect. 8.4). Ju uses WZ terms for GEZ, namely *ajikar* for eGEeZ, a tabooed category of spouse, and *salirae* for eGEyZ, the preferred category of spouse. Further terms for these specifications are badly needed from other groups. The current information is listed below:

i.   *yar* GEBms (GEGss?)   ii. *goi* eGEyGos
iii. *sangat* eGEyGos   iv. *salirae* eGEyZ (Ju)
v. *ajikar* eGEeZ (Ju)

Two more categories remain to be discussed briefly in this level. CEP is now usually a variant of Indic *samdhi(n)*, but Sa, Mu and Ho seem to have an independent term, namely *bala* (unless this too is Indic, being connected lexically, though not semantically with *bara*, *bada*—see PssG(E), below). In Sora, we find two undeniably symmetric prescriptive features (ms assumed) with some terms, in that CEF is *marengeru* (also MBS, FZS, and possibly Dravidian; see above) and CEM is *tonan* (also Z); there is also *parui*, glossed as CEP by Vi. There are few specific Munda terms for spouse, but instead a large number of Indic loans (for example, Sora, R *dokri*, from Oriya; Sa *bahu*, from Hi *bahu* SW), circumlocutions and allusive descriptions (e.g. Sa, Mu *orak-hor* 'man of the house'; Mu *herel* 'adult male'; Sa, Mu, Kh, B *gomke*, *gumke* 'master, big man'); and adoptions of other Munda terms, especially those for child (e.g. R *kun*, Mu *kuri*, *honjar*, Sora *kumyar*; note also R *kimo-boi*, 'bride'). Such devices reflect in part the name avoidance enjoined between a married couple. Also to be noted are Sora-Gorum *menraq* H, and NM *era*, woman, wife. Mu, Ho, Sa *hirum*, *hirom*, Asur *mirom* are all 'co-wife', second wife, though in Kw terms for sister are used, a clear reference to the junior sororate (see sect. 6.5).

In +2 there are two principal terms. PF is *ta*, *tata*, *ntaq* etc. (R, Gq, Mu, Ho, Sa, Kh; FF in Asur and Kw; the Sora term is *jojo*) and PM is *yayu* etc. (KM, Kh; Sora *yoyo*, *yuyu*), *jia* (Sa, Mu, Ho, Asur; FM in Kw). Although the first of these resembles forms in some Indic and Dravidian languages, both terms in fact have cognates throughout AA (Parkin forthcoming), a widespread distribution suggesting that they are ancient and fundamental. There is a tendency to apply both terms to PPG categories also, using absolute sex as the criterion, so that PF = PPB, PM = PPZ. This does not apply to Ju, which in any case lacks both roots. This language has Indic loans instead, which are also found as synonyms elsewhere, namely *nana*, *nani*, *aja* and *aji* (unless this is Munda—see above, eZ). These too are classificatory: e.g. Kw *nana/i* are also recorded as FZHP. Some NM also have *bura/-i* ('old man, old woman').

The regular KM term for CC is found in Gb *ileqei*, R *iqlei*, *igle*, Gq *agle*, and in Gm *iqleng*, which is prefixed to show sex of referent. Also connected is Sora *uleng*, an alternative to *yaya*, *jaja*, also recorded for CC (not in Vi). Kher has *jai*, which usually appears in compounds with *kora* (lit. 'boy'), *kuri* (lit. 'girl'), and *han*, *kon*,' child', as in Mu, B, Ho and Kora; Ho also has the term in an isolated form, as does Bh (DD). The main NM term for CC, though (according to ZZ 4), is represented by Sa *korar*, Ku *kurar*, *kular*, and it may be present in the KM language Gm (*koron*). CM has *bokdu* (Kh), *bokolap*, *bokosen* (Ju), all connected with *boko*, yG (see above). The Indic loans *nati*, *natin* frequently appear, especially in NM and CM. CC terms are also applied to GCC categories and—sometimes in combination—to affinal specifications in both +2 and –2.

There are a considerable number of equations between +2, –2 and/or ego's level. Ju is particularly well endowed with these, some being applied to the +4 and –4 levels also. Where ego's level is split by age, the elder specification goes with the senior of these levels, the younger with the junior. Thus we have *aji*, eZ, +2, +4; *bokorae*, yZ, –2, –4; *sango*, WeB, +2, +4; *inibou*, WyB, –2, –4; *ajikar*, WeZ, +2, +4; and *salirae*, WyZ, eGEyZ, –2, –4. *Somondi* and *tiurae* are applied to +2, +4, as well as to CEF and CEM—senior kin, because of the respect due to the specifications that are in ego's level. The sexual distinction is also maintained: e.g. a female ego classes SS with yB (*boko*) and SD with yZ (*bokorae*).[7]

Other languages have similar equations. My original suggestion of connecting NM *jia* (PM) with *jai* (CC; Parkin 1985: 708) has been rejected as doubtful (ZZ 4), though Bhattacharya has *jia* as CC in one article (1966: 38). Nonetheless Mu has *bura*, *nana* PF, CS, *buri*, *nani* PM, CD. Mu, Kw and Sa have *aji* eZ, PM (FM in Sa), Bh has *dada* eB, CS (cf. Beng. *dada* eB, PF) and Gb has *mining* eZ, PosGD, MM. In Sa *gorom* (Mahali *gadam*) 'namesake' is used in address to both CC and PP (a clear reference to the naming of children after their ssFP—see Ch. 10), usually in compounds with words for mother, father, girl, boy, old man, old woman. In Kh, *bokdu* CC is clearly from *boko* etc. yG, though this root is only found in EG terms in ego's level in Kh today. Sora *yaya*, *jaja* (CS, CD) resemble *yoyo*, *yuyu* (PM), *jojo* (PF), and although the difference in vowel may rule out a direct etymological connection, their similarity may be explicable otherwise (e.g. as echo words). Only in Mahali are there any independent +4/–4 terms, namely *gambuda/-i* (+4), *gamkora/-kuri* (–4), and even these are clearly compounds.

7.3 Adjacent Levels

Such equations are also to be found in the opposing generation set, based on the levels adjacent to ego's, to which we now turn, starting with +1. *Ba*, *aba*, *apa* are the standard Munda terms for 'father', and although similar to Indic *baba*, *bapa*, Tamil *appa*, Urdu *abba* etc., they are probably not related to any of them; however, the Munda forms with the voiced consonant may have been influenced by Indic.[8] In Sora and Gm there is a separate term, *wang, ayan.* The standard Kher term for 'mother' is *enga* (also *inga, anga*); also connected is Ku *an-*, a reduced form of *ayang* only appearing as a bound form with the possessive suffix, e.g. *ante* 'your mother'. A variant is Mu *eang,* which appears in KM as *(i)ang, (i)ong* etc. Kh has *ayo,* and the Ju form, *buin,* is also in this series (ZZ 5).

The PG(E) terms are consistently arranged in symmetric prescriptive fashion, and although there is little lexical consistency throughout the Munda family in this terminological area, the semantic references even of Indic loans has been altered to display this sort of symmetry. In Kher, *gungu* (Sa *gongo,* except in Bouez) is applied to PessG(E) in Sa, B and Kw, to FyB and MyZH in addition in Ho,[9] to FyB in addition in Mu, and to PeG and PessGE in the Hasada dialect of Mu. Kw and the Naguri dialect of Mu have *bada/-i, bara/-i* (probably Indic), and Hasada has *kuku,* all as exact synonyms of *gungu* as PessG(E), the former set providing sex-specific alternatives. This also appears in B, Asur and Kh, as PessG(E), and Gq *baha,* FeB, MeZ, may be linked with it. Possibly there was no relative-age distinction in this part of the terminology at one time, the entire PssG(E) field being covered by these terms, for today PyssG(E) is usually an Indic term: *kaka* is FyB, MyZH (FyB only in Indic and B), *kaki* is MyZ, FyBW (only FBW in Indic, only FyBW in B), and *masi, mosi* is MyZ in Bh, B (MZ in Indic). Only Mu and Ho have independent Munda terms here, respectively *garin* and *gawain,* glossed as MyZ, FyBW. Sa has the more usual *kaka, kaki* here, but also uses Sa and Indic terms for parent, prefixed with *hudin* ('small'; the antonym of this word, *marang,* is used in a similar fashion as an alternative to *gongo*). Ku has a similar device for PessG(E), namely *khat-ba, khat-mai, khat* meaning 'big'; *ai* is M, MyZ. PyssG(E) terms are often recorded for step-parents also, a reference to junior levirate and sororate (sect. 6.5): e.g. in Kw, HZHP = PyssG (*kaka/-i*) in symmetric prescriptive fashion, and the terms also cover step-parents.

In CM and KM, even though the terms are lexically different, we do not find a markedly different pattern. In particular, there is again evidence of innovation in this field, though here the discrimination of relative age depends on internal semantic development rather than outside loans. As in NM, PessG(E) terms are

Munda (except possibly in Kh) and refer to the whole of this field; they usually vary for absolute sex of referent, but only grammatically, namely Kh *bada/-i, bara/-i* (perhaps Indic), Ju *atir, atirae,* R, Gq *busa(n) (boi),* possibly Gm *takur, ukur,* and Sora *entalaij* (MeZ, FeBW; also GD in some references; see below for male specifications). Kh uses Indic terms for PyssG(E), except that *mij* (recorded as FyBW, but also as MeZ, perhaps an error) is probably Munda, perhaps connected with Mu *misi* Z. Ju has *san(o)bui* (lit. 'little mother', *san* being Indic) for the female categories in this field, using *dadi* (lexically identical with Hi, Bihari etc. *dadi* FM) for the male ones. R *tabuk* (FyB) and *umbuk boi* (MyZ, FyBW; *boi* = 'woman'), cognate with Gq *thabo* (FyB, MyZH) and *mbo* (MyZ, FyBW), are related pairs (ZZ 16). Zide (1958: 14) suggests that the morpheme *-buk* may be derived from *boko* yG. It is not possible to establish any connection between Gm *takun* (FyB) and *ua* (FyBW), but the former, like *takur* (FeB) may be connected with Gq *taq* and hence with Proto-Munda *tata* (both PF). This is strongly suggested by Sora, wherein *tata* is FeB, MZH (but not PF in Sora), while *yaya* (MyZ, FyBW) is almost identical with *yayu* (PM, PPZ). Thus in KM there seems to have been some tendency for PP (and occasionally sibling or parent terms) to invade the PssG(E) (especially PssyG(E)) area of the terminology. Movement is unlikely to have been in the reverse direction, in view of the wide distribution of these same +2 terms, both in Munda and in other AA. (There is no similar tendency in the reciprocal descending levels, i.e. from –2 to –1.) Finally, Sora FyB, MyZH is *kibong* (Vi) or *dada* (FF in Hi, Beng., etc., PF in Gm, but FeB in Oriya, Sora's nearest Indic neighbour).

Before examining PosG(E) we will look at the terms for EP, in which field there are basically two categories, EF and EM; that is to say, there is no distinction between husband's and wife's relatives, so that the field is symmetrically organized. EM is *hanar* in Kher (Ho *hoyar*), *kankar* in Ku; CM has *kinkar*, KM *kinar* etc. EF terms, though slightly more diverse, are cognates too, namely Sa *hoenhar*, Mu etc. *honyar, honhar*, Ku *kumkar*, Ju *kuinkar*, Sora *kumar, kunyar*, R *ngkui*. In Kodaku, EP shares terms with PP, the only such example in Munda.

We turn now to PosG(E). Kher has *kuma* (Sa FZH; Mu FZH, MB; Ho FZH, MB, WF), which, despite the similarity of its first syllable to some of the above terms for EF, is unlikely to be the same root (N.H. Zide personal communication), so that except in Ho we are unable to reconstruct a fully prescriptive equation here. More universal is the use of Indic or Dravidian *mama/-o/-u* [10] for both MB and FZH, a synonym in the above languages for *kuma* and like it offering an equation typically associated with symmetric prescriptive terminologies, yet one which does not normally include the further, characteristic affinal specifications except in Kw (also WF) and Ho (also WF, eZHF). Ho has the most comprehensive symmetry of this type in the +1 level. Although *kuma* is restricted to MB, FZH and WF, *hoyar* is applied to all of these, as well as to HF, and even *mamu* refers here to FZH and EF, having lost its sole designation in Indic as MB; moreover, *hoyar hon* (lit. 'father-in-law's son'), is used for FZS. Sa too is an exception, but in another sense, namely in distinguishing FZH (*kuma*) from MB (*mama*), though elsewhere it preserves the usual symmetry, this being one of the very few asymmetric prescriptive features anywhere in Munda terminologies. As in Kher, PosG(E) is usually a loan in Ku, CM and KM. Kh and Ku have *mama/-u/-i* for all the categories in this field. In Ju and KM this root is applied to male specifications only, though Elwin (1948: 68 and n.1, *contra* McDougal) gives Ju *mamu* as EF also, and this is the case with Gb *mamung* too (Claudia Gross, personal communication). In Ku, FZ and MBW are also *phuphu* (Hi FZ) or *kaki* (which is FBW in Indic), but only *sasu* appears in Ju (connected with terms for EM in Indic, perhaps) and *nanni* in Sora (Hi, Bihari MM). R, Gq and Sora have *wang, uon, anang* for FZ and MBW, the Gq form also being EM. One source gives Ju *ating* [connected with *atir(ae)*, PessG(E)] as FZ, MBW. This root can be compared with Gm *mata, ating* FZ, MBW, EM, a diagnostic symmetric prescriptive equation. Also, like Ho, Gm has the equation FZH = MB = EF, but unlike Ho uses only loans for it (*mama, satra*, as synonyms); Gq has the same equation, with the term *maon*.

In both Gm and Gq, the above terms exist alongside the regular *kinar, kehar*, as EM. In Kher, one finds *hatom, hatam* (Indic or Dravidian according to Bch 29) for FZ, MBW, and Indic *mami* (MBW only in Indic) occurs frequently as an alternative. Kw *mami* and Ho *hatom* are also WM and thus synonyms of *hanhar, hanar*, giving a full symmetric prescriptive equation. In contrast to PssG(E), the PosG(E) field is virtually unmarked as regards relative age.

Turning now to the reciprocal −1 level, we find that the term for 'child' is a cognate in all Munda languages, and indeed it is exceedingly widespread in other AA also, being easily the most widely occurring kin term in this language family (Parkin forthcoming). As far as Munda is concerned, the forms are Kher *hon, han, hopon,* Ku *kon, kor,* Ju *konon,* Kh *kondoq,* KM *on, odu-on, oqon* etc. *Hopon,* found only in Sa and B, may once have been a plural form, but today it is used mainly as a synonym of *hon* (*Encyc. Mund.* 1801). In NM sex is shown by suffixation (*-kora,* 'boy, male'; *-kuri, -je, -era,* 'girl, female'), this possibly being a later development (Zide 1958:12). Sora has *dangriyo* (D), *gabruvan* (S), in addition to *on.*

In the collateral –1 area, (E)ssGC is the reciprocal of PssG(E), and (E)osGC is that of PosG(E), and as in the +1 level we find a tendency to split the former (but to a much lesser degree the latter) by age. The Munda terms for (E)yssGC are frequently connected with those for the reciprocal +1 category (PessG(E)). Thus we have *gungu, gongo* (Ho, B, Mu, Sa, Kodaku; Mu also has *kuku*), *bada/-i* (Asur, Mu, Kh; possibly Indic or Dravidian), *tata* and *entalaij* (Sora), and *atirkon, atirchindae* (Ju; Bch 29 connects these with Kher *hatom* and thus traces them simultaneously to terms for MZ and FBW, and to Indic and Dravidian, but neither hypothesis is very plausible; see below). Ku has *kosre, kosrej* (not in +1), which, like *bada/-i,* denotes gender only grammatically. As in the PssG(E) field, the split according to relative age in (E)ssGC seems to be fairly recent, the original terms being confined to the junior half of the –1 level. A number of devices have been adopted to deal with the new senior categories (a mirror image of the +1 situation), only Ju having a purely independent term, *oturo.* The most prominent of these are the adoption of Indic *bhatija/-i* (BC in Hi, Bihari), which is found in Mu, Asur and Kh; the creation of compounds from other, usually Munda terms, as in Mu, Sa, B and Ho; and the use of terms for 'child' (Munda or Indic), found above all in Ho. The latter may be a vestige of a fully symmetric prescriptive terminology. It does not always discriminate relative age, being applied sometimes to the junior half of the category also, perhaps an indication that relative age discrimination is a secondary innovation. In KM virtually no age discrimination has been reported in this field except in Sora, where (E)ssGC usually seems to be equated with C, an equation compatible with and common in symmetric prescriptive terminologies. In Sora, however, this holds good only for ssGC, since EssGS and EssGD are respectively *kinnarbiyon* and *edir(ba)baion.* The latter is probably Munda, but otherwise of uncertain etymology (it may be connected with Ju *atir*, of similar but wider meaning). The final morphemes of both are probably cognate with Gb, R *buyan, biyan* (B, yB), not found in isolation in Sora.

As with the reciprocal PosG(E) field, (E)osGC is less commonly split by age. Kw, Mu, Ho and Ju have independent terms, respectively *giru, gere* (suffixed with *-kora, -kuri* to indicate sex), *gaing* and *goblekon, goblesendae*. Sa has *homon* BCws, the same term becoming GCws, HGC in Ho. According to an early article by Zide, this is cognate with Ku *kon* etc. (1958:13), but it also bears a resemblance to R, Sora *amonsej*, Sora *amonsil* eBC (ws?). Apparently, both are from terms for 'child' plus *-m-* infix (ZZ 11), and they both have cognates elsewhere in AA (Parkin forthcoming). Elsewhere, we find devices similar to those mentioned in the previous paragraph, especially the formation of compounds from other Munda kinship terms, as in Mu and Sa, and the adoption of Indic *bhanja/-i*, as in KM, Kh, Sa, Ho, B and Kw. Maybe as a result of bilingualism, there is some tendency, especially in KM and Bh, to restrict this term to ZC, its meaning in Indic, leaving terms for 'child' or Indic *bhatija/-i* to cover BC, and thus obscuring any relative-sex denotations (unless these are ill-recorded). Generally, however, terms for 'child' rarely feature in this field, and indeed they would be restricted to the ss specifications in the theoretically reduced form of a symmetric prescriptive terminology. Sa has *kumang-kora/-kuri* for WBC, the first part of which also occurs as FZH, MB. This is the only instance of an equation between any PosG(E) and (E)osGC categories apart from Ju *goblekon, goblesendae* (see below for +1/–1 equations).

Turning to the CE field, we find that SW is regularly *kimin (-to, -dae)* in NM, CM and GRG, perhaps connected with Gm *konun* and Sora *kaon, koin;* this may be related to the *kin* in CM and KM terms for EM (the final *-kar* in these terms is an affinal morpheme) through the addition of the *-m-* infix (ZZ 11). Ju has *buirae*, from *bui* M. DH is *ara* in Mu, Ho, B, Kw, Asur and Ku, *aram* in CM, *arain* in Sa, *arion* in Gb, with R *arju* and perhaps Gq *rujua*, Gm *ranya*, Sora *ream* connected also. This root is absent from Bh, which uses Indic *jamai*, a term which, in the more usual form *jawae*, is found throughout Munda as a synonym of *ara* etc. Indic *damad* is also found on occasion, which in Kw is also SWB. Neither of the Munda roots for CE can be connected lexically with those for (E)osGC to offer a fully symmetric prescriptive equation (a situation mirroring the usual absence of equivalence between the reciprocal +1 areas of the terminology), though the fact that ZC is often a loan suggests that such an equation was made at one time. Only Gq and Sora have evidence of such an equivalence, the former with *machoa* (probably Indic), the latter with Indic *bhanja/-i*, which both exist alongside the regular Munda forms. This may simply be due to bilingualism, but possibly there was an innovation—i.e. the splitting of the old symmetric prescriptive equations—for which an Indic term has been adopted. As already noted, most CE terms are also used for yGE, which is common in north Indian terminologies and probably derives from them in Munda.

The +1 and –1 collateral pattern can be set out as follows:

  i. Kher *gungu*, Kher, Kh *bada/-i*, Ju *atir* PessG(E), (E)yssGC
     (different terms in KM)
 ii. Some NM *gawain* etc. PyssG(E) (mostly Indic terms otherwise)
iii. Kher *kuma* MB, FZH (and WF in Ho) (mostly *mama* otherwise)
 iv. KM *wang* etc., some Kher *hatom*, Ju, Gm *ating* FZ, MBW
     (and EM in Gq, Gm; WM in Ho; mostly *mami* otherwise)
  v. **kankar* EF
 vi. **kinkar* EM
vii. 'Child' or Indic terms etc. for (E)ssGC
viii. *homon, amon-*; Kher *gaing* etc. Ju *goble-* (E)osGC
 ix. *kimin* etc. SW (cf. ego's level)
  x. *ara* etc. DH (cf. ego's level)

Apart from Sa *jae-* (in combination) there are no independent terms confined to the +3/–3 levels, such terms being either Indic sibling terms (Bh and especially B, Kw; often used in compounds for the +3 levels in Indic also), compounds of Munda terms (Sa, Sora), or the Munda terms for PG categories. As we have seen, Ho, Mu *gungu*, Mu, Asur *bara/-i* are found in each of the four levels +3, –3, +1, –1, and in Bh in +3, +1 and –1. Juang has many examples of equivalence between these same levels: *atir* FeB, +3 males; *atirae* MeZ, +3 females; *atirkon* yBS, –3 males; *atirchindae* yBD, –3 females. *Sasu* (FZ) and *mamu* (MB) link all four levels (*mamu* is also MBSS), as do *konchalan* (D), *buirae* (SW) and *aram* (DH). *Sanobui* (MyZ) is also present in –1 (FZSD, MBSD) and –3. *Goblekon* (ZS) and *goblesendae* (ZD) also cover FFZC, FMBC.[11] Although McDougal calls this 'discontinuous Omaha' (1963: 140), the pattern has more to do with a systematic equivalence between alternate generations, to which I return below.

7.4 General Features

In fact, the Munda terminologies are characterized more by a symmetric prescription than by anything else. There are very few equations or distinctions suggesting an asymmetric prescription,[12] nor are we dealing with non-prescriptive terminologies of any sort. The few equations linking consecutive levels have nothing to do with so-called 'Crow-Omaha' principles, the most common of them (CE = yGE) most probably being attributable to the influence of north Indian terminologies. Apart from the exceptions given in note 12, the symmetry of all the terminologies in all levels is remarkable, matrilateral kin regularly being equated with patrilateral kin and wife's relatives with husband's relatives.

Although Munda terminologies have enough of the diagnostic equations in the medial three levels to enable us to call them symmetric prescriptive, this applies mainly to consanguineal specifications, seldom to affinal ones. Hence they differ in this, and in other respects, from Dravidian terminologies (which have the same sorts of equation but extend them to affines) and lean more towards the standard north Indian pattern. Essentially, though, they (and certain neighbouring Indic and Dravidian terminologies) have to be described as separate systems (see Figure 3b).

The KM and Ho terminologies are, on the whole, closer to Dravidian than CM or the rest of NM. In the latter group, most of the characteristic symmetric prescriptive equations are found in the +1 and –1 levels, both of which confine them to consanguineal referents and exclude affines. Thus for +1 parallel kin we can establish the equations FB = MZH and MZ = FBW, but for +1 cross kin only MB = FZH ≠ EF and FZ = MBW ≠ EM. Since there are usually separate terms for parents (rather than the same terms being used for both P and PssG(E)), the characteristic pattern is P ≠ PssG(E) ≠ PosG(E) ≠ EP. On the other hand, in KM and occasionally other languages (Ho, Kw, Ju) affinal specifications are at least sporadically equated with PosG(E). Similarly, ego's level has a generational pattern in NM and CM as far as consanguines are concerned, for G = PssGC = PosGC; in KM, by contrast, PosGC is

	male	female	male	female	affines
+2	PF/PM				compounds
+1	F FB	FZ MBW	MB FZH	M MZ	EP
0	Ego; B PssGS PosGC EGE/EGEG/GEGE	(Ego) Z PssGD PosGD	EG/GE/GEG/CEP/E (different terms)		< <
−1	S BS EZS	D BD EZD	ZS EBS	ZD EBD	CE
−2	CC				compounds

Figure 3b. *Typical NM and CM terminology*

The symmetric prescriptive pattern is recognizable but much modified, especially in ego's generation set (i.e. including +2 and −2) and in the creation of many separate affinal categories.

more likely to have a separate term. There is regularly, however, a separate set of terms for siblings-in-law in all branches. In the −1 level, cross and parallel kin are again regularly distinguished, so that for a man BC = WZC and ZC = WBC, while for a woman ZC = HBC and BC = HZC. In NM (including Ho) and CM, lineal kin and affines are again kept separate from parallel and cross kin respectively, so that C ≠ (E)ssGC ≠ (E)osGC ≠ CE. In KM, however, lineal and parallel kin are generally not distinguished, so that the pattern is usually C = (E)ssGC ≠ (E)osGC ≠ CE. This is not an exact mirror image of the situation in the reciprocal +1 level in KM, though it is in the other branches. The +2 and −2 levels regularly merge all kin types in Munda, though distinctions can always be made with compound terms.

Relative-sex structuring is thus quite pervasive, even in ego's level, where it is generally applied directly to alter, e.g. ss/osG, but also in such a specification as GEGos. In +1 and −1 the principle is applied to linking kin—in other words, it is the cross-parallel distinction. Another feature commonly found is relative age, but this is not quite so pervasive. It is applied liberally in ego's level, but elsewhere mainly to parallel rather than cross kin, i.e. to PssG(E) rather than PosG(E) and (E)ssGC rather than (E)osGC.

Many of these distinctions are made with the aid of obvious loans, usually from Indic languages, though the origin of some Munda kin terms is not entirely clear, and a few are clearly Dravidian in origin. Thus in +1, PyssG(E) usually uses Indic terms, as does (E)essGC, especially in NM and CM. This suggests that relative-age discrimination, at least in these levels, is not an original feature of the terminologies, since such loans must have been absent at some period. In this respect, it is significant that KM, the area which is probably the most conservative linguistically, has virtually no relative-age discrimination in the (E)ssGC area, though the reciprocal +1 area is much like other Munda. Similarly, the widespread use of *mama/-i*, a loan whatever its source (see note 10), for PosG(E) raises the possibility that these specifications were once conflated with EP in a neater symmetric prescriptive pattern. This happens anyway in KM and Ho, though admittedly we also have Munda lexis for this specification in NM and so alternatively this distinction may be older. Similar remarks can be made about the reciprocal −1 level, where Indic *bhanja/-i* is regularly used for ZC, which would be conflated with CE categories in a purer symmetric prescriptive terminology. Here again, however, there are separate terms for ZC (especially ZCms) in KM and Ho, which have AA cognates and are therefore not loans. Thus there would also appear to be a longstanding distinction between (E)ssGC, (E)osGC and CE in most Munda terminologies.

Nonetheless, there are a number of places in these terminologies where one feels that relative-age discriminations have been introduced or a prescriptive equation breached with the aid of a loan or occasionally some other device. Ego's level seems to have relatively few loans with this particular significance, even though it too has evidently changed, mainly in the conflation in most terminologies of *all* cousin categories, cross as well as parallel, with siblings. However, there is plenty of other apparently Munda lexical material here, all of which is applied to sibling-in-law categories (EG, GE, GEG, but not EGE, which = G). In a more truly prescriptive system, of course, these would be seen primarily as cross cousins, or perhaps as potential rather than just actual affines, and it is likely that the original terms for cross cousins are to be found among the terms currently used for these specifications. The best place to focus on in this connection would seem to be those that currently stand for GEG categories, since these are often reported in connection with marriage preferences (see sect. 8.4). Their significance lies, amongst other things, in the fact that, like PosGC specifications but with even greater immediacy, they express a situation in which two groups of siblings intermarry; the difference is that unlike PosGC categories, any reference to the immediately preceding generations is omitted in arriving at the relationship involved (see further, sect. 8.5).

Generally speaking, it is the affinal categories that have retained the original Munda terms through these changes, while the consanguineal ones have adopted Indic loans, where these are present. The affinal terms also seem to be more consistent from one terminology to another in the three medial levels. EP and CE terms, for instance, form a remarkably consistent series, even though there are some doubts over the inclusion of some terms within it.[13] The same is true of a number of sibling-in-law terms, but terms for collateral kin in these levels, even the Munda ones (*gungu*, for example), mostly have a distribution limited to one branch or even one part of a branch. Like most affinal terms, however, terms for lineal kin and for the +2 level vary less. This may mean that the affinal terms are the truly fundamental and original ones rather than those which stand for cross kin—and in a purer symmetric prescriptive terminology these would have a cognatic as well as an affinal reference.

I am now more certain than I was formerly (1985: 717) that what distinguishes Munda terminologies from the theoretical symmetric prescriptive model can be accounted for in terms of the current alliance system of the Munda. This will only become fully apparent when the relevant data on alliance is presented in Chapter 8. Here, however, it can be noted that there no longer seems to be any great disparity between terminology and alliance, mainly because positive marriage rules—of a sort—now appear to be the norm rather than the exception among the Munda. In the case of NM and CM, the matter was originally obscured by paying too much attention to cousin categories, whereas it is more usefully directed elsewhere, specifically to GEG ones, as I have already indicated. In the case of KM, it now appears clear that most if not all groups have some form of cross-cousin marriage. This change of viewpoint has been greatly aided by the appearance of new data on some groups, and this has occasioned a rethinking of data on the others.

Conversely, I am now less certain that relative-age discrimination in these terminologies reflects exclusively the practices of junior levirate and junior sororate (cf. Parkin 1985: 717–18), though clearly these remain significant. It remains clear that, in the EG/GE fields, terminological age discrimination can be correlated with similar discrimination in behaviour and in marriageability (see respectively Ch. 9 and sect. 8.3). Thus joking relationships are expected between EyG and eGE, and the os categories may marry, in what will be a secondary marriage for at least one of them. Conversely, relationships (especially if os) between EeG and yGE are characterized by avoidance or at least restraint, and marriage is quite out of the question. Thus in behaviour, EeG is assimilated to EP, and yGE to CE, and this is reflected terminologically, though not with direct equations in the case of the former pair. Since stereotyped relationships between the +1 and –1 levels are also uniformly ones of restraint and avoidance, relative age cannot be concerned with behaviour here. So why should it matter at all in this level, given also that ego virtually never marries into it?

To answer this in terms of secondary marriages, we need to view the whole matter cross-generationally. Generally, a male ego may contract a second marriage with either his eBW or his WyZ. To his children, these are FeBW and MyZ; to the latter, these children are (former) HyBC and eZC (ws) respectively. Focusing on a female ego produces the converse formulae (i.e. male becomes female and vice versa), and regarding both egos in respect of their tabooed relatives produces the inverse ones (i.e. senior becomes junior and vice versa). From ego's point of view the main cross relatives of these levels, who to him are WB, ZH and HZ, constitute one half of a ss link and so cannot marry in any case. Hence their part of the terminology lacks relative-age distinctions. This contrasts with the EG/GE fields, the whole of which are split according to relative age, since here the terminology has to cope not just with secondary marriages, but also with differences in behaviour which affect os and ss relationships equally.

The fact that age discrimination in the EG/GE fields is achieved with Munda lexical material whereas that in the +1 and –1 levels relies heavily on Indic loans might suggest that it was present earlier in the former than in the latter areas of these terminologies, and even that this reflects the borrowing of secondary marriages (in their modern form, at least) from Hindu society. The problem is, however, that the distinction between parallel kin who are distinguished by relative age and cross kin who are not is one that is found in many other prescriptive terminologies in other parts of the world; and although secondary marriages may account for or be a cultural expression of this terminological feature in India, it cannot explain it globally. More probably, therefore, it is to be connected simply with status and age within the family and sibling group is societies in which one's elder brother is often virtually equivalent to one's father and one's elder sister to one's mother. This sort of distinction might also be significant cross-generationally in a joint family, hence its application to PssG(E). PosG(E) kin types would be less affected, because they would tend to be living elsewhere.

The third major characteristic of these terminologies, apart from prescription and relative age, is the extent to which they distinguish sets of alternate generations, namely ego's, +2, −2, versus +1, −1, +3, −3. This is found not only in actual equations in a number of terminologies but also—in NM and CM, at any rate—in the circumstance that of the main five levels, ego's, +2 and −2 tend to merge cross and parallel relatives (though terms for affines in ego's levels are distinct), while +1 and −1 tend to keep them apart. However, it is probable that this difference was not present in the terminologies originally, which on comparative grounds would have had separate cross-cousin terms and possibly cross-parallel distinctions in +2 and −2, as in some similar terminologies (Kariera, for example, though not usually in Dravidian; see Dumont 1966 [14]).

It no longer seems necessary to explain the contrast as regards ego's and the +1 level through a difference in perspective in the arranging of marriages (cf. Parkin 1985: 716). Instead, the particular characteristics of each level can and should be seen in the light of alliance as it obtains today among these groups. Thus in ego's level cross-parallel distinctions have disappeared where, and because, cross cousins can no longer be married, so that they have become merged with lineal and parallel kin, already unmarriageable (see sect. 8.4; the original argument might nonetheless be valid in other societies with such terminological disparities). In KM, of course, this contrast is less marked, for there are some separate cross-cousin terms and some cross-cousin marriages.

The equations between alternate levels, however, are probably original and of long standing. They may, in fact, be more extensive than they at present seem to be—it may be no coincidence that the group which has such equations in abundance, the Juang, also happens to be one of the best documented. The reasons for seeing them as fundamental will be dealt with in the last chapter (Ch. 11), and other, more sociological expressions of this same theme will also be dealt with later (in Chs. 9 and 10). But first we will deal with affinal alliance, of which these terminologies can be regarded as the linguistic expression.

Chapter Eight
Affinal Alliance

8.1 Introduction

The distinctions that Munda kinship terminologies make between cross and parallel relatives in the +1 and −1 levels allow them to be seen as representing 'elementary structures' or 'prescriptive' terminological systems, even though this pattern is not always followed in other levels, and despite the near-uniform separation of affinal from cross specifications. Indeed, there is explicit evidence of such systems in respect of some groups, and although for others the evidence seems weak, it can be argued that its significance is greater than has hitherto been realized.

8.2 Agnates and Affines

Affinal exchange takes place between different groups of agnates, the effective units being clans or clan segments or villages (the latter often having an agnatic core; see sect. 5.2 ii). Most, perhaps all Munda tribes dichotomize agnatically defined groups according to the criterion of marriageability. However, the exact ways in which they do this differ somewhat (though details are lacking in most cases). A list of the most important classifications is given in Table 1. The terms require some discussion, since the columns in which they appear are defined only in the minimal sense as marriageable and non-marriageable: there are a number of variations in their exact reference. One of them, *kutum(b)*, even appears on both sides of the table (though never in the same language). This and *bondhu/bandhu* are both of Indo-European origin, and their various meanings are discussed at some length by Inden and Nicholas. The principal contemporary meaning of Bengali *kutumb* is 'affines, allies (of a male)', which in certain contexts includes maternal kin. These are otherwise *jñati*, a category which also includes agnates but excludes a woman's affines. According to Fruzzetti, *kutumb* refers to 'the people to whom one gives daughters in marriage

Table 1. *Designations for marriageable and non-marriageable kin groups among the Munda*

§ = Indo-European term

Tribe	Non-marriageable	Marriageable
Santal	§nij pera, §jatia pera	§bandhu pera, §kutum, sangin pera, balasaka
Mundari	hagako, §bhayad	§kutum, kupul nata
Ho	hagako, §bhayad, §kutum ko	kupul ko, bala §bondhu
Kodaku	§gotia	pahuna (§?)
Korwa	§kutum	?
Kharia	§bhayad	§kutumb
Juang	§kutumb	§bondhu
Sora	tap-rungkun	?
Gadaba	§bhai, §kuttum	§bondhu
Remo	?	§bondhu
Gataq	nairamoan	§moita

and from whom one takes wives for one's sons, being people with whom one does not share blood.' However, Sanskrit *kutumba* and therefore Bengali *kutumb* can also be used as alternatives to *jñati* and may therefore include agnates. Although this is a subsidiary meaning in Bengali, the same root is equivalent to *gosthi*, the agnates of one family, in certain other parts of India, which would explain its primarily agnatic meaning in Juang, Ho and Gadaba. *Bandhu* has had a similarly varied history, originally referring to maternal relatives and, by the sixteenth century, 'affines'. Today it usually denotes 'friend' in Bengali, implying the absence of any agnatic or indeed cognatic relationship and therefore signifying 'marriageable', its basic meaning in Munda languages too. Inden and Nicholas appear to consider all the Bengali categories they discuss as ego-centred, but this nowhere seems to be true of the Munda: the Juang and Gataq classifications certainly refer to group-to-group relations, and other Munda appear to follow them in this.[1]

The Juang distinction between *kutumb* and *bondhu* applies to clans and their major segments (local descent groups or LDGs) and also to villages, but not to discrete moieties.[2] *Bondhu* refers to marriageable units, i.e. potential and actual affines. *Kutumb* covers agnates (including LDGs of the same *bok* or clan), but it also includes certain groups which are neither *bondhu* nor agnatic. These are generally descent groups which were formerly in a *bondhu* relationship with ego's but which have ceased to be so because of a quarrel. Henceforward they become *kutumb*—not because they are now suddenly agnatic but because they are no longer marriageable. These quarrels characteristically involve a boundary dispute and appear to be quite common. Most villages have myths to explain their *kutumb* clan becoming *bondhu*, apparently a case of reclassification following a 'wrong' marriage.[3] Other conceivable reasons might be segmentation leading to complete separation, or simply patching up a quarrel,[4] though McDougal reports no actual instances of either.

The effect is to rule out the possibility of the Juang having a true dual organization of the sort proposed by Rivers elsewhere in India. McDougal states clearly: 'Each LDG maintains affinal alliances with several other LDGs' in such a way that 'the *kutumb-bondhu* dichotomy does not result in the division of the society into two exogamous moieties.' There is thus a degree of flexibility in the distinction and an absence of the society-wide division between the two sorts of descent groups that one would find with dual organization. The contrast can be shown diagrammatically:

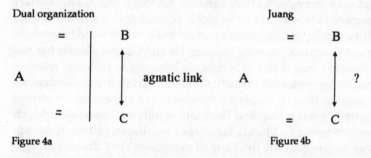

Figure 4a

Figure 4b

In Fig. 4a, if clan A has an affinal relationship with two clans B and C, then by virtue of the division into discrete, exogamous moieties the relationship between B and C must be agnatic. In the Juang case, however, this neat division is lacking: just because LDG A has a *bondhu* relationship with both B and C, this does not mean we can predict the relationship between B and C, which might be either *kutumb* or *bondhu*. Nor can we predict the nature of the relationship between A and C if that between A and B happens to be *bondhu* and that between B and C *kutumb*:

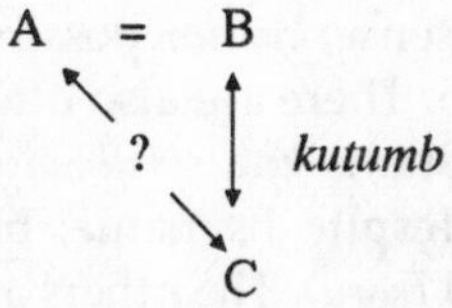

A = B

? ↓ *kutumb*

C

Figure 4c

A and C might be classed as each other's affines, as they would be in dual organization, regardless of actual alliances, but they need not be. McDougal attributes this to the fact that there are only two designations available to the Juang. However, this is no less true of dual organization, in which the distinction is between 'affinal' and 'agnatic', reflecting the discreteness of the moieties and therefore of the categories; any quarrel between affinally related clans that ended their alliance would leave them in a relationship of potential affinity, since they would remain in opposite moieties. Among the Juang, however, it would be changed—the dichotomy is strictly between 'marriageable' and 'non-marriageable', and the latter includes not only 'agnates' but also those with whom one has quarrelled, i.e. both those closest to oneself and those from whom one is at the greatest possible distance within the society, with whom even intermarriage is undesirable. To some extent, the classification depends on the actual pattern of alliances, according to which certain referents may be classed as either *bondhu* or *kutumb*. For example, MZD would be *bondhu* and thus marriageable if her mother had married into a descent group that was *bondhu* to ego's, but she would be *kutumb* and thus banned if her mother had married into a *kutumb* group—which might be ego's own.[5] With dual organization there would be less uncertainty built into things: MZD would necessarily be an agnate, given patrilineal descent and the marriage of one's MZ to an agnate. Hence Juang society is not a system of dual organization, since affinal and agnatic groups do not oppose one another in a simple way and do not form two mutually exclusive units.

What is true of the Juang also seems to be true of other Munda, though the material is less detailed. I will review the situation group by group.

Gadaba *bondhu* villages are those of existing and potential marriage partners, and the term means affines in general as opposed to *somdi* which, *pace* Izikowitz, has its usual Indic meaning here of

CEP. Gutob *bhai* is the standard Indic term for 'brother', and its use here seems to apply to agnates in the wider sense, *kuttum* possibly being restricted to one's own descent group. There are also other categories which exclude intermarriage. One is the *sorubhai* or village community, not strictly agnatic despite its name, but defined by partaking of the same ritual food *(soru)*. The others are not agnatic either but refer to certain ceremonial relationships: the *moitur* relationship, between individuals or villages, and the *pan- jabhai* relationship, between villages only. The Gadaba regard *sorubhai* as closer than *moitur*, these as closer than *panjabhai*, and these as closer than *bondhu*, the most distant of all within their society. The Gataq dichotomy is between *nairamoan* or 'brothers' and *moita* or 'friends', i.e. marriageable kin.[6]

Sora *tap-rungkun* has a still more restricted meaning, referring to one's own lineage only, i.e. to one's closest agnates within the *birinda* or maximal descent group (one of its glosses is 'my rice-brothers'). Kodaku *gotia* is similar in that it means fellow clan-mates, while *pahuna*, which is opposed to it, apparently means 'affines'. Kharia *bhayad*, also based on the common root for 'brother', may have a similarly restricted meaning.[7]

The same may be true of Mundari and Ho *hagako* (= *haga* 'brother' plus *-ko* plural marker). In Mundari, for instance, *haga* refers to one's own clan and more particularly to the narrower agnatic groups formed by one's village agnates and, narrower still, one's potential inheritors in default of a direct heir. *Kili* co-members refer to each other as *haga* ('brother') or *misi* ('sister') and one's own lineage is one's *bhayad*. *Kupul* or *kupul nata*, which is opposed to these, means 'relation by marriage', though there is also a distinc- tion between *nare* ('near') and *sangin* ('far') *kupul*. The boundary is between the second and third degrees from ego and this is sig- nificant for the conduct of alliances (see sect. 8.4). *Kutum* refers to potential rather than actual affines: 'all persons belonging to mar- riageable clans are *kutum*. The term *kupul* is applied only to those persons with whom [an] affinal relation has been established.'[8] In Ho, *bala-bondhu* means strictly 'allies' in the usual north Indian sense and is therefore equivalent to Mundari *kupul*, whereas *kupul ko* are all those who are not cognates rather than just 'allies', which seems to correspond more to Mundari *kutum* (cf. the Juang). Bouez hints that the Ho today prefer the former and are less certain about the exact reference of the latter, though he himself sees the term as expressing 'exchange' on etymological grounds. As in Mundari, *hagako* and *bhayad*, its Indic-derived equivalent, appear to refer to one's own lineage only,[9] leaving *kutum ko* to cover the non-marriageable classification in the wider sense. Bouez is rather contradictory as to its meaning, saying at one point that it is definable only in opposition to *bala-bondhu* (thus implying simply 'non-allies'), at another that it depends on patrilineal affiliation (so excluding matrilateral kin, even though some such groups are non-marriageable).[10] Nonetheless, since it is said to include MZD, who is unmarriageable but matrilateral, perhaps the former interpretation is to be preferred. It also includes FZ when taken alone, which indicates that the classification may have different boundaries according to context. However, the sense is a collective one, even though *bala* when used alone is a kin term meaning CEP (= Indo-European *samdhi*).[11]

In Santali, the word *kutum* is used to refer to the following relatives, all affinal or uterine specifications: FZH, ZH, DH, MB, MBC, MZ, MZC, WP, WG, WMB, CEP, BWP.[12] This may not refer to all Santal areas, for the term is apparently absent from Mayurbhanj and Keonjhar. In Mayurbhanj and Santal Parganas the dichotomy is between *jatia pera* (non-marriageable, cognates) and *bondhu pera* (marriageable kin), with *bhayad* also being used for agnates. Bouez does not mention *kutum* for Keonjhar. Here, allies in general are *balasaka*, a term equivalent to *sangin pera* or 'far relations'. Most nearer collaterals, cross as well as parallel, are *sor pera* or 'near relations', which appears to distinguish all cognatic kin, uterine as well as agnatic, from affines. Although FZH is explicitly excluded from this category, all of ego's mother's brothers are included, classificatory as well as genealogical. One's agnates are *nij pera* or 'true relatives'. However, the term *pera* is used very loosely of 'relations' in the sense of 'same people', and its exact meaning depends on context and preliminary qualifiers. For instance, *pera sagai* defines 'true relations' in opposition to *hatu sagai* or 'village relations'. Similarly, *santal pera* refers to the Santal as a whole, since the entire tribe is mythically descended from the same pair of primaeval ancestors. For the Santal of Keonjhar, therefore, the agnate-affine distinction that all Munda appear to make ceases to apply outside the particular context of marriage: cognation ultimately encompasses affinity. For Bouez this is an important, fundamental contrast between Santal and Ho, for whom the agnate-affine distinction is more significant.[13]

None of these dichotomies is in itself sufficient to determine exactly which particular kin types are marriageable and which are not. The 'marriageable' or 'affinal' category is the one from which ego will draw his or her spouse, but this will contain genealogically defined referents and even whole genealogical levels (especially +1 and −1) that are excluded from marriage, as well as any prescribed category of marriage partner. We turn to these matters in the rest of this chapter, seeing also how they unite these societies by linking the discrete descent and local groups into which they are otherwise divided.

8.3 Kin Types and Marriage Choice: Prohibition and Permission

All Munda prohibit members of the nuclear family—parents, siblings and children—as spouses and sexual partners. This prohibition normally excludes step-children also, though Elwin records an exception among the Sora of a man marrying his step-daughter, to which no one objected, since they were 'of different blood'.[14] Since cousins are ordinarily equated terminologically with siblings, they too are frequently excluded from marriage. This applies especially to parallel cousins, though occasional marriages with MZD may be tolerated in certain groups, for which the panch may impose a fine. Among the Juang this would be possible if MZ had married into a *bondhu* group, but McDougal recorded no actual cases. It is definitely not allowed by the Ho, for whom MZD is included with the *kutum ko,* nor by the Sora, nor by the Santal, for whom she is a *sora pera* (see previous section).[15] FBD marriage, of course, would amount to endogamy of the agnatic group and even, possibly, the household, and for this reason is nowhere tolerated. As for cross cousins, we will see in the next section that first cross cousins are generally excluded, and though more distant ones may be allowed, the preference is often framed to specify an affinal rather than the usual cognatic category. Other referents of ego's level that are excluded are EeG and yGE, which are therefore assimilated in this respect, and often terminologically (though not in Kharia and Juang—see Ch. 7), to EP and CE respectively, both firmly tabooed in marriage. This contrasts with the possibility of marriage between EyG and eGE, which in the case of HyB–eBW marriage is often virtually a requirement. This is partly to be explained by the assimilation in many contexts of eG to P (i.e. to a lineal +1 referent) and therefore of EeG to EP (i.e. to a +1 affine), hence the assimilation of the reciprocal yGE categories to CE. But a woman's marriage to HeB (as his yBW) or a man's marriage to WeZ (as her yZH) would also involve the contradiction that the children of the second marriage (WeZ) would be younger in age than those of the first but senior in status, being the children of the elder of two siblings; and WeZ would herself be 'junior' to her yZ, who had married first.[16] EGE, EGEG, GEGE and CEP categories are also excluded, such as WBW, WBWZ, ZHZH and CEPos among the Santal and WBW among the Sora.[17] Some GEG ones are allowed, however, and indeed seem to be the preferred category in most North and Central Munda groups (see next sect.).

There are a number of reports of marriages into the +2 and –2 levels being allowed, either in reality or according to tradition. A good example are the Juang where despite the genealogical distance involved, referents in these two levels may be of roughly the same age (see next sect.), though elsewhere a marked difference in age may constitute an impediment, the formal rules notwithstanding. However, ethnographers often write as if ego may marry his own grandparents, and this is very doubtful: we can at least be certain that referents who are lineally connected are generally excluded, since they would normally be seen as parallel, not cross relatives, and in some cases will be agnates. Ethnographers may have been confused by cases in which a prescribed or permitted category includes some +2 or –2 specifications as well as some from ego's level and therefore assumed that the whole of these outer levels could supply a spouse for ego. At least one Munda group, the Asur—a low caste which seems to have no positive marriage rules—does not allow marriages between these levels.[18]

Generally, referents in either of the adjacent levels (+1, –1) are strongly tabooed as marital or sexual partners. The exceptions all seem to be rare contingencies compensating for the absence of the usual second-spouse category (see sect. 6.5). Majumdar frequently reported the possibility of marriage to MZ among the Ho, and also of marriage to ZD, though this was 'not much favoured'. Chattopadhyay later refuted his data concerning MZ by enquiry in Seraikella and Kolhan, pointing out that not only is one's MZ of the same generation as one's mother, but also that if she is younger she is a potential spouse for one's father (as his WyZ), while if she is older she is tabooed for both father and son. However, while the latter comment can be allowed to stand, the former would not necessarily constitute an objection. Despite Majumdar's specious reasoning[19] and the fact that marriage to any MZ would violate the usual rules barring marriage with both parallel relatives and members of adjacent levels, Bouez tends to confirm Majumdar with his own, more recent data. This concerns MyZ only, who can be a second spouse for ego, especially if widowed. Bouez interprets this in one part of his book as the sororate deferred for one generation, though he also calls it a 'marginal practice'.[20] Dhan, herself a Ho, implicitly confirms Majumdar in respect of ZD marriage in saying that WeBD, though a −1 referent, is a possible alternative to WyZ as a second spouse.[21] Some Gadaba may institutionalize ZD marriage as their norm (see next section on all these examples).

There are other cases in which a −1 referent may be a substitute for WyZ. Among the Mahali, WZD may be a second spouse for ego if no WyZ is available. There may be a similar situation among the Korwa, though Majumdar's data needs to be used with care. He gives a picture of them being a very inbred group, indicating that the lines of exogamy are drawn only round the nuclear family and closest agnates (i.e. including FBC and BD), so that marriages can take place with MZ, FZ and ZD, though they are all very infrequent. This is partly contradicted by a later report of Bhandari, who explicitly rules out MZ and MBW.[22] Elwin reports the possibility of marriage to one's mother's co-wife among the Sora, which—given the fact that most second wives are yZ or HeBW to the first, through junior sororate and junior levirate—may amount to another example of normal secondary marriages deferred to the next generation. This becomes more evident in other passages in the same chapter, though Elwin appears to contradict himself within a very few pages. At one point he says that 'a Saora is expected to marry his elder brother's widow and even his father's elder brother's widow'. However, elsewhere he implicitly supports Sitapati's earlier statement that it is father's *younger* brother's wife who is involved by saying that 'a widow is expected to marry her husband's younger brother or one of an elder brother's sons, if there are no younger brothers'. Thus HeBS is a possible second spouse for a female ego (this specification is, of course, the reciprocal of FyBWws).[23]

Archer gives a complete list of the relationships the Santal consider incestuous: P/C, B/Z, CE/EP, PG/GC, PGS/PGD, PP/CC, PPG/GCC, HeB/yBW, FBW/HBS, MBW/HZS, WMZ/ZDH, BSW/HFB, SWZ/ZHF, WBW/HZH, WBWZ/ZHZH, CEM/CEF, DHZ/BWF, WBD/FZH (but cf. Bouez, above), step-parent/step-child and step-brother/step-sister. Incest with close relatives (and with EP or EeG) leads to 'irreversible' expulsion, whereas incest with classificatory relatives is less serious, readmission being possible for a fine.[24] A similar list of prohibited spouses is given for the Birjhia Asur: Z, PGD, PZ, step-mother, step-sister, MBW and GD. For the Ho, incest is a matter of being linked to the same agnatically linked cemetery, and breaches of this rule necessitate excommunication. Among the Gataq, relations between mother and son or EP and CE are more serious than those between father and daughter or between male ego and yBD, yBW or WeZ.[25]

Thus the overall pattern is one in which +1 and –1 referents are almost totally excluded as marriage partners, except for some rare exceptions that are mostly substitutes for the usual category of second spouse. Also prohibited are many referents—parallel and close kin especially—in ego's level and the +2 and –2 levels. However, it is only in these levels that marriage is at all possible, and it is here that we must look for any prescribed category of spouse.[26]

8.4 Regular Affinal Alliance: The Data

Ho

As we saw in sect. 4.2, the Ho have a large number of *kili* or exogamous clans, each divided into sub-clans, and each village is associated with a single clan, whether in myth or reality. Thus there is a strict rule of village exogamy, which can only be broken in those comparatively rare cases in which a village has more than one clan. Between villages, alliance is asymmetric. One's actual MBD is equated terminologically with one's sister and is unmarriageable—Chattopadhyay recorded only two examples out of a sample of 147—but marriage with a classificatory MBD, such as MFBSD, is said to be the preferred form. This particular specification ensures the continuity of alliances generation after generation while avoiding first cousins, as Majumdar confirms: 'When a man marries in the Andi form, his children are usually married to the family or Killi of his father-in-law.' MFBSD is, of course, the daughter of mother's patrilateral male parallel cousin (though still a cross relative herself), and thus she belongs to the same patrilineal descent group as ego's mother and MBD (see Fig. 5).

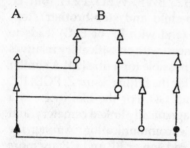

Figure 5. *Ho MFBSD marriage*

The men of all three generations of descent group A marry women of descent group B, but of different collateral lines. However, collateral males of A may marry into descent groups other than B, for it is customary, though by no means necessary, for marriage to take place between groups of two or three *kili,* so that any particular clan may maintain alliances with more than one other. Although the circle of alliances has widened in modern times, 'a man usually marries within the Pir or within a reasonable distance from the village'—and the *pir* is, of course, a clan-based unit (see sect. 5.2).[27] However, it is still not completely clear whether the Ho system is to be seen as an asymmetric rather than symmetric one. Bouez gives no term for MFBSD, the supposed preference in alliance, but on the basis of the overall symmetry of the terminology it is likely to have a patrilateral reference also. We cannot even be sure whether these specifications have separate terms or whether, like all cross cousins, they are classed with siblings (see sect. 7.2). Furthermore, in a sample of marriages, Bouez recorded only 20.7% (48 out of 237) with a classificatory MBD, though it is not always clear exactly what the remainder consisted of. Possibly they obey the same direction of alliance, for there were only eleven marriages that clearly violated this principle, three of which were with a 'FZD', for which a double brideprice is paid. None of Bouez's informants seemed to regard FZD marriages with approval: in such cases 'the informants tend to hide rather than emphasize the classificatory tie.' Chattopadhyay says that they are banned, but significantly Dhan, herself a Ho, excludes only the genealogical FZD and allows classificatory ones.[28]

Bouez does regard as symmetric those marriages which take place *within* a village in which there is more than one clan. In his sample, these numbered 29 or 12.3%, of which 18 were sister-exchange marriages without brideprice or any other prestations—in other words, alliances involving the intermarriage of a set of siblings. The relevant category is most probably eGEyGos: Dhan tells us that yBWeZ and yZHeZ are permitted as spouses, while yZHyZ is not, and in such systems yGEeG are the complements of eGEyG (see Fig. 6; also sect. 8.5 below).

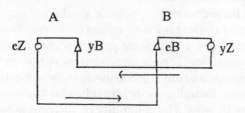

Figure 6. *Ho symmetric exchange between descent groups within the same village*

The arrows show the direction in which the women move at marriage. From the point of view of the two younger siblings, this is eGEyGos marriage; from the point of view of the two elder siblings, this is yGEeGos marriage.

In these cases siblings must marry in age order. Moreover, joking relationships, which commonly express the possibility of marriage where they occur between os referents (see sect. 9.1), exist with eBWyG and yBWeG, while avoidance or respect relationships, which typically signal taboos on marriage among the Munda, exist with eBWeG and yBWyG. Finally, such direct exchanges seem to take place simultaneously, and they immediately close the alliance cycle, being rarely continued or repeated in later generations. As we shall see, this set of circumstances is often found together with preferences for eGEyGos categories among the Munda. Bouez contrasts them with asymmetric exchange among the Ho, which takes place between villages and is continuous. The Ho themselves explain this with reference to the separatist tendencies of clans within the same village and insist on the immediacy and complete symmetry of exchange in such cases in order to preserve village unity: this might be threatened if a permanent, asymmetric relationship between clans were established, especially if, as seems likely, particular clans are localized in different hamlets within the village. Generally, however, village exogamy is required as a complement of clan exogamy and of the normal identity of clan with village, and breaches of this rule can bring forth a heavy fine even within multi-clan villages. Bouez himself does not seem entirely convinced of the 'asymmetry' of the Ho system, arguing that they seek to efface asymmetry in alliance through ritual and prestations. For instance, he sees the asymmetry between wife-givers and wife-takers as being nullified by the high brideprice that obtains here, and one of his own informants told him that there was no 'high' or 'low' among allies.[29]

Despite these doubts, the preferred ideology of exchange among the Ho clearly envisages the repetition of the previous alliances of particular villages and descent groups without a delay in subsequent generations. There is no general restriction on the mother's clan in marriage, and one tends to marry in the same descent group as one's father, though in a different collateral line in order to avoid actual cross cousins. The continuity of alliances is backed up by financial and other sanctions. It is ego's MB who is expected to find him a suitable bride and help with the wedding expenses, and if either wishes to contract an alliance elsewhere he must compensate the other. Dhan reports some marriage between alternate levels.[30]

Santal

The Santal also have indications of established patterns of affinal alliance. Generally, the rules concerning cross-cousin marriage exclude first cousins; and some writers exclude cross-cousin marriage altogether—one (Kochar) only in the lifetimes of the respective parents.[31] There is also usually some interdiction on uterine descent groups, though ethnographers disagree as to which level.[32] At all events, there are clearly restrictions on repeating the marriages of one's father, especially if cross cousins cannot marry in the lifetimes of their parents. There are some areal differences in this large tribe, and we start with Keonjhar.[33]

Santal clans are much larger and less localized than those of the Ho and there is no strict rule of village exogamy, but Bouez again sees symmetric and asymmetric principles in evidence here. He views the 'asymmetric' aspects of the Santal marriage system not as a product of regular affinal alliance, as among the Ho, but as a result of status differences between clans. In themselves, these are founded on agnatic filiation and origin myths and are independent of affinal alliance. This would mean that marriages take place hypergamously as in north Indian society rather than hypogamously as in systems of generalized exchange, but in fact, he says, both forms are involved. While elder sons should marry hypergamously—perhaps because of their position in the sibling group—there is more freedom for younger ones, and these tend to marry hypogamously, though this is a matter of practice rather than of formal rules. Thus elder sons marry into clans of inferior status, younger sons into clans of superior status. This can be shown diagramatically, thus:

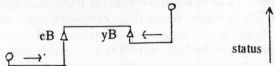

Figure 7. *Santal alliance: age order and status*

From the point of view of affinal alliance, this merely shows women marrying into the agnatic group from more than one direction and does not enable us to be certain as to the preferred direction of alliances. The preferred spouse is actually denoted by the Indo-European term *sangat*, namely eZHyZ,[34] a category which in itself suggests an overall symmetry of exchange, i.e. two men exchanging their sisters:

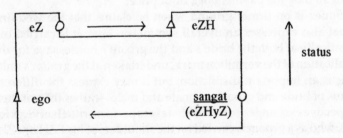

Figure 8. *Santal alliance*: sangat *marriage*[35]

Bouez argues that ego's eZH has the status of a Brahman at ego's wedding and is therefore not only a wife-taker of ego but also his superior; hence the first marriage is a hypergamous one. However, since eZH remains a superior in giving his yZ to ego, the second marriage is hypogamous. He regards these two patterns of exchange as merely aspects of a common underlying system, in which there is a neutralization of asymmetry, especially in the fact that elder siblings of both sexes are involved in hypergamous marriages, young siblings in hypogamous ones.

One is inclined to doubt this on initial acquaintance with the data. One problem is the fact the MB and FZH have separate terms (*mama* ≠ *kuma*). In other parts of the ritual ZH is inferior (see below) and in Bodding's dictionary ZH is equated with the low-status 'village ryot' in one entry (*lari manjhi*).[36] Furthermore, in the first case (Fig. 7) the overall symmetry is simply a product of the juxtaposition of two opposite asymmetric principles, whereas in the second (Fig. 8) it is expressed in the categorical injunction itself (eZHyZ). Again, Bouez argues that prestations and ritual nullify the asymmetry. The brideprice itself is quite stable compared to that of the Ho, since the alliance groups themselves have a relatively stable status—or at least do not depend on the flux of alliances, as among the Ho. Bouez finds it significant that it is balanced by an equivalent counter-prestation, though one excluding money. This does not really suggest absolute symmetry between alliance groups, since in return for a brideprice the wife-takers receive not only a prestation equivalent to it but the bride as well. But the arrangement does appear to be a compromise between north Indian hypergamy and the prestations usual to hypogamy, since the complete asymmetry and non-reciprocity of the former is mitigated by the payment of a brideprice.

Bouez is on firmer ground when he claims that the wedding ritual also expresses an overall symmetry. First, it is carried out identically at both the bride's and the groom's house, save for the application of the vermilion mark, undertaken at the groom's only. This is an important distinction, but it may express the different status of bride and groom—female and male—rather than of their respective exchange groups. Wife-takers perform ritual services for ego, who as a groom is carried on the shoulders of his FZH or eZH, and this indicates inferiority in terms of generalized exchange; but in terms of hypergamy wife-takers are superior, and in other parts of the ritual these two referents are assimilated to Brahmans. Similarly, MB is superior to ego in terms of affinal alliance and cannot eat the leavings of his ZS; but he can eat those of any other male relative, and as a matrilateral relative he is inferior to ego. Thus ritually speaking, inferiority balances superiority for both wife-givers and wife-takers. Similarly, children may be fostered to either MB or FZH. Both help ego to marry, FZH by piercing his ears,[37] MB by helping him find a wife and alone accompanying him to his prospective in-laws for the initial negotiations (though FZH may substitute for MB in default).

Thus the *sangat* relationship and the ritual and economic aspects of alliance all express an overriding symmetry of exchange among the Santal of this area. Another aspect of this may be the temporary nature of *sangat* alliances, which may be repeated by the other agnates of ego's generation but are not perpetuated in subsequent ones. Indeed, one has to await the lapse of three generations before renewing any previous alliance, and a Santal avoids the descent groups of his M, FM, MM and FFM, as well as his own, in choosing a spouse.[38] The only extension allowed is into the following generation, but this does not amount to repetition: it consists instead of marriage between ego's son and ego's WyZ (i.e. between a man and his MyZ), a rare practice but one preserving in some measure the confining of alliances to the same generation in that at least the women concerned are both of that generation (Fig. 9; see also previous section). This closure of alliances after each generation resembles the direct exchange of Ho marriages that take place within the village (q.v.), and it is also found among the Mundari (q.v.). It contrasts with the immediate repetition of alliances among the Ho in the regular form, which is not found among the Santal. Even among the latter, however, there may be a rule of repetition after the lapse of the required number of generations (as among the Mundari), and thus stability of exchange in the long term here too.

According to Carrin-Bouez, the Santal of Keonjhar and neighbouring Mayurbhanj form one group as regards alliance, with the same clans and sub-clans, but she tries to draw a distinction be-

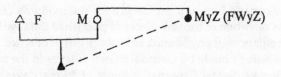

Figure 9. *Santal MyZ marriage*

tween the two areas nonetheless, though without giving details. She seems, however, to be referring to the absence of hypergamy in the latter area, where the regime 'operates on an absolutely symmetric basis'. Again there is no marriage between actual cross cousins or their descendants (we are not told for how many generations) and thus a ban on the immediate repetition of alliances.[39]

Further north, in Santal Parganas, Santal alliances appear to be asymmetric rather than symmetric. Gautam clearly states the preference to be for marriages between MMBSD and FFZDS, which is different from the Ho one. Here, one marries into one's mother's mother's descent group and avoids that of one's mother and therefore actual MBD (Fig. 10).

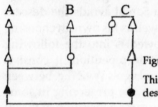

Figure 10. *Santal MMBSD marriage*

This necessitates more than two descent groups.

Gautam says:

> A marriage of this type is greatly esteemed, because of the genealogical distance between the lineages of the bride...and the bridegroom.... At the same time it expresses the matrilateral preference which the Santal always have.

This would mean that the repetition of any particular marriage is delayed for a generation. Gautam talks of a 'three-generation marriage formula', and he is supported here by Biswas, who says that 'a Santal can marry a girl who is three...generations apart'. These formulations presumably include the generations of the original marriage and its repetition as well as the 'delayed' one. They clearly contradict Kochar's hint of a preference for the mother's clan in marriage, as does one of the few pieces of published data we have on how the alliances of any Munda tribe work out in practice. This consists of a survey made by Gausdal in two villages in the north, one near Dumka, Santal Parganas (sample of 49 marriages), the other just over the border in Birbhum (a sample of 25). The survey examines the clan and sub-clan affiliations of husband, wife and

HM in the stated sample of marriages. In the first village there were only seven cases (14 per cent) in which wife and HM came from the same clan, and only two (4 per cent) in which they came from the same sub-clan. In the second village there was just one case (4 per cent) of wife and HM belonging to the same clan (but to different sub-clans). Adding the two sets together, we arrive at percentages of 11 per cent and 3 per cent respectively for shared clan and sub-clan out of the total sample of 74 marriages—an impressive display of the low level of immediate continuity in alliances in this area. Scrutiny of the data also shows a tendency for members of the same (sub-)clan to disperse their alliances among other (sub-)clans (there are three instances in the Dumka data where two men of sub-clan A have married two women of sub-clan B, perhaps to be interpreted as classificatory brothers marrying classificatory sisters).

Gautam says that there is no objection to direct exchange, which even has a name (*golainti*) and can involve cross cousins, but it is nonetheless rare when compared with the asymmetric exchange involved in MMBSD marriage. These

are preferred rather than those of 'direct exchange', firstly, because such marriages provide a gap between generations and secondly because the brideprice is repaid to the mother's clan. The social standing of such marriages is also enhanced by the fact that they are not disliked by the neighbouring Hindus.

Reference is made to *bandhu* villages or hamlets in calculating the possibility of an alliance. Gautam also says that 'marriage preferences [are] associated with a ranking order of the clans', which must be a reference to status differences due to affinal alliance, since elsewhere he excludes North Indian hypergamy from this area. He calls the relationship between (classificatory?) MB and ZS 'a privileged relationship...in terms of ritual performance and responsibility', including MB helping ego find a bride. As with Bouez's Ho data, we do not have a term for the preferred category and therefore cannot tell whether it would cover any patrilateral specification also. Here too, however, asymmetry is suggested by the fact that MB and FZH have separate terms, as in Keonjhar (again, *mama* ≠ *kuma*). Some +2 and –2 categories could least traditionally be taken as marriage partners here.[40]

Mahali

The closely related Mahali are generally said to ban or dislike cross-cousin marriage because of Hindu influence. It is very rare and never arranged, but simply the result of elopement or capture. Only sixteen out of a sample of 356 marriages were with a cross cousin, eleven of them with MBD and five with FZD. Some informants favoured it because of the prior knowledge they had of the bride and because it serves to keep property intact. Others disliked it because of the nearness of the relationship and the increase of authority it gives to MB, as WF, and also because it does not fit in with the wishes of many Mahali to rise in status. Intra-village marriage is common here, but even inter-village marriages take place only within a fairly short distance: nearly 55% of a sample of 369 wives came from within five miles and nearly 80% from within fifteen miles.[41]

Mundari

As with the Santal, the Mundari have similar rules against the immediate repetition of marriages. Each village tends to be uniclan, so that alliances take place between villages, apparently symmetrically. Several alliances may be made in the same generation between the same exchange groups, but they may not be repeated in subsequent ones so long as the mutual visits that result from them are maintained, and this may be several generations. The gap is typically of three generations, during which time these affines are *nare kupul* or 'near affines'; in other words, marriage is banned between the children, CC or CCC of any woman or pair of females of the same natal clan. In the fourth generation, however, they become *sangin kupul* or 'distant affines' and hence marriageable once more. Although Choudhury claims that there are no preferences for particular villages or clans in marriage, Yamada says that the repetition of alliances after this interval 'has rather the nature of a rule', for they have to be sought where a previous relationship by marriage can be traced. In calculating the possibility of alliances, reference is made initially to villages rather than to *kili* names. While there is ignorance even of one's own *kili* name on occasion, and regularly of one's wife's, one's knowledge of the villages from which spouses have come is much greater and may extend to the whole village (women are often known by the names of their natal villages). According to Sachchidananda, 'Among the Munda[ri] generally, the prerequisite for marriage is the existence of some kinship relationship (*kutumb*), direct or indirect, between the negotiating parties'. One should ideally marry into a village where there has been a previous alliance, but three generations before—. one where *nare kupul* have recently become *sangin kupul*. Most alliances are made into geographically close villages, usually those within about twelve miles (the distance tends to be greater in those areas with uniclan *parha*: see sect. 5.3), and according to Icke-Schwalbe 'at least four clans...are join[ed] together in a closed marriage circle'. Nonetheless, *kili* names are still compared to ensure they are different, for breaches of clan exogamy can entail future difficulties for the rest of the village in finding spouses.[42]

Pfeffer records the term for the prescribed category as *teya* for a male ego and *iril* for a female ego, but this is problematic for a number of reasons. First, the specifications generally recorded for these two terms are usually of significance only in secondary marriages (respectively eZH and HyB), and therefore can hardly be the main prescription. Secondly, the only gloss he gives for *teya* is a *male* kin type (and actually in a *Ho*, not a Mundari kinship vocabulary), despite the fact that this is supposed to be the marriage preference for a male ego. It is in fact more likely that the prescribed term is *goi* (BWZms, ZHZms; also *sangat* according to Sachchidananda—cf. the Santal), who are known to be potential marriage partners and with whom there is the major joking relationship. There is also some sister exchange, though immediate cross cousins are excluded, being classed with siblings as *haga*, and in accordance with the rule of delay 'fourth cross-cousin marriage [is] recognized'.[43] In this respect, therefore, the Mundari alliance system is not to be seen as an expression of preferred FZD marriage, as Lévi-Strauss claimed in *The Elementary Structures of Kinship*, especially since the rule of delay is of three generations, not one, as in the ideal model of such a system.[44] The overall symmetry of the Mundari system is suggested by the actual pattern of alliances, while the marriage ceremony also stresses the equality of status between wife-givers and wife-takers, and between bride and groom.[45]

Birhor

Williams mentions both BWZ marriage and sister exchange as the most common options here, and this is confirmed by Adhikary's more recently collected data. Probably, on comparative grounds, the first option is really one for eBWyZ, and although this in itself denotes a unilateral preference, it is cancelled out by the preference for sister exchange. Williams suggests that this system is intended to keep sons in the *tanda* in a situation of rather fluid *tanda* membership, but it is more likely to be a system of regular affinal alliance. He continues:

> the equivalence of the exchange is assured by immediate exchange of 'sisters' between two men who are seeking spouses. Once this has been successful, other marriages are easily arranged by similar exchanges between these bands for the remainder of the generation.

We are not told whether or not there is a rule of delay in subsequent generations before these alliances can be renewed, but this is strongly suggested by 'the rule that one does not marry a relative' (by which Williams presumably means a fairly close genealogical relative), and by the fact that ego cannot marry a cross cousin in the lifetime of either his or her respective parents, except by paying a fine to the panch. Roy suggests that this is due to the great respect owed to MBW (as a +1 relative), but it would seem to have more to do with a system of affinal alliance; indeed, Roy himself talks of persistent intermarriage between the same two or three clans. Alliances within the *tanda*—which is probably at least to some extent patrilineal (see sect. 4.2)—or into any *tanda* which contains near relatives are excluded, as are actual cross cousins. Williams concludes:

> the marriage rule in practice among the Birhor effects the maintenance of marriage affiliation with surrounding groups in a long-standing situation of some territorial fluidity, much as does the rule of cross-cousin marriage in a situation of territorial stability.

In other words, just like ordinary cross-cousin marriage, BWZ marriage plus rules of delay in renewing alliances can still act to generate and preserve society-wide links—even though the genealogical and chronological distances are greater.[46]

Korwa

Majumdar discusses the possibility of cross-cousin marriage here and comes to a positive conclusion as far as the past is concerned. Much of his evidence hangs on the relationship between MB and ZS, who must compensate one another with prestations in the event of an alliance being made elsewhere than between themselves, and groom and bride have to spend one night in the former's mother's brother's house before proceeding to that of the groom. Such reports are not in themselves implausible, but Majumdar is often unreliable, and apart from Deogaonkar he is not supported in his conclusions as to MBD marriage by later writers. In one place he explains the above facts as a survival of a former period of 'matriarchy' and elsewhere conveys a picture of the Korwa as a very inbred group falling apart under modern pressures, with only the nuclear family, FB, BD, FBS and FBD being barred in marriage. Contrary to all this, Bhandari and Srivastava and Verma between them rule out all cousins, cross as well as parallel, and MZ and MBW. The rule of clan exogamy, which despite Majumdar does obtain here, would rule out any agnate, though Majumdar's interpretation is to some extent supported by Sandhwar and Deogaonkar, who say that in practice there is frequent clan endogamy due to lack of knowledge even of the name of one's own clan (cf. the Mundari, above).

Bhandari, writing of the Korwa of Dudhi, gives the most complete picture of the kin types preferred in marriage, which cover the +2 and −2 levels as well as ego's:

ms	ws
FZHM (*nani*)	FZHF (*nana*)
MM	MF
WMM	HMF
MZHM	HMZHF
WMZHM	
	yBWeB
ZHyZ	eZHyB

SWBD	SWBS
SWBSW	SWBDH
DD	DS
DSW	DDH

That there is a strong preference for the marriage of a female ego to yBWeB (or for a male, eZHyZ) is suggested by his statement that 'one's sister's husband can be one's wife's brother only' and by the fact that WeB and eZH have the same term (*bahnoi*). These, and Bhandari's further statement, that one's SWB should marry one's daughter, so that SWB and DH are both *damad*, suggests symmetric exchange. He also says that there are not many exchange marriages, and in Palamau Sandhwar recorded only four out of a sample of 73. Following him, it would seem that the preference for women is for eZHyB (*goi*), with whom marriage is very easily undertaken and with whom there is the most marked joking relationship. *Goi* is clearly reciprocal (i.e. it also covers eBWyZ ms) and is glossed in one unpublished source as 'a girl in wife's category, female friend'. Given this, therefore, and the symmetry of the terminology, there is unlikely to be an ideology of asymmetric exchange here. There is no cross-cousin marriage among the Kodaku sub-group either: 'Marriage by exchange is approved, but such unions are seldom reported', though the ban on marriage with any genealogical relative of the mother indicates a prohibition on the immediate repetition of alliances. Marriages take place with nearby villages no more than sixteen miles distant on average.[47]

Other North Munda

Less evidence is available on the remaining North Munda groups. Marriage to cross cousins or BWZ is explicitly excluded from the Asur, nor are there any marriages between members of alternate generations here. Thus there appear to be no positive marriage rules, though except among the more highly Hinduized Asur of the Jobhipat area some *ad hoc* exchange marriages may still take place as a means of avoiding brideprice. Among the Birjhia Asur, villages are more important than clans in regulating marriage, and the fact that the grandchildren of a couple may marry suggests the repetition of alliances with a generational delay here too. Certainly *goloant* marriages between two brothers and two sisters are allowed, but they are inauspicious and therefore unpopular and have no brideprice, though the other standard rituals are carried out. As with the Korwa, inadvertent breaches of clan exogamy occur because clan names are not very well known.[48] This is true of the Korku too, according to Fuchs. First and second cross-cousin marriages are banned here and blood relations avoided up to the fourth generation, but marriage again becomes possible in that generation. There is some circumstantial evidence that the preference is for a GEG category: Ali remarks that, as is usual among the Munda, one cannot marry WeZ, even if she happens to be eBW, a set of circumstances indicating the marriage of two brothers to two sisters (BWZ marriage) in age order (see Fig. 11). However, exchange marriages are also allowed.[49]

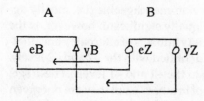

Figure 11. *Asymmetric exchange with eBWyZ marriage*

Many Bhumij groups, even the more Hinduized, and especially in Orissa, are said to allow cross-cousin marriage without regarding it highly, though in Manbhum it is prohibited. According to Das: 'Two brothers may marry two sisters without any restriction—the younger may marry the elder sister while the elder brother [can marry] the younger one'; but this would be wholly exceptional for a North Munda group, since it would entail eGEeG and yGEyG marriages. There is no cross-cousin marriage among the Kora.[50]

Kharia

Roy and Roy stated some fifty years ago that 'all sections of the Kharias practise cross-cousin marriage', 'although now very close relatives of the class are generally avoided'. Forty years later Bahadur claimed there was none, but it has been confirmed a little more recently by Vidyarthi and Upadhyay. Alliances are repeated after the lapse of one generation, at least among the Dudh Kharia. Consonant with this, certain GEG categories are allowed: Roy and Roy give these as eBWyZms and ZHBws (eZHyBws?), while Vidyarthi and Upadhyay talk about sister exchange as well as two brothers marrying two sisters, both of which are said to produce some terminological confusion. Kharia marriages generally take place within a short geographical range, usually within six kilometres from the village and rarely more than twenty kilometres distant. Marriage with MPZ is said to be allowed but very rare, which probably applies to marriages between alternate levels generally.[51]

Juang[52]

McDougal, the chief ethnographer of the Juang, calls their alliance system 'one of classificatory sister exchange' or 'prescriptive symmetric alliance'. The exchange unit is not the clan as such but the local descent group (LDG), which often means the village also. As we have seen (sect. 8.2), all these units are classed as either *bondhu* or marriageable and *kutumb* or non-marriageable (i.e. mostly agnatic, but not exclusively so). Equally significant, however, is the horizontal division of Juang society into sets of alternate genealogical levels, so that ego's level is identified with the +2 and –2 levels, which form a set in opposition to the +1 and –1 levels. These sets are known as *bhaiguli* ('a group of brothers'), but they are not given specific names. In principle, 'men marry females of *bondhu* descent groups who belong to their own generation moiety', and although certain specific referents in this class are banned to ego as marriage partners, the requirement to take one's spouse from it is basic. To take a wife from one's *kutumb* would be *bogodung* or incestuous; to take a wife from the opposing generation set (i.e. from the +1 and –1 levels) would be *jenkani*, a term covering all sexual improprieties that are not incest, including adultery. This system superimposes a generational, horizontal dichotomy over the vertical, descent-ordered one, but it does not amount to a classic four-section system, any more than the *kutumb-bondhu* dichotomy constitutes dual organization: each LDG has alliances with several others, and there is no grouping of the 38 LDGs or 18 clans into larger units that might be seen as the marriage classes of a four-section system.

There can be no marriage with women in the category *ajikar* (i.e. WeZ, eBWeZ, eZHeZ; also WFFZ, FMeZ, SSWeZ, FFZHeZ, FFZHBSD, FFBWBSD), even though they are all *bondhu* and of ego's generation set (this is the usual prohibition of EeG and eGEeG among the Munda). However, spouses can be taken from elsewhere in this class (i.e. *bondhu* plus ego's generation set). The preference in first marriages is for a woman in the category *salirae* (eBWyZ, eZHyZ; also WyZ, WBSD, FMyZ, SSWyZ, ZHyZ, FFZHyZ), but those in the categories *na* (PM, MFZ, FMBSD) and *bokosini* (CD, FFZSD) are virtually equivalent to them, the three being closely associated with one another. Other possible categories are *aji* (MBD, but also eZ) and *bokorae* (FZD, but also yZ), but these are less preferred. Classificatory cross cousins can be married, but although McDougal's informants disagreed over actual PosGD, it seems that these should ideally be avoided. Thus 'the exchange of spouses between intermarrying groups usually takes the form of linked marriages between pairs of siblings.' One generally avoids repeating the marriages of one's close agnates of the preceding generation (F, FB, FZ etc.) and should instead repeat that of a classificatory eB, especially a member of one's *kutumali* or minimal clan segment. McDougal cites avoidance of terminological conflict as the main reason for this. Repeating the marriages of the previous generation implies marrying a close cousin of some sort, and since close cousins are denoted by the same terms one uses for siblings, this would involve a reclassification of kin types for the principals and their near relatives. This is not necessary if one repeats the marriage of a classificatory elder brother or an equivalent +2 relative such as FFB or, for a female ego, FFZ (FFZH = eZH terminologically, and probably FFBW = eBW also): provided sets of siblings marry in age order, as usually happens, then a male ego's wife will automatically be a *salirae*. Also, ego should ideally use matrilateral terms to refer to *bondhu* women of the +1 level, i.e. the affines of the previous generation—one's mother is a *bondhu* relative, for instance—while he should refer to *bondhu* relatives of his own and the +2 and –2 levels with affinal terms. Since ego should also use affinal terms for his own affines, especially wife's parents, a terminological conflict would arise if ego's level were to repeat the marriages of the previous generation—e.g. his WF might also be his MB, as FWB.

McDougal's statistics broadly accord with these rules and preferences. 54% of first marriages in his sample were with a *salirae*, i.e. they repeated the marriages of a classificatory elder brother, though only 4% were with any of the +2 or –2 specifications of the category. The few cases of marriage with a *na* or *bokosini*, a mere 4%, were generally the second of a pair of exchange marriages and thus seem to have been undertaken to close the exchange cycle, perhaps in cases where no *salirae* was available for the second marriage. Only 3 per cent repeated the marriages of close agnates of the previous generation in being with an actual MBD, though a further 21 per cent were with a classificatory cross cousin.[53] There were no marriages with an *ajikar*, the one *bondhu* category of ego's generation set which is barred to him. However, there were a surprising number of marriages into adjacent generations, despite this being a violation of the formal rules and of the categorical injunctions. These formed 18% of the total: 9 with MyZ, 9 with a *goblesendae* (ZD, eBWBD, eZHBD) and one each with an *atirae* (FMBD) and *atirchindae* (classificatory yBD, but in this case actual BDSD). Deviant marriages are nonetheless tolerated, partly because of an overall shortage of marriageable women (they marry earlier than men) and partly because the categorical rules begin to lose their force when one reaches more distant relationships. According to McDougal, such 'violations occurs with some frequency, but they require adjustment of pre-existing relationships, the system of classification being based on the assumption that persons of opposite [generation] moiety do not marry.' The children belong to the opposite generation moiety to their father, as with regular marriages, but the terminological classification of one's spouse's kin is modified so as to correspond with that of a correct marriage. However, there are limits to the success this has, since

> this adjustment results in some inconsistency when relationships with kin or affines of a *bondhu* LDG are traced through an inmarrying spouse originally belonging to the opposite moiety from that of her husband, since their classification by moiety will be the reverse of that obtaining in relationships traced through the other inmarrying spouses.

McDougal seems to place more stress on eBWyZ as the preferred partner, especially in emphasizing the requirement to repeat the marriage of an 'elder brother'. This impression may be unintended, for it would mean that exchange here was asymmetric (Fig. 11, above) and would be contrary to McDougal's statement that 'the system is consistent with sister exchange', i.e. the exchange of women between descent groups within each generation. Alternatively it may be that this sort of exchange applies mainly at the level of the overall system, i.e. that of the village or LDG, while eBWyZ marriage, an asymmetric system, is the preferred form at the *kutumali* level. In other words, individual exchanges are asymmetric, but when collected together appear as symmetric between descent groups and villages as a whole (Fig. 12a). There may also be a contrast in the frequency of repetition according to the level of agnatic grouping. McDougal states that

> each village maintains relatively continuous marriage alliances with a small number of local units. In any particular generation most of the village marriages will be with these groups, but the remainder among a wide range of other groups.

This seems to conflict with other data of his showing delays of at least two and more probably three generations before the repetition of alliance, and with his statement that there is 'no long-term recognition of relations of consanguinity'. Here too, however, the contradiction might be resolved by postulating greater discontinuity between lower-order segments than at the LDG or village level (see Fig. 12b).

The foregoing applies mainly to primary or first marriages: different preferences exist for second marriages, namely for 'a widow of the class *kuli* or *na*;' above all, 'the widow of a "grandfather", provided she is of the right age, is...a preferred second spouse. Moreover, instances of such unions are not uncommon.' Also permitted, but 'considered less desirable', are marriages with one's *kimingdae* (classificatory yBW, SSW), except one's own yBW, who, as virtually everywhere among the Munda, is strongly tabooed. Since 'for most purposes *kuli* and *na* are treated as a single unit', this preference amounts to the usual Munda practice of junior levirate but assimilating eBW (*kuli*) to certain +2 equivalents (*na*). However, the fact that the preference is for +2 referents in this class (*na*) suggests that eBW (*kuli*) is rarely actually married, and McDougal also says that second wives are rarely *salirae*, since they are usually taken from a different descent group from one's first.

The marriage ritual also expresses a contrast here. In any single marriage, wife-givers are regarded as superior to wife-takers. This is reflected in the terms for cross cousins, in which MBC are equated with elder siblings, while FZC are equated with younger siblings, and in the fact that one may not eat with one's wife-takers. 'However, because the two groups related by a *bondhu* alliance

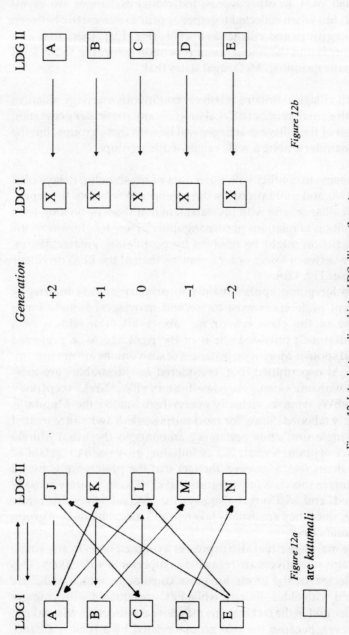

Figure 12 *Inter-kutumali and inter-LDG alliance (Juang)*

Figure 12a shows asymmetric exchange between any two kutumali, but symmetric exchange between LDGs.

Figure 12b shows kutumali X receiving wives from different kutumali in each generation, but still with continuity of alliances between LDGs.

exchange brides their relative status is situational: one of the two groups is superior on one occasion, the other on a different occasion' (perhaps this refers to the repetition of ritual, as with the Santal and certain other groups). Moreover, the asymmetry due to relative age clearly overrides that between wife-givers and wife-takers: on meeting his yZH a WeB should be saluted first, but a WyB should salute eZH. Overall, then, the ideology of Juang affinal alliance stresses symmetry rather than asymmetry between wife-givers and wife-takers.

The only respect in which villages are dependent on one another is in the obtaining of spouses, because of the assumed and to a large extent real agnatic ties that make up the typical village. In view of their near-autonomy, 'inter-village relations...center on intermarriage' alone, so that the marriage system constitutes virtually the sole operational linkage between agnatic groupings throughout Juang society. Brideprice is paid to the village rather than the girl's family in the first instance, though of course the latter will receive a share of it along with all other villagers. Affinal ties are also more important than uterine or matrilateral ones, and the non-repetition of alliances from one generation to the next must mean that these rarely correspond for any particular ego. But for this reason affinal ties are themselves temporary, since they are not used to obtain the spouses of future generations, and this also applies to the cognatic ones they create in ensuing generations (see above). Hence reference is made to categories and to the *kutumb* or *bondhu* status of particular villages in choosing a spouse. In addition, nearby villages are avoided in marriage because of actual or potential boundary disputes and the ease with which wives can return home if dissatisfied (such separations happen anyway in about 10% of marriages). Adjacent villages that have exchanged brides are especially prone to quarrel and some will be *kutumb*, so brides are taken from non-neighbouring villages that are not too distant—the average distance is about four miles. Over a longer period than a single generation the main ties would seem to be those between *bondhu* villages at a moderate distance, and the chief means of maintaining these is not pre-existing affinal links but the periodic mutual dancing visits, which provide the best opportunity for staging the capture of brides, the chief means of spouse selection among the Juang (see sects. 6.2, 6.4).

Koraput Munda

The Gataq seem to have symmetric spouse-exchange. According to Guha *et al.*, MBD is declared to be the preference by the Gataq themselves, though in practice she is often avoided, in which case a youth's MB must be compensated with a payment called *monghure* and must approve any alternative match; similarly, however, a FZ receives a share of the brideprice as compensation if her BD should marry someone other than her son. Furthermore, Siddiqui, one of Guha's collaborators, mentions elsewhere 'selection of spouse from among the cross cousins of either of the two types', and marriage is allowed into one's mother's clan.[54]

The Remo were excluded by Elwin from having cross-cousin marriage, and he compared them with the Gond in this respect:

> not a single informant had married his mother's brother's daughter or even a more distant cousin than that...in such striking contrast to...the Gond tribes immediately to the west.

However, there are some indications that they may have an alliance system broadly similar to the formal rules of the Juang, while in some areas there may be marriage to actual cross cousins. Kin in alternate generations to ego's are also a part of the prescription.[55]

Pfeffer describes the general Gadaba situation as one of continuous symmetric alliance involving bilateral cross cousins. Wife-givers or *rilauñi* are distinguished from wife-takers or *riã*, the former being superior. Symmetric exchange obtains between all *bonso*, though the village *kuda* are the actual alliance groups (see sect. 4.2). According to Chandra Sekhar:

> The surname known locally as *intiperu* plays an important role in...marriage alliance. *Menarikam* (marrying mother's own brother's daughter) and *edurumenarikam* (marrying father's own sister's daughter) are in vogue.

Thus symmetric exchange is indicated here too. These terms are clearly Telugu, though the Kathera are Munda speakers according to the author. He also says that 'marrying one's own and cousin['s] sisters' daughter is also permitted.' This is very unusual for a Munda group, though it is, of course, well known among

Dravidians in south India. His Gadaba are in Andhra Pradesh and are, therefore, the most southerly Munda, and they may have come under local Telugu influence in this respect.[56]

Among the Gorum, 'cross-cousin marriage is preferential, not obligatory', the first cross-cousin being excluded and immediate repetition of alliance banned.[57] The latter rule also applies to the Sora, who (especially in the wealthier families) have a 'three-generation' avoidance rule, though this seems to include the first and repeated generation as well as the delayed one. One's mother's *birinda* or at least *tega* (see sect. 4.2) is certainly avoided in selecting a marriage partner. Although Elwin stated that 'cross-cousin mar-riage...is not allowed', Sitapati excluded only first cousins and mentioned classificatory MBD marriage, in which he is supported by Chowdhury. This on its own would entail a unilateral direction in the transfer of women, but the Sora also ban WBW in marriage. This suggests a symmetric ideology of exchange, in which WBW would be a classificatory sister, rather than an asymmetric one, in which she would be a wife-giver's wife-giver and therefore not prohibited in marriage, at least not as a 'sibling'. According to Vitebsky, cross cousins are ideally not available, though some, especially the higher-status Gamang, will marry them. Altogether, this suggests avoidance of close kin in marriage together with some repetition of alliances in the long term.[58]

Despite many unanswered questions, therefore, there is plen-ty of evidence of regular affinal alliance among the Koraput Munda.

8.5 Regular Affinal Alliance: Interpreting the Data

Although much of the evidence is indirect, circumstantial and incomplete, it would appear that most Munda tribes have systems of regular affinal alliance. The Munda-speaking low castes, how-ever—at least the Asur, Kora and Mahali—appear to have an open, complex, non-prescriptive alliance system instead; possibly they have abandoned 'cross-cousin marriage' in order to reinforce their claims to caste status. Most of our discussion will focus on the former group, especially since the extent of regular affinal alliance among the Munda has not hitherto been fully appreciated, despite their prescriptive terminologies.[59] The essential data are given in Table 2.

Table 2. *Categories specified in affinal alliance among the Munda*

Tribe	Specification (term where known)	Generational delay
Santal	eZHyZ, possibly eBWyZ in south (sangat); MMBSD in north	3 (1 in north)
Mundari	GEZ (goi)	3
Ho	MFBSD; eGEyZ (in multi-clan villages only)	none (at least 1 in multi-clan villages)
Korwa	eGEyG; eZHyB (goi); yBWeB	?
Birhor	eBWyZ, but with sister exchange	at least 1
Birjhia Asur	GEG?	?
Korku	eBWyZ	3
Bhumij	PosGC	1 or 3
Kharia	eBWyZ; eZHyB	1
Juang	eGEyZ (saliray)	1 or 3
Gataq	PosGC	1 or none
Remo	PosGC; PPosGCC?	1
Gadaba	(P)PosGC(C) (eduru) menarikam	1
Gorum	(P)PosGC(C)	1
Sora	'MBD' + ban on WBW	1

In a number of cases a particular category of spouse is specified. This is sometimes reported as a kin term, sometimes as a genealogical specification. In many cases the ethnography does not explicitly talk of prescription or of positive marriage rules, but only of permitted and prohibited categories; but the data and circumstances covering these groups so much resemble those concerning the groups for which we do have positive data as to make it highly likely on areal grounds that they should be included too. In many cases there is a rule of delay in renewing alliances, and sometimes we are forced to rely on this to a greater degree than we would like as evidence. However, this can still be justified, since these rules imply the renewal of alliances after the period of delay has passed, which in the case of the Mundari and Gadaba we know to be explicitly enjoined. Even were this not the case, they generally seem to accompany the positive data we have on regular systems of affinal alliance among the Munda. Indeed, it will be argued not only that they are an essential part of these systems, but also that they have their own categorical prescription—typically eGEyGos, found in whole or in part in most North Munda and both Central Munda tribes.

In fact, it can be claimed that over half the prescriptions or preferences reported among the Munda are for a category of this sort and not for some sort of cross cousin, the category so often associated with regular affinal alliance in the anthropological tradition. Most Munda instances of regular cross-cousin marriage are concentrated in Koraput, and indeed all the Koraput Munda tribes seem to have such systems. However, there are also examples further north, namely the Ho and some Santal and Bhumij. Most of the reports cite cross-cousin specifications rather than terms. Only once are cross-cousin terms reported in connection with a prescription in the literature (see Gadaba), though independent terms exist elsewhere in this area (further north, of course, Munda terminologies usually equate cross cousins with parallel cousins and siblings).

Most instances of 'cross-cousin marriage' among the Munda appear to specify the bilateral cross cousin, and thus although some particular alliances may in practice be unilateral, the basic ideology of exchange in all these cases should be regarded as symmetric. Such exchanges need not be simultaneous, of course; it is enough that women may be both given to and taken from the same alliance groups. It is true that the Ho and Santal of the north are said to have an asymmetric preference, namely one for a matrilateral cross cousin, though we do not know the term for the specified category in either case; in the former there is evidence that the overall ideology is still a symmetric one, and in the latter we still do not have sufficient information to judge exactly what happens. Nowhere, however, does affinal alliance seem to have a fundamentally asymmetric ideology, such as the *mayu-dama* rules Leach describes for the Kachin (1945).

Most cross-cousin specifications, whether in Koraput or Bihar, seem to be for a second cross cousin; first cross cousins are usually excluded (this is explicitly the case for some groups, such as the Ho and Santal, while in others uncertainty remains). Such a rule of avoidance means, of course, not repeating the alliances of the previous generation, i.e. imposing a delay of a generation (at least) before those alliances can be renewed; and this is exactly what we are told about the alliance systems of the Gorum and Sora. A similar effect may be produced by the sometimes-reported rule against marrying a cross cousin in the lifetime of his or her parents (Birhor, Santal).

The rules of delay are one way (though not the only one, as the Ho case makes clear) of avoiding marriages with a near cross cousin. But the extent of the delay also appears to have significance as to whether it is a cross cousin who will be stipulated at all or a GEG specification. The difference is a real one but ultimately these two options can both be seen as aspects—perhaps diachronic developments—of a common fundamental structure. To show this properly, let us examine the position of all the affines of ego's level in the light of the ideal two-line or symmetric prescriptive kinship terminologies with which the actual Munda terminologies are to be associated.

In an ideal symmetric prescriptive terminology—i.e. one which merges affines with cross kin and keeps these distinct from parallel kin—any GEG specification would appear as a cross cousin (see Fig. 3a in Ch. 7). The same would be true of the EG and GE specifications from which second spouses are preferentially drawn among the Munda, though here the dichotomy in terms of relative age excludes one half of them, namely yBW and WeZ (except among the Remo—see above, sect. 6.6). Conversely, the super-categories EGE, EGEG and GEGE would, under such circumstances, be equated with siblings and parallel cousins, as would the specification CEPos (e.g. DHMos is a classificatory sister); and in fact EGE = G equations are quite common among the Munda (see sect. 7.2); EGEG and GEGE specifications are recorded much less often, but they too tend to be equated with siblings. In the few reports we have relating to marriage possibilities, one finds that these categories are always explicitly banned in marriage (CEPss is admittedly a cross cousin on this basis, but ss referents do not marry in any case). For instance, the Santal forbid marriage with WBW, WBWZ, ZHZH or CEPos and the Sora with WBW (sect. 8.3). (In an ideal three-line terminology or asymmetric alliance system many of these specifications would have different positions from lineal kin.)

Munda kinship terminologies rarely equate PosGC with EG, GE or GEG specifications, so they cannot be regarded as equivalents or possible substitutes for one another, much less the same genealogical positions. However, it is evident that marriage possibilities regarding the GEG categories correspond with the overall symmetric prescriptive pattern that the terminologies exhibit, like the prohibitions concerning EGE, EGEG and GEGE ones. The only exceptions are when the specification is for BWZ alone, which in itself expresses asymmetric exchange (two brothers marrying two sisters); but these are rare and often inadequately reported. This asymmetry is anyway nullified when the specification also covers ZHZ (sister and brother marrying brother and sister, i.e. symmetric exchange).

There are a number of other possible variations on these models whereby sets of siblings intermarry according to their relative ages, but the available evidence suggests that only two are found among the Munda. Although differing in the mode of transfer of women (unilateral in Fig. 13a, bilateral in Fig. 13b), they resemble each other in enjoining marriages in age order, so that eG always marries eG and yG marries yG.[60] The other possible systems would disrupt this pattern because eG would marry yG and vice versa, as in Figs. 13c, 13d and 13e, so involving a certain disparity of age for one married pair but not necessarily for the other. In other words, even assuming one married pair to be of roughly the same age, the marriage of the other would unite the eG of one spouse with the yG of the other. It is not that marriages between the eG of one set and the yG of the other would be totally out of the question; but if the age discrepancy is to be avoided, then one marriage of this sort, even if between near age-mates, would rule out its repetition (as in Fig. 13c) or reciprocity (as in Figs. 13d and 13e) by the other pair of siblings. Only Figs. 13a and 13b avoid this problem while ensuring the continuity of alliances within the same generation.

Figure 13. *Models of affinal exchange through marriage to GEG categories* (the = sign indicates only marriage in the Figure.)

Allowed:

(a)   Asymmetric (eB = eZ and yB = yZ)

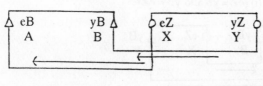

A = X, i.e. A = yBWeZ	X = A, i.e. X = yZHeB
B = Y, i.e. B = eBWyZ	Y = B, i.e. Y = eZHyB

(b)   Symmetric (eZ = eB and yB = yZ)

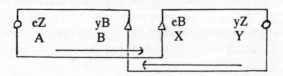

A = X, i.e. A = yBWeB   X = A, i.e. X = yZHeZ
B = Y, i.e. B = eZHyZ   Y = B, i.e. Y = eBWyB

Thus in (a)   A does not marry yBW (Y), though Y is also WyZ
                  B does not marry WeZ (X), though X is also eBW
                  X does not marry yZH (B), though B is also HyB
                  Y does not marry HeB (A), though A is also eZH

In (b) there is only one set of marriage possibilities, because there is only one male and one female on each side; the other categories are same-sex ones.

(a) and (b) are distinguished in the mode of transfer of women (unilateral or bilateral); they are united in insisting that eG = eG and yG = yG – if eG = yG, then the second possible marriage is excluded by the rule of marriage in age order.

Disallowed:
(c)   Asymmetric (eB = yZ and yB = eZ)

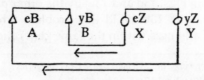

A = Y, i.e. A = yBWyZ   X = B, i.e. X = yZHyB
B = X, i.e. B = eBWeZ   Y = A, i.e. Y = eZHeB

(d)   Symmetric (i) (eZ = yB and yB = eZ)

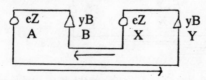

A = Y, i.e. A = yBWyB   X = B, i.e. X = yBWyB
B = X, i.e. B = eZHeZ   y = A, i.e. Y = eZHeZ

(e) Symmetric (ii) (eB = yZ and yZ = eB)

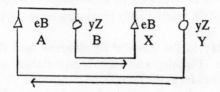

A = Y, i.e. A = yZHyZ	X = B, i.e. X = yZHyZ
B = X, i.e. B = eBWeB	Y = A, i.e. Y = eBWeB

Thus in (c)A does not marry X (WeZ, yBW)

B does not marry Y (WyZ, eBW)

X does not marry A (HeB, yZH)

Y does not marry B (HyB, eZH)

Though marriage between B and Y is normally allowed, this model would involve a banned marriage (between X and A).

There is only one set of possibilities each in (d) and (e).

In all of these, therefore, whether symmetric or asymmetric, both marriages would entail eG marrying yG; one of these can normally take place, but it would exclude the other.

And in practice too, we find the reports we have concerning this matter regularly exclude eGEeGos and yGEyGos as spouses while allowing eGEyGos and yGEeGos. But as for actual preferences, only those falling whin the eGEyGos field are in fact reported. This is also because of the rule that sibling sets marry in age order, i.e. eG always marries before yG, especially if they are ssG. The trouble with this formulation is that it assumes that there is always an eG who has married first, which raises the question of which specification *he* is being guided by. One which specified yGEeGos under these circumstances is literally nonsensical, since if eG should always marry first, this would postulate a marriage that had not taken place. Nonetheless, it would sensibly express the elder sibling's marriage in terms of the system once both had taken place. The solution to this conundrum is, of course, that these preferences represent wide categories for which the genealogical minimal specification is insufficient—one repeats the marriage of a classificatory eG at least as often as, probably in reality more often than, one's actual eG. Thus what the preference really expresses is that alliances should follow a common direction within the same generation but should not be repeated in subsequent ones nor themselves repeat those of the immediately preceding ones—typically the previous one or three.

Both the rules of delay in the renewal of alliances and the preferences for particular GEG categories are to be associated with symmetric exchange alone as far as the Munda are concerned. They can also be connected more directly, although there is some difference according to whether the delay is of one or of three generations: for in practice, one-generation rules are associated with either PosGC or GEG specifications, while three-generation ones tend to be restricted to the latter. In conventional analyses of systems of regular affinal alliance the route to a marriageable cross cousin proceeds through the preceding generations, either directly back to a +1 referent (e.g. MB) or through a +1 referent to a +2 referent (e.g.MMB) etc., and then to a cross-sex sibling, before descending again to ego's own level. Rules of delay, on the other hand, focus attention almost necessarily on one's own generation, since one cannot refer directly to the alliances of the previous generation—or even the previous three, depending on the rule—in arriving at the specified category: they have taken place elsewhere. The same is true of exploiting GEG preferences, since they are not traced through previous generations at all and are by definition confined to one's own. It may be argued that one can still refer back to previous generations, given that rules of delay are always regular ones—which in its turn suggests the equally regular renewal of alliances after the lapse of the stipulated period. This may indeed happen when the delay is of only a single generation, but with a delay of three we begin to come up against the problem of the limited genealogical knowledge that the Munda are generally reckoned to have.[61] The analyst may be able to see cross-cousin marriage in such systems, but this is due more to the influence of the anthropological tradition over him than to a just view of the indigenous conception of the system. The repetition of a cross-cousin marriage in only the fourth generation, for instance, would involve specifications of the order FFFFZSSSS and FFFFZSSSD.[62] It can be doubted whether any tribal is going to be able to trace such links in practice, and we have seen that McDougal specifically says that there is 'no long-term recognition of relations of consanguinity' among the Juang.[63]

It is here that the significance of the marriageable/non-marriageable dichotomy becomes evident, and of the frequently reported reference to particular villages rather than particular kin types that has to be made in calculating alliance possibilities in the first instance. Once one such alliance has been established as proper, it is easier simply to repeat it with the aid of prescriptions that refer to the existing generation and to that alone, rather than tracing several generations back. A Juang does not and probably cannot with any ease refer directly to any previous alliance in choosing a spouse, for the alliances of his generation are peculiar to it and are not those of any previous generation before the fourth, in most cases. All he needs is a *bondhu* female of the right category (*salirae*), preferably from an eGEyGos specification, and perhaps mainly a classificatory eBWyZ. The rules of delay that are associated with the specification of GEG categories greatly lengthen the links involved in tracing, let alone repeating, the alliances of a previous generation, and thus make the idiom of cross-cousin marriage difficult to employ in calculating potential alliances. It is much simpler to phrase the preference in terms of a category designating potential and actual affines of ego's generation that are structurally analogous to cross cousins.

These rules of delay have consequences for the actual terminologies of the Munda. First, they ensure the terminological separation of affines from cognates, since these will not coincide in any generation near to ego if the rules are followed: e.g. mothers' brothers will only exceptionally be wives' fathers. A second example is the merger of cross cousins with parallel cousins and siblings in most Munda terminologies. This is non-prescriptive theoretically, but it corresponds with the usual prohibition of near cross cousins in marriage among the North and Central Munda. This is less true of Koraput, where classificatory cross cousins are the usual preference. Here, there are more likely to be separate terms for cross cousins and cross-parallel distinctions in the +1 level (see Ch. 7). This does not mean that MB and WF will necessarily be identical individuals: among the Gadaba they may or may not be, but even if they are, the roles of MB and WF are kept distinct in the wedding ritual.[64]

Most of our discussion has concentrated on 'elementary structures' or 'prescriptive alliance' systems, but there are some Munda-speaking groups who appear to have no prescribed

category of spouse and no system of regular affinal alliance, namely the Asur, Mahali and Kora, all low castes rather than tribes. This
may mean that the Turi, another Munda-speaking low caste, are to
be associated with them, but this needs further confirmation. At all
events we should be aware of the possibility, especially with the
more Hinduized Munda.[65] Apart from these cases, Munda kinship terminologies, all basically symmetric prescriptive, mostly
govern symmetric exchange in affinal alliance, as their own pattern
logically suggests. Although by some conventions they are
anomalous for symmetric prescriptive ones and might even be
doubted to be of that type, the sorts of equation they make are basic,
and their correlation with the facts of alliance to a considerable
degree of detail can be seen to be greater than hitherto realized and
cannot seriously be doubted.

This correlation has not, however, generally been recognized for
what it is, largely because of too great an obsession with 'cross-
cousin marriage' to the exclusion of other possible expressions of
regular affinal alliance. The basic reason why there are so few
reports of cross-cousin marriage in the Munda ethnography is not
that there are few examples of 'elementary structures' here, but that
the specifications involved are often not expressed in terms of cross
cousins at all, but in terms of certain affines of ego's generation that
are fundamentally analogous to them—not genealogically, nor
even terminologically as far as the present-day terminologies are
concerned, but in the more general sense that they both inherently
express a situation in which two groups of siblings intermarry. The
difference is that the notion of cross-cousin marriage is predicated
on the tracing of links through preceding generations which are
themselves the product of previous marriages—in other words, on
the continuity of alliances into the immediately following generations. The notion of sibling's spouse's sibling marriage is not
predicated thus, and among the Munda GEG specifications are
regularly associated instead with breaks in the continuity of alliances, though continuity is nonetheless preserved in the long term by
the ultimate renewal of alliances, and in the short term in other
ways (prestations, dancing visits, etc.).

It is for this reason that the Munda systems cannot be seen as
involving regular FZD marriage (*pace* Lévi-Strauss; see previous
section and n. 44). One cannot totally rule out the possibility that
some groups have a declared preference for classificatory FZD in

marriage, especially in areas of contact with Dravidian groups. But the reversal of the direction in which women are transferred with each generation that is envisaged by the model of such a system is not at issue in what I have just been discussing. Repeated FZD marriage would constitute a continuous alliance system, despite the reversal, since women would be transferred in every generation in one direction or the other. Among the Munda, however, the alliance is broken for one to three generations, or at any rate not maintained through the transfer of women in these generations. Also, there are no examples among the Munda where FZD, classificatory or real, is reported to be the preferred spouse, and FZD terms are normally shared with siblings. Quite apart from these considerations there are, of course, theoretical doubts concerning the status of repeated FZD marriage as a separate class of alliance system anyway.[66]

Such breaks lead, of course, to the dispersal of the alliances of a particular descent group among several other descent groups. Lévi-Strauss (1966) associated dispersed alliance with so-called 'Crow-Omaha' terminologies and therefore effectively disqualified them as an 'elementary structure'. However, this line of reasoning can hardly be sustained in the present case, since Munda terminologies have no such features. In addition, it is not, in fact, uncommon for societies with prescriptive terminologies to disperse alliances among different kin groups.[67] However, what are involved in these cases are either 'subsidiary rules' or a mere behavioural tendency. In Barnes' view: 'What is actually at issue is a rule *absolutely* prohibiting...repetition within a given degree. Of course, no such rule is compatible with prescriptive alliance nor with a positive form of affinal alliance.'[68]

As regards the second observation, the Munda material actually suggests the opposite. Although there are prohibitions on the immediate repetition of alliances, there are also prescriptive terminologies whose more particular features can be explained in terms of the alliance system; evidence that certain kin categories are prescribed in marriage, some with a recorded term; some evidence that the breaks in affinal ties are only temporary—always a definite number of generations (one or three); and evidence that the renewal of such ties is jurally enjoined (no marriage to someone previously unrelated; marriage into a specific village or descent group). All this allows us to consider at least the possibility of their longer-term continuity, while the stress on multiplying such links between the same alliance units within each generation indicates regularity rather than randomness in the formation (or renewal) of alliances. There is still the basic distinction between marriageability and non-marriageability, but one does not marry into the same marriageable set all the time. Thus the Munda have found a third way of 'refreshing standing ties' apart from maintaining 'extensive ritual and economic links' or devising a 'Crow-Omaha' terminology,[69] i.e. they refer initially to the village-cum-agnatic group in seeking an alliance and then enjoin subsequent marriages in that generation in terms of the relationships set up by the first one. What is noteworthy is that they regulate affinal alliance by referring not to genealogy, but to classification—to the marriageability of a village or descent group and/or a terminological category. This does not suggest the randomness which led Lévi-Strauss to exclude dispersed alliance from the class of elementary structures. The Munda show exceptionally clearly the inappropriateness of genealogical thinking in recovering indigenous conceptions of kinship that has bedevilled studies of such structures in anthropology, despite its analytic convenience.

The Munda material also reminds us that there is a radical difference between alliance dispersal as a fundamental aspect of the system and alliance dispersal as merely one of its secondary aspects. Whether subsidiary rule or behavioural tendency, what Barnes has in mind is the practice whereby many societies in Southeast Asia with regular asymmetric affinal alliance prefer or insist that each member of a group of ss siblings (including usually parallel cousins) marries into a different alliance group. This need not of itself lead to the violation of prescriptive rules, since the stipulated category will typically cover a large number of individuals in all available alliance groups, but nor is it entailed by them. The successors in the immediately following generation will, of course, be able and perhaps required to repeat these alliances, in so far as demographic factors allow. Here, therefore, diachronic continuity takes precedence over the unity of the sibling group. Among the Munda, it is the reverse: diachronic continuity is disrupted, but sibling-group unity prevails in forming alliances (of course, it is the dispersal of alliances that is important rather than sibling-group unity). This second method is very similar to that associated with 'Crow-Omaha', at least to the extent that there is no continuity in the immediately following generations. It is also to be found in parts of north and west India. Unlike Munda, however, neither of these examples entails prescription.[70]

A final problem is Pfeffer's comparison of the Juang with the Aranda, the stock example of the well-known eight-section systems of Australia, in which a male ego marries a second cross cousin and his group symmetrically exchanges women with two others in turn.[71] Certainly there are close parallels: the rules of delay of the sort in operation among the Munda ensure that, here too, ego's group needs at least two others to ally with. Also, to describe the Aranda prescribed category as a second cross cousin may be yet another distortion of the indigenous view brought about by our own genealogical bias. However, the Juang do not have the eight sections of the Aranda, just a relativized dichotomy between marriageable and non-marriageable. Moreover, no Munda terminology can be seen as four-line in the manner of the Aranda one. Although the existence of separate affinal terms may conceivably account for a third line in the +1 and −1 levels (cross and parallel representing the other two), no fourth line is identifiable, since all cross kin are regularly conflated together, regardless of collateral distance (see Figure 3b). In ego's level the basic distinction is generally not between lines in a prescriptive terminology but between those terms which combine affinal and cognatic specifications and those which cover only the former. In fact, the pattern of ego's level is not at all prescriptive, but if anything generational. The only possible part of any Munda terminology that could be considered four-line is the +1 level of the Santal one, wherein MB and FZH are distinguished—and the Aranda themselves actually merge these two specifications.[72]

Confirmation of the view of Munda kinship set out here will have to await the collection of better data on them, but I hope at least to have provided some sort of framework for future research on the topic. There is another aspect of Munda kinship which is noteworthy, however, and this is the evidence of a special sense of identity between alternate generations. This has already been pointed out in this and the previous chapter, and it is a theme I return to in the next two.

Chapter Nine
Alternate Generation Equivalence

9.1 Behaviour

Generally among Munda groups, stereotyped behaviour patterns can be dichotomized as follows: those requiring reserve and decorum and possibly total avoidance including a ban on sexual relations and marriage between os referents; and those allowing jocular behaviour and general familiarity, with the possibility of marriage and/or a degree of sexual licence between os referents—what the ethnography usually calls 'joking relationships'. The first are obligatory on both formal and everyday occasions and may entail some asymmetry of status, though among the Munda this is mostly a matter of seniority versus juniority rather than superiority versus inferiority. The second are mandatory on formal ceremonial occasions and 'may be viewed as a form of ritual';[1] they usually entail equality and symmetry. Thus there is a basic dichotomy between reserve and familiarity, avoidance and jocularity, and to some extent status asymmetry and symmetry in expected forms of behaviour. Both are equally applicable to cognatic as well as affinal relationships, though the latter are characteristically more strongly marked than the former. However, they can be distinguished from each other because they apply to different sets of generations. Thus reserve is associated with relationships between adjacent levels (especially +1 and –1) and familiarity with those within a level and between alternate levels (+2/0/–2). There are some exceptions, especially concerning ego's level, within which there are some relationships entailing restraint, even avoidance. However, even these can be accounted for through their assimilation to one or other adjacent level in respect of behaviour and also to some extent terminologically.

Starting with relationships between adjacent generations, these are almost exclusively ones of restraint and sometimes of total avoidance, covering both cognates and affines in the +1 and –1 levels.[2] Thus there is no joking relationship between parent and child and indeed a degree of avoidance: for instance, Juang children should not take part in dancing with their parents, and an eldest son should not even witness his mother dancing. Similarly, the Korwa prohibit dancing with FyB, FyBW, MB, MBW, FZ and FZH, and a male ego completely avoids the female specifications among these referents. There are slight differences between ego's relations with matrilateral kin compared with patrilateral kin. Ego's father is pre-eminently the locus of authority, and his FB may also be involved in this role, especially if he is the actual head of the family. However, one's mother's jural role may be a little different—less severe, etc.—than one's father's. Also, MZ and MZH have no particular jural role in respect of ego.[3]

This is less true of ego's MB. Although the strongly marked MB-ZS relationship or avunculate reported from Africa, Oceania etc., is not really present among the Munda, MB and ZS may still have a ritual role in relation to each other. For instance, among the Gadaba and Korku, it is a MB who performs the first hair cutting ceremony of his ZS when the latter is one year old, and who disposes of the hair by throwing it into a water source. Roy and Roy refer to 'the special importance and authority which attaches to the mother's brother' among the Kharia, he being the person who places the ring on ego's finger when ego is being married, and he has other roles at ego's wedding, carries out ego's first hair-tying and, among the Dhelki Kharia, officiates at ego's naming ceremony. One's MB also has a ritual role at Korwa weddings. Among the Juang, he has no special duties in respect of his sister's children's marriages, but his village should receive a share of meat after any hunt and a gift of alcohol when his sister's son becomes a ritual elder, while the rite of purification after a funeral must be carried out by an unmarried boy from the village of the deceased's MB.[4] Only among the Ho is a joking relationship between MB and ZS reported—and the Ho direction of alliance has asymmetric features not found among most other Munda. Among the Santal the relationship is one of avoidance, and a Santal will accept food from any other Santal except his ZS. Nonetheless, the MB of the chief mourner (and therefore generally the WB of the deceased) must be present at the rite disposing of the bones of the dead in the river Damodar.[5] For other Munda the relationship appears to fall between these two poles, being characterized by respect rather than avoidance, and it is mostly symmetric—there is none of the asymmetry in favour of the ZS that is found in the classic avunculate.

There are some exceptions to this overall pattern of respect to + 1 referents. Santal women have a joking relationship with FZH, for whom WBD is a possible but rare second spouse, but this seems to be restricted to this group.[6] Among the Ho, relationships between kin classed as *gungu*, a term applied widely to parallel kin in the +3, +1, –1 and –3 levels, are ones of neutrality rather than either joking or avoidance. This is perhaps because of the term's wide range, often used even to persons with whom one's relationship is unknown or uncertain. Some joking also takes place between +1 and –1 referents among the Juang. Although there is no formal joking relationship with FyB, FyBW or FyZ here, one can dance with these kin types, something not allowed with FeB, FeBW or FeZ. Moreover, many classificatory fathers' younger brothers will be younger than ego, and this tends to undermine the respect relationship that should exist between them. This means that there is some joking in practice with FyB, but this in its turn may increase the latent hostility between adjacent generations and lead to fights. However, the joking is of a different quality from the mandatory ritual form, not least because it is never obligatory. While ritual joking can be physical as well as verbal, with direct bantering between the sexes and no offence to be taken, this joking is only verbal and between males, with only indirect reference to cross-sex referents, and never in their presence; offence is a distinct possibility if one goes too far. Such 'indirect joking...does not constitute a formally defined joking relation'; it takes place only 'in informal gatherings of males', not in more highly ritualized contexts, such as marriage ceremonies, in which adjacent generations are formally opposed to each other. Thus the Juang maintain the basic dichotomy too, which is formally expressed on ritual occasions, with deference and avoidance being shown by the –1 level to the +1 level, and stereotyped joking and feigned aggression between most referents of ego's own and alternating levels; but there are also more informal occasions when it is expressed through a contrast in the nature of the joking itself to +1 and one's own level. It is not at all clear whether this is unique to the Juang or found with other Munda tribes also.[7]

There are no exceptions as regards +1 and –1 affines, however, and respect and avoidance is especially marked between them. To a Juang, for example, affines are more important than maternal kin, and even if he should marry into the same village as his father,

which is rare here, his WF will be more important to him than his
MB. Between all CE and EP categories, but especially os ones, there
is normally mutual reserve and avoidance of each other's names,
and sometimes total avoidance.[8] For a Juang, the relationship
between HF and SW is one of strong respect, but not actual
avoidance, though it is considered to be similar to that between
mother and child and therefore has the greatest measure of taboo
in sexual matters. Relations between DH and WP are also ones of
great respect, though they are here the axis of certain ritual prestations between villages: for example, on becoming a ritual elder ego
sends meat and alcohol to his WF's village and receives paddy in
return. GCE-EPG relationships are to be included here, such as the
relationship ZSW-HMB among the Kharia, in which avoidance is
very marked; they would be related as classificatory FB and BD in
a symmetric prescriptive terminology.[9]

There is some evidence that restraint marks relationships with
the +3 and –3 levels also, as might be expected, since they alternate
with the +1 and –1 levels. Among the Asur, relationships between
PPP and CCC are characterized thus, and this group, as well as the
Mundari, Ho and some Bhumij, also have terminological equations
between all or most of these levels (see sect. 7.3). However, the
Birhor and Korwa have relationships of joking and familiarity
between PPP and CCC, and these two groups, as also other Bhumij,
use Indic sibling terms for these levels.[10] This may simply reflect
the influence of neighbouring Indic terminologies, many of which
use sibling terms in compounds for +3 referents. On the other hand,
it may be that these referents, who are at an even greater distance
from the locus of authority (the +1 level) than the +2 level, are
sometimes assimilated in behaviour to the latter rather than the
former.

We remain with familiarity in turning to relationships between
members of alternate generations, which normally apply to the
whole of these two levels and are only slightly tempered by the
small amount of potential authority held by one's PP. Such
familiarity is especially marked in os relationships of this kind, for
example classificatory MF-DD among the Gataq, where not even
sexual relations are banned. Indeed, marriage between these two
levels is an option in many groups, and mutual joking frequently
makes allusions to imaginary situations of this kind. Among the
Ho too, the more marked joking relationship is with MF rather than

FF. Similarly, among the Juang there is no joking between FF and SD—they are agnates, i.e. *kutumb*, in the direct line, and so cannot marry—but classificatory MF and DD are *bondhu* relatives and potential marriage partners, and hence there is a joking relationship between them. The FM-SS relationship is similarly one of potential marriage here, since it is assimilated to the eBW-HyB relationship, eBW being in theory a possible second spouse, though in practice a +2 equivalent (FFBW etc.) is preferred if of the right age. Still with the wider categories, the HFF-SSW, MFZ-BDC and FMZ-ZSC relationships of the Juang are all characterized by mild joking but not sexual intimacy. However, some of these wider specifications suggest the need for respectful behaviour because of terminological equivalence with a tabooed relative of ego's level. An example is the Juang category *ajikar*, which includes EeZ, a tabooed category, but also the +2 and –2 categories WFFZ, FMeZ, SSWeZ and FFZHeZ, to whom similar if perhaps less marked behaviour is considered appropriate. The Birhor explicitly associate the joking relationship between grandparents and grandchildren with the rebirth of the former in the latter (see Ch. 10).[11]

Although ego's level is largely associated with relationships of familiarity, if not outright joking, it is also within it that the most rigid and important avoidance relationships are to be found, namely those between EeG and yGE. Characteristically, a male ego will treat with the greatest reserve his WeB, yZH, WeZ and yBW, and he must avoid any physical contact or direct communication with any of them, or reference by name to them in conversation with a third party. Typically, even glances and physical proximity should be avoided also, and marriage and sexual relations with female relatives in these fields are totally out of the question; they should not even remain in the same room together.[12] A female ego should adopt exactly the same behaviour with her HeB, yZH, HeZ and yBW. However, in practice ss relationships here are less severe that os ones. A female's relationship with her HeZ seems to be the least sensitive in this field, and a man and his WeB may have a fairly easy relationship (see the Juang, below). The requirements of avoidance need not prevent a widow and her children from finding support and shelter from her HeB if necessary.[13]

There are some exceptions to the above rules in the literature. Among the Remo, HeB and yBW have a symmetrical joking relationship, for they are preferential second spouses here, reversing the normal Munda pattern (see sect. 6.5). There is some mild joking between classificatory, but probably not actual yBW and HeB among the Juang also, for whom a classificatory (but never actual) yBW is a possible second spouse, though preferred less than +2 equivalents of eBW. There is also some mild joking here (and among the Korwa) between a WeB and his yZH, though WeB, being senior, is superior, so that yZH should greet first.[14] Highly marked joking relationships characteristically occur between the opposing pairs of EyG and eGE, who may joke together and act as one another's confidants, while os referents may even indulge in sexual intrigue, since they are potential spouses. Sexual relations between HyB and eBW may take place quite openly, even in one's elder brother's lifetime, but this is not universally the case; some groups, like the Juang, dislike the practice, and among the Santal 'the elder brother's wife is respected as [one's] mother'. A man's relationships with his WyG are the freest in Juang society, though again they should not lead to sexual relations between eZH and WyZ. However, this clearly reflects Juang dislike of pre- and extra-marital sex generally rather than being an aspect of this particular relationship: as elsewhere among the Munda, os eGE and EyG referents are potential second spouses, and joking characteristically refers to sexual matters; but actual sexual relations with eBW in the lifetime of eB would, at least here, be regarded as adultery. As for ss relationships of this sort, that between WyB and eZH is basically symmetrical, but although a wife-giver, WyB is apparently regarded as junior, so should greet first (cf. WeB, above).[15]

Taken together, the dichotomy between relations of reserve and joking among EG and GE referents is clearly connected in part with the marriageability of particular kin types through junior levirate and junior sororate (sect. 6.5). An exception which proves the rule is found in Elwin's account of the Remo, where jocularity occurs between HeB and yBW, the relationship between HyB and eBW being one of reserve. Yet here, as we have seen, it is the senior levirate that occurs instead, so that marriageability and the dichotomy in behaviour are *both* reversed. Among other Munda, the junior sororate is generally less important and less frequent than the junior levirate, the former often being virtually mandatory; and this is reflected in the fact that the familiarity between

WyG and eZH is frequently milder than that between HyG (especially HyB) and eBW.[16]

Marriageability may also account for the contrast in behaviour between ss referents in this field, since they are affines. It is clear that the avoidance that marks EeG-yGE relationships is more characteristic of relationships with adjacent levels than of those within one's own, and one can argue that, as regards behaviour, these referents are generally assimilated to the +1 and −1 levels, according to relative age. The Birhor, for instance, are said to regard the relationship between HeB and yBW as analogous to that between father and daughter. However, as Fuchs remarks of the Korku, it would be truer to see them as assimilated to EP and CE instead (eB/F equivalence within the same family).[17]

Some GEG relationships also entail avoidance and reserve. Among the Juang, these are eBWeZ-yZHyG and eZHeZ-yBWyG, these pairs being equated terminologically in behaviour to WeZ-yZH (the first of each pair is an *ajikar*). Among the Ho, ego must maintain the same sort of reserve towards eBWeG and yBWyG, 'because', says Dhan, 'they do not belong to his age group'. Other relationships within this field entail the possibility of joking and familiarity, including eBWyG and yBWeG among the Ho, eGEyG among the Kharia, ZHBms, eZHyZms, eBWyBws and eZHyB among the Korwa, and ZHZ, ZHeB and BWB among the Kodaku. The Korwa os relationships here are especially marked as indicating marriage preferences. Similarly, for the Mundari the most marked joking is with *goi* (BWZms, ZHZms) and *eyar* (BWBms, ZHBms). As for the Santal, Kochar includes yBWZ and ZHeB as joking partners, but Culshaw excludes them both. If we had a little more information, we might in fact find that both were right because referring to slightly different specifications, i.e. Kochar to yBWeZ and yZHeB, Culshaw to yBWyZ and eZHeB. The specifications above are given as recorded and cannot be regarded as complete. Nonetheless, it seems that relationships with eGEyG and yGEeG categories generally entail some familiarity whereas those between yGEyG and eGEeG entail avoidance, or at any rate reserved behaviour, which reflects the marriageability of GEG referents according to relative age (the former group are, of course, frequently cited as the preferred marriageable category among the Munda; see previous chapter).[18]

Relationships between spouses and siblings are generally ones of equality and familiarity rather than joking specifically. However, some degree of decorum is appropriate to elder siblings, who are potentially surrogate parents and thus virtually equivalent to +1 referents. In particular, one's eB is, in these patrilineal societies, the family heir, and younger siblings may be treated as children by him to some extent, or at least be expected to obey their elder brothers. Among the Juang there is reserve between eB and yB but also some latent tension. Part of this is due to the fact that although eB is assimilated to father, especially if actually family head, ego nonetheless has a joking relationship with eBW. Relationships between brothers and sisters and between sisters alone are more symmetrical but still exclude marked joking. Classificatory brothers also have a more symmetric relationship than real eB and yB: a classificatory eB is saluted on formal ceremonial occasions, but there is no question of superordination or subordination. There is also symmetry between cross and parallel cousins, and a joking relationship between male parallel cousins and all cross cousins. Classificatory os cross cousins are in a minor way potential spouses, though rarely the declared preference, and it is thus significant that such joking relationships are less marked than those with affines who are potential spouses. Relationships between os parallel cousins are ones of reserve, however, no doubt to signal that they are tabooed in marriage, and Gautam mentions parallel cousin avoidance among the Santal also. This group are also said to avoid eZ (presumably males only), but the Mundari have no avoidance rules regarding osG. Among the Kodaku there should be no 'exaggerated familiarity' to cousins, who are assimilated to siblings in behaviour. Singh implies that joking relationships are more marked with unmarried than with married siblings, and this may be generally true. Avoidance relationships between os referents are more marked than those between ss ones, presumably because the possibility of violating the rules concerning marriage only arises in the former, not, by their very nature, the latter.[19]

Among at least some Santal, a joking relationship exists between MMBSD and FFZDS, these being potential spouses in the north of their area. Other groups are reported as having cross-cousin joking relationships, such as the Juang (above), Gataq and Mahali, or, less usually, with just a matrilateral female cross cousin, as with the Ho.

The latter also have a relationship of avoidance with FZD, though this appears to be restricted to the genealogical FZD only. The Mundari have no cross-cousin joking relationships, since cross cousins may not marry. Cousins by marriage are apt to be avoided, especially cross specifications, who are classificatory siblings in terms of regular symmetric spouse exchange. Recorded examples include WMBD-FZDH and He(PGC)-y(PGC)W among the Kharia and MBSW-HFZS among the Korwa; the second Kharia pair might also be assimilated to the HeB-yBW relationship as regards parallel cousin specifications.[20]

A lesser degree of reserve concerns ego's relationships with EGEos (i.e. the affines of one's affines), such as HeZH-WyBW and HyZH-WeBW among the Santal, though they too can be considered classificatory siblings and indeed are seen as such, according to age. Jain says that 'parity and comradeship' mark relationships with one's EGEss, as between pairs of WZH and HeBW-HyBW among the Asur and between WeZH-WyZH and HeBW-HyBW among the Mundari.[21] Whether in north Indian society or in systems of regular affinal alliances, pairs of WZH will tend to regard each other as equals, since they have taken brides from the same family or other alliance group. As far as the EGEG and GEGE fields are concerned, we know only that the relationship between HeZHB and BWyBW among the Santal is also one of avoidance. These specifications can also be seen as classificatory siblings or as analogous to the HeB-yBW relationship. Finally, we must consider the relationship between pairs of CEP, i.e. those whose children have married one another. This is one of equality, but often tempered by mutual respect and mutual name avoidance, the inclusive form of the dual personal pronoun being used instead. Avoidance may be total with CEPos, for such referents are classificatory siblings and therefore tabooed in marriage, but a Korwa male can apparently indulge in mild joking with DHM as well as DHF.[22] There is also limited joking between all CEP referents, os and ss, among the Juang, though the wife-givers seem to be of slightly higher status.[23] Gadaba os *somdi*, however, joke much more demonstrably, with mutual assaults with cow dung and water, despite the fact that they may not marry.[24]

Thus although name avoidance is an intrinsic part of many relationships, it does not necessarily imply a relationship marked by avoidance and absence of familiarity in other respects: husband

and wife will use a circumlocution when addressing or referring to one another, even though their relationship in Munda society is broadly one of equality. Among the Juang, kin terms or teknonymy are used to seniors, one's spouse and os joking partners, the latter being potential spouses, whereas names are used to juniors, and this is probably generally true of the Munda. Birhor spouses switch from kin terms to teknonymy after the first child is born in addressing or referring to one another. Kin terms rather than names may also be used of or to junior affines, suggesting that the respect due to them as affines overrides their inferiority as juniors.[25] Marriage need not alter pre-existing kin terms, but neither do divorce or widowhood necessarily alter the forms of address and behaviour between individuals who were formerly related by marriage. For example, among the Mahali one continues to call one's DH *jawae*, even after the divorce or death of his wife, and any subsequent wife of his is called *hapanera* or 'daughter'.[26] Among the Korwa, however, 'name taboos are removed after the death or divorce of the spouse or the relation with regard to [whom]...the taboo exists.' With the Birhor, any conflict over address and the appropriate behaviour to follow is settled by the panch for a fee, for although there may be more than one possibility in both, only one is allowed at any one time in each. From the examples given by Malhotra, it would seem that the nearest relationships generally override the more distant, though avoidance overrides joking (WeZ-yZH rather than eBW-HyZ). There are two rites involved, the first to decide which relationship to follow, the second to drop the others, half of the fee (Rs. 2.50) standing for each. Breaches of relationship taboos are dealt with by the village or clan panch.[27]

As with marriageability, therefore, but more comprehensively so, behaviour can be dichotomized according to generation, restraint and avoidance applying to adjacent levels (+3, +1, –1, –3), privileged joking and familiarity with alternating ones (+2, 0, –2) (see Fig. 14). Ego's level is itself dichotomized in the same way, but most if not all the avoidance relationships here can be assimilated to those concerning the adjacent levels. There are some variations in this pattern from tribe to tribe, and Bouez dismisses the normal dichotomous view as far as the Ho are concerned, seeing a continuum as more appropriate. Somers expresses a similar view about the Santal, where 'actual behaviour ranges over a long continuum of slight variations from extreme freedom to extreme

Joking relationships etc.	Restraint and avoidance
+2	
	+1
	EeG; eGEeG (eG)
EyG, eGE eGEyG, yGEeG PosGC G; E	EGEG, GEGE (EPGC, PGCE) FZD (Ho) EGE; CEP
	yGE; yGEyG (yG)
	−1
−2	

Figure 14a. *Behaviour stereotypes among Munda groups*

Allowed	Prohibited
+2*	
	+1
	EeG; eGEeG
(PosGC) EyG, eGE yGEeG, eGEyG	G, PssGC (PosGC) EGE, EGEG, GEGE CEP
	yGE; yGEyG
	−1
−2*	

Figure 14b. *Marriageability of genealogical levels among Munda groups (opposite sex only) (* not if in direct line)*

reticence'. Moreover, 'these differences do not suggest a hierarchy of statuses; there is nothing in the behaviour to imply superiority or inferiority.'[28]

The Juang, by contrast, provide on the whole a good example of the dichotomy. Relationships between the +1 and −1 levels are asymmetric in terms of seniority-juniority, though not necessarily, if at all, in terms of superiority-inferiority. They require respect, and although there are some gradations in intensity, not even the mild, indirect joking with FyB is ever mandatory—there are no formal ritual occasions on which it takes place. Similarly, there are exceptions to the normal symmetry of the set formed by the +2, 0 and –2 levels. Both sorts of relationship—joking and respect—are more marked in relation to affines than to cognates; only to the former is honorific speech necessary, whatever the approved behaviour. The *kutumb-bondhu* dichotomy (see sect. 8.2) and the marriageability of particular referents also modifies the pattern. A male Juang can joke with any male in his *bhaiguli* or generation set except his own eB, though joking is more marked with *bondhu* than with agnatic relatives. A female Juang can joke with any *bondhu* female of her generation set; there is no particular avoidance of her sisters etc., who are *kutumb*, but no established joking with them either. Across the sex line there is no joking with *kutumb* relatives, regardless of generation set, owing to the incest taboo. Thus joking is restricted to members of the same generation set who are both *bondhu* and potential spouses (e.g. excluding one's *ajikar* EeZ etc.). Strictly speaking, this means potential spouses for the whole local descent group and generation set rather than just ego:

> The unmarried females with whom a man jokes belong to the category of potential spouses for the members of his LDG and moiety, and to the same category as the inmarrying spouses already recruited. Those of appropriate age are his own potential spouses, but this is a fact of less significance.

These generation sets are, of course, social, not biological, and there may be age discrepancies, as we have seen with fathers' younger brothers, who are ego's +1 relatives genealogically yet may, in fact, be younger in age. Overall 'there...is little difference in the age composition of the two moieties.' The antagonism between the opposed generation sets is strong and can lead to fights, in which alternate generations support one another against adjacent ones. However, the opposition between generation sets as wholes relates only to some ceremonial occasions; on others, juniors and seniors are distinguished by the former showing formal respect to the latter.

Therefore, although the dyadic relation between particular generations of opposite moiety [i.e. generation set] is asymmetrical, that between the two moieties considered as units is symmetrical. This symmetry is expressed by means of reciprocal indirect joking between males of opposite moiety [i.e. 'FyB' and 'eBS'].

Thus the dichotomy is sociocentric rather than egocentric, although the contents of particular relationships are focussed on ego. This means too that it has an integrating as well as a discriminating effect. Ego is identified with other members of his own *bhaiguli* not only through the behaviour expected of himself, but also by the fact that this should be shared by the other members of his *bhaiguli*. The dichotomy is also expressed terminologically, in the sense that no term equates referents from both generation sets.[29] The address terminology follows the same dichotomy but even more starkly, choosing one strategic term for each adjacent generation (father, son, etc.), but one for the whole of the alternating set (i.e. all +2, −2 and 0 level males are 'brothers'), reflecting the equality and familiarity appropriate to the latter, and the authority structure inherent in relations between lineal kin in adjacent levels.[30]

9.2 Ritual and Alternate Generations

Among the Juang, dancing is an example of the same dichotomy, since inter-village dancing is analogous to cross-sex joking and is obligatorily associated with it. Similarly, Remo dances bring together boys and girls in relationships of potential affinity with the old women of the village and in opposition to parents, though young husbands may also take part. Juang myth and ritual also express the unity of alternate generations that behaviour broadly signifies. In the marriage ritual, the bride is lifted on to the shoulders of either her 'eBW' or 'FM' in the ceremony offering her to the groom's village, and it is the groom's 'eBW' or 'FM' who leads the bride to give the groom a ceremonial bath. At one stage in the ceremony it is said that 'a girl has entire freedom with her husband's younger brother and a grand-father with his grand-daughter'. Classificatory eBW and FM are equivalent in other rites, such as the first sowing of hill rice and the paying of homage to the Raja of Keonjhar. Finally, PP and CC are associated together in the Juang myth explaining the origin of death.[31]

This ritual equivalence can be found in other Munda tribes also. Writing of Mundari weddings, Basu says:

> When the bridegroom's party returns home with the bride, it is customary for the elder sister or the grandmother to accompany them and stay for a short period (i.e. 3 days) in the bridegroom's house and go back with the couple.

Among the Santal a midwife and her assistant should belong to the mother's own level or the +2 level, not the +1 level, 'because it is not fitting for the woman in childbirth to express her nakedness before anyone who belongs to the generation of her own parents'. During the actual birth, 'She is supported at her back by one of the women, who again must be either two generations removed from her or else be of her own generation'. In at least part of the Santal area, and in other groups also, a child's ear-boring—frequently essential for marriage or cremation—should be carried out by its grandparent, though in Keonjhar it is done by FZH.[32] A fundamental expression of this association is that concerning reincarnation, to which we turn in the next chapter.

In a broader sense, the Juang equivalence of grandparents, siblings and grandchildren in opposition to fathers and children as regards expected behaviour and affinal alliance corresponds to the ritual divisions of the village, and indeed the two systems are considered comparable by the Juang themselves.[33] The focus of the village is the *majang*,[34] which though in a general sense is a men's house—women are admitted only exceptionally—is mainly associated with the unmarried youths (*kongerki*) and old men (*kamando*) of the village. Opposed to them are the heads of family (*bowntay*), who, though not restricted from the *majang* in the way that women are, are less involved in its affairs. However, the distinction is not just one of age—of youngsters and old men versus the mature: it is also respectively one of ritual power versus secular authority and of low sexual activity and lack of procreative power versus a high level of both. This dichotomy helps explain the disapproval of pre-marital sex among the Juang: the mature group are pre-eminently heads of family, a prerequisite for which is marriage, whereafter young men leave the *majang;* and for a youth to have sexual relations before marriage would conflict with his ritual status. Very young children, who are under the close protection of their fathers, have little to do with the *majang* as individuals until they (if male) begin to sleep there regularly, though they may be taken there by their fathers in the daytime earlier in life.

There is a parallel sequence of women's groups: young *selanki* and old *kamandorayki* are opposed to mature *mabhuniki*. The status of the latter two depends on that of their husbands, and a girl ceases to be *selanki* and becomes a *mabhuniki* on becoming a mother, not strictly at marriage. Again, sexuality is important, for only sexually inactive women may enter the *majang*. The village *selanki* actually sleep elsewhere, normally in the homes of widows, and usually in no single organized way like the *kongerki*, but like the *selanki* of *bondhu* villages they take part in *majang* activities. Thus the 'ritual' group is characterized by a tendency to minimize sex differences, whereas the 'secular', 'married' group stresses them: females of the latter group are the only people who are actually excluded from the *majang*.[35] Symmetric joking relationships tend to apply right across the 'ritual' group, even where some members are in the +1 or –1 kinship levels (except for close links), and similarly with asymmetric relationships with the 'married' group (cf. the occasional marriages with +1 and –1 referents here, above, sect. 8.4). Unmarried juniors refer to the 'married' group as 'parents' and are guided in their secular duties by one of them. Conversely, they refer to the ritual elders as 'grandparents' and are associated with them in actual rites. The elders are intermediaries with the spirits and are sometimes assisted in this and in the first mango rite by the juniors. It is the latter that should carry the corpse of a ritual elder, and the final purificatory rite after death should be carried out by an unmarried boy of the deceased's mother's brother's village; ritual elders and women are not present during cremation, which is polluting.[36] Among the Remo too, married women should not sleep in the dormitory, though here and in many other tribes widows and even female divorcees may return to it (see sect. 6.1).[37]

Chapter Ten
Reincarnation

Reincarnation in India is conventionally associated with the Hindu (or textual) doctrine of *karma*, but it is also an aspect of tribal eschatologies. Some ethnographers almost automatically interpret these beliefs as the debased result of Hindu influence,[1] whereas others, perhaps more plausibly, suggest that it is them to which the Hindu doctrine must ultimately be traced. Basically, though, they are of a very different character and must be regarded as independent, the more so since analogous, even identical beliefs are found in tribal societies in other parts of the world. Fundamental to them is, once again, the conceptual unity of alternate generations.

Tribal eschatologies characteristically recognize at least two 'souls'—sometimes more. One contains the personality of the deceased and is eventually merged into the general body of largely anonymous ancestors. The other apparently lacks a full personality, though it may retain some physical and even psychological characteristics. It is more significant as the animating life-spirit, whose loss constitutes death. It is this which is reincarnated and really should be termed 'soul substance' to distinguish it from the personalized soul; it is this I shall concentrate on here.

Santal

There are several souls or soul substances within the body or *hormo*. Carrin-Bouez mentions a number of them:

> In the body, only the skeleton is conceived as immortal, thanks to the *maran ji* ('big breath' or 'principle of life') which gives it life and which dwells in the bones of the skull. The other *ji*, called 'little breath' (*hurin ji*), dwells in the stomach and shelters the *roa*, the 'soft soul'.

The latter leaves the body after death and enters a plant or animal body. Different again is the *umul* or shade, which leaves the body in sleep. After death, the spirits of ancestors (presumably the *maran ji*) are called (*agil*) *hapram* and they eventually turn into the *bonga* that are worshipped at major festivals (unless they are the souls of those died inauspiciously, who becomes *bhut bonga*, more malevolent).[2] According to Hodson the deceased person is eventually born into the same family, the particular ancestor being discovered by divination. Culshaw and Carrin-Bouez are more doubtful that reincarnation is involved here. The latter bases her opinion on a comparison with the Hindu form of reincarnation and on the fact that the *maran ji* becomes a *bonga*, whereas the *hurin ji* is merely ephemeral. However, the comparison is unnecessary and misleading, for as the author herself seems to realize, there is more than one possible theory of reincarnation. Her own informants seem to have been united in rejecting the Hindu version.[3] The *hurin ji* may not, in fact, be so ephemeral, since it is also concerned with the regeneration of the species. Conversely, the *roa* may be reincarnated, as it is in rice plants.[4] Other authorities on the Santal are less equivocal about reincarnation, or that naming is connected with it. Gautam says that 'those who go to heaven come back to earth in the third generation as a "Hor" (man or a Santal). This is also clear in the practice of name-giving, since children are named after the grandparents who are reborn in them.' And according to Hansda, who from his name appears to be a Santal himself:

> They believe that [the] new-born babies are the prototype of the grandparents and that a baby resembles the figure, the posture and the activities of the grandparents concerned. In [the] case of deceased grandparents whose name is inherited by a baby, it is believed that the same soul is...in the baby and hence first preference is given in selecting the names to the deceased grandparents.[5]

Generally, the first son is named after his FF, the second after his MF, the third after FFeB, the fourth after MFeB, then FFyB, MFyB, etc. The same pattern, *mutatis mutandi*, applies to daughters.[6] PG(E) names may be used if there are many siblings, or if one of these referents has been dead for a long time without his or her name being inherited, but the preferred names are those of an alternate generation in the patriline. However, if a child cries incessantly it is thought to have been given the wrong name, one other than that of its true ancestor, whose intervention is the cause of the child's crying. Usually, this is deemed to be a matrilateral relative seeking to have its name chosen against the wishes of the agnatic relatives. However, the latter have priority, for naming is one of the rites that admits a child to its father's clan and sub-clan. The *ojha* or shaman solves the problem and presumably carries out all divination in respect of birth and naming.[7]

The inherited name is the 'private' or 'inner' name,[8] and it is little used in practice for fear of doing harm to its owner, with whom it is intimately identified. Everyone also has an 'upper' or 'outer' name or nickname for daily use,[9] and also to avoid confusion if the grandparent concerned is still alive, or so that name taboos can be circumvented.[10] Indeed, a child will never be addressed by this private name if his namesake is still alive. These nicknames change and were originally borrowed from Hindus or Moslems or taken from the place or time of birth. They too, however, are becoming subject to inheritance in the traditional Santal manner; for instance, Culshaw mentions the case of a Santal receiving both the private name and the nickname of his FFeB.[11]

Thus naming and reincarnation are both expressions of the alternation of generations among the Santal. This is also evident in the mound of earth which is erected as a temporary alter as part of the final rite of purification in relation to the dead. *Sal* leaves are planted in a row upon the altar representing the Creator (*marang buru*), followed by the mythical ancestral couple (*prodhol haram* and *prodhol budhi*) and the household god (*orak bonga*), followed by three human beings, one from each of ego's set of alternate generations: *gorom ayo* (PM), *bokoea* (B), and *jae kora* (CS). The alternation between death and (re)birth is expressed in the *sika* or cicatrization marks with which Santal youths decorate their forearms. These give them their identity as Santal males and are necessary for a 'good death' and to become a *bonga* or spirit. They are always of an odd number, which is itself associated with life or *jion*, whereas even numbers are associated with death or *moron*. The first mark denotes life, the second death, the third renewed life through reincarnation, and so on.[12]

Mundari

In life, individuals are said to have two souls, a *roa* and a *ji*. Both are immortal, but while the former can leave the body (e.g. during sleep), the latter must remain there; it is equated with *mon* 'mind', possession of which distinguishes humans from animals. After death, both *roa* and *ji* leave the body. The former escapes from the grave immediately after death and remains on earth, first becoming a *umbul* [13] or shade, which wanders freely until the disposal of the corpse. It is then brought back to its earthly home in the *umbul ader* ('returning home of the soul') rite, in which flour and ashes are spread on the ground to detect its return (this does not apply to the inauspicious dead). The *umbul* thereafter becomes a *bonga* or spirit and is merged with the general body of ancestral spirits or *ora-bon-gako*. It has both beneficient and maleficient powers over the living it has left behind and is therefore honoured with all other *bonga* in the month of Mage (= Hindu Magh). However, it is also dependent on the humans it left behind for food, which it obtains by causing them harm, so that they have to offer a sacrifice. Bhowmik and Chaudhuri describe the *ji* as 'a kind of airy substance, which leaves the body after death' through the nose or mouth or eye. Since it was Haram, the Creator, who originally gave it to men and thus gave them life, it probably returns to him initially after death. It is more immaterial than the *roa* but is reincarnated in some member of the deceased's family, especially a grandchild, the eldest son and daughter having precedence.[14] Accordingly, the personal name is inherited also,[15] though it is often avoided in everyday use, nicknames being used instead. The name-giving ceremony, called *eksia* or *sakhi* (the latter means 'namesake'), is performed after the post-partum purification ceremony and is carried out by women only. In the traditional system, children are named after FP or FG (both sexes), preferably the former.[16] There is an element of divination, however, the method used being to place some grains of rice or leaves of grass in water and to call out a series of names, that being called out when the grains or leaves come together being the one chosen. One child was named after his FMyB, after the names of FFF, MFeB, MeB, FF and FFeBS had all been tried in this way and rejected. There is a *sakhi* or *mita* relationship between the child and the relative after whom it has been named, who may or may not be alive. It is he or she (or his or her heir) who buys the pin for the child's ear-boring ceremony, essential for its spirit to reach the ancestors after death.[17]

Asur and Turi

According to Das Gupta:

> Every Birjhia has a guardian spirit, which is called the Gono or Chhain, 'spirit shadow'. A Gono may be dead or...living, [a] close or distant relation, male or female. It gets 'hold' of the child as it comes out of the mother's womb. The Manti alone can find out the Gono of a new born child through his magic.... If so desired the Manti can also change the Gono...',

though *gono* names are generally those of +2 relatives. A similar situation obtains among other Asur, where grandsons are named after FF and where those after whom a child is named are called *gonon*, a term which is explicitly compared by Leuva to Mundari *sakhi* or 'namesake'; times or days of birth are other sources of names. However, names can be changed by rice-in-water divination if they prove unsatisfactory. Leuva quotes from an informant to provide an example:

> Divination revealed that Kandra, my deceased father, would like to have his name perpetuated and so we immediately changed the name of the son from Mangra [Tuesday] to Kandra.

Leuva adds:

> It is not improbable that this practice was originally meant either as a means of divination to discover which of the deceased ancestors was reborn in the person of the infant, or as a means of securing for the child the protection of the spirit of the deceased ancestor, whose name was thus appropriated.

The Turi name children after a relative by 'rice-grain-in-beer' divination.[18]

Birhor

A person has three souls, one of which joins the ancestors, the other two being reincarnated in a new body, though not necessarily in a Birhor: one is male, the other female. The former leaves the body during dreams, while the latter remains in the body; if both leave, death ensues. The *sakhi* is the sponsor and namesake of the child, who need not belong to the same family, nor even be alive. If alive, it is he who takes the child in his lap for the ear-boring ceremony, which is an initiation for the child and must take place before a person's death to ensure a proper burial. The *sakhi* also helps anoint the guests with oil. The name-giving ceremony involves three grains being placed in water with a blade of grass, one grain and the blade of grass being witnesses, the other grains being any ancestor and the child itself. The grains are changed each time the process has to be started again:

if the name selected is that of a relative whose name is tabooed to the baby's mother, a second name, sometimes derived from the day of the week on which the child was born, is selected. Each and every Birhor is found to have two names—one his ordinary name and the other his secret name.

Grandparents are believed to be reborn in their grandchildren, and this is linked with the joking relationship they have: 'The Birhors believe in re-birth and it is supposed that the grandchild replaces the grandparent and so [a] free, frank joking relationship exists between them.'[19]

Korku

The Korku also distinguish the personalized soul from the soul substance or *jiv*. The former is installed in a memorial tablet and if neglected may become a *bhut* and harm the living in revenge. The latter returns to Bhagwan (if the individual had been married properly) and it does not harm the living. It is subject to reincarnation at least a generation after death; corpses are marked to see if the spirit returns in an infant, and new-born children are examined for such marks accordingly. Children are named after the recently dead, on the fifth or eleventh day after birth.[20]

Korwa

The Korwa also believe in the reincarnation of ancestors in new-born children, though 'one can only get a child according to the good will of *Bhagwan*, the Supreme God'. While there is naming after the days of the weeks or months, or after the seasons, ancestral names are also used, those of patrilineal ancestors for male children, those of matrilineal ancestors for female children. According to Majumdar, 'the third or fourth generation bears the name of the first one', and he associates this with reincarnation. Until they receive a given name, male children are called *babu* and female children *maiyan*.[21]

Ho

A Ho has two souls, the *marang ji* ('big soul') and the *roa* or *hudin ji* ('little soul'). It is the *roa* whose departure causes death and dreams, but after death it is brought back home to the *ading* (the inner, private sanctum where the souls of deceased ancestors reside) with the aid of the *ra-a-nadar* ceremony (the sprinkling of rice on the floor to detect the soul's return). There is some disagreement as to whether reincarnation is involved. Chattopadhyay and Ray-Chaudhuri deny it, and in this they are echoing Hodson, but Majumdar suggests that this was at least the traditional idea: 'The grandfather reappears after death in the role of the grandchild, and the names of children are selected in accordance with the sequence of death in the family.' Some ancestors do not deserve reincarnation, however. Bouez indicates that it is the *roa* that is involved here, for this is reincarnated in a plant, animal or human, but he omits further details on this point. If he is right, it means that the Ho are an exception to the usual situation among the Munda in that the same soul which is reincarnated is also that which is brought back home, but in other respects they clearly resemble other Munda in their ideas.[22]

Children are named after a deceased relative or friend (*sakhi-jana* or *suku-jana*) or both (e.g. the *sakhi* may share his name with one of the child's ancestors), but usually after a +2 referent (patrilateral or matrilateral; sometimes FG or a +3 referent). The choice of name may depend on the grain-in-water method (see Mundari) or on body marks, and a corpse's forehead is marked with dots alternatively in vermilion and rice-paste to aid recognition of his future reincarnation. The naming after a *sakhi* is usually intended to cement an already existing relationship, and if a child is named after a living person, that person makes the child a prestation. If all heritable names prove unsuitable, the child is named after a day of the week.[23]

Kharia

There is a distinction of souls between the *jiom*, which is reborn after a period with the ancestors, and the *longae* or *chhain*, which returns to the *ading* or house shrine shortly after the funeral rites have been performed. Children are named after ancestors, the +2 level being preferred and patrilateral relatives having precedence over matrilateral; naming is associated with reincarnation. The child's namesake is called *mita*, and he or she (or his or her heir, if deceased) is important in the final birth purification rite, which is continuous with the name-giving rite: specifically, he ties a cotton thread around the child's waist, washes his feet, and gives him presents. Among the Dudh Kharia he also performs the child's ear-boring ceremony, which is essential for the latter's eventual incorporation with the ancestors. This is a form of initiation into the tribe, and if the child dies before it has been carried out its soul cannot join the ancestors; its body will be buried not in the burial ground, but at some isolated spot outside. Here, the *jiom* returns to the ancestors rather than the Supreme God, and the personalized soul remains in the house shrine, but other details conform to the usual Munda situation.[24]

Juang

According to Elwin:

> Some Juang say that men have five *jiv* (soul or life-force...), in the mouth, ears, eyes, nose and chest. When a man sleeps, the *jiv* in the mouth, ears and eyes go out to wander through the world; whatever the mouth tastes, or the ears hear or the eyes see is a dream. The chief of the *jiv* is in chest; if this leaves the body the man dies.

He continues: 'except under Hindu influence they have no idea of rebirth.' However, he also says that to see a grandmother in a dream means that a girl will be born in the family, to see a grandfather a son, and that at least the head of the household is reborn in his son's son:

> When the elder finally makes up its [*sic*] mind to be reborn, it sends a dream saying: 'Formerly she was my daughter-in-law;

now she will be my mother'.[...] 'Sometimes the father has a dream in which an Ancestor appears to say who has been reborn in the child. When they name the child it will cry if it is not correct and the Ran-uria then has to be consulted.

Elwin's uncertainty seems to be the result of his view that Hindu influence is significant, but all the elements of the tribal version are present. Chattopadhyay and Ray Choudhuri claim that the Juang do connect name-giving with reincarnation, and at least in Keonjhar they name children after a deceased agnate of the +2 generation, the umbilical cord being cut by the FM or FFZ of the child. Grandparents and grandchildren also appear together in the myth explaining the origin of death.[25]

Sora

The soul, *puradan* or *jibo* (from Oriya), can leave the body in sleep, dreams, shamanistic trances, etc., and may cause disease. Although the body and person die, it is not destroyed by death, and it controls the individual's mental and moral actions. At death it becomes a shade or *kulman* (Elwin has *kulban*) and remains near its home, before going to live in the underworld as an ancestor following the *guar* ceremony, which takes place a few days or weeks after death.[26] It is essential to life, for it is identified with the heart and can never leave the living body.[27]

According to Elwin,

the Saoras...insist that there is no real reincarnation; there is not a rebirth of the person, but only of the name. But the name itself has a kind of real existence, and the ancestor or tutelary who gives a name to a human child does in some way live in it, even though he continues another life in the Under World.

And elsewhere he says: 'it must be admitted that the language used at a name-giving ceremony [he attended] at Singjangring in 1950 was undoubtedly suggestive of a belief in a real rebirth.' Elsewhere, too, he says that certain rites honouring ancestors give them 'some kind of further life on earth by the naming of children after them', and a number of times he refers explicitly to the rebirth of a particular grandparent in his grandson. And since a second death is expected just as much as a second birth, the process is clearly a cyclical one. Sitapati's statements concerning reincarnation are much more confused, but he too appears to accept that the idea exists, since he associates ancestral spirits with grandparents.[28]

Children may be named after days of the week as well as ancestors. In the latter case, precedence is given to the +2 level on both sides of the family, sons generally being named after FF, and there are also nicknames. 'Names are often given in dreams, especially when an ancestor desires that kind of semi-reincarnation that follows the bestowal of his name.' The shaman may be called in if a child cries excessively or refuses its mother's milk, and he usually gives the reason as a particular ancestor wishing the child to bear his or her name. Similarly, 'a common cause of sickness for young children and their parents is the desire of a dead ancestor to perpetuate his name, and in some way reincarnate part of himself, in one of his descendants.' It is significant that the classes of shaman and shamanin which carry out divination concerning name-giving, respectively the *guarkumbaran* (or *sanatung kuran*) and *guarkumbaroi*, are also those that deal with the dead.[29]

Remo

The Remo acknowledge two souls. The *sairem* or shade remains near the earth after death and cause problems for the living so it is propitiated, indefinitely. It can eat earthly food, unlike the *siorem* or *jiwo* ('soul'), which returns after death to Singi-Arke (literally 'sun-moon') or Mahaprabhu, and with which it seems to be identified here (unlike in other groups). Life in the Land of the Dead is similar to that on earth, and it will come to an end too, in reincarnation in a child of the same clan, possibly after a period residing in an animal—a cow or a dog, according to merit; the inauspicious dead are not reincarnated, however. The child is given the same name as the ancestor, whose identity is discovered by divination: the child is offered a piece of straw while a series of names is called out to it, the correct one being signalled by his or her clutching the straw (the name of a day of the week is applied if this is unsuccessful). Corpses are marked with charcoal and oil, in the belief that the reborn child will have the same marks and can thus be identified more easily. Elwin regards Remo reincarnation as a Hindu-derived idea, but it is clearly the usual self-contained tribal version in all essentials.[30]

Gataq and Gadaba

The Gataq also distinguish the *saharem* (shade) from the *jivon* (soul): 'The former lives at the place where the body was burnt, while the soul goes to its creator Maprohu in the sky.' The Gadaba are said to have two souls, one harmless, the other dangerous, both being called by the Desia term *dhumba*. At death, the harmless soul immediately enters the deceased's SW, eventually being reborn in the ensuing generation, i.e. −2 from the deceased. This applies to both males and females, given that the latter join the lineages they marry into. Rebirth thus takes place in the same lineage, and as a member of the same sex. This depends, however, on settling the dangerous *dhumba*, the object of the spectacular *gotr* rite which takes place every generation or so. The Gadaba name children after the day of the week on which they were born, or else after +2 ancestors, but in either event they regard them as the latter's reincarnations.[31]

A number of elements can be identified as composing these tribal eschatologies, namely the distinction of soul substance (usually called *jiv* etc.) from the personalized soul; reincarnation of the former, while the latter eventually becomes merged with the anonymous and undifferentiated body of ancestral spirits; and the assumption of the names of the deceased by their reincarnations.

The name *jiv* is clearly Indic and the concept shares many features with the Hindu *jiv*, including reincarnation and origination with the Supreme Being (in the tribal case Bhagwan, Mahadeo, Singi-Bonga, Singi-Arke etc.); its destiny is different, however. In particular, it is subject to perpetual rebirth in the same family, most often being transferred between grandparent and grandchild (or at least between the +2 and −2 levels). Accordingly, it assumes most importance at rites of birth and, more especially, of naming, in contrast with the personalized soul, which receives most attention in the rites of death and is the subject of most concern after death. This concern is due to the potential danger of the personalized soul to the living, but the *jiv* is life itself: while it can leave the body temporarily in illness or in sleep (dreams are its adventures during the latter), its permanent departure constitutes the death of the physical body and impels the personalized soul on its journey to the ancestors. Yet the *jiv*'s departure *from earth* is only temporary: sooner or later it returns.

Apart from explicit statements by tribal informants concerning reincarnation, there is also the evidence of naming practices, which generally exhibit a preference for naming children after +2 referents (though other referents may be invoked instead). The individual usually has other names and nicknames in addition to his 'real' name, and sometimes not even the latter may, in fact, be inherited. But the 'real' name—whatever its source, and especially if inherited—seems to have a semi-sacred, or at least a private quality. It is rarely used in everyday circumstances, partly to avoid the attention of evil spirits, and partly to avoid the name taboos that might otherwise arise.

There is, of course, a potential contradiction between, on the one hand, belief in the reincarnation of grandparents in their grandchildren, and on the other, the fact that a grandparent may still be alive at the grandchild's birth. This need not, of course, be perceived as a contradiction, for it may be circumvented by referring to mythology or through ritual action or by invoking 'the commonly encountered discrepancy between the event of physical death and the social recognition of it'.[32] Among the Munda, it may lead to the inference that a different relative (one from the +3 level, perhaps, or a +1 collateral) must have been reborn in the child. However, there is frequently uncertainty as to exactly which relative this is, and in order to establish this, some sort of divination has to be carried out. Another indication may be marks on the child's body resembling those borne by a deceased ancestor, and sometimes corpses are marked with vermilion, oil, rice-paste or charcoal in order that their future reincarnations may be recognized. As a last resort, a different sort of name may be chosen, or a nickname applied temporarily. These alternatives may also come into play if there are many children, since there will be occasions where they outnumber the available grandparents. Nonetheless, there is a distinct tendency for individuals to be reborn in their lineal descendants two generations away wherever possible. There seems to be particular concern that this should apply to first-born children, who commonly receive the names of their same-sex father's parent.[33] This preference for agnates over matrilateral kin should occasion no comment in these mainly patrilineally organized societies. Parents are never reincarnated in their own children, however, for fear of fatal consequences for either or both (see next chapter).

There remains the problem of deciding how far, if at all, these ideas concerning reincarnation constitute a *belief*, especially since doubts have been expressed as to whether, and in what circumstances, the concept has any meaning at all (Needham 1972). However, they clearly amount to a *representation* that is closely tied to the social structure at many points. What this means for the Munda and their place in the anthropology of India will be discussed in the final chapter.

Chapter Eleven
Munda Kinship in Context

From all the foregoing data two particular aspects can be isolated as fundamental to Munda social organization. One is the equivalence of alternate generations, which should be seen not as a series of traits linked by a common theme, but as a single idea with a number of possible expressions, namely in some of the equations made by the kinship terminologies; in the contrast between relationships involving joking or familiarity and relationships involving respect or avoidance; in the substitutability of particular kin types in ritual action; in certain ritual representations; in the marriageability or non-marriageability of particular kin types; in the transmission of the name and soul substance of a grandparent in his or her same-sex grandchild; and in the rules delaying the immediate renewal of alliances, which are always of an odd number of generations (whether three as in the north or one as in Koraput).

The other fundamental aspect of Munda societies is the ideology of repeated symmetric affinal alliance, which is expressed in the kinship terminologies as well as in actual alliances to a large degree. The latter are symmetric at least in that there is never a feeling that one should not both give and take wives to and from the same alliance group in the same generation. This symmetry is notable and seems to be maintained even in the north, where alliances are dispersed in such a way that they cannot be renewed between the same exchange groups within the lifetime of an average individual. Although single marriages are, of course, generally unilateral (the reciprocity is far from being always simultaneous), the symmetry may be marked even on these occasions in ritual ways or with prestations.

This symmetry links the two aspects I have isolated, for it is no less apparent chronologically than laterally. The links between alternate generations amount to an expression of equivalence—even an identity—between kin types which allows us to postulate that there are really only two generations recognized in these societies. These generations perpetually revolve around and replace one another, grandchildren being (re)born as grandparents die—a cyclical representation instead of the unending ladder of generations familiar to us in the West. This is by no means unique to the Munda in South Asia, and similar observations regarding this sense of unity have been made for the neighbouring Dravidian-speaking tribes and the Tibeto-Burman-speaking Sherpa of Nepal.[1] In alliance and terminology also, the Munda share much with neighbouring tribes—especially the North and Central Munda with certain North Dravidian and Indo-European-speaking ones, a comparison which can even be extended to Meghalaya (see below, Appendix II). Conversely, the Koraput Munda have close parallels with Central Dravidian tribes.

Yet as Radcliffe-Brown noted long ago,[2] all aspects of alternate generation equivalence are extremely widespread globally, though neither universal nor necessarily appearing together in the same societies. The link between alternate generations on the basis of behaviour—of an easier relationship between grandparents and grandchildren than between adjacent levels, which normally centre on the jural role of a father or other +1 referent—is exceedingly common and has often been noted. Name inheritance from the +2 level to the –2 level is also widespread in all sorts of societies, being found even in European ones and their extensions overseas. In some societies, however, these are just single aspects of a whole complex of parallel ideas which is fundamental to the social structure. In the Munda case, this can readily be appreciated from the fact that the equivalence preserves the cross-parallel distinction as regards marriage and kinship terminology, but preferentially, at least, unites agnates as regards the reincarnation of soul substance and names; the dichotomy in behaviour also reflects marriageability.

This complex is also found outside India, in areas very remote from it. Hocart recorded it in Fiji in 1931. Other examples occur in the Amazon Basin and in Australia. A recent comparative book on the Guiana region of South America (Rivière 1984) delineates a situation very similar to middle India, involving two-line symmetric prescriptive terminologies, many with +2/ego's level/–2 equations; the possibility of marriages between kin in alternate generations; alternate generation divisions based on the 'recycling of names and souls' from grandparents to grandchildren; and a narrowly ordered concept of time. Especially mentioned are the Ye'cuana, Panare and (outside the Guiana region proper) certain

Tukanoan groups, and the Kaxúyana are reported to regard life and death as 'alternating forms of expression'. In connection with the state of Pirá-Paraná, Christine Hugh-Jones writes: 'ideally speaking, each alternate generation consists of the very same names and the very same souls...ideally, one father-son tie is severed by the death of the father just before the son is himself transformed into a father.'

Australia is also famous for alternate generation equations and symmetric prescriptive terminologies (2– and 4–line) and for kinship systems the classic example of which is that of the Kariera, in which the cross-parallel distinction of generation sets results in a fourfold structure with each name being repeated every other generation. Reincarnation is less in evidence here, being reported only from the north and northwest, and its existence even there has provoked controversy (over the Aranda, for example). Nevertheless, the alternation of generations is most apparent as 'an equivalence often expressed during ritual and ceremonial activities'. Among the Walbiri, for example, marriages are allowed (though not necessarily highly thought of) between a male ego and his MFZ or DD, both of whom belong in the same section as MBD. They are also potential wives for his FF and SS, who are themselves equated respectively with his eB and yB. Names have a private quality, and there is name-sharing between the pairs FM and SDws, MF and DSms, and MM and DD, as well as some belief in reincarnation.[3]

Comparisons between India and Australia are nothing new, though they have been criticized in recent years, especially in Dumont's dismissal (1970) of Radcliffe-Brown's attempts to compare Australian and south Indian societies (1953). However, in *central* India circumstances are different, and it is here, if anywhere, that comparisons with Australia are feasible. This relates to Dravidian- and Indo-European-speaking tribes in this area as well as to Munda ones: that is to say, most to some degree base their social organization on this fundamental opposition between two sets of alternating generations. This is shown especially by Grigson's ethnography on the Hill Maria and Elwin's on the Baiga, but it is also evident from other reports on the area, however piecemeal.[4]

This means that, *pace* Bouez, we cannot talk of a distinct 'Munda kinship model': too much is shared by the Munda and their

Dravidian and Indo-European neighbours (alliance, kinship terminology, reincarnation, descent, inheritance, village structure; see
Appendix II); conversely, there are differences of detail within
Munda—especially between Koraput Munda and the rest.[5] But
because of its widespread occurrence, the opposition of generations can hardly be considered the product of cultural influence
through contact between the areas concerned, many of which have
only known contact, if at all, through the agency of European
expansion in the last few centuries. As far as India is concerned it
cannot be the product of Hindu influence either, partly because it
is essentially alien to Hinduism (see further below), and partly
because Hindu influence could not explain such values as they
exist in South America or Australia. Thus the explanation has to be
sought elsewhere, with reference both to a wider humanity and to
the evolution and erosion of these values in some human societies.

Early attempts to explain the opposition—through the affective
feelings that were supposed to exist between grandparents and
grandchildren, or through double descent theory—have long since
been abandoned. Accordingly, when Aberle assembled some of
the relevant terminological data in 1967, he felt compelled to call
the result 'a finding in search of a theory' (1967: 273). However, this
is no longer the situation as regards either the kinship or the
reincarnation aspects of the theme. I will discuss recent theory
regarding each in turn and then attempt to relate them to the
Munda and their situation within India.

Needham has frequently expressed the view that historically the
starting point in the evolution of terminological systems is most
probably represented by those which, in his language, sort jural
statuses into two lines, i.e. those also known as symmetric prescriptive, bifurcate merging or restricted exchange. This is partly because of their lexical economy and internal consistency, and partly
because his studies of actual terminologies and alliance systems
have never suggested to him that it is possible to derive them from
anything else. The progression is always from the simplest to the
more complex, though later stages may vary in the type of their
complexity—they may have more lines, for instance, or show lineal
unity.[6] In fact, the transition from simple to complex is not
sufficient by itself to account for the hypothesis. Cognatic kinship
terminologies are not really more complex than two-line symmetric prescriptive ones, they are just differently constructed; and

at least one common form of classification, that known as 'Hawaiian' or, better, generational, could be said to be simpler still, with a single term for each sex in each level. But the principles used by both are non-prescriptive: one also needs to invoke, therefore, the basic dichotomy between prescriptive and non-prescriptive. Most anthropologists who have dealt at all with the matter would with little hesitation put prescriptive before non-prescriptive in any grand scheme of evolutionary development. The really significant thing about prescriptive two-line terminologies, therefore, is that they are the simplest conceivable attested terminologies within that larger class of terminological systems that itself claims an evolutionary priority.

However, more recent theoretical work by Allen[7] suggests that those symmetric prescriptive terminologies which also equate members of alternate generations are more fundamental still, because they are even simpler—i.e. the number of terms required would be reduced if such equations were made consistently. Indeed, if full classificatory equations were also present and sexual distinctions ignored or relegated to the purely linguistic (e.g. by affixation or inflection for females), then theoretically no more than four terms would be required, distinguishing cross and parallel in each of two levels—one's own (including +2, –2 etc.) and that adjacent to one's own (+1, –1 etc.). The model is given the name tetradic, to indicate its fourfold structure. The author admits that no attested terminology actually has this theoretical minimum, and he locates the model in ethnographic prehistory. Analytically, however, it is a rarification of all the principles associated with symmetric prescriptive terminologies, leading to 'the only *truly* elementary structures'.[8] Not all symmetric prescriptive terminologies have such equations, of course,[9] but this in itself supports the theory that they are very fundamental and also the most unstable type of equation—i.e. they are the first to dissolve under circumstances of change.[10]

The same author has (with others) also drawn attention recently to an earlier attempt to place various concepts of the person in an evolutionary sequence, this being the subject of Marcel Mauss's last major piece of work.[11] In it, Mauss draws a distinction between the concept of the person (i.e. its cultural representation, which has nothing to do with individual perception) which is most usually found in tribal societies (*personnage*), and those which have succeeded it in the great literate civilizations especially. The complex surrounding *personnage* typically consists, in Mauss's view, of a stock of names recycled through the generations; a stock of souls similarly transmitted, the connection between the two being such that they seem almost homologous; and the fact that they commonly, though not invariably, oscillate between members of every second genealogical level. The *personnage* is a role, a representation (of an ancestral line, or of a totem)—hence the possession, masks and dancing which Mauss also mentioned. It has been progressively individualized by civilizations great and small ever since, a process which Mauss represents as evolutionary stages, but which could just as easily be conceived as alternatives.[12] His view of the finitude of names and souls has not proved generally sustainable,[13] and the claim that certain sorts of society lack any concept of the individual has repeatedly been questioned. However, the constituent parts of the complex can certainly be discerned—not necessarily in total—among the Munda and in other parts of India, as well as globally, as we have already seen.

What needs to be stressed in the present context is the perpetuation of souls and names through regeneration; the historical priority of the *personnage* in Mauss's theory; and its logical and often actual association with symmetric prescriptive terminologies and the patterns of affinal alliance these suggest. A similar attempt to set a sequence specifically in relation to reincarnation in India has recently been made by Obeyesekere.[14] He defines the key distinction between tribal reincarnation beliefs and the better-known Hindu, textual doctrine of *karma* as an ethical one, in that in the latter the form of one's future reincarnation depends on the accumulated merit (or lack of it) of one's previous lives. On the other hand, where reincarnation is normally a matter of the inheritance of soul substance from ancestor to descendant it is difficult to envisage merit influencing the process, as it does, of course, with *karma*: if every soul substance has essentially the same fate, regardless of the circumstances of its life, moral concerns are excluded. This ethical neutrality leads Obeyesekere to suggest that the doctrines of rebirth and the transmigration of souls were not original to *karma*, in the sense of being internally generated, but that they had a tribal—or in his own words, 'preliterate'—origin:

The Indian religious philosophers can be credited, not with the inventions of the rebirth theory, but rather with transforming the 'rebirth eschatology' into the 'karmic eschatology', through a process of speculative activity which I label 'ethicization'.

This means, however, that heaven is only a temporary abode, and rebirth back into a world full of suffering negates any sense of it being the reward for a good life. Consequently, the ethicization of reincarnation belief leads logically to the further doctrine of *moksha* or liberation from the endless cycle of rebirths as the goal leading to *nirvana*. Ethicization is thus a phase in 'the course of religious evolution' later than that of reincarnation in the simple sense, i.e. as found in preliterate or tribal societies; it is analogous to Mauss's later 'person' rather than his *personnage*.[15]

The worldwide (though not universal) distribution of these ideas, as well as their reduction to one common underlying theme and the evidence of some historical priority for them and for the social forms they order, all suggest that they are due to fundamental properties of the human mind of the sort much written about by Lévi-Strauss and, more recently, Needham. This further helps to undermine the cultural autonomy of the Munda on the global stage, but again it guarantees their autonomy ultimately from high-status—i.e. Hindu and caste—values within India. The influences produced by the latter are real, but they belong to historical time and are nearer the surface of tribal consciousness. They do not account for all aspects of these societies' values and cannot have stimulated those that go deepest and whose origins are very probably bound up with human prehistory itself. To show this more fully, let us examine the data relating to the rise and development of the karmic doctrine of reincarnation within India against a tribal background.

As it occurs in Munda and other tribal societies in India, reincarnation differs from the Hindu doctrine of *karma* because of the absence of any ethical component. Here, it is the manner of one's death, not the worth of one's life, that is the qualification for rebirth; only those who die inauspiciously (e.g. prior to initiation, or by suicide or witchcraft etc.) may be excluded from reincarnation, and in these cases it is not lack of merit that disqualifies them but ritual imperfection or incompleteness. Moreover, reincarnation is, of course, an object of desire here, not of dread. These facts in themselves suggest that the tribal view is not simply a distortion of the Hindu one. To a certain degree, indeed, one can argue the opposite.

Although it is not possible to trace any actual connection with tribal antecedents along the lines suggested by Obeyesekere, one can trace the origin and development of the doctrines of *karma* and rebirth into this world in the Hindu texts in such a way as to suggest that they most probably developed wholly within India. It seems to be generally agreed that neither doctrine is present in the early Vedas, where even entry into the next world is a matter of correct ritual, not of the worth of one's actions.[16] In fact, both doctrines begin to appear only in the Upanishads. Transmigration of the soul is first recorded in the sixth- or seventh-century BC *Brhadaranyaka Upanishad* (vi, 2) as a Kshatriya-derived theory taught to the Brahmans only subsequently, and the ethical component provided by *karma* first appears as a secret theory in the same text (iii, 2). The doctrine of transmigration is reiterated—this time as a revelation by Yama as the god of death—in the *Katha Upanishad* (I.i, 20–9), and it received general acceptance only from the time of the later Upanishads onwards. There is also a reference in the *Brhadaranyaka Upanishad* to the infinity of the name (iii, 2), a quality found in the tribal version too.[17]

It must be doubted, therefore, that the Indo-European-speaking invaders brought these ideas with them, especially since no other related people is known to have had anything similar (except for the ancient Greek idea of metempsychosis or transmigration).[18] Moreover, they do not appear to have originated in Brahmanical circles. Indeed, it may well be that it was the lower castes that provided them with their route into the Hindu world generally, in view of the other parallels that can be found between tribal and low-caste society in social organization, myth, ritual etc. At all events, the balance of evidence suggests that the karmic doctrine had post-Vedic and non-Indo-European antecedents, and that it most probably originated in the tribal theories of rebirth and the recirculation of souls. From here, these would have entered caste society, probably in part through the common process whereby tribes are known to transform themselves into castes at the bottom of the hierarchy. Subsequently, they would have become the subject of philosophical speculation by Hindu religious thinkers working within them; but the raw material they used was most probably the eschatological beliefs of local tribal communities.

The probability that it is tribal reincarnation that has influenced *karma* rather than the other way round is also strengthened by evidence that, as with kinship, the evolution of these ideas has not been unidirectional or of similar scope, even within India. First of all, there is evidence that the unity of alternate generations is found in some higher-status Indian societies as well as in tribal ones. According to Marten:

> In the Central Provinces [today, Madhya Pradesh], it is generally believed among Hindus that a dead person will be reborn in the same family within three generations. The grandfather dies and the grandson is reborn. [...] If a birth and a death occur simultaneously in a family, transmigration is believed to have taken place.

Fürer-Haimendorf, too, says that: 'Many a Hindu of today believes...that a dead man may be reborn in a grandchild...'. Tiemann, referring to the Jat of Haryana, says: 'A woman regards her life as fulfilled...when she "can see the face of her son's son".' Finally, Sedlar, referring to the Hindu householder of the upper three varnas, remarks: 'Once he had grandchildren, he was regarded as having completed his duty to society; he entered the third stage of life and became a hermit in the forest', that is, the stage preparatory to complete renunciation, which itself involves one's own social death as a prerequisite.[19]

Elsewhere, however, there is an identity between *adjacent* generations, which is quite impossible for the Munda and other tribal societies. Jaini remarks that 'the idea that a man is in some sense identical with his son is well known to Hindu literature', and it is also mentioned in Manu.[20] This perhaps refers above all to his eldest son, who will inherit his authority and control over the family and light his pyre after his death. But sometimes a more direct identity is expressed. Among the Kochhar of the Punjab, for instance, the father is deemed to be reborn in his eldest son, and funeral rites are held for the former in the fifth month of his wife's pregnancy; the couple are then remarried after the birth.[21] Among many upper-caste groups a child's *jiv* is thought to come from the father during sexual intercourse, having returned to earth in the rain, from where it enters the food plants utilized by humans.[22] These examples suggest that reincarnation beliefs among Hindus do not form a unified body of belief, indeed that they are even more diverse than tribal ones (some Hindu groups even deny the doctrine of reincarnation altogether). The latter are on the whole much more coherent, and they certainly cannot be been simply as debased versions of the doctrine of *karma,* nor as dependent upon it in any way.

A similar evolutionary process can be postulated for kinship. The conventional distinction as regards both terminology and alliance is that between north and south India, the former being non-prescriptive in both respects and governed by hypergamy, the latter having prescriptive terminologies and established preferences for particular kin types in marriage, and for isogamy, i.e. equality of status (in terms of the caste hierarchy) between alliance groups. This convention, however, covers only those groups (admittedly the mass of Indian society) which can somehow or other be recognized as castes: it omits tribal groups completely and therefore leaves out some significant variations in kinship systems within the sub-continent.

On the usual evolutionary scale (discussed above), which sets prescriptive kinship systems before non-prescriptive ones, the south Indian kinship model is more likely to have represented the original state of affairs in India than the north Indian one. However, as Trautmann has pointed out in discussing Dravidian kinship (1981), this southern model differs from the Central Dravidian one—and by extension, the middle Indian, tribal one—in that its terminologies lack alternate generation equations. Even though, like Munda, some of these terminologies do not make consistent cognate-affine equations (and Kurukh, in Ranchi, even merges cross cousins with siblings), in respect of the vertical equations they are the closest of all Indian systems of kinship to Allen's fundamental tetradic model. Following this model, we should accord them a historical priority even over those of south India (i.e. the South Dravidian branch plus some similarly constructed Indic terminologies of the region).

In fact, as I argue elsewhere (Parkin 1988a) there is good evidence to suppose that the Central Dravidian terminologies were the Dravidian standard at a time of greater linguistic unity for the language family as a whole; and that the south has lost some of the expressions of alternate generation equivalence, especially in terminology, but also in alliance, for marriage to a classificatory eZD (a –1 relative) is very common and frequently expected (unlike further north, in Munda, Indo-European, and Central and North Dravidian). Nonetheless, the south remains prescriptive. The Munda suggest another line of development, especially as regards the variation between Koraput Munda and North and Central Munda. Of the Munda kinship systems, it is the former that are closest to Central Dravidian in having a greater quantity of fully prescriptive equations (i.e. between cross kin and affines) and marriages between close kin (first or second cross cousins).[23] The Central and North Munda systems (and the local North Dravidian and Indic ones—see Appendix II) are at one remove in breaking the cognate-affine equations and dispersing alliances through a three-generation marriage rule; yet they retain alternate generation equations—in some cases (e.g. the Juang) to a greater extent than Koraput Munda—can still be regarded as prescriptive terminologically, and have marriage rules specifying particular kin types and/or long-term continuity in the formation of alliances. However, the former are crucial steps along the road to a non-prescriptive system. Given the establishment already of the dispersal of alliances to avoid close kin, to remove prescription one only needs the abandonment of any sense of obligation to renew alliances after the lapse of the required number of generations, together with terminological adjustments breaching the symmetric equations that unite parallel kin types in one term and cross kin types in another. Add to this a status inequality between wife-givers and wife-takers to ensure that no direct exchange is possible, even in a later generation, and you have in its essentials the north Indian kinship system.[24]

This means, of course, that as with reincarnation, so with kinship, the prescriptive systems of India cannot be derived from the high-caste ideology, even though it has clearly modified them. Dumont, of course, tried to distinguish north from south Indian kinship through the different influences that caste has exercised on them.[25] Perhaps the difference is also (or instead) an example of a more worldwide (though again not universal) tendency for prescriptive systems to move towards the non-prescriptive (e.g. China, Sumba[26]). Much more work (especially fieldwork) would be needed to establish this firmly in India, but the Munda provide in many ways the best material and opportunity for doing so, since they combine undoubtedly prescriptive kinship systems with some that have begun to move away from that model and yet others (the Munda-speaking low castes) which have evidently passed that barrier altogether. The problem can thus be studied within one group of peoples who, since they are linguistically related, are likely to have been more unified at one stage and thus to have shared much of their history and culture together.

Appendix I
The Nihal

The Nihal were introduced at the end of Chapter 2 as a group of interest to Munda scholarship because of the possibility that their language is related in some way to Munda, though perhaps only co-ordinate with it within AA. This question has yet to be resolved, but this short appendix aims to recognize their potential significance for Munda studies generally by discussing the little ethnography available on them, especially that relating to kinship.

Groups called Nihal are found on the borders of Maharashtra and southwestern Madhya Pradesh, especially in the Kandesh, Nimar, Buldana, Berar and Amravati districts, and, according to Fuchs, even as far away as the northwestern parts of Madhya Pradesh. Hermanns lists a number of sub-groups named after areas (Nahar, Towä, Bhilapur, Taor and Nimari) who can all intermarry and interdine. Conversely, de Candolle divides them into three endogamous sections (Balahi Nihal, Pahari or Dukhia Nihal and Rhagwansi Nihal, in order of increasing status), though many seek to pass as Korku. They claim originally to have been one group with the latter, having been outcasted because they do not preserve Hindu food taboos like the Korku. The Korku deny this, however, and say that the Nihal have always been separate from and inferior to them. They accordingly require them to stay in separate hamlets, outside Korku villages, under their own *jat patel* or caste headmen; they rarely become village headmen themselves, because of their low status. There is little interdining or intermarriage with the Korku, though unmarried Korku may take cooked food from a Nihal. There is also reported to be some marriage between Korku men and Nihal women in Melghat, which leads to outcasting today, though in the past the children of such unions were admitted as Korku. This, in fact, has been one mechanism of the assimilation of Nihal to Korku and of the former's consequent decline.

The other local groups rank the Nihal below the Bhilala, Bhil and Korku in the local caste hierarchy and above the Balahi, though they themselves regard the Bhil as well as the Balahi as their inferiors. Depending on area, they have a number of caste-like occupations: herdsmen, field and village watchmen, woodcutters, farm labourers, only occasionally being farmers or landowners in their own right; they also hunt and fish. They were often employed as soldiers by local rulers in the past, and some apparently continue the criminal activities which made them notorious in these times. In the west they have a reputation as 'gifted magicians'. It may have been their criminality that led to their massacre by Sindia's soldiers early in the nineteenth century, and it is only since then that they have been in a position of subordination to the Korku, for whom a number are village watchmen and whose language has strongly influenced their own. Nihal is the standard designation in the literature; it may be connected with *nahar* 'tiger, lion'. They call themselves Kalto.[1]

Comparatively few of those classed as Nihal actually speak the language of that name, only 1196 being cited in the 1951 Census and 1167 in the 1961 Census (689 in Maharashtra and 478 in Madhya Pradesh; Stampe says less than 2,000). The rest use either Marathi or the Nimari dialect of Hindi or Korku instead. 'All Nihals except children are bilingual in at least one of these neighbor languages, and it is possible to classify Nihali dialects in terms of Hindi, Marathi, or Korku mixture', though 'there is no tendency to lay aside Nihali in favor of the neighbor languages', presumably because of its value as an argot, whatever its origin (see Ch. 2). According to Stampe, Nihal speakers are found in Buldana district, Maharashtra and East Nimar district, Madhya Pradesh. A slightly earlier source indicates speakers further west, between Sandwa, Khargon and Bikangaon (Madhya Pradesh), though there is now some doubt over this—in a footnote, Stampe states that his data, which came from Aasha Mundlay, the most recent researcher among the Nihal, should supersede all previous statements on their location. The 'purest' Nihal is said to be that of the village of Teli, 25 miles (40 km) east of Burhanpur and just northwest of the Gawilgarh Hills.[2]

In comparing the Nihal with the Munda, it will be as well to start with their kinship terminology. The chief source for this is Kuiper, who collected together all the previously published data on the language in a long article published in 1962. I have unfortunately not seen more recent material (especially by Mundlay, which remains unpublished), which would almost certainly be able to fill some of the remaining gaps. Nonetheless, the data we do have is of sufficient interest to discuss here (see Table 3).

Table 3. *Nihal Kinship Terms*

(§ = Indic loan)

+1 level

aba, ba, eba, a	F	
baba§	FeB, FZH	
ay; may (ayrere)	M	not IE (Kuiper 1962: 298); Ku?
bhaga may§	MeZ, FeBW	
mavsi§	MyZ	
kaki§	FyBW	
kaka§	FyB, MyZH, FZH	
mama§	MB, FyZH	
mami§	MBW	
dukri may§	FZ	
phuphu§	FyZ	
birtom	EF	–*om* may be an affinal suffix, of unknown origin (but cf. Ho *hapanum* 'bride'); cf. ego's level and –1
napyom	EM	

Ego's level

basi-gita	B	see below for *gita*
bommoki	B (plural?)	cf. Ku *bumbuki, bumbaku,* Mu etc. *boko* yB
(bhaga§) day, dada	eB	connected with *dado*? All from or via Ku
sunu (§?)	yB	cf. Indic *sana* etc. 'small'; Sk *sunu* S
bai (§?)	Z, eZ	cf. Indic *bhai* B; present in Bhil also
gita	yG, WyBW	cf. Sa *gida, gadar* 'little children' or Ku *ganda* 'boy'
kalatell	WeB, WeBW (dual?)	origin unknown
birtom	WeZ, HeB, HeBW	origin unknown; cf. +1 level, EF, –1, WBS
napyom	HeZ, WeBW	origin unknown; cf. +1 level, EM
ilur	HyB	cf. Munda *ilil* etc.
aji (§?)	HyZ	possibly Munda
karyom	eBW	origin unknown; –*om* possibly affinal
ovari	yBW	origin unknown; connected with Indic *bahu* etc.? Also in –1 level
teya	WG	cf. Munda *tenya* etc.
atho	H	origin unknown; cf. Ku *dhotha*
kol	W	origin unknown; cf. Kui *kola* 'bride', Kharia *konsel,* Mu etc. *kuri*

−1 level

palco, palcu, palicho (§?)	S	
beta§	S	
lana§	S (plural?)	cf. Hi *landa* 'boy'; also Kw *lani* (not in Ku)
bacura?§ bac(h)e-gita §	youngest son	cf. Hi *bacca*. see under yG for *gita*
pirju, perijo	D	origin unknown; not from Ku
bakari §, lanna§	C	cf. above, *bacura, lana*
dai-na palcu-re (§?)	eBS	
bhanja§	ZS	
ovari	SW	cf. ego's level, yBW
birtom	WBS	cf. ego's level and +1

No terms have been recorded for the +2 and −2 levels or any remoter ones, so we can consider only the three medial levels; there are similarities in detail with Munda throughout (see Ch. 7). The +1 level contains mainly Indic loans, but a number of them link PG(E) specifications in the manner of an ideal symmetric prescriptive terminology, i.e. *bhaga may* MeZ, FeBW, *kaka* FyB, MyZH (but also FZH) and *mama* MB, FyZH. However, there are no equations involving MyZ, FyBW, FZ or MBW, all of which have separate terms. No term is recorded for MeZH, while FeB shares *baba* with FZH, a synonym of *kaka* in the latter sense. As with Munda, the principle of relative age applies more to PssG(E) than to PosG(E). Terms for EP are independent (*birtom* EF, *napyom* EM) and are apparently indigenous rather than loans; they also cover certain specifications in other levels, namely HeB, HeBW, WeZ and WBS (*birtom*) and HeZ and WeBW (*napyom*), thus resembling Munda.

In the −1 level there is less evidence of prescription, but there is a lineal equation with *palcu* S, eBS. ZS is *bhanja*, as in Munda a separate and Indic term which may have replaced an indigenous term once applied to DH also. No term for the latter specification is recorded in Nihal, but *ovari*, probably of indigenous origin, links SW and yBW. Ego's level lacks concrete evidence of symmetric prescriptive equations, there apparently being no separate term for any category of cousin, though since no term for the latter is actually recorded we cannot tell whether siblings and cousins have the same terms. The principle of relative age pervades this level to an even greater extent than the +1 and −1 levels. In all these respects the Nihal terminology strongly resembles Munda, though this may reflect the close association with the influence of Korku or general areal characteristics rather than membership of the Munda language sub-family as such.

Though this information is patchy enough, we have even less in the way of relevant ethnography.[3] There is no cross-cousin marriage,[4] and marriages into one's mother's clan are also prohibited. As we saw in section 8.4, this amounts to a ban on the repetition of one's father's marriage. Whether this means that the normal rule of alliance specifies a GEG category cannot be determined, though there is some evidence that this may be true of the neighbouring Korku (sect. 8.4). The terminology also tends to support such an interpretation, at least to the extent that EP terms are separate from those for +1 cross kin, indicating that the latter never become affines because ego never repeats the marriages of his +1 agnates. The ban mentioned by de Candolle on marriage or sexual relations with one's BW may actually refer to yBW, as is common in central India: it is certainly regarded as serious, since expulsion is the penalty. Most marriages are by choice and by brideprice or service, though de Candolle mentioned one case of 'husband purchase', from the Dhertelai area. The amount of brideprice is usually decided by the panch or village headman; the latter must also approve the match itself. The marriage ornaments may be inherited (from the bride's mother, presumably) or purchased with money provided by the youth's family. Adultery is punishable by fines or banishment. Divorce is simple, but needs the panch's consent. Polygyny is allowed up to six wives, though this must very largely be a purely nominal figure.

There are the usual totemic, patrilineal, exogamous clans; many of the totems are of trees, not animals, plant totems being generally common in this region.[5] The eldest son succeeds to his father's jural role but has no particular advantage in the inheritance of property. Daughters may inherit marriage ornaments and their future wedding expenses if still unmarried, but their receiving any inheritance, and the amount of it, depends on their father's discretion. Possibly there is no name inheritance here, for names are chosen by the Brahman, who also selects the most auspicious day for weddings and officiates at them and at funerals. Little, therefore, seems to distinguish the Nihal dramatically from the Korku and other Munda as regards social organization.

Appendix II

Alliance and Kinship Terminology of the Oraon, Mal Pahariya, Maler, Bhuiya, Hill Kharia and Khasi

The main features described in sect. 8.4 for most North Munda groups are not confined to the Munda, but are also found among certain of their Dravidian- and Indic-speaking neighbours and among the sole Mon-Khmer-speaking group in the Republic of India, the Khasi. This appendix presents brief notes on the situation concerning affinal alliance and terminology in each of these groups.

The Kurukh (Oraon to outsiders) are found in Chotanagpur, in close proximity to the Mundari, and in Bengal. They have come under considerable Mundari influence in both religious matters and social organization. Some even speak Mundari rather than their own Dravidian language, and the Kurukh kinship terminology shares with many Munda ones the incorporation of the possessive personal pronoun in the kin term, though by prefixation rather than suffixation as in Munda. The terminological pattern itself resembles Central Dravidian rather than North Munda in the complete separation of adjacent levels and in having more completely prescriptive +1 equations (MB = EF, FZ = EM etc.); but there are no separate terms for PGC, cross or parallel, and there are some equations between alternating levels (+3, +1 and –1). The system of alliance strongly resembles that of the Mundari, with *gotra* exogamy, four-*gotra* marriage circles, no marriage to first cross cousins and ideally no renewal of alliances within the ensuing three generations, but in practice the delay lasts as long as mutual visiting is kept up (cf. the Mundari). There is also some direct and presumably non-repeatable exchange of women.[1]

The closely related Maler are found further north, in the Rajmahal Hills, Santal Parganas, and number some 53,000. They are known as Sauria or Pahariya by outsiders, though the latter is also used of other local groups. Descent, succession and inheritance are all patrilineal. There are lineages, called *byare*, with some ritual unity, but the exogamous, totemic clans found elsewhere in the

area are absent. 'Marriage is permissible where no blood relationship can be traced.' There is no cross-cousin marriage, and marriage partners 'should not be related to each other up to three
generations on both father's and mother's sides'. However, it is not
clear what is the focus of alliance: it can hardly be the village, since
there is no rule of village exogamy. Verma hints at a preference for
the mother's side in the fourth generation, but he is not very clear.
Although Malto is a Dravidian language closely related to Kurukh,
the terminology has only slight vestiges of a 'Dravidian' typology,
exclusively in the +1 level. Thus there are symmetric prescriptive
equations involving PssG(E), but MB ≠ FZH, and some PosG(E)
terms are merged with PssG(E) ones.[2] The full consanguineal
pattern in +1 is as follows:

pipo	FeB, MeZH; FeZH in some dialects
dada	FyB, MyZH, FyZH; FeZH in some dialects
peni	MeZ, FeBW
kale	MyZ, FyBW; FyZ in some dialects
pinso	FeZH
bnarha	FeZH
moma	MB
momi	MBW
chacho	FeZ; FyZ in some dialects

The neighbouring Malpahariya are largely Bengali speakers
(though some speak Malto) and number some 40,000. They and the
10,000 Kumarbhag resemble the Malto closely in marriage rules
and kinship terminology, with no clans or cross-cousin marriage
and marriage only beyond the fourth generation.[3] The pattern of
their cognatic +1 terminology is as follows:

jetha	FeB, MeZH, FeZH
kaka	FyB, MyZH
jethi	MeZ, FeBW, FeZ
kaki	FyBW
mosi	MyZ
mosa	MyZH
mama	MB
mami	MBW
pisi	FyZ
pisa	FyZH

Thus Sarkar's data on the Malpahariya closely resembles Vidyarthi's on the Malto and suggests that, *pace* Trautmann, an unusual equation in the latter's data (*dada* FyB, FyZH) was not simply an error.[4] Both terminologies preserve symmetric prescriptive equations for parallel kin while separating and to some extent isolating MB and MBW (FZ and FZH tend to be merged with parallel kin). However, this does not signal the emergence of a three-line prescriptive system so much as suggest transition from symmetric prescriptive to standard North Indian (cf. Parkin 1990).

The Hill Bhuiya are an Oriya-speaking group found in Keonjhar and living in close proximity to the Juang, with whom they share a number of features and have a common mythological origin (see Ch. 2). The focus in choosing alliance partners is the village, there being a distinction between *kutumb* ('same blood', hence forbidden in marriage) and *bandhu* (marriageable) villages; such clan names as do occur among these groups have little or no exogamic significance. However, there is apparently no rule of delay here. 'The children of two sisters may...intermarry, provided one party belongs to a Kutumb group and the other to a Bandhu group', and cross-cousin marriage is allowed, as is BWZ marriage (cf. the Juang, sect. 8.4). According to Roy, the plains Bhuiyas do not recognize the *kutumb-bandhu* distinction but allow both cross-cousin marriage and MZD marriage, only agnates being banned. Bouez, by contrast, rules out cross-cousin marriage here but confirms that it takes place in the hills. In Seraikella too, 'the Hinduized Bhuiyas...regularly practise cross-cousin marriage' (apparently just MBD marriage). Like Kurukh, the Hill Bhuiya terminology given by Roy has alternating generation equations (in +3, +1, –1; and +2, ego's level) and the rigorous separation between adjacent generations that is characteristic of the Central Dravidian terminologies. There is a similar group in Mayurbhanj, who are called Bhumij but speak Oriya. They disapprove of cross-cousin marriage (though it does occur) and prohibit marriage within one's mother's clan within three degrees, or even five 'if the relationship between the families is still maintained'; thus there is a rule of delay in renewing alliances.[5]

Also in Mayurbhanj and surrounding areas are the Oriya- and Bengali-speaking Hill Kharia, who must be distinguished from the Munda-speaking Kharia further north (see Ch. 2). In some of these areas they have no clan systems, and in others clan names are ill known and have little or no exogamic significance. According to Roy: 'the Mayurbhanj Kharia may marry in his own village, in his own *gotra* or clan, in his own *padit* [i.e. family surname] and his own *sangya* [totemic clan name]', the only prohibition being 'marriage between near kin'. However, Hari Mohan mentions a ban on relations up to the third generation, and Sinha says that the lineages of FZ, MZ, MB and FMB are avoided in marriage. Here too, the mechanism concerning alliance focuses on the village, not the clan. Villages and families are divided into *kutumb* (here, marriageable) and *bhayad* (tabooed, agnatic) groups for purposes of both marriage and commensality. 'The only restriction to marriage is that a Kharia must not marry in a family with whom *no* previous relationship by marriage either of his own or of some related family (*Bandhu-basia*) can be traced, nor in a family very closely related' (my emphasis)—i.e. alliances should be renewed eventually. Roy and Roy speculate on the presence of cross-cousin marriage in the past and say that it is still allowed, though 'now very close relatives of the class are generally avoided'. MZD marriage is allowed if there is no agnatic relationship but is very rare. These seem to be classificatory specifications, at least in part (see p. 125, where mother's cousin's daughter's marriage is mentioned). Only agnates and 'true cross cousins' are firmly banned. Although traditions of common descent are maintained, a common totem and common village are generally considered to be evidence of consanguineal relationship. Consequently, especially in the Mayurbhanj Hills, 'Kharias generally do not marry in the same village or settlement, though it is not now forbidden, as such, by customary law'. Today, there is some marriage by exchange as well as some cross-cousin marriage.[6]

The Khasi are located in Meghalaya, some distance from the main Munda concentrations. Their Mon-Khmer language is connected with Munda through Austroasiatic, but they differ from the Munda in having matrilineal succession and inheritance (bilateral among the War sub-group) and matrilineal exogamous descent groups, called *kur*. However, their affinal alliance resembles that of some North Munda groups. There are no preferences for particular clans in marriage, and marriage between cousins generally seems to be disliked, though it is allowed under certain circumstances. Unfortunately, ethnographers mostly fail to agree on what these circumstances are, though this may to some extent reflect differences between the several sub-tribes into which the Khasi are divided. Thus the War Khasi appear to ban MBD marriage entirely, though it may take place according to a recent study by Das Gupta, who contradicts earlier authors explicitly here. The Lyngngam, who trace their origins partly to the neighbouring Tibeto-Burman-speaking Garo, do not recognize it as fully legitimate. Many writers point to a rule of delay in arranging marriages with either MBD or FZD. According to some, this cannot take place in the lifetimes of the fathers of the girl and the youth respectively; otherwise these ascendants might die.[7] In fact, according to Chattopadhyay there can be no marriage by a girl to her MBS even after her MB has died, because of his status in the household in this matrilineal society, though this does not apply to FZS, since FZ lives elsewhere. This is supported by Das Gupta's more recent work, according to which the transfer of women should be unilateral (i.e. there is MBD marriage only). It is also suggested by the fact that sister exchange is banned or at least discouraged, as well as by the ban on FZD marriage, though the latter may not be significant in this respect in view of the rarity of first cousin marriages here. Most of these statements actually seem to apply to first cousins only. The War Khasi allow FFBDD, FFZDD and MMBDD as spouses, as well as cousins in the third etc. descending generations from two brothers. Parallel cousins and +1 referents are generally banned, however. According to Hodson and Natarajan, marriage with anyone related to one's father within three generations is banned. Instead, it would seem that certain GEG categories are marriageable. Nakane mentions GEZ marriages, though she also states that 'there is no structural continuity'. However, this statement may apply to the immediately following generation and neglect the possibility of renewal in the long term. Khasi kinship terminologies are symmetric prescriptive in the +1 and −1 levels, and to a greater degree than Munda in some dialects, with PosG(E) = EP and FBW = MZ equations and the pattern C = ssGC ≠ osGC = CE. Ego's level is more generational, not only cross and parallel cousins but also siblings-in-law sharing terms with siblings in most dialects, affinal specifications normally being suffixed only. However, War has a separate term (*kynum*) for MBS, FZS, ZH and WB. There is complete generational separation throughout.[8] More work should clearly be directed at Khasi affinal alliance in the light of these considerations.

The mountainous fringes to the north of the Indian sub-continent may eventually prove to have systems similar to those of the North and Central Munda. Although little comparative work has as yet been published on the kinship of the Tibeto-Burman speakers of the region, Toffin avers that 'similar combinations of north Indian and "Iroquois" elements also exist in the Himalayas and the Chittagong Hills', e.g. among the Kulunge Rai.[9] Further west, in the Karakorum, the symmetric prescriptive terminologies of the Indic language Shina and the isolate Burushaski also have striking resemblances with North and Central Munda, especially in the absence of cross-affine equations and the generational pattern of ego's level, though we know next to nothing about affinal alliance in this area.[10]

Notes

Notes to Chapter One

1   In addition, there is the Tai language Khamti and its purely ritual relative Ahom in Assam and one language of uncertain affiliation, Nahali or Kalto in western Madhya Pradesh; the latter may, however, eventually prove to be related to Munda (see Ch. 2 and Appendix I).

2   In the case of Dravidian, this is limited to just one language, Brahui, spoken in the Kalat area of Baluchistan, in Pakistan.

3   Largely thanks to Sten Konow, *contra* F. Hahn on the Dravidian theory and V. Thomsen and G. von der Gabelentz on the Australian theory. See *LSI* IV: 2ff., 15ff.

4   E.g. 1959, 1960, 1963, 1966.

5   See the references in Pinnow 1963: 140; also Bhattacharya 1970b.

6   Critics have included Sebeok 1942, Kuiper 1948, and Emeneau 1954. Schmidt's exclusion of Vietnamese and inclusion of the Austronesian Chamic languages of south-central Vietnam are now recognized to be wrong. Also, his 'Malacca' (now Aslian) languages are generally considered to form a separate branch of AA, co-ordinate, like Nicobarese, with Munda and Mon-Khmer. See Diffloth 1974 for the best recent account.

7   E.g. Kinnauri, Dhimal, Limbu, Bahing, Rong (Przyluski 1924: 399; see also the brief account in Kuiper 1966: 63ff.).

8   Maspero 1948. The 'Austroasiatic' examples he cites are in fact from two Austronesian languages, Malay and Cham.

9   E.g. Nigam 1971.

10   Schmidt 1906; Benedict 1942, 1966–7, 1976.

11   E.g. Heine-Geldern 1928, 1932; Fürer-Haimendorf 1943b, 1945a.

12   Roy 1912: 49–50; 1935b: 220–1.

13   E.g. Shafer 1954; Karvé 1965; Roy 1912.

14   Bouez 1985; Parkin 1984: sect. 5.2.

15   See, for example, Culshaw 1949: 16.

16   See Dumont 1959: 66–7: 'outwardly the Saoras [*sic*] maintain their autonomy, and consequently have not submitted to the intricacies of pure and impure, while inwardly they admit the prestige of their neighbours' (ibid.: 74).

17   See Das and Uberoi 1971: 36–7, 38–9.

18   1957: 9, original emphasis; ibid.: 8. The part about tribes having lost contact was soon dropped (1959: 60), and later still we are told that the second remark should have been attributed 'to Marcel Mauss speaking in his idiosyncratic fashion' (1962b: 121 n.3).

19   A good example is his essay 'The Conception of Kingship in Ancient India' (1962a).

20   Godelier 1973: 93; Bouez 1985: 15; also Orans 1960: 20.

21   Cf. Bailey 1959: 98–9. Dumont's actual demonstrations of his model consist essentially, of course, of structuralist analyses of caste society, so to suggest he is being diffusionist here may seem bizarre. I mean only that as far as the tribes are concerned this is the logical implication of his initial, programmatic model: he made no subsequent analytical attempt to show how they were actually integrated into the caste system, so we are not able to assess how his structuralism would have coped with them in practice. Dumont certainly accepts the fact of cultural borrowing and the diversity associated with it (e.g. 1957: 9, 15, 20–1), but he prefers to stress the way these influences have been incorporated by Indians themselves—a by no means negligible consideration in itself, but not one at issue in the present argument.

22   See, for example, Dumont 1966b, 187ff.

23   Cf. Dumont 1971: 76 n.42.

24   1985: 19ff.

25   For example, Dalton 1872, Risley 1891, and Russell and Hira Lal 1916.

26   See Ponette 1978: Foreword and p.14.

27   1955: 50.

28   Cf. Dumont's review article (1959) of Elwin 1955.

Notes to Chapter Two

1   Standing 1976: 275; Przyluski 1930: 199; cf. Tedesco 1943: 16 n.71; 1945: 82–3; also Thieme-Breslau 1939: 135, 136.

2   It is nonetheless recorded once as an ethnonym (Roy 1912: 359n.).

3   E.g. Oriya *kolho* means 'hypocrite' (Bouez 1985: 39, 212 n.2).

4   Roy 1912: 358.

5   After Zide and Zide 1976: 1298.

6   Zide and Stampe 1968: 377 n.15). Bhattacharya's alternative suggestion (1975: 100–1), that Sora and Gorum (North Koraput) be linked with Central Munda rather than South Koraput, does not seem to have prevailed.

7   It was originally intended to use only the proper ethnonyms, i.e. the names used by the people themselves, but it was realized that this would create problems, since many of them are very similar, even identical, especially in North Munda groups.

8   Indic languages are those Indo-European languages spoken in India, which form just one part of the Indo-Aryan branch of the language family.

9   Karvé 1965: 315.

10   Pinnow 1966: 181–2; Ali 1973: 41; Stampe 1966: 76; Karvé ibid.; Roy 1912: 75; Hermanns 1966: 55; Fuchs 1988: 24.

11   Sahay 1977: 11; cf. Ali ibid.; Hermanns ibid.

12   Quotation from Stampe ibid.; also Ali 1973: 42–3; Vidyarthi and Rai 1977: 161; Dixit 1966: 5; Hermanns ibid.; Fuchs ibid.: 25–7.

13   Konow 1908: 70.

14   Stampe 1966: 78; Pinnow 1966: 81; Leuva 1963: 22; Grierson in *LSI* IV: 128, 137.

15 Only the Gond and Bhil are more numerous (*pace* Deliège 1981: 118, who considers the Bhil only the third largest tribe in India), and neither of these seems to be regarded, or to regard themselves, as quite so unified as the Santal (see especially Deliège 1980 and 1981 on the diversity of the various groups called 'Bhil').

16 Bouez 1985: 8, 81–2; Datta-Majumdar 1956: 23; McDougall 1977: 301; Gautam 1977a: 242.

17 The Damodar is called Nai or 'river' by the Santal, to distinguish it from *gada* or ordinary rivers (Culshaw 1949: 3–4, 155).

18 Datta-Majumdar 1956: 19; Mahapatra 1977: 358; Bouez 1985: 82.

19 Gautam 1977b: 369; Datta-Majumdar 1956: 30; Gausdal 1960: 12; Bista 1972.

20 Datta-Majumdar 1956: 33–4.

21 Bahadur 1977: 27; Vidyarthi 1964: 20; Roychoudhury 1963: 32; Prasad 1961: 143–4; Fuchs 1973: 170–1; Sengupta 1970: 4–8; Chakraborty and Kundu 1980: 87; *LSI* IV: 32. Mahali is also the name of a Birhor clan (Roy 1925: 92).

22 Prasad 1961: 198–9; *LSI* ibid.

23 Mahapatra 1980: 28.

24 Quotation from Gautam 1977b: 372; also Troisi 1979: 24; Gausdal 1953: 3; Prasad 1974: 13; Bouez 1985: 81.

25 'Santal' is certainly better established in the academic literature. Although the Mundari also call themselves *hor*, they are clearly distinct from the Santal; the latter consider the Mundari to be inferior and 'as more "savage" than themselves', partly because of differing ritual attitudes (see Carrin-Bouez 1986: 100).

26 Fuchs 1973: 172; Roy and Roy 1937: 163; Gausdal 1953: 52; Campbell 1953: 507; Bodding 1935b: 257; cf. *munda* as used by the Mundari (above).

27 Bhowmik 1980: 52; cf. 'Kherwarian', above.

28 Sachchidananda 1979: 77; it is pronounced *mura* is Manbhum (Sinha 1962: 63).

29 Roy 1912: 61, 66ff., 123–7, 134, 175–9, 227ff., 290ff.; *LSI* IV: 79.

30 Quotation from Standing 1981: 221. Also Stampe 1966: 78; Cook 1965: 4; Kuiper 1965: 54–5; *Encyc. Mund.*: 1763, 2911.

31 Bouez 1985: 43; Sachchidananda 1979: 77; Choudhury 1977: 22, 25. Khangar is also the name of a Birhor clan (Roy 1925: 91).

32 On Hoffmann, see Ponette 1978: Foreword and p.14. Choudhury is often out of step with other writers on this group on points of detail. Sugiyama's book was subjected to a scathing review by Jordan-Horstmann (1972), the main burden of which was that it did nothing to supersede Roy's work of fifty years earlier.

33 Chatterjee and Das 1927: 1; Stampe 1966: 79; Majumdar 1950: 1; Pfeffer 1982a: 31, 79; 1983: 91; Stampe 1966: 80; Roy 1912: 127–30; Chattopadhyay 1964: 13; Majumdar 1950: 4–6, 9–11; *Encyc. Mund.*: 1763.

34 Mazumdar 1927: 42; Gautam 1977a: 31; Roy 1935a: 3; Prasad 1962a: 72.

35 1939: 2–3, 53. On Bhumij distribution generally, see Roy 1935a: 1–2, 37; Das Gupta 1966: 95; Sinha 1957: 23; 1958a: 23; 1962: 37–8; Ray Chowdhury 1929: 96–7; Sahu 1942: 104: Das 1931a: 46ff.

36 Nigam and Dasgupta 1964: 188, 195; Das 1931a: 46–9; Das Gupta 1966: 95; Sinha *et al.* 1969: 134. In 1931, Das stated that only slightly over a third of all Bhumij spoke the language of the name (37.37%). These were mostly in the parts of Bihar and Orissa mentioned above (1931a: 51).

37 Das 1931a: 24n.; Ray Chowdhury 1929: 99; Sahu 1942: 101; Mandelbaum 1970: 603. 'Bada' and 'Sano' are also found among the Gadaba (16, below).

38 In the former group, Martel 1979: 106; Roy 1925: 60–1; Pinnow 1966: 181–2; Bose 1971: 33; in the latter group, Stampe 1966: 79 and Grierson (*LSI* IV: 80, 102).

39 Standing 1976: 281; Stampe ibid.; Martel ibid.; Leuva 1963: 3; Adhikary 1984: 17.

40 Sen 1955: 113; Stampe 1966: 79; Bouez 1985: 8; Adhikary ibid.

41 Chakraborty 1978: 30–1: 1979: 5–6; Roy 1925: 43ff.; Sen 1965: 47.

42 Ali 1973: 66; Singh 1977a: 38; Singh and Danda 1986: 1–2.

43 Stampe 1966: 80; Leuva 1963: 23; Rizbi 1977: 47; Vidyarthi in Sandhwar 1978: 10, 20; Hari Mohan 1979: 79–80; Singh 1977a: 39; Singh and Danda 1986: 2–3.

44 Rizbi ibid.; Singh and Danda 1986: 19 n.3.

45 Gupta 1964: 132; Rizbi ibid.; Sandhwar 1978: 18, 28; Rosner 1967: 218–19. In Palamau, however, there are seven endogamous Korwa sections (Gupta ibid.), their names varying from informant to informant. Sandhwar gives two separate lists: Dhari, Sinduria, Paharia or Birjhia, Koraku, Agaria, Kharia or Tisia, Guywing; and Dhari, Sinduria, Paharia, Tisia, Birjhia, Sinduria, Mandiyar (1978: 35). Deogaonkar lists the Dih, Pahari, Agaria and Dand in Madhya Pradesh (1986: 13).

46 Leuva 1963: 1; Jain 1958: 27; Elwin 1942: xxvii, 58ff.; Bhattacharyya 1953a: 13.

47 Leuva 1963; 3 and Ch. 1; Roy 1926.

48 Roy 1926: 149; Bhattacharyya 1953a: 1; Leuva 1963: 2; Das Gupta 1978: 26–8, 67; Elwin ibid.

49 Elwin 1942: 64–5; Das Gupta 1978: 27, 66–7; Roy 1926: 148; Jain 1958: 31, 33; Prasad 1962b: 105; Icke-Schwalbe 1983a: 31–2 n.2.

50 1963: 21ff., 70ff.

51 Quotation from Das *et al.* 1966: 105; also Fuchs 1973: 172.

52 Pfeffer 1983: 91. Bouez points out that tribes are usually regarded as of higher status than low castes even by high castes in this area (1985: 30).

53 Jordan-Horstmann 1972b: 565; Rosner 1956: 44.

54 Das 1964: 20–1; Roy 1915: 10; Ghosh 1966: 81.

55 Datta 1933: 107.

56 Quotation from Roy and Roy 1937: 14; also ibid.: 1–7; Vidyarthi and Upadhyay 1980: 6–7, 11–12.

57 Roy and Roy 1937: 29–36; Roy 1935b: 220–1, 225; Vidyarthi and Upadhyay 1980: 7; according to the latter, *dudh* also refers to an earth support for a cooking pot. 'Kharia' itself also refers to a Korwa endogamous group (Sandhwar 1978: 35), a Scheduled Caste in Tripura (Vidyarthi and Upadhyay ibid.) and a Birhor clan (Roy 1925: 91), and in lower Midnapore it is a vulgar word for Muslims (Bhowmik 1980: 53).

58 Vidyarthi and Upadhyay 1980: 9; Dasgupta 1978a: 91, 94–6. The word 'Thar' denotes any tribal dialect of Bengali in Manbhum.

59 Quotation from Roy 1935b: 223; also Roy and Roy 1937: 10, 31, 38; Pfeffer 1983: 91.

60 Stampe 1966: 74; Roy and Roy 1937: 18, 19; Vidyarthi and Upadhyay 1980: 10.

61 On the first derivation, see Dasgupta 1978a: 94; on the second, Roy and Roy 1937: 25; Sahay 1977: 11, 13.

62 See Roy and Roy 1937: 24–5; Bhowmik 1980: 52, 54–5. Although 'bird' is *konter* in Kharia today, the latter suggests that this is derived from **kher*, through *k(h)enter*.

63 Vidyarthi and Upadhyay 1980: 12–14.

64 Ibid.: 11, 19; Das 1931b: Preface and p.19.

65 Stampe 1966: 75.

66 Cf. Birhor *thania* 'settled' (above, 6).

67 Bose 1929: 51–3; Elwin 1948: 16, 23–4; McDougal 1963a: 4, 6.

68 McDougal 1963a: 5, 6, 328. Gonasika means literally 'nostrils of the bull', a reference to a passage in the Juang origin myth (ibid.: 328 and n. 1).

69 Elwin 1948: 7 n.1; Dasgupta 1978b: 1 n.1; Bose 1929: 50; Voegelin and Voegelin 1966: 21.

70 McDougal 1963a: 5; Patnaik 1964: 23, 26–7; Dasgupta 1978b: 69, 73.

71 McDougal 1963a: 6, 12–14; Elwin 1948: 42.

72 Elwin 1955: xx. 'This "V" is a Telugu intrusion' (Yeatts 1931: 286).

73 Grignard 1909: 18.

74 Prasad 1961: 231, 235; Fuchs 1973: 11, 176; Bhowmik 1963: 7; Elwin 1955: 4–6.

75 1927: 10, 11, 17.

76 Stampe 1965: 332–3; Sitapati 1938: 57–8; 1939: 157–8; Roy 1927: 323; Piers Vitebsky, personal communication.

77 Vitebsky 1980: 47.

78 Elwin 1955: 50ff.; Sitapati 1939: 167–8.

79 Elwin 1955: 8–9; also Sitapati 1939: 157, 167–8; Choudhury 1963–4: 101–2; Munro and Sitapati 1931: 200; Subbarayan 1948: 64; Piers Vitebsky, personal communication.

80 Stampe, 1965: 333 n.10, 337; Zide 1969: 413; Subbarayan 1948: 58; Bhattacharya 1954: 45; Satpathy 1963–4b: 165; Izikowitz n.d.: 129.

81 1976: 1259.

82 Bhattacharya 1957: 2; also Burrow and Bhattacharya 1962: 45–6; Emeneau 1969: 338–9; Ramadas 1931: 160; Majumdar 1939: 6. Bhattacharya makes it clear that the Ollar were known earlier and recog-

nized as Dravidian speakers, but the information had apparently been obscured from scholarship through being buried in census reports and official gazetteers. The Gadaba themselves do not use their own ethnonym to refer to the Ollar, which suggests that the use of 'Gadba' for the latter in the earlier literature was wrong (Claudia Gross, personal communication).

83   Cf. Subbarayan (1948: 56): 'Bodo is also called Boda from Bodaluvade, the fibre which is used in the Gadaba cloth.' 'Boro' is Desia, 'Moro' is Gutob (Claudia Gross, personal communication).

84   Fürer-Haimendorf 1943b: 149–50; Bhattacharya ibid.: Thusu and Jha 1972: 161; Mohanty 1973–4: 132; Izikowitz n.d.: 129.

85   Thusu and Jha ibid,; Deka and Pattajoshi 1975: 228; Singh 1972: 102; Subbarayan 1948: 56.

86   Chandra Sekhar 1964: 5, 29; Roy 1927: 308; Singh ibid. *Kathera* is Telugu for 'scissors', these being used for the ceremonial hair-cutting at marriage (Subba Rao 1965: 63).

87   Quotation from Subbarayan ibid.; also Sahu 1942: 108; 1953: 61; Bose 1950: 173; Ramadas 1931: 162. Thusu and Jha 1972: 168 n.1; Izikowitz ibid.

88   Zide 1969: 412, 413; Fürer-Haimendorf 1945b: 328 n.2; cf. Pfeffer ms.; Claudia Gross, personal communication.

89   Stampe 1965: 338 and n.16; Tripathi 1973: 326; Claudia Gross, personal communication; Mohanty 1973–4: 153; Pfeffer 1984b: 232.

90   Mazumdar 1927: 16; Ramadas 1931: 161; Subbarayan 1948: 55; Sahu 1942: 108; 1952: 468, 470; 1953: 61, 62; Chandra Sekhar 1964: 5.

91   Sahu ibid.; Burrow and Bhattacharya 1962: 46; Claudia Gross, personal communication.

92   Elwin 1950: 2–3, 6–7; Fürer-Haimendorf 1943b: 161; Das 1956a: 106; Stampe 1965: 332, 340.

93   Elwin 1950: 1; Bhattacharya 1968: xxx; Voegelin and Voegelin 1966: 21. Presumably *remo* is equivalent only to *vir* in these two languages, since there are separate ethnonyms.

94   Claudia Gross, personal communication.

95   Stampe 1965: 341; Fürer-Haimendorf 1945b: 8; 1954: 178; Guha *et al.* 1970: i, 1–2; Subbarayan 1948: 58. The final *-q* in Gataq represents the glottal stop.

96   Guha *et al.* 1970: 1; Mohanty 1981–2: 1. This seems a more likely spelling than Gntare, which is nonetheless printed in both sources.

97   Fürer-Haimendorf 1945b: 328; Mahapatra 1976: 815. According to Stampe (1965: 341) there are less than 2,000.

98   'The Dires...show few of the essential features of Austroasiatic culture.... Essentially they belong, however, to the same stratum as the Reddis' (1945b: 332); 'there is a definite cultural and to a lesser extent racial similarity between the two tribes' (ibid.: 8), though, Fürer-Haimendorf thought, the latter had come under Telugu, the former under Austroasiatic influence.

99   Also spelt 'Nahal', occasionally 'Nehal', in earlier works, but Zide's group appears to prefer 'Nihal' (see Stampe 1966: 391 n.4).

100 Bhattacharya 1956: 245.
101 Quotations respectively from Zide 1969: 428 and Kuiper 1962: 287–8; also Pinnow 1963: 151; Aasha Mundlay, personal communication.
102 See Zide 1969: 413.
103 On these groups, see Das *et al.* 1966: 74, 117; Prasad 1961: 172–5, 205–9, 315; Gautam 1977a: 31–3; Vidyarthi 1964: 20; Bhowmik 1963: 7; Fuchs 1973: 111. Standing confirms the presence of Mundari-speaking low castes in parts of Ranchi (1976: 17).
104 *LSI* IV: 79; Chatterji 1923: 452; Griffiths 1946: 1; Roy 1912: 21; Prasad 1961: 315.
105 E.g. Chatterji ibid.; Majumdar 1950: 23–4; but cf. Majumdar 1961: 65.

Notes to Chapter Three

1 E.g. the Mundari (Sugiyama 1969: 37–8). The land rights of Munda descent groups are given fuller treatment in sect. 4.3 (ii).
2 Sinha 1958a: 90. On these matters generally, see McDougal 1963a: xxi, 29–30, 39–41, 52–3, 62 n.1, 287–8, 311, 313 (Juang); Guha *et al.* 1970: 84 (Gataq); Bouez 1985: 42 (Santal and Mundari); Elwin 1950: 9 (Remo); Patnaik 1970: 190–1 (Sora). On the Mundari, see also Yamada 1970: 23ff., 250ff.; Sugiyama 1969: 37–8; Jha 1964: 28–9; Icke-Schwalbe 1979: 64–5.
3 Williams 1968: 128–30; also Chakraborty 1979: 6. See sect. 4.2 for a fuller discussion of the *tanda*.
4 Roy 1925: 44. Vidyarthi 1960: 525.
5 Roy 1925: 43ff.; Martel 1979: 108; Sinha 1958a: 93; 1960: 57.
6 Roy 1926: 149; Rosner 1967: 218–19; Sandhwar 1978: 18, 277, 278; Singh 1977a: 38, 42; 1977b: 96; Hermanns 1966: 59; Singh and Danda 1986: 63.
7 Yamada 1970: 30ff.; Standing 1976: 44, 63, 282.
8 Izikowitz n.d.: 130; Orans 1959: 218; Sachchidananda 1964: 26.
9 See above. Many hunting and gathering groups trade forest products for cultivated food with local settled populations, e.g. the Orang Asli in West Malaysia.
10 Roy 1926: 148; Leuva 1963: 2, 44; Elwin 1942: 64–5; Prasad 1961: 197–9.
11 Mohanty 1981–2: 3; Patnaik 1964: 23, 26–7; Bahadur 1977: 27; Sengupta 1970: 4–5.
12 Das 1964: 20–1; Mohanty 1963–4: 176; cf. Roy and Roy 1937: 24–5.
13 See Bouez 1985: 30.
14 On the Sora, Choudhury 1963–4: 102. On the Santal, Bouez 1975: 111–12; Gausdal 1960: 12; Pfeffer 1984a: 41–2. Quotation from Bose 1971: 20.
15 Orans 1965; Banerjee 1981; Dhan 1961: 45, 52–3; Mohanty 1981–2: 3.
16 Elwin 1950: 22; 1955: 61; Sachchidananda 1981: 216.
17 Izikowitz n.d.: 130.
18 Quotation from Datta-Majumdar 1956: 86; see also Gautam 1977a: 136. On the Kharia, Roy and Roy 1937: 213–15.
19 See Dhan 1961: 59–61; Vidyarthi and Upadhyay 1980: 115; Standing

1976: 93; Bhandari 1963: 80; Elwin 1948: 25; Sengupta 1969: 3.

20 Dhan ibid. Other ethnographers (Bouez 1985: 71, 127; Chatterjee and Das 1927: 27) suggest that she is completely a part of neither her natal nor her husband's descent group, though the application of the vermilion mark transfers her ritual duties from her natal to her husband's home and she can opt to be buried in the ossuary of the former if she desires. However, this may be just a quirk of interpretation. Dhan is herself a Ho, so at least her account deserves respect on that score.

21 Choudhury 1977: 30; Jordan-Horstmann 1972a: 282; Standing 1976: 222.

22 Roy 1925: 101.

23 McDougal 1963a: 97, 274; 1964: 342.

24 Roy and Roy 1937: 166, 187, 271–4, 283; other examples are the Birhor and the Santal (Roy 1925: 148; Bouez 1975: 124; Mukherjea 1962: 215–16).

25 Elwin 1950: 24–5, 100–1; Fürer-Haimendorf 1954: 178.

26 Piers Vitebsky, personal communication; Hermanns 1966: 135; Singh and Danda 1986: 33.

27 Gautam 1977a: 80–1, 158, 229 n.4; Singh and Singh 1976: 36; Culshaw 1949: 84, 158; Gausdal 1953: 5; Bouez 1985: 118–19, 125.

28 Culshaw 1949: 124; Fürer-Haimendorf 1943a: 171.

29 Parry 1979: 150ff., on Kangra in northwest India. The distinction between joint and extended families is strictly speaking, of course, that between families constituted around a set of brothers and/or agnatic parallel cousins, shallow in lineal depth, and those with a lineal depth of, typically, three generations, with or without collateral agnatic lines. However, the chronological fluidity of domestic organization means that this distinction too is very much one between ideal types rather than actual domestic arrangements.

30 Orans 1959: 218; Chakraborty 1972: 105. Among similar examples, two surveys of Korwa households show 70% and 54% respectively of nuclear families, but a significant number of extended families was also recorded in the second case (Rizbi 1977: 50; Sandhwar 1978: 84). Similar examples among the Mahali, separated by ten years, show a variation from 9.9% joint or extended (Sengupta 1970: 50) to 40% (Chakraborty and Kundu 1980: 88).

31 Gautam 1977a: 86, 88. Saha, writing of the Santal of Midnapore (1972: 22), gives *mit tukui* as the designation for a family of any size who cook their meals on the same hearth.

32 Quotation from Vidyarthi and Upadhyay 1980: 149; see also ibid.: 106; Vidyarthi 1960: 552; McDougal 1963a: xxii, 85, 87. Kodaku *oda* means both 'nuclear family' and 'house' (Singh and Danda 1986: 34–5, 41).

33 E.g. the Ho and Korwa (Bouez 1985: 54; Sandhwar 1978: 83; Singh 1977a: 41).

34 McDougal 1963a: 93.

35 Williams 1968; Vidyarthi ibid.; Malhotra 1963: 315.

36   Turner 1967: 192; Elwin 1955; cf. Chaussin 1978: 169.
37   Choudhury 1977: 47, 56; Yamada 1970: 270–1; Carrin-Bouez 1986: 41
      n.49; Bouez 1985: 115–16; McDougal 1963a: 119; Roy 1925: 141.
38   McDougal 1963a: 116; Somasundaram 1949: 38; Roy 1925: 139.
39   Ali 1973: 45; Rizbi 1977: 50; Sandhwar 1978: 39, 84, 113.
40   Chaussin 1978: 174; Bouez 1985: 94; Sugiyama 1969: 43.
41   Guha *et al.* 1970: 84 on the Gataq; Dhan 1961: 56, 60 on the Ho.
42   Examples are the Santal, Ho, Kharia and Mundari (Mukherjea 1962:
      170–80; Chattopadhyay 1964: 25; Roy and Roy 1937: 120–1; Yamada
      1970: 259–60).
43   E.g. Gautam 1977a: 104; Choudhury 1977: 56.
44   McDougal 1963a: 110.
45   First quotation from Culshaw 1949: 11, second from Mohanty 1981–2:
      6; see also Sandhwar 1978: 113; Carrin-Bouez 1986: 29; Danda 1962:
      309.
46   Culshaw 1949: 147; Mukherjea 1962: 217.
47   E.g. among the Korwa and Kharia (Rizbi 1977: 59; Vidyarthi and
      Upadhyay 1980: 160). Among the Mahali, he can continue to inherit
      from his own father (Sengupta 1970: 106).
48   Troisi 1979: 172–3; Culshaw 1949: 147.
49   Troisi 1979: 171–2; Mukherji 1964: 69; also Gautam 1977a: 105, 122;
      Das Gupta 1978: 143.
50   Roy 1912: 429–35; Yamada 1970: 264–5; Choudhury 1977: 37–8, 50–1,
      56; Standing 1981: 227.
51   1963a: 104.
52   Possible, for example, among the Kharia (Vidyarthi and Upadhyay
      1980: 160) and Santal (Biswas 1956: 93), but not the Korwa (Sandhwar
      1978: 39).
53   Bouez 1985: 122; Dhan 1961: 56.

Notes to Chapter Four

1   See Kuper 1982.
2   Cf. Bengali *kula*, a patrilineal descent group tracing its origin from a
      single ancestor (Inden and Nicholas 1977: 4–5).
3   Turner 1966: 163; Gausdal 1953: 48. Gautam is out of line with other
      writers on the Santal in describing it as a clan (1977a: 79). It also means
      'uncultivated or fallow land' in Santali (Gausdal ibid.).
4   In Mayurbhanj, Santal clans are called *padit*, the *paris* being sub-clans
      (Mukherjea 1962: 110). Bodding suggests tentatively that *paris* is from
      Bihari *paris* 'touch', or from *parasiya* 'neighbouring' (1935b: 597),
      though it should also be compared with Gondi *pari* 'clan' (Fürer-
      Haimendorf 1956: 503). The *paris* are also referred to as *hormo* or
      'body' by Santal (Kochar 1970: 49).
5   In Bengali this is largely synonymous with *kula* but stresses a shared
      name rather than an ancestor (Inden and Nicholas ibid.).
6   Orans 1965: 10; Fuchs 1966: 214; Sengupta 1970: 16.
7   Elwin 1948: 25; McDougal 1963a: 65.

8   I give their names in alphabetical order to avoid prejudicing the account which follows: Baske, Bedea, Besra, Core, Hansdak, Hembrom, Kisku, Marndi, Murmu, Pauria, Soren and Tudu (see Pfeffer 1984a; Gausdal 1942: 434–9; 1953; Biswas 1956: 62ff.: Prasad 1974: 68).

9   Culshaw 1949: 69, 94–5. He says that the name Bedea is not known in Bankura, where the missing clan is known as Donka or Bhaduli.

10   Gautam (1977a: 79, 229 n.2) suggests that they are simply a group that has become Hinduized.

11   Kochar 1970: 50; Gausdal 1960: 125–6.

12   Orans 1965: 10; Bouez 1985: 87, 109; Carrin-Bouez 1986: 27; Somers 1977: 75. Bouez's lists omit, in addition to Bedea, Core and Pauria.

13   Carrin-Bouez 1986: 27, 33. For details of the occupations, see ibid.: 77ff. and Prasad 1974: 68. Somers' informants in Santal Parganas had no knowledge of these traditional occupations (1977: 76–7).

14   Gausdal 1960: 18, 32; Bouez 1985: 87, 108; Culshaw 1949: 70; Gautam 1977a: 81–2.

15   Bouez 1975: 111, 112; 1985: 89, 90; Carrin-Bouez 1986: 21–2, 27; Datta-Majumdar 1956: 41.

16   First two quotations from Carrin-Bouez 1986: 25, 28, 41 n.47; Gausdal 1960: Biswas 1956: 73–4; Bouez 1985: 125 n.9, 176; Kochar 1970: 42; Somers 1977: 76; Gautam 1977a: 81.

17   1985: 31, 175; also Carrin-Bouez 1986: 27, 37.

18   Bodding 1935: 750; Gautam 1977a: 83; Bouez 1975: 114; Orans 1965: 11n. Only once does Bouez use the term in relation to Santal sub-clans in this area (1985: 105).

19   See the lists in Gausdal 1953 and 1960: 210ff.; Biswas 1956: 64–7; Campbell 1953: 588–9.

20   Gausdal 1942: 431; Bouez 1985: 91.

21   Among the Santal the term *khil* seems to be restricted to these two *khut*; Carrin-Bouez translates it as 'lignée' (1986: 93), and it does not seem to be as extensive as the Mundari unit of the same name (see below), which is analogous to the *paris*; cf. above. n.3.

22   Bouez 1975: 114–15; Gausdal 1953: 22, 37–8, 52, 58–9, 63; 1960: 210.

23   Bouez 1985: 88, 90, 133; Gautam 1977a: 83.

24   1975: 114–15; 1985: 93–4.

25   Orans 1960: 13; Carrin-Bouez 1986: 30; also Bhowmik 1971: 69.

26   'Neither the clan, the sub-clan, nor the local lineage is endogamous.... Indeed, all are exogamous and it is only the entire tribe which in some respects is equivalent to a Hindu caste' (Orans 1960: 20). Gautam also says that the *khut* is strictly exogamous (1977a: 85).

27   Bouez 1975: 114–15; 1985: 93–4, 215 n.8; Gausdal 1953: 19–20; Culshaw 1949: 84; Kochar 1970: 50ff.; Gautam 1977a: 85–6; Carrin-Bouez 1986: 60 n.5, 76ff., 89 n.30. Gausdal gives the following explanation for the secrecy of *khut* names: 'Even uttering the name of such a Bonga [divinity] may cause him to appear and cause the greatest calamity. The names are therefore only used when an appropriate offering is presented.' He regularly describes the *khut* as 'sacrificial clans', thus distinguishing them from the *paris* or 'ancestral clans'.

28   Bouez 1985: 176; Sachchidananda 1956: 53ff. The Santal float the bones of the dead away on the river Damodar after cremation and do not erect memorial stones like many other groups (Culshaw 1949: 153, 155–6).

29   Quotation from Gautam 1977a: 85–6, 103; Gausdal 1953: 10.

30   Somers 1977: 78–9, 87–8; Campbell 1953: 101; Bodding 1932: 345; Kochar 1970: 54; Orans 1965: 11.

31   1934: 54, 507, 508. In Bengali, *gosthi* refers to a much more restricted group, namely the *kula* or clan members of the household (Inden and Nicholas 1977: 8).

32   1970: 51ff. Gautam equally confusingly glosses *khut* indifferently as sub-clan or lineage (1977a: 83).

33   Bouez 1985: 177.

34   Sengupta 1970: 16–25.

35   Roy 1912: 131n., 400, 406ff.; Sachchidananda 1979: 340–2.

36   Yamada 1970: 263, 386–7; Choudhury 1977: 26–7, 33; Sachchidananda 1979: 107–8.

37   Standing 1981: 225–6; Bouez 1985: 39; Jordan-Horstmann 1972a: 282. Choudhury also identifies 'sub-clans' in an intermediate position (1977: 31, 33), but since these can have separate *sasan* from the parent clan they may in reality be new clans in process of formation through segmentation.

38   Quotation from Standing ibid.; also *Encyc. Mund.*: 2380–1; Bouez 1985: 42; Choudhury 1977: 29; Yamada 1970: 279; Icke-Schwalbe 1979: 64–5.

39   Sugiyama 1969: 109–10; Standing 1981: 227. *Khewat* is the legal term; the co-members are called *ora'renko* ('people of the house') in Mundari.

40   Standing 1976: 92; 1981: 226–7; Choudhury 1977: 34, 37, 38–43; Roy 1912: 107, 392; Sugiyama 1969: 95–6, 101, 109–10; Yamada 1970: 376, 387. Icke-Schwalbe (ibid.) identifies the *kili* with the *sasan*.

41   Jordan-Horstmann 1972a: 282.

42   *Encyc. Mund.*: 2380–1. As with the Santal, the term *khut* may be unknown in the south: Carrin-Bouez describes very similar units as extended patrilineages (1986: 28) but gives no generic name for them.

43   Bouez 1985: 31, 47, 54, 75, 176; Dhan 1961: 42, 43; Majumdar 1950: 92; Chatterjee and Das 1927: 48.

44   Bouez 1985: 31, 46–53; Majumdar 1950: 92–3; Dhan 1961: 63–4; Chattopadhyay 1964: 15.

45   Rizbi 1977: 51–2, 59; Sandhwar 1978: 39–42, 113, 334 n.29 (quotation from last reference). Vidyarthi and Rai (1977: 157) also mention sub-clans, but these may be the same as the lineages.

46   Singh 1977a: 41; Singh and Danda (1986: 33, 35) claim there is nothing between *goti* and *oda* (nuclear family).

47   Roy 1925: 90–2, 115–16; Sinha 1968: 81; 1958b: 87, 89; Martel 1979; Williams 1968; Malhotra 1963: 313–14; Chakraborty 1979: 12.

48   On the Bhumij, Sinha 1962: 46; 1966: 20; Das 1931a: 21; Ray Chowdhury 1929: 102. A list of Bhumij clans is given by Das (ibid.:

61–1), one of Bir Asur clans by Leuva (1963: 64). For similar lists of Korku clans, see Hermanns 1966: 179, Fuchs 1966: 214–15; 1988: 171–4, and Dixit 1966: 5.

49   McDougal 1963a: 65ff., 121, 144, 414, 428, 435–7; 1964: 321–2; Bose 1971: 55–6 (on Dhenkanal). Lists of Juang clans can be found in Bose 1929: 47–8 and Elwin 1948: 25. The quotations are respectively from McDougal 1963a: 68, 70, 74.

50   Roy and Roy 1937: 127ff., 143–4; Bouez 1985: 32.

51   *Bonso* is from Indic *vamsha* (literally 'bamboo', whence 'family, lineage'; Turner 1966: 652), which in Bengali, for instance, is a virtual synonym of *kula*, though expressing shared bodily substance rather than a shared dead ancestor (Inden and Nicholas 1977: 4–5); cf. Korwa *bans*, above.

52   Guha *et al.* 1970: 56, 58; Mohanty 1981–2: 5. According to the former, the Monkey and Goat totems reported by Ferreira (1965: 257), Elwin (1950: 28) and Fürer-Haimendorf (1945b: 329) for this area are not found among the Gataq.

53   Guha *et al.* 1970: 56, 58, 63; Mohapatra 1963–4: 128; Fürer-Haimendorf 1945b: 330. See also sect. 8.2 on the question of dual organization among the Munda generally.

54   Fürer-Haimendorf 1943b: 163; 1943a: 168–9; *tsoro* is from Sanskrit *caru*.

55   Elwin 1950: 8, 21–34; cf. Claudia Gross, personal communication.

56   Quotations from Fürer-Haimendorf 1954: 178 and 1943a: 163; also *idem* 1945b: 331; 1954: 177f.; Fernandez 1969: 34–6; Elwin 1950: 32–3.

57   Fürer-Haimendorf 1943b: 151; Elwin 1950: 28; Chandra Sekhar 1964: 5; cf. Pfeffer ms; Claudia Gross, personal communication.

58   Pfeffer ms; Claudia Gross, personal communication. This new information modifies earlier data in Pfeffer 1982a: 48; 1983: 96; and 1984b: 232–3. Data in other sources (Izikowitz n.d.: 131, 137; Somasundaram 1949: 38–9; Satpathy 1963–4a; 152–3) are so patchy and confused that they are probably best disregarded. See sect. 8.4 i for other Gadaba categories.

59   Satpathy 1963–4b: 165; Pfeffer 1982a: 91; 1983: 95–6; Elwin 1950: 28.

60   Elwin 1955: 50, 52; Choudhury 1963–4: 102; Chaussin 1978: 169; Vitebsky 1980: 64; personal communication; Sitapati 1939: 192, 194.

61   Piers Vitebsky, personal communication. Chaussin (1978) sought to distinguish the *birinda* ('lignée') from the 'lignage', or localized subdivisions of the former when it grows too large to occupy a single hamlet. Vitebsky, however, is adamant that this never happens and that the distinction is a false one.

62   Elwin 1955: 53, 141, 153; Piers Vitebsky, personal communication.

63   Elwin 1950: xii–xiii; McDougal 1964: 324–5.

64   Fuchs 1966: 218; Ferreira 1965: 77, 123; Elwin 1948: 26–31; Roy and Roy 1937: 123n., 145–6; McDougal 1964: 321–2.

65   Fuchs 1966: 214; Majumdar 1950: 91; Bouez 1985: 47.

66   E.g. the Santal, where this is usually done by a father's sister's husband (Bouez 1985: 118–19, 122; Carrin-Bouez 1986: 73), the Kharia

(Roy and Roy 1937: 283; Vidyarthi and Upadhyay 1980: 129) and the Mundari (Choudhury 1977: 74).

67 E.g. the Mundari, Korku, Asur and Korwa (Yamada 1970: 384ff.; Fuchs 1966: 217; Das 1956b: 144; Hari Mohan 1979: 88, 91; Bhandari 1963: 80).

68 Fuchs 1966: 251; Orans 1965: 10; Kochar 1970: 44.

69 Singh 1978: 30–1. There are usually at least two lineages in each Mundari village, but they are invariably closely related segments of the same clan (see sect. 5.2).

70 Yamada 1970: 7, 298ff., 387; Sugiyama 1969: 86ff., 112ff.; Roy 1912: 66ff., 115ff.; Choudhury 1977: 28; Sachchidananda 1956: 54–5; Jordan-Horstmann 1972b: 566–7.

71 See Standing 1976: 52, 65, 73–4, 90, 285.

72 Bouer 1985: 43; Standing 1981: 236; Singh 1978.
Chatterjee and Das 1927: 7, 40; Majumdar 1950: 5, 7, 12, 89, 102–3; Dhan 1961: 43–4; Bouez 1985: 44.

74 McDougal 1963a: 68; Roy and Roy 1937: 140, 162b–3, 172–5, 194, 327; Sachchidananda 1953: 187.

75 Gautam 1977a: 102–3; Martel 1965: 344–5; Bouez ibid.; also Kochar 1965: 6; Somers 1977: 38–42; Saha 1972: 9–10.

76 Elwin 1955: 50–2; Sitapati 1939: 167–8, 194–5; Chaussin 1978: 179. See Ch. 2, 13, for the meanings of *gamang* and *buyya*.

77 Guha *et al.* 1970: 63; Mohanty 1973–4: 154.

Notes to Chapter Five

1 Guha *et al.* 1970: 87; Bose 1971: 55–6; McDougal 1963a: xxii, xxiv, 62, 85; 1963b: 184–5; Turner 1967: 189; Chaussin 1978: 171, 178, 180; Standing 1981: 225.

2 1977: 107–8, 133.

3 Bodding 1935b: 324; Hrach 1978: 94; Singh 1980: 221.

4 McDougal 1963a: 179, 450; Pfeffer ms.; *baro bhayki* is in fact an Oriya term.

5 See the comments in Sugiyama 1969: 143; Sachchidananda 1979: 189; Chaussin 1978: 178–9; Gautam 1977a: 71, 100; Sengupta 1970: 188, 193; Rizbi 1977: 57; Sandhwar 1978: 114; Dhan 1961: 41, 45, 74–5; Guha *et al.* 1970: 88; Singh and Danda 1986; 27, 81.

6 Quotation from Hrach 1978: 94.

7 Roychaudhury 1961: 1, 4; Singh 1980: 227; Sandhwar 1978: 224, 227; Sengupta 1970: 198.

8 Biswas 1956: 154; Gautam 1977a: 98, 267.

9 See, for example, Chaussin 1978: 178.

10 Gupta 1977: 179; Singh and Danda 1986: 77.

11 Quotation from Standing 1981: 233; also Sengupta 1970: 188; Somers 1977: 85; McDougal 1963a: 370ff.; Claudia Gross, personal communication.

12 Elwin 1948: 32; 1950: 180; Satpathy 1963–4a: 153; Srivastava *et al.* 1971: 17; Fuchs 1988: 185.

13 E.g. among the Korwa and Gataq (Mohanty 1981–2: 9; Rizbi 1977: 54).

14 Singh 1980: 224; Gautam 1977a: 93.

15 Elwin 1948: 32; Bouez 1985: 215 n.9; McDougal 1963a: 63, 195. Elwin says that the Juang *padhan* and *dihuri* are hereditary, the *bhuitar* being appointed by 'general consent' (ibid.: 33), but his data are older than McDougal's and were collected under difficult circumstances.

16 Their exact role and powers may vary from tribe to tribe. Carrin-Bouez (1986: 139), for example, hesitates to draw too close a comparison between the Santal *ojha* and the various classes of Sora shaman described by Elwin (1955). I use the word 'shaman' only advisedly here, merely to point out the existence of ritual specialists of this general sort among the Munda.

17 Elwin 1950: 161; Kochar 1965: 11.

18 E.g. among the Remo (Elwin 1950: 160). Some shamans are in practice the children of others nonetheless; others may be from other tribes.

19 Elwin 1950: 160, 188–9; 1955: Ch. 5; Sinha 1958b: 90; Danda, cited in Gupta 1977: 179–80.

20 Datta-Majumdar 1956: 46; Culshaw 1949: 79–80; Kochar 1965: 10, Gausdal 1953: 49, 54. The above is the gloss given in most authorities, but Carrin-Bouez calls him a 'boundary priest' ('prêtre des limites'; 1986: 48).

21 Singh and Danda 1986: 88–9; Rizbi 1977: 60; Majumdar 1944: 37, 61; Danda 1971: 103; Sandhwar 1978: 37; cf. n.19.

22 Fuchs 1973: 172; Das Gupta 1978: 72–3. The name Baiga is used indifferently as 'priest' and as an ethnonym, as in Elwin 1939.

23 His significance is indicated by his name, *jog* (from Bengali), meaning 'world, society'. On his role, see Mukherjea 1962: 152–3; Culshaw 1949: 9–10; Datta-Majumdar 1956: 46; Somers 1977: 95; Kochar 1965: 9; 1970: 106; Gautam 1977a: 91, 229 n.16; Carrin-Bouez 1986: 31, 126 n.11; Martel 1965: 315.

24 Quotations respectively from Gupta 1977: 176 and Sengupta 1970: 29; on the Korwa, Rizbi 1977: 54–5.

25 Chaussin 1978: 178.

26 E.g. Roy 1912: 117; 1925: 63–5; Roy and Roy 1937: 163; Chatterjee and Das 1927: 9; McDougal 1963a: 194; Sugiyama 1969: 86.

27 McDougal 1963a: 63 and n.1, 64, 194, 388; Rout 1969–70: 85. The former, representative role of the *podhan* is now undertaken by the village *member* (an Oriya loan from English) of the modern *gram-panchayat* (McDougal 1963a: 64).

28 E.g. among the Korwa and Birhor (Gupta 1977: 176; Bouez 1985: 30–1). Among the Santal the *naeke* (village priest) can act as the *manjhi* (village headman) but not vice versa (Carrin-Bouez 1986: 98). In Dumontian terms, therefore, priestly authority encompasses secular power here, as in Hindu society (see Dumont 1966b).

29 Sinha 1962: 38, 48; 1966: 9; Dhan 1961: 74; Rout 1969–70: 84; McDougal 1963a: 195; Gupta 1977: 179.

30 Quotation from Bouez 1985: 94; also *idem* 1975: 114; Carrin-Bouez

1986: 92–3; Gautam 1977a: 90; Sengupta 1970: 179.

31   Datta-Majumdar 1956: 31, 122–2; Culshaw 1949: 7; Somers 1977: 38–42; Elwin 1955: 50–2.

32   Elwin 1948: 33; their own funerals have special ritual rules.

33   E.g. the Ho and Mundari (Sachchidananda 1956: 53–5). The *sasan* is absent from the Santal—see above, Ch. 4, n.28.

34   Sachchidananda ibid.; Carrin-Bouez 1986: 17–18; Culshaw 1949: 80, 153; Elwin 1950: 8; Mohanty 1973–4: 135.

35   Martel 1979: 107; he argues that this indicates some Birhor having been sedentary for a long time, though this does not necessarily follow, in view of the quite restricted area of their wanderings.

36   Sugiyama indicates that among the Mundari both *gitiora* and *akhara* are associated with the *tola* or hamlet rather than the village (1969: 125, 132).

37   E.g. the Gataq, Korwa and Mahali (Guha *et al.* 1970: 5; Singh 1977a: 41; Sengupta 1969: 108).

38   McDougal 1963a: 104, 245, 259; Vidyarthi and Upadhyay 1980: 15.

39   Yamada 1970: 260; Majumdar 1950: 101.

40   Izikowitz n.d.: 131 and n.4; Elwin 1950: 11; cf. Martel 1965: 344; Bouez 1985: 211 n.37.

41   E.g. the Juang (McDougal 1963a: 53, 313).

42   See above. This is in contrast to hunting-and-gathering groups in many other parts of the world, among whom death rites are often extremely perfunctory (see, for example, Woodburn in Bloch and Parry 1982).

43   Quotations from McDougal 1963a: 66f.; also Bouez 1985: 54.

44   Quotations respectively from Fürer-Haimendorf 1945b: 331; *idem* 1954: 178; and Elwin 1950: 24–5. On the Gadaba, Mohanty 1973–4: 135; Pfeffer ms.

45   Quotation from Choudhury 1977: 29; also Bose 1971: 55–6; Sachchidananda 1979: 188; Sugiyama 1969: 99; Majumdar 1950: 96, 101–4; Elwin 1950: 8, 28; 1955: 51; Claudia Gross, personal communication. The Gadaba *kuda* may not strictly speaking be descent groups extending throughout the society, but within the village they tend to be agnatically defined (see sect. 4.2). *Contra* other writers on the Mundari, Yamada rules out *khut* localization (1970: 279–80).

46   Majumdar 1944: 35; Bhandari 1963: 86; Sandhwar 1978: 221, 335 n.64; Das Gupta 1978: 67–8, 73; Guha *et al.* 1970: 63.

47   Standing 1976: 36–7, 358.

48   Sengupta 1970: 200; Singh 1977a: 43; Singh and Danda 1986: 77.

49   McDougal 1964: 322.

50   Roy 1912: 120, 412–17; Choudhury 1977: 1–5, 28, 112; Carrin-Bouez 1986: 31; *Encyc. Mund.*: 3278, 3311; Yamada 1970: 362–4; also Choudhury ibid.; Sachchidananda 1979: 196; cf. Singh 1978: 30; Standing 1976: 94.

51   Roy 1912: 417–18; Choudhury ibid.; Sachchidananda 1964: 25; 1979: 198–9.

52   Standing 1976: 125, 135.

53 Quotation from Navlakha 1959: 30, 33; also Ray Chowdhury 1929: 98–9.

54 Chattopadhyay 1964: 14; Dhan 1961: 41, 76; Bouez 1985: 42, 76; Dasgupta 1983: 42; Chatterjee and Das 1927: 8–9; Majumdar 1950: 12, 102–3; Gupta 1977: 172.

55 McDougal 1963a: 58–62, 66, 250ff., 316, 370ff., 382–5, 430; 1964: 321–3; Rout 1969–70: 4, 88.

56 Not to be confused with the *manjhi* or village headmen, though like them they are hereditary figures (Bouez 1985: 86).

57 Carrin-Bouez 1986: 31ff.; Bouez 1975: 110; 1985: 85–6; Troisi 1979: 64–6; Orans 1965: 10; Somers 1977: 103–5; Culshaw 1949: 11; Datta-Majumdar 1956: 94–5. Kochar says they are government appointees today (1965: 12).

58 Singh 1980: 225–6; Somers 1977: 105–6; Gautam 1977a: 98; Hrach 1979: 95; Troisi 1979: 66; Carrin-Bouez 1986: 32–3, 42 n.56. See also sect. 5.4, below.

59 Illegitimate children have no totemic name and are therefore ritually anomalous; they are given a fictive father in order to provide them with one (Carrin-Bouez 1986: 42 n.57).

60 Bouez 1985: 131–2, 215 n.16; Datta-Majumdar 1956: 47; Sachchidananda 1979: 196. There is a *pargana bonga*, sacrifices to whom are the responsibility of the *kudam naeke* (Bodding 1935b: 356; Gausdal 1953: 54).

61 Quotation from Roy and Roy 1937: 172–5; also Vidyarthi and Upadhyay 1980; 161ff.

62 On the Sora, Roy 1927: 322–3; Vidyarthi and Rai 1978: 20. On the Korwa, cf. Sandhwar 1978: 223 with Gupta 1977: 176. On the Gataq, Guha *et al.* 1970: 86.

63 Gautam 1977a: 266; Choudhury 1977: 123; Standing 1976: 114; Chaussin 1978: 178; Hari Mohan 1982: 39.

64 Choudhury 1977: 105, 123ff.; Sugiyama 1969: 138; Yamada 1970: 361–3; Somers 1977: 108–9; Sandhwar 1978: 220.

65 Gupta 1977: 176; see also Vidyarthi and Upadhyay 1980: 163, on the Kharia. Other government organizations with which tribals come into contact include the Development Block and the police *thana* (Troisi 1979: 66–8).

66 1912: 120; see also Kochar 1970: 44–5; 1965: 19.

67 Bouez 1985: 31, 43–4; Carrin-Bouez 1986: 13; McDougall 1977: 300; Roy 1912; Jha 1964: 29–30, 33ff.; Sinha 1962: 42, 46–7, 61.

68 Datta-Majumdar 1956: 47; Gautam 1977a: 94–5; Orans 1965: 22. *Sendra durup* or 'hunt sitting' is an alternative term (Kochar 1965: 13). Mukherjea seem to regard the Hunt Council and the meeting on the Damodar as separate (1962: 158–9).

69 Quotation from Hrach 1978: 96; also Singh and Singh 1976: 39. The *dihri* is only concerned with disputes arising out of the hunt itself (Troisi 1979: 66).

70 Singh 1980: 227; Troisi ibid. According to the latter this is the only body that can excommunicate, though this contradicts Bouez, who

states that the *parganait* also has this power (see previous sect.). Possibly there is a regional difference, for Bouez worked in Keonjhar, Troisi in Santal Parganas.

71   Roy 1925: 76–7, 118–19; Elwin 1950: 183; Guha *et al.* 1970: 84–5; Standing 1976: 129–30.

72   E.g. the Korwa (Rizbi 1977: 57) and the Korku, where this leads to expulsion (Hermanns 1966: 158–9).

73   Quotation from Standing 1976: 15–16; also Bahadur 1977: 11, 24; Sinha 1962: 43; Bouez 1985: 212 n.1.

74   On the Gadaba, Mohanty 1973–4: 132. On the Birhor, Roy 1925: 118–19; Malhotra 1963: 311–13. On the Kodaku, Singh and Danda 1986: 32, 43.

75   Sengupta 1966: 75; 1970: 99–100; Gautam 1977b: 378; Chattopadhyay 1964: 21; Bouez 1985: 111–12; Carrin-Bouez 1986: 21.

76   1937: 58, 87; 1950: 124.

77   Subbarayan 1948: 64.

78   Standing 1976: 17, 19. They also despise the Birhor as scavengers (ibid.: 281). The Sora also tend to avoid marriage with artisan low castes (Elwin 1955: 9).

79   See Mandelbaum 1970: 64.

80   Dhan 1961: 78.

81   Dasgupta 1978a: 14; Orans 1959: 237. While the Santal themselves have no internal ranking by dietary habits or other criteria, in Santal Parganas they are accorded a place in the local hierarchy by their neighbours, ranking above the Maler but below the Mal Paharia (both Dravidian-speaking groups found in the Santal Parganas): the latter abstain from beef and observe other ritual rules more strictly than either of the other two tribes (Gautam 1977a: 379; Prasad 1974: 74).

82   Dasgupta ibid.

83   See Bouez 1985: 30.

84   It is less offensive for males to marry into such a caste than females, since their children do not suffer any stigma (Guha *et al.* 1970: 73, 93).

85   Rout 1969–70: 4. This sort of thing is found elsewhere in India, e.g. beef-eating Untouchables ranked lower than tribals in the former State of Madras (Dumont 1966b: 110, after Risley).

Notes to Chapter Six

1   Leuva 1963: 90; Roy and Roy 1937: 223.

2   Quotation from Roy 1925: 99, 143; also Rizbi 1977: 57; on the Mundari, see Sachchidananda 1979: 105.

3   Majumdar 1937: 86; 1950: 123. Here, not only humans but also objects such as fishing nets and hunting weapons are ritually 'married' to ensure their effectiveness.

4   Hermanns 1966: 134.

5   As with the Ho, Kodaku and Korwa (Majumdar 1950: 111–12; Sandhwar 1978: 60–1; Rizbi 1977: 56; Singh 1977a: 43; Singh and

Danda 1986: 26, 42); among the latter the adoption of adult clothes is the only change.

6   Datta-Majumdar 1956: 87; Gautam 1977a: 138–9; Biswas 1956: 91; Culshaw 1949: 129–30; Troisi 1979: 166; Mukherjea 1962: 190, 195.

7   Sugiyama 1969: 125; Elwin 1948: 114; Fürer-Haimendorf 1943a: 172.

8   Majumdar 1950: 140; Vidyarthi 1958: 80.

9   Majumdar 1944: 56; Sandhwar 1978: 86–7, 109–10; Guha *et al*. 1970: 81, 100–3; Leuva 1963: xiii, 89; Pandye 1962: 93.

10 Guha *et al.* ibid.; Rizbi ibid.; Standing 1976: 15; cf. Elwin 1950: 120; Singh 1977a: 43; McDougal 1963a: 208–9; Singh and Danda 1986: 32, 38.

11 Majumdar 1950: 101, 130–1; Danda 1971: 101; McDougal 1964: 341–2; Sengupta 1970: 188; Singh and Singh 1976: 39; Singh 1977a: 44; Guha *et al.* 1970: 62.

12 On the first two, see Roy and Roy 1937: 224–5; Rout 1962: 171; but cf. Das 1979: 189. Most Juang in Keonjhar, much less Hinduized, marry at 18–22 (men) or 16–18 (women) (McDougal 1963a: 164). On the Bhumij, see Ghosh 1916: 273; Sahu 1943: 173; Das 1931a: 6–7.

13 As regards the former group, Mukherjea 1962: 196 on the Santal of Mayurbhanj, Bahadur 1977: 56 on the Mahali, and Sachchidananda 1964: 45–7 and Choudhury 1977: 81 on the Mundari; as regards the latter group, compare Elwin 1955: 54 on the Sora with Roy 1927: 333 and Sitapati 1939: 189.

14 Gataq, Sora, Mundari and Ho brides also tend to be older, Santal, Birhor, Kodaku, Gadaba and Bhumij brides younger (Chakraborty 1980: 82; Subba Rao 1965: 63; Das 1931a: 7; Pfeffer 1982a: 34; Sitapati 1939: 195; Sachchidananda 1964: 54; Choudhury 1977: 81; Majumdar 1950: 126; Singh and Danda 1986: 50; Elwin 1950: 116–17; Troisi 1979: 167). Troisi thus contradicts Biswas (1956: 74–5), who says the Santal have no fixed pattern. There is disagreement over the Kharia (see Roy and Roy 1937: 226 versus Vidyarthi and Upadhyay 1980: 166) and Korwa (see Majumdar 1944: 53–6; versus Rizbi 1977: 57 and Sandhwar 1978: 62).

15 Pfeffer 1982a: 34; 1983: 102–3.

16 McDougal 1964: 331.

17 On the Juang, McDougal 1964: 328, 340; 1963a: 95–6. On the Turi, Rosner 1956: 45.

18 See, for example, Biswas 1956: 74–5; Datta-Majumdar 1956: 42; Sandhwar 1978: 104.

19 Rizbi 1977: 56; Singh 1977a: 44; Hari Mohan 1961: 302; Majumdar 1950: 134.

20 E.g. the Juang; see Elwin 1947: 301, 303; Fürer-Haimendorf 1950: 129, 140; also Guha *et al.* 1970: 102.

21 First quotation from Elwin 1947: 314; second from Fürer-Haimendorf 1943a: 172; see also *idem* 1950: 129.

22 McDougal 1963a: 104, 220ff.; 1964: 340; Fürer-Haimendorf 1985: 91. Elwin (1948: 96) says that the youths visit the girls here too, but having lost his notes he was forced to rely on the 'preliminary'

investigations he carried out for his book on the Muria *ghotul* (1947) in making this statement.

23 E.g. the Mundari and Remo (Sugiyama 1969: 127; Fürer-Haimendorf 1943a: 169; Elwin 1950: 7).

24 See, for example, Mishra 1981–2: 34.

25 Fürer-Haimendorf 1950: 142; McDougal 1963a: 89, 101; Guha *et al.* 1970: 102; Sugiyama 1969: 125; Elwin 1947: 315. See also sect. 9.2.

26 E.g. the Mundari, Gataq, Kodaku and Gorum (Sugiyama 1969: 126; Rani 1957: 74; Guha *et al.* 1970: 102; Singh and Danda 1986: 26; Satpathy 1963–4b: 165).

27 On the Santal and Mahali, Culshaw 1949: 9–10; Elwin 1947: 291–2; Mukherjea 1962: 137; Sengupta 1970: 98. On the Korwa, Majumdar 1944: 40. On the Korku, Driver 1892: 131. On the Sora, Sitapati 1939: 190 and Piers Vitebsky, personal communication, versus Fürer-Haimendorf 1950: 128.

28 Roy 1925: 243, 551; Majumdar 1937: 8; Sachchidananda 1956: 56; Elwin 1947: 306. Quotation from Roy and Roy 1937: 78.

29 Fürer-Haimendorf 1950: 142; Roy 1931: 387; Elwin 1947: 303, 309.

30 McDougal 1964: 342; Standing 1976: 211.

31 1963: 96–7.

32 Quotation from Bouez 1975: 122; also Das 1965: 10; 1967: 6.

33 Das 1931b: 27; Bouez 1975: 123–4. Among the Juang, other villagers and even affines and maternal kin resident outside the village, especially MB, FZH and GEF, are expected to contribute something, though less than the closest agnates (McDougal 1963a: 253–4).

34 Hermanns calls the Korku *gonom* a 'compensation for [loss of] the bride' rather than a true brideprice (1966: 136), but it seems to be quite high here.

35 Majumdar 1961: 244; 1937: 102–6; Dhan 1961: 67; Bouez 1985: 67, 71; Sinha 1968: 80; Williams 1968: 130; Sandhwar 1978: 67; Chattopadhyay 1946: 47–9.

36 Standing 1976: 90; Parkin 1984: 122–3.

37 McDougal 1963a: 104, 245, 259.

38 Gautam 1977a: 133; Mukherjea 1962: 201; Datta-Majumdar 1956: 43; Culshaw 1949: 138, 143; Bouez 1985: 117. The Ho have no return prestations (Bouez 1985: 133).

39 On the Bhumij, Banerjee 1962: 19. On the Korwa, Majumdar 1944: 14, 54.

40 Called *andi* by the Ho (Dhan 1961: 67), *arandi* by the Mundari (Standing 1976: 210), *kirin bahu bapla* by the Mahali and Santal (Chakraborty and Kundu 1980: 89; Datta-Majumdar 1956: 88), *raibar bapla, duar bapla, diku bapla* or *duar itut' sindur* by the Santal, or *sarige bariat* if the vermilion is applied in front of the bride's, not the groom's house (ibid.; Orans 1959: 229ff.), *toso* by the Gataq (Guha *et al.* 1970: 65), *gotang kania* or 'path marriage' by the Juang (McDougal 1963a: 283), *sebung* by the Remo (Elwin 1950: 90, 96; Fürer-Haimendorf 1943a: 171) and *beao* by the Korku (Hermanns 1966: 134–5). The Korwa have several forms, namely *biaha, dolkadhi, telmakhani* and *tharra* (in des-

cending order of expense), though there is an areal difference, the second being found in the plains, the third and fourth in the hills, and only the first in both (Sandhwar 1978: 67–8, 271).

41 E.g. the Ho (Majumdar 1950: 134). Among the Santal the gap between the first visit of the boy's parents to the girl's and the engagement must be an odd number of days (Bouez 1985: 123).

42 Sengupta 1969: 5; Prasad 1974: 81; Vidyarthi and Upadhyay 1980: 140; Guha *et al.* 1970: 110; McDougal 1963a: 244, 452.

43 Sengupta 1970: 103; Bhandari 1963: 102; Saha 1972: 22; Bouez 1985: 70; Gautam 1977a: 126; Singh and Danda 1986: 50.

44 This is not a universal practice (the Ho do not do this) and it may have been borrowed from Hindu society (see Bouez 1985: 124).

45 Gautam 1977a: 158, 229 n.4; Bouez 1985: 71–2; Culshaw 1949: 158. According to Beck (1967: 558), it is the repetition of the rite at the groom's home which signifies incorporation of the bride among the Kharia.

46 Guha *et al.* 1970: 118.

47 Majumdar 1937: 274; Orans 1965: 58ff.; Gautam 1977a: 125; Majumdar 1950: 132; Mahapatra 1980: 27.

48 The less elaborate forms of marriage are not always regarded as of low status. Among the Mundari, elopement marriages and the marriages of widowed and divorced people are usually regarded as equal to the *arandi* form in status and inheritance rights if a brideprice has been paid and witnessed (Standing 1976: 211).

49 This is called *lokor* by the Korku (Hermanns 1966: 134, 154), *oportipi* or possibly *rajikushi* by the Ho, though the latter may be slightly different (Dhan 1961: 67), and *haram bariat* or *tunki dipil* by the Santal (Orans 1959: 229ff.). Another example is the Juang *tonkay oti*, literally 'to take a basket', a reference to the basket of rice which accompanies the bride's party (McDougal 1963a: 239). *Idigosha*, or *duar lebet*, with the brideprice deferred, seems to be the Mahali version (Sengupta 1966: 77; Chakraborty and Kundu 1980: 89).

50 See, for example, Bouez 1985: 113; Chatterjee and Das 1927: 53; Das Gupta 1978: 144–5; Hermanns 1966: 157; Gautam 1977a: 109, 124; Sandhwar 1978: 69.

51 This is called *udulia* by the Gadaba and Gataq (Satpathy 1963–4a: 153; Mohanty 1981–2: 6), *dhori para* by the Juang (McDougal 1963a: 238–9) and *angir* by the Mahali (Chakraborty and Kundu ibid.). Majumdar regards it simply as 'marriage by mutual consent, without any ceremony or payment of brideprice' (1950: 138; also Chattopadhyay 1964: 22).

52 Elwin 1948: 96; Sengupta 1966: 77; Sitapati 1939: 190; Bouez 1985: 117; Choudhury 1952: 91, 104–5.

53 E.g. the Juang, Gadaba and Ho (Elwin ibid.; Subba Rao 1965: 64; Majumdar 1950: 136).

54 Bouez 1975: 123. The Gataq call this variation *sagarta* (Guha *et al.* 1970: 118).

55 Or by forcing her to eat rice among the Remo (Elwin 1950: 86, 92, 96).

56 Roy and Roy 1937: 270; Das 1931b: 25; Bouez 1975: 124.
57 E.g. the Mundari, Sora, Korwa and Gadaba (Ghosh 1967: 406; Sitapati 1939: 190; Majumdar 1944: 53; Srivastava and Verma 1967: 54–5; Subba Rao 1965: 64–5).
58 Leuva 1963: 91–2; Majumdar 1950: 135, 140; Bouez 1975: 124; Guha *et al.* 1970: 110. It is called *itut' sindur* or *itut' bapla* by the Santal (*sindur* is a reference to the vermilion mark), or *or agu* in the case of simple marriage by capture (Orans 1959: 229ff.; Troisi 1979: 172), *guboi* or *ndelia* by the Gataq (Guha *et al.* 1970: 65, 118), *guboi* by the Remo (Fürer-Haimendorf 1943a: 171), and *aurapar* or *tana* by the Mahali (Chakraborty and Kundu ibid.).
59 McDougal 1963a: 220ff., 237–8, 248–9, 269, 273–4; Elwin 1950: 90, 96; Fürer-Haimendorf 1943a: 171–2.
60 On this form, see Troisi 1979: 172; Roy 1925: 145–6; Roy and Roy 1937: 271; Datta-Majumdar 1956: 44–5; Bhandari 1963: 95, 97; Das Gupta 1978: 145; Gautam 1977a: 123. The practice is called *boloen* ('to enter') by the Korku (Hermanns 1966: 158; Dixit 1966: 14; the woman's entry into the house must be by the back door, not the front), *anander* by the Ho (Dhan 1961: 67), *ghar mechrano* by the Mahali (Chakraborty and Kundu 1980: 77), *gasiarmundi* by the Gataq (Guha *et al.* 1970: 117), *paisamundi* by the Gadaba (Satpathy 1963–4a: 154) and *dhuku* or *duka duki* by the Korwa (Sandhwar 1978: 70; Deogaonkar 1986: 39–40). A woman who does this is called *dhukni* in Mundari and Santali, from Hindi *dhukna* (Pandey 1966: 42; Campbell 1954: 289), *dhuku-dhani* in Korwa (Deogaonkar ibid.), and *gandamnaboi* in Sora ((Vitebsky 1979).
61 Dixit 1966: 12–14; Hermanns 1966: 155–6; Srivastava 1976: 289–90; 1979: 82; Majumdar 1930: 114–15; 1944: 14, 54. On the Korwa, see previous section.
62 Roy 1925; 148; Mukherjea 1962: 218; Majumdar 1926: 15.
63 On these two types of marriage, see Datta-Majumdar 1956: 44; Biswas 1956: 83; Mukherjea 1962: 215; Gautam 1977a: 124; Bouez 1975: 124–5; 1985: 115 (Santal); and Roy 1925: 149 (Birhor). Mahali *kirin bahu bapla* looks like a very similar term, but it is actually the name for the regular form of marriage ('bought-wife marriage'; see above, note 40).
64 Biswas 1956: 83; Mukherjea 1962: 213.
65 Bouez 1985: 113; Mahapatra 1980: 27; Orans 1959: 232–6.
66 1948: 96; McDougal does not even mention it.
67 McDougal 1963a: 237–9; Chakraborty and Kundu 1980: 89.
68 Orans 1959: 231; Leuva 1963: xiii, 89.
69 Hermanns 1966: 160; Beck 1967: 557.
70 Leuva 1963: xiii, 100–1; Jain 1959: 33; Rosner 1956: 46; Bhattacharyya 1953a: 11; N. Prasad 1961: 228. S.S. Prasad (1962b: 104) simply says that it is very rare among the latter.
71 Bhattacharya ibid.
72 Sachchidananda 1964: 56; Elwin 1950: 114; 1948: 104; Fürer-Haimendorf 1943a: 172; McDougal 1963a: 96, 274.
73 See Bouez 1985: 126; Sengupta 1970: 132; Bahadur 1977: 50–1; Roy

and Roy 1937: 278; Bhattacharyya 1953b: 6.
74 Quotation from Culshaw 1949: 147; see also Bouez 1985: 126.
75 McDougal 1963a: 276. See also below.
76 Datta-Majumdar 1956: 45; Elwin 1955: 56; Roy and Roy 1937: 185, 278; Choudhury 1977: 94; Bahadur 1977: 42–3, 56; Sahu 1943: 174; 1953: 62; Dhan 1961: 67; McDougal 1963a: 274–9. Among the Kodaku, elder children go with the father, younger children with the mother (Singh and Danda 1986: 54), and this may be typical.
77 Rout 1962: 175; Elwin 1948: 105; McDougal 1963a: 98, 278; 1964: 334 n.10. Once again, we see the concern of village authorities with proper kinship behaviour.
78 Troisi 1979: 169; Culshaw 1949: 147; also Choudhury 1952: 112; Singh and Danda 1986: 53.
79 Guha et al. 1970: 125; Datta-Majumdar 1956: 45; Culshaw ibid.; Troisi 1979: 168; Bouez 1985: 125; Elwin 1955: 56.
80 Bouez 1975: 124; Mukherjea 1962: 215–16; Roy and Roy 1937: 271–4; Roy 1925: 148. This means, inter alia, that she will not be able to help any subsequent husband with the domestic ritual (Bouez 1985: 113).
81 Bhattacharyya 1953a: 11; Sachchidananda 1979: 132; Gautam 1977a: 122; Elwin 1948: 105; Rout 1962: 174; Choudhury 1977: 94; Majumdar 1937: 89; 1944: 53–4; 1932: 268; Sandhwar 1978: 110.
82 Chatterjee and Das 1927: 27; Chakraborty and Kundu 1980: 89; Choudhury ibid.; Rizbi 1977: 58; Gautam 1977a: 122.
83 Quotations respectively from Culshaw 1949: 146, McDougal 1963a: 240–1, 281, and Elwin 1950: 96; also Roy and Roy 1937: 185; Guha et al. 1970: 123; Bhattacharyya 1953b: 6.
84 See on these matters, Rout 1962: 171, 174; McDougal 1963a: 280–1; Kochar 1963: 54–5; 1970: 78–9; Troisi 1979: 169 and n.21; Mukherjea 1962: 196–7; Chatterjee and Das 1927: 41; Guha et al. ibid.; Chattopadhyay 1964: 16, 22; Sengupta 1968a: 67; 1970: 113; Bahadur 1977: 41–2; Sandhwar 1978: 334 n.39; Singh and Danda 1986: 57. Among the Korku such marriages are called adha urag sageba, literally 'to take half the house' (Hermanns 1966: 157).
85 See Culshaw 1949: 146; McDougal 1963a: 334; Elwin 1948: 96; 1955: 56; Dhan 1961: 61, 69; Bhandari 1963: 96; Kochar 1970: 78–9; Ray Chowdhury 1929: 107; Choudhury 1977: 80–1; Ramadas 1931: 168; Guha et al. 1970: 66; Satpathy 1963–4a: 153); Sengupta 1968b: 68–9; 1970: 122–4. The quotation is from Mukhopadhyay 1976: 19.
86 Dhan 1961: 69; McDougal 1963a: 280; Hermanns 1966: 157.
87 Elwin 1955: 56; Sitapati 1939: 193, 195.
88 1950: 96, 116–17, 131.
89 See Pfeffer 1982a: 34; 1983: 102–3; apparently also referred to by Bouez, talking about the Ho (1985: 72).
90 Das 1931a: 12; Ali 1973: 43; see also below.
91 Manu ix, 57–70; see also Das 1962: 229–30.
92 See Prince Peter 1963.
93 Culshaw 1949: 146; Bhandari 1963: 96; Choudhury 1977: 80; Rout 1962: 171; Elwin 1948: 105; Rosner 1956: 46.

94   Elwin 1950: 114, 116–17; Fürer-Haimendorf 1943a: 172; Majumdar
      1950: 124; Dhan 1961: 54; McDougal 1963a: 282.
95   McDougal 1963a: 279; 1964: 331 n.9.
96   Elwin 1948: 96; McDougal 1964: 331; Bhandari 1963: 96; Chattopad-
      hyay 1964: 19; Majumdar 1937: 88; Sengupta 1968a: 68–9; 1970: 113,
      122–4; Choudhury 1977: 81; Das Gupta 1978: 144; Singh and Danda
      1986: 57.
97   Sengupta 1970: 113; Bouez 1985: 79–80, 106, 119; Dhan 1961: 71. See
      also sects. 8.3, 8.4 on this last point.
98   Sengupta 1970: 119; Guha et al. 1970: 82; Ali 1973: 43. The Korku rule
      presumably applies to cases in which WyZ is also yBW.
99   McDougal 1964: 331 and n.9; Sengupta 1968b: 66–7. See also sect. 8.4.
100   Quotation from Elwin 1950: 125–6. Elwin encountered one Sora
      village where 'every married man had at least two wives' (1955: 56).
      See also McDougal ibid.; Elwin 1948: 104; 1950: 114, 116–17; Roy and
      Roy 1937: 116, 274; Gautam 1977a: 125; Troisi 1979: 167; Bouez 1985:
      113; Biswas 1956: 218; Roy 1912: 227ff., 290ff.; Sahu 1943: 173; Majum-
      dar 1950: 124; Singh and Danda 1986: 35.
101   Quotation from Datta-Majumdar 1956: 81–2, on the Santal; also
      Choudhury 1977: 80; Guha et al. 1970: 127; Choudhury 1952: 88;
      Sengupta 1970: 113; Bista 1972: 139.
102   Sengupta 1970: 110; Sachchidananda 1964: 67; Elwin 1955: 56–7;
      McDougal 1963a: 282; 1964: 331 n.9; Hermanns 1966: 160.
103   E.g. in Bengal and Gujarat; see Fruzzetti 1982: 111–12 and van der
      Veen 1973 respectively.

Notes to Chapter Seven

1   There are three terminologies for which we have no data, namely
      Turi, Juray and one of the Gataq languages (see Ch. 2). The sources
      for the analysis in this chapter are mainly those listed in my thesis,
      in which extensive tables of Munda kin terms can also be found
      (Parkin 1984: Ch. 6 and Appendix). Additional references are Zide
      and Zide forthcoming (ZZ); Vitebsky 1979 (Vi); Pfeffer 1982a: 21, 77;
      McDougal 1963a: Ch. 4; Sachidananda 1979: 348; Fuchs 1988: 165–6;
      and Singh and Danda 1986: 59, 112–13. The analysis is a revised
      version of one which first appeared in *Man* 1985: 707ff., and I grate-
      fully acknowledge the permission of the Director of the Royal
      Anthropological Institute to republish passages from it here.
      Some of the lexical forms and etymologies I proposed in the original
      version have since been criticized (Zide and Zide forthcoming), and
      although I consider that most of the criticisms strengthen rather than
      weaken the anthropological arguments I was trying to make, they
      have been taken into account in making this revision. I am grateful
      to the authors for making a manuscript copy of their paper available
      to me (page numbers which follow 'ZZ' in the text below refer to this
      manuscript, from which the starred forms have also been taken).
      Hopefully, this revision brings us closer to a truly accurate account

of Munda kinship terminology, but the final word will have to await the appearance of the remaining papers on the linguistic aspects of Munda kin terms, including proto reconstructions, that the authors have promised. I am also grateful to Piers Vitebsky for supplying me with data on Sora kin terms. Forms marked Bch are from Bhattacharya 1970a, the accompanying numbers referring to his entries, not to pages.

The language abbreviations used in this chapter are as follows:

AA	Austroasiatic	GRG	Gutob-Remo-Gataq	Ku	Korku
B	Birhor	Hi	Hindi	Kw	Korwa
Beng	Bengali	IE	Indo-European	Mu	Mundari
Bh	Bhumij	Ju	Juang	NM	North Munda
CM	Central Munda	Kh	Kharia	R	Remo
Gb	Gutob	Kher	Kherwarian	Sa	Santali
Gm	Gorum	KM	Koraput Munda	SM	South Munda
Gq	Gataq				

Asur, Ho, Kora and Sora have been left unabbreviated. 'Indic' refers to the Indo-European languages spoken in India. For kin term abbreviations, see Preface.

2   It is hypothetically possible that Munda equivalents for these terms once existed but have disappeared since the loans were adopted. This is very unlikely, however, principally because of the regularity with which the loans are applied to the same categories throughout the family of terminologies. Other parts of the terminologies of some of the more Hinduized groups (Bh, Kh, Asur, Kw) *have* undergone this sort of lexical replacement, but this is not relevant to the present discussion.

3   Vitebsky 1979 and personal communication. See also Chaussin 1978: 177, though her statements are not entirely clear. These equations cannot be seen as so-called 'Crow-Omaha', since they are applied to cross kin on both sides; moreover, the –1 specifications have alternative terms, as classificatory GC.

4   Karvé 1965: 277, 284; Trautmann 1981. There is some uncertainty about the Remo term, since after checking Elwin's data (1950) in the field, Fernandez reported that 'the term "*Marenger*" was unknown to my informants' (1969: 30, italics in the original).

5   See McDougal 1964: 329, Table 1.

6   The difference is that in the senior part the devices used are similar but not identical to other compounds for the kin and affines of one's +1 affines, e.g. Ho *kaka-honyar*, means '*honyar*'s *kaka*', i.e. EFyB (ZZ 15; the *Encyc. Mund.* has numerous such examples). This is not quite the same as *bauhonhar, ajihanar*, for although the prefixes suggest siblings of EP, the specifications these terms refer to are in fact their children: e.g. *ajihanar* is '*hanar*'s daughter', not her sister (i.e. '*hanar*'s *aji*').

7   McDougal 1963a: 128 and n.1, 137–8; see 1964: 329 for other examples.

8   Zide 1958: 11; Bhattacharya 1966: 35.

9   Bouez indicates that in Ho it is used more widely still, especially in address, to classificatory +2 or –2 referents and WeZH (1985: 57, 59).

10   The ultimate origin of *mama* is uncertain and may be either Indic or Dravidian. In Indic it usually appears as MB, but in Dravidian it tends to have the full symmetric prescriptive range of MB = FZH = EF (Trautmann 1981). This same distinction is found between different Munda languages, indicating that in KM *mama* is a loan from Dravidian, but in NM a loan from Indic.

11   McDougal 1963a: 128, 132, 138, 140; 1964: 329.

12   Only two are clearly recorded: Sa MB ≠ FZH and Ju MBC ≠ FZC (see text).

13   This consistency of affinal terms contrasting with the variability of many cognatic terms (especially for collaterals) is also evident from Szemérenyi's work on Indo-European kin terms (1978).

14   Dumont is mainly right in seeing the +2 and –2 levels as being completely merged in Dravidian, but there are exceptions, namely Mappilla, Gommu Koya and Hill Maria (see the tables in Trautmann 1981: 170, 189, 196).

Notes to Chapter Eight

1   Inden and Nicholas 1977: 8, 15–17, 117–19 nn. 1, 4, 7, 8; Fruzzetti 1982: 15, 23, 42–3, 149. Parry remarks (1979: 138) that *kutumb* means only agnates in Kangra, though referring also to 'non-agnatic cognates and affines' in Malwa in central India (after Adrian Mayer).

2   On the Juang generally, see McDougal 1963a: 75–6, 81–2, 246, 316; 1964: 323, 328–9.

3   1963a: 82; 1964: 328–9.

4   See McDougal 1963a: 246.

5   McDougal 1963a: 132 n.1. In some cases, McDougal's informants were not even sure whether particular villages or clans were *kutumb* or *bondhu* to their own (1963a: 437), though in part this may be due simply to ignorance. Roy thought that only ego's group was *kutumb*, all the rest being *bondhu* (1935: 135), but this is clearly an over-simplification (he was working with a neighbouring group at the time).

6   On the Gadaba, Claudia Gross, personal communication; Mohanty 1973–4: 146; Singh 1977a: 102; cf. Izikowitz n.d.: 133, 137. On the Gataq, Guha *et al.* 1970: 56ff.

7   *Gotia* is possibly from Indic *gosthi* or 'agnatic household'—see Inden and Nicholas 1977: 8; also Chaussin 1978: 172; Piers Vitebsky, personal communication; Singh 1977a: 42; Roy and Roy 1937: 174.

8   Quotation from Choudhury 1977: 61; see also ibid.: 26, 40, 57–8; Standing 1981: 225; Sugiyama 1969: 95, 1970: 385; Roy 1912: 418.

9   See Chattopadhyay 1964: 15.

10   Cf. 1985: 54 and 79–80.

11   Ibid.: 55, 133.

12   Kochar 1970: 62–3; Mukherjea 1962: 137. Gautam and Kochar call the

kutum a '(non-unilineal) kindred' (Kochar ibid. and p. 37; Gautam 1977a: 134), but it is not clear whether or not they mean by this an ego-centred group.

13   Bouez 1985: 97–9, 177; Kochar 1970: 54, 62; Gautam 1977a: 79, 107, 146; Mukherjea 1962: 137–9, 144.

14   1955: 53; also Das Gupta 1978: 130; Sitapati 1939: 193.

15   Roy 1925: 125–6; Roy and Roy 1937: 125, 223, 226; McDougal 1963a: 132 n.1; Bouez 1985: 133; Piers Vitebsky, personal communication.

16   Chattopadhyay 1964: 21.

17   Archer 1974: 84–6; Elwin 1955: 53; Sitapati 1939: 193.

18   Jain 1958: 31.

19   Majumdar claimed that since there was no separate term for MZH this specification must be equivalent to ego, so that ego's wife was also his MZ! (1924: 200; also 1937: 89; 1950: 126). He retracted his statement about MZ marriage on one occasion (1926: 153). Cf. Chattopadhyay 1964: 19ff.

20   1985: 79, 80. Further on (p. 135), when comparing the Ho and Santal, he seeks to assimilate it to the preferred, *sangat* marriage of the latter through assimilation of ego's father to his elder brother—i.e. one's *sangat* or eBWyZ is assimilated to FWyZ, i.e. MyZ. However, this is a less satisfactory explanation, since it assimilates an occasional practice to a regular preference, so that what 'is fully realized among the Santal' becomes merely 'an implicit model' among the Ho.

21   1961: 71. WeBD and ZD are terminologically equated here, as *gaing* (Majumdar 1950: 176).

22   Sengupta 1970: 113; Majumdar 1932: 267; 1944: 56; Bhandari 1963: 100.

23   Elwin 1955: 53, 56; Sitapati 1939: 193.

24   Archer 1974: 85–6; Bouez 1985: 131, 215 n.16; see also Hermanns 1966: 158–9.

25   Das Gupta 1978: 130; Bouez 1985: 76; Guha *et al.* 1970: 122.

26   Marriage prohibitions also result from the fictive kinship created through ritual, since the principals thereby become classificatory siblings and their own relationships are re-ordered accordingly with respect to one another. See, for example, Sengupta 1966: 75; Gautam 1977a: 120; Elwin 1950: 37–8.

27   Quotation from Majumdar 1950: 125–6; also ibid.: 93–4; *idem* 1937: 88–9; Bouez 1975: 121 and n.7; 1985: 60–1, 66; Chattopadhyay 1964: 20–1.

28   Bouez 1985: 66ff.; Chattopadhyay 1964: 21; Dhan 1961: 70–1.

29   Bouez 1985: 66ff., 75, 116–17, 155–6, 177; Chattopadhyay 1964: 15, 21; Dhan 1961: 70–2; also Dasgupta 1983: 43.

30   Bouez 1985: 75; Chattopadhyay 1964: 19, 21; Majumdar 1950: 125; Dhan 1961: 70, 72–3. Dhan's report on inter-level marriage is worth citing: 'I found one such case in village Lemre. Bende Champia...married his father's...father's wife...after his death. Bende is 30 years old and his grandmother is 28 years old.'

31   Culshaw 1949: 172; Kochar 1963: 49; 1970: 39; Bhowmik 1971: 171;

Mukherjea 1962: 139; Fürer-Haimendorf 1985: 113.

32   Gausdal, following Risley, claims that there can be no marriage into one's mother's *khut* or sub-clan (1953: 8). Kochar (1970: 53) says that marriage is possible into one's mother's sub-clan but not lineage, Datta-Majumdar (1956: 41) that marriage is possible into her sub-clan but not clan, and this is apparently supported by Bhowmik (1971: 169). Bouez contradicts himself in his monograph (see 1985: 105 versus 189), though he now recognizes some restriction, a change from his 1975 article, in which he said 'no prohibition falls on the mother's clan' (1975: 119).

33   The account of the Keonjhar Santal is based on Bouez 1975: 119, 120, 122–3; 1985: 79–80, 106–25, 133, 189–90; also Kochar 1970: 62; Mukherjea 1962: 146.

34   Bouez records this term ('friend' in Indic languages) as eGEyGos when listing kin terms (1985: 101), but he gives only the specification eZHyZms when discussing alliance *per se*. He is supported by some other writers on the Santal. Mukherji mentions the existence of a joking relationship with both ZHZ and ZHB (ms only?), whom he calls *iril kuri* and *iril kora* respectively (1964: 69). Fürer-Haimendorf says that a Santal may marry eBWZ but not yBWZ (presumably eBWyZ but not yBWeZ; see 1985: 113).

35   This is a modified version of Bouez's Figure 12 (1985: 110) and has been chosen because it shows relative age and status clearly. However, the *alliance* structure is essentially the same as in Figure 6 (the Ho, above), i.e. one of symmetric exchange.

36   1935b: 73.

37   Mukherjea, who also worked in Orissa, says a grandmother should do this (1962: 189).

38   Pfeffer 1983: 119. Thus this is an expanded version of the 'four-*got* rule' of north India (Tiemann 1970), in which avoidance is limited to the *got* or descent group of one's father, mother, FM and MM only. This imposes a delay of just two generations, so that only one's SSS can repeat one's own marriage, i.e. one can repeat the marriage of a FFF but no one nearer.

39   Carrin-Bouez 1986: 19, 30, 41 n.50, 65–6. Her book is mainly concerned with matters of ritual, so we have only scattered references to alliance to go on, not a full analysis.

40   On these two paragraphs, see Gautam 1977a: 107–11, 116–18, 124, 1977b: 371, 379; Biswas 1956: 73; Kochar 1970: 43; Gausdal 1953: 96–7. The quoted passages are from Gautam 1977a: 109, 110.

41   The statistics are respectively from Sengupta 1970: 100, 113, 116 and *idem* 1969: 108–9; also 1966: 76, 99–102; 1968a: 65; Roychoudhury 1963: 32.

42   Standing 1976: 86, 93; *Encyc. Mund.* 2381, 3827; Yamada 1970: 384–6; Jordan-Horstmann 1972a: 282; Choudhury 1977: 76ff.; Sachchidananda 1979: 114; 1957: 8, 113; Icke-Schwalbe 1979: 64. Choudhury tends to contradict Yamada's interpretation in saying that one can marry into one's mother's clan, excluding MZ or step-mother.

This suggests the possibility of renewing alliances in the immediately following generation, without any delay. Bouez suggests that there is a gap of only one generation (1985: 149–50), but he is relying here on the supposed precedent provided by the Juang, not on direct evidence. Choudhury's further statement, that it is not usual to confine marriages to particular villages, does not necessarily contradict Yamada, for it may signal an avoidance of particular villages associated with the generational delay, not simply a random pattern of alliances. Yamada himself says that occasional instances of *kili* endogamy do occur and are tolerated, which is understandable if *kili* names are generally ill known.

43   Quotations from Icke-Schwalbe 1979: 64; Pfeffer 1982a: 79, 86 on the kin terms; also Sachchidananda 1979: 90, 348; Choudhury 1977: 58, 62, 66–7; Das 1965: 10, 12.

44   Lévi-Strauss 1949: 529–31; cf. Parkin 1983: 80–2; Bouez 1985: 150. See also next section.

45   Standing 1976: 211; *Encyc. Mund.* pp. 1987.

46   Williams 1968: 127, 130–1; Roy 1925: 125–6; Adhikary 1984: 57–8.

47   On these two paragraphs, Majumdar 1932: 267–8; 1944: 14, 33, 56–7; Bhandari 1963: 80, 88, 90, 91, 93, 96, 100; Srivastava and Verma 1967: 54; Sandhwar 1978: 39, 43, 44, 69; Hari Mohan 1979: 88–91; Singh and Danda 1986: 43–4, 57; Deogaonkar 1986: 34, 38. The quotation concerning the Kodaku is from Singh 1977a: 42. Among the Korwa the marriage priest is characteristically a 'sister's husband' (a wife-taker) (Bhandari 1963: 104).

48   Leuva 1963: 68, 91; Jain 1958: 31, 33, 35, 37; Das Gupta 1978: 130, 144–5; Bhattacharyya 1953a: 10; Das 1956b: 114; Roy 1917: 570.

49   Fuchs 1966: 216–17; 1988: 176–7, 239–40; Hermanns 1966: 135, 157; Ali 1973: 43.

50   On the Bhumij, Das 1931a: 12; Chatterjee and Das 1927: 55; Pfeffer 1982a: 58; Banerjee 1962: 19; on the Kora, Das 1964: 45.

51   Roy and Roy 1937: 157, 158, 160–1, 223; Bahadur 1977: 24; Vidyarthi and Upadhyay 1980: 117, 120, 132; Pfeffer 1983: 101.

52   This section is based on McDougal 1963a: xxiv, 74, 76, 81–2, 129–39, 155–64, 168, 259, 274, 408, 428–9; 1963b: 185–6; 1964: 319, 322, 328–31, 334, 342; also Elwin 1948: 49.

53   1963a: 159–66. In 1948, Elwin recorded a figure of 52% of marriages with MBD (1948: 96), though Rout (1972: 171) supports McDougal in saying that actual MBD is avoided.

54   Guha *et al.* 1970: 80, 82–3, 109, 119; Siddiqui 1976: 5–6; Mohanty 1981–2: 6.

55   Elwin 1950: xiii, 36; Pfeffer 1982a: 53, 86, 1982b: 51; 1983: 96, 102, 118; personal communication.

56   Pfeffer 1982a: 48 (after P.K. Mishra); 1983: 96, 102; 1984b: 233; ms and personal communication; Claudia Gross, personal communication; Chandra Sekhar 1964: 14–15.

57   Pattanayak 1968: 255; Pfeffer 1983: 96, 102, 118.

58   Sitapati 1939: 193; Pfeffer 1983: 102; Chowdhury 1963–4: 102; Elwin

1955: 53; Piers Vitebsky, personal communication. Chaussin's statements here (1978) rely heavily on a distinction between 'lignée' and 'lignage' (see sect. 4.2), which Vitebsky rejects as false.

59   This does not mean that the matter has been ignored, only that the search for such systems has to some extent been misdirected. My own earlier statements on this point (e.g. Parkin 1985: 717) now seem unnecessarily tentative in seeing them as untypical of the Munda. It will be shown below that this view ceases to be tenable once one moves away from focusing only on so-called 'cross-cousin marriage' and looks more widely at all the other possible expressions of such alliance systems. In what follows, my view of the relationship between terminology and alliance in prescriptive systems is essentially that put forward in Needham 1973.

60   Pfeffer has stressed the importance of the elder-younger distinction in these societies and has argued that seniority is often equated with consanguinity (1982a: 77; 1983: 107).

61   See, for example, McDougal 1963a: 428; 1964: 324–5; Elwin: 1950: xii–xiii; Pfeffer 1982a: 43; Roy and Roy 1937: 147.

62   Cf. Pfeffer 1982a: 85.

63   1963a: 428.

64   Claudia Gross, personal communication.

65   The Birjhia Asur may eventually prove to resemble the other North Munda groups, however; see previous section.

66   See, for example, Needham 1962: Ch. 5. Needham's objections turn essentially on the instability of any system which reverses the direction of alliances with every generation; the fact that no independent terminological principles are known which formally express the system; and the likelihood that in practice such a system would be indistinguishable from regular symmetric affinal alliance ('bilateral cross-cousin marriage'), in which exchange is anyway likely to be staggered, for simple demographic reasons (present unavailability of suitable women to give in exchange, for example). Thus debts of women are always outstanding, and the frequently reported preferences for a classificatory FZD as marriage partner—common as is well known in south India—though they must be accepted as social facts, in reality express merely that 'our group are currently owed a woman by our affines for one given previously'.

67   See, for example, Needham 1962 on the Purum; Barnes gives other examples from Indonesia, namely the Tanimbar Islanders and the Karo Batak (1976: 389).

68   Barnes ibid., original emphasis.

69   Ibid.

70   On north and west India, see Tiemann 1970; Kolenda 1978; Parkin 1990. In the relation between preference and prescription, the first situation is not dissimilar to the unilateral preferences within a bilateral classification that are so commonly reported from south India.

71   1982a: 53, 61ff.; 1983: 101, 109.

72   Korn 1973: 29, after Strehlow.

Notes to Chapter Nine

1 McDougal 1964: 345. See sects. 8.3 and 8.4 on the marriage preferences and prohibitions mentioned in this chapter.
2 McDougal 1964: 333–4; Chattopadhyay 1964: 16–17; Biswas 1935: 49.
3 McDougal 1963a: 102ff.; Sandhwar 1978: 45; Choudhury 1977: 63–4; Roy 1925: 126, 135; Jain 1958: 31–2.
4 Roy and Roy 1937: 117, 158–9; Vidyarthi and Upadhyay 1980: 117; Satpathy 1963–4a: 153; Hermanns 1966: 129; Sandhwar 1978: 39; McDougal 1963a: 131.
5 On the Ho, Bouez 1985: 65. On the Santal, ibid.: 103, 112 n.5, 117, 123; Carrin-Bouez 1985: 73; also Kochar 1963: 52, 54, though his statements are rather contradictory and he later said that Santal children may be fostered to MB or FZH (1970: 62).
6 Mukhopadhyay 1976: 13; Bouez 1985: 103; also Mukherji 1964: 69.
7 On the Ho, Bouez 1985: 57, 64. On the Juang, McDougal 1963a: 106–7, 147; 1964: 335–7.
8 McDougal 1963a: 130; Bhandari 1963: 94; Chattopadhyay 1964: 16–17. Not among the Asur (Jain 1958: 33). Bouez distinguishes respect from avoidance as far as the Ho relationship with EF is concerned: 'one avoids rather than respects a father-in-law, and the respect one shows him is due not to his status as an ally, but as an elder' (1985: 63).
9 McDougal 1963a: 105–7, 133–4; Roy and Roy 1937: 160.
10 Malhotra says specifically that 'the behaviour pattern follows the kinship terminology' (1963: 324); see also Jain 1958: 36–7; Bhandari 1963: 94.
11 On the Juang, McDougal 1963a: 108–9, 131; 1964: 329, 334. On other groups, Guha et al. 1970: 76–7; Biswas 73; Roy and Roy 1937: 160; Choudhury 1977: 66; Dhan 1961: 72; Singh 1977a: 42; Malhotra 1963: 318. Further examples come from the Korwa (see sect. 8.4, where Korwa marriage preferences are listed).
12 E.g. Guha et al. 1970: 76; Datta-Majumdar 1956: 82; Roy 1925: 137–8; Choudhury 1977: 66.
13 See, for example, Sugiyama 1969: 55, 63.
14 Elwin 1950: 64n., 114, 117; McDougal 1963a: 113, 135; Bhandari 1963: 90, 94.
15 The quotation is from Biswas 1956: 54–5; also McDougal 1963a: 113, 135–6; 1964: 334; Kochar 1970: 78–9. On the different forms of salutation used by the Santal, see Culshaw 1949: 12–13.
16 See, for example, Choudhury 1977: 64–5; Bhandari 1963: 90.
17 Roy 1925: 127; Fuchs 1988: 167. To a certain extent this is reflected terminologically; see sect. 7.2.
18 McDougal 1963a: 136; 1964: 329, 332; Dhan 1961: 71–2; Roy and Roy 1937: 159–61; Bhandari 1963: 90, 93–4; Sandhwar 1978: 43; Choudhury 1977: 66; Kochar 1963: 52; Culshaw 1949: 134; Singh and Danda 1986: 57.
19 Jain 1958: 33–4, 36–7; Rizbi 1977: 53; Choudhury 1977: 54, 63; Sen-

gupta 1970: 92–3; McDougal 1963a: 109–10, 112, 131–2, 410; 1964: 332, 334; Gautam 1977a: 108; Mukhopadhyay 1976: 19; Singh 1977a: 42; Singh and Danda ibid.: 43.

20 Gautam 1977a: 117; Guha *et al.* 1970: 81; Mohanty 1981–2: 8; Sengupta 1970: 94; Dhan 1961: 70–2; Bouez 1985: 65; Sachchidananda 1979: 90; Roy and Roy 1937: 159; Vidyarthi and Upadhyay 1980: 118; Sandhwar 1978: 44.

21 Kochar 1963: 52; Dhan 1961: 72; Jain 1958: 33, 34, 37–8; Choudhury 1977: 64–5. Malhotra says that the Birhor have an avoidance relationship with HeBW, a joking relationship with HyBW (1963: 316ff.), but this is countered by the fact that these two categories are reciprocals—unless, as seems unlikely, there is a marked asymmetry in their relationship, of the sort noted for the avunculate by Radcliffe-Brown (cf. the Asur, above).

22 Choudhury 1977: 65; Chattopadhyay 1964: 16–17; McDougal 1963a: 138; Bhandari 1963: 94. On the Santal, cf. Kochar 1963: 52 and Mukhopadhyay 1976: 19; also Culshaw 1949: 13.

23 McDougal ibid. McDougal seems to be mixing up his data here, for he indicates that SWF, the wife-giver, is inferior to DHF, the wife-taker—according to him, the former should salute first and is often called *sano* (Oriya 'little') *somondi*, whereas DHF is *kuba* (Juang 'great') *somondi* (1963a: 137–8). This would accord with north Indian hypergamy, but in all other respects, what asymmetry there is in the Juang alliance system relates to usual affinal alliances—wife-givers superior to wife-takers.

24 Claudia Gross, personal communication.

25 Bhandari ibid.; Chattopadhyay 1964: 19; Choudhury 1977: 75; Jain 1958: 36; Bhowmik 1971: 175; McDougal 1963a: 97 n. 1; Malhotra 1963: 316; Burrows 1915: 111.

26 Sengupta 1966: 82–3. This must refer to the usual marriages, which are *not* with an MBD. In the rare instances of MBD marriage there is no change in the kin term used for MB (Sengupta 1970: 96).

27 On the Korwa, Bhandari 1963: 86, 95; on the Birhor, Malhotra 1963: 320–1, with examples at ibid.: 324.

28 Bouez 1985: 63–4; Somers 1977: 69. Nonetheless, a contrast in behaviour may be applied to village officers. There is a joking relationship between Santal village youth and the *jog-manjhi* (sec. 5.2), while the *manjhi* or headman is owed the respect due to a father (Gautam 1977a: 92–3).

29 In this respect, Juang and Kharia are atypical of the Munda, whose terminologies otherwise regularly equate yGE with CE (sect. 7.3; the terminology as a whole is, of course, focused on ego).

30 On the Juang, McDougal 1963a: 129, 141–50; 1964: 332ff.

31 The quotation is from Elwin 1948: 103; also ibid.: 107–8; 1950: 88–9; McDougal 1963a: 236, 247, 252, 358, 365; 1964: 334–5, 339ff.

32 The second and third quotations are from Culshaw 1949: 123–4; also Basu 1972; Mukherjea 1962: 189.

33 McDougal 1963a: 420; on what follows, see also ibid.: Ch. 6 and pp.

332ff., 352ff., 423–5, 431; also 1963b.

34   This is what McDougal (1963a) calls it. According to Elwin it is called *darbar* or *mandagarh* and 'flourishes in Keonjhar, but has generally decayed in Pal Lahera and Dhenkanal' (1948: 73).

35   Although McDougal does not mention the fact, it is also true that sexually active women will mainly be wives of householders and therefore recent incomers. Possibly they are therefore regarded as ritually dangerous, a danger which passes as their husbands become ritual elders, by which time they are completely integrated into the village community. Young girls, of course, are village agnates until they marry and move away.

36   Here too, Elwin is at variance with McDougal, saying that 'the older men carry the body out of the village. It is often considered advisable that the younger boys should not go, "for they may die"' (1948: 110).

37   Elwin 1950: 75.

Notes to Chapter Ten

1   E.g. Elwin 1950: 202ff.; Culshaw 1949: 159–60.

2   Carrin-Bouez 1986: 67, 89 n.17, 170 n.2; also Kochar 1963: 60ff.

3   'The concept of "reincarnation" *as expressed in Hinduism* seems strange to them, which they demonstrate by saying that the Hindus "have no ancestors"' (1986: 75, my emphasis; see also ibid.: 67, 71–2; Culshaw 1949: 159–60; Hodson 1921a: 1).

4   Bouez 1985: 72.

5   Gautam 1977a: 150; Hansda 1983: 184.

6   This system is completely reversed in the case of *ghar-jawae* marriages in the sense that the names of maternal kin take precedence (Datta-Majumdar 1956: 87). However, this is from the point of view of that particular marriage only: the maternal line is still an *agnatic* line when seen over several generations, the anomaly being simply the result of this uxorilocal marriage (see sect. 3.3).

7   Hansda ibid.; Mukerji 1964: 69; Troisi 1979: 61; Bouez 1985: 121; Culshaw 1949: 127–8; 1941: 125.

8   *Mul* or *bhitri nutum* (Troisi 1979: 162). According to Bodding, *mul* means 'principal, original, real' (1935b: 336), while *bhitri* means 'inside, inner' (1932: 414). Gautam says that this name is only used in ritual (1977a: 114).

9   *Bahna* or *cetan nutum* (Troisi ibid.); *bahna* means 'nickname' (Bodding 1932: 175); *cetan* means 'upper', but also 'superficial' (ibid.: 519–20).

10   For example, without a nickname a grandmother would not be able to address or refer to her grandson, since she may not use the name of her husband, whose name the child now bears.

11   Hansda 1983: 186, 188; Troisi 1979: 162 and n.13; Culshaw 1949: 129: 129. Twins are given Hindu names.

12   Gautam 1977a: 140–1; Troisi 1979: 165–6; Mukherjea 1962: 191–2. The Mundari appear to connect odd numbers with death (see Roy 1912: 463, 466). Both they and the Birjhia Asur make *sika* marks (Choud-

Notes 273

hury 1977: 74; Das Gupta 1978: 129), but it is not clear if a pattern is used. The Kharia also make them, apparently of an odd number, on the left forearm (Vidyarthi and Upadhyay 1980: 130).

13   *Umbul* is a Mundari word, but the others are Indic loans; *roa* is from Oriya, in which it means 'rice seedling'.

14   *Encyc. Mund.*: 2055, 3616ff.; Topno 1955: 719ff.; 1978: 15–21; Bhaduri 1944: 150; Bhowmik and Choudhuri 1966: 102; Exem 1978: 86; Sachchidananda 1979: 90; Shrivastava 1957: 67; Sugiyama 1969: 90.

15   This is less likely with more Hinduized Mundari. Today, names may either be Mundari (which includes those referring to physical characteristics and qualities) or Hindi or Sadri (Hindu deities, names of days, months, seasons, festivals) or even biblical, because of missionary influence (Topno 1970: 172). Standing even reports that naming after a pre-chosen friend or relative has replaced naming after ancestors here (1976: 193–4), but the latter seems to be the original practice.

16   Sugiyama 1969: 61, 90; Chaudhuri 1966: 129; Mundri 1956: 70. Choudhury gives a different order, namely MP, FP, other agnates (1977: 72).

17   Banerjee 1969: 81; Choudhuri 1966: 129; Mundri 1956: 70–1; Choudhury 1977: 72–4; Sugiyama ibid.

18   Das Gupta 1978: 125, 126; Jain 1958: 31; Leuva 1963: 84–6; Rosner 1956: 46.

19   Quotations respectively from Roychoudhury 1964: 24 and Malhotra 1963: 318; also Roy 1925: 234–5, 238–40, 253ff.

20   Chattopadhyay and Ray Choudhuri 1958: 126; Hermanns 1966: 125, 134, 173; Fuchs 1988: 221, 287, 296 *Pace* Fuchs (ibid.: 287), the Korku probably search for marks in a heap of flour in order to see whether the personalized soul has returned to the family hearth, not to divine reincarnation; cf. the Mundari.

21   Quotations respectively from Sandhwar 1978: 48, 57 (italics in original) and Majumdar 1944: 51–2; also Rizbi 1977: 56; Deogaonkar 1986: 42–4, 53.

22   Ray *et al.* 1954: 293–4; Majumdar 1950: 47, 193, 207–8; Sarkar 1919: 139–40; Bouez 1985: 73; Chattopadhyay and Ray Choudhuri 1958: 113; Hodson 1921a: 3. Those who do not 'deserve' reincarnation may be the inauspicious dead rather than the immoral dead; cf. the Remo, below.

23   Majumdar 1950: 187–9; Chattopadhyay and Ray Chaudhuri 1958: 113–14, 119–20; Sarkar 1919: 136–8; Chatterjee and Das 1927: 24.

24   Roy and Roy 1937: 209–15, 283, 293; Chattopadhyay and Ray Choudhuri 1958: 126. Among the Dhelki Kharia, ear-boring is done by two members of the Muru clan, or at any rate from a clan different from that of the child.

25   Elwin 1948: 68, 107–8, 112, 141–2; Chattopadhyay and Ray Choudhuri ibid.; McDougal 1963a: 98–9.

26   According to Vitebsky, it simultaneously becomes absorbed by the spirit responsible for its death (1980: 48–9, 64).

27   Elwin 1955: xxii–xxiii, 65–6, 73, 226–7, 334, 505–6; Sitapati 1940–1:

127; 1943: 4–5; 1948–9: 37–8. Vitebsky (personal communication) reports he found no reference to the two souls mentioned by Elwin and Sitapati.

28   Elwin 1955: 73–6, 142, 387ff.; Sitapati 1940–1, 127; Piers Vitebsky, personal communication.

29   Elwin 1955: 73–4, 131, 226, 358ff., 387–90, 499; Piers Vitebsky, personal communication. The *guar* rite incorporates the *kulman* with the ancestors; the name is from *gu* to plant, plus *ar* 'stone' (Elwin ibid.: 359).

30   Elwin 1950: 104, 134, 202–4, 214, 217; Fürer-Haimendorf 1943b: 167. Elwin could not locate *siorem* in the sense of *jiwo*, but he encountered the same word as 'testicles' and speculated that as with the Baiga, this is the seat of the 'soul' (presumably the *jiwo*).

31   On the Gataq, Fürer-Haimendorf 1945b: 330. On the Gadaba, Pfeffer ms; Claudia Gross, personal communication. According to the latter, the *gotr* is concerned with removing sorrow, not danger, from the living.

32   Bloch and Parry 1982: 13.

33   See, for example, Sugiyama 1969: 90. This suggests that first-born children have the main responsibility for ensuring that the pool of ancestral souls is recycled, and that younger siblings are less significant in this respect.

Notes to Chapter Eleven

1   Trautmann 1981: 199, 233; Allen 1976: 587, postscript; see also Parkin 1988a.

2   1950: 28ff.; also Mauss 1938.

3   On these two paragraphs, see Hocart 1931; Rivière 1984: Ch. 4 and pp. 98–9; Henley 1982: Ch. 4; Hugh-Jones 1979: 164–5; Ashley-Montagu 1937; Meggitt 1965: 144–5, 148, 279, 317. The second quotation is from Meggitt 1972: 74.

4   Grigson 1949; Elwin 1939; see also Parkin ibid.

5   Bouez 1985: 175. He is basing his view on only four groups, the Ho, Santal, Juang and Bhuiya—and the last of these are Indic speakers.

6   See, for example, 1967: 46; 1968, especially pp. 326, 333; 1974 passim; 1980a, especially pp. 54ff., 74ff., 79; 1980b, especially pp. 43ff.

7   1986; also 1982, 1989a, 1989b.

8   1986: 105, original emphasis; also ibid.: 91, 96, 107.

9   E.g. South Dravidian terminologies (Trautmann 1981).

10   Allen 1986: 99–100.

11   Mauss 1938; Allen 1985.

12   I.e. synchronically (see Allen 1985: 42).

13   A possible exception are the Gadaba, and perhaps other groups in Koraput (Pfeffer ms, and personal communication).

14   1968, 1980; he makes no actual reference to Mauss's earlier work.

15   Quotation from Obeyesekere 1980: 138; also ibid.: 148; 1968: 12, 17–18.

16   Obeyesekere 1980: 156ff. Certain specified mythical figures, such as Mitra, may achieve reincarnation (Head and Cranston 1977: 36), but

this is clearly exceptional. Among modern writers, only O'Flaherty so much as hints at the possibility of a Vedic origin for *karma* (but only through the notion of re-*death*), and even she admits that rebirth on this earth does not feature there (1980: 3ff.).

17 See Basham 1975: 78; Parrinder 1973: 78; 1970: 225.

18 Fürer-Haimendorf 1953: 45; Sedlar 1980.

19 Quotations respectively from Marten 1911: 159; Fürer-Haimendorf 1953: 47; Tiemann 1970: 172; and Sedlar 1980: 35. On the last point, see also Dumont 1960: 44 n.18, 45; Das 1977: 35; Manu vi, 2.

20 Jaini 1980: 229 n.27; Manu ix, 8;also *Aitareya Brahmana* vii, 13.

21 Rose 1902: 278–9.

22 O'Flaherty 1980: 19–20; Jaini 1980: 221; Parrinder 1973: 78.

23 Thus in kinship as in language (Zide and Stampe 1968) the Koraput Munda are more conservative.

24 I argue these points at greater length elsewhere (Parkin 1990). One of the notable things about north Indian kinship terminologies is the large number of terms and the consequent isolation of many kin types which would be merged with others in either a prescriptive or many a Western terminology—e.g. the specification MB has its own term and is usually distinct from FZH, FB, MZH and EF. This is especially true of the +1 and –1 levels, and of affines in ego's level, even though in ego's level characteristically PGC = G. It is as if the prescriptive equations, e.g. F = FB ≠ MB, have been completely broken but not yet reassembled as in many Western terminologies, where, for example, FB = MB ≠ F.

25 See 1983: 165ff. for his most recent statements on this question; also 1966c.

26 See, for example, Fêng Han-yi 1937 on China and Needham 1980b on Sumba.

Notes to Appendix I

1 On this and the previous paragraph, de Candolle 1961: 752ff., 766ff., 783; Hermanns 1966: 57; Kuiper 1962: 243–5, 274–5; 1966: 57; Bhattacharya 1956: 245; Fuchs 1988: 24–5, 180, 185, 195, 204.

2 Quotations from Stampe 1966: 394–5, after Aasha Mundlay; also Zide 1969: 428; de Candolle 1961: 752–3 and n.9; Kuiper 1962: 243.

3 All from de Candolle 1961, especially pp. 774ff., and Fuchs 1988: 180–1, unless otherwise stated.

4 Thus de Candolle, and Fuchs 1988: 180; but cf. Russell and Hira Lal 1916 iv: 260.

5 Ferreira 1965: 77.

Notes to Appendix II

1 Roy 1915: 2, 346–50, 351 and n., 356, 485–7; *LSI* IV: 79; Trautmann 1981: 143–6 (who mentions 'a preference for marriage with non-relatives', by which he presumably means that close genealogical

referents are banned); Icke-Schwalbe 1979: 65; 1988: 272.

2   Quotations respectively from Sarkar 1935; 252–3 and Vidyarthi 1963: 61; also *idem*: 1 and n.1, 58, 68–9, 78, 103, 218; Bainbridge 1907–10: 44, 54; Sarkar 1934: 248, 257–9, 263; Verma 1959: 67, 75, 85.

3   Sarkar 1937; Verma 1960: 9, 10, 16.

4   1981: 146.

5   Quotations respectively from Roy 1935a: 142, Chatterjee and Das 1927: 55, and Ray Chowdhury 1929: 102; also ibid.: 106–7; Roy ibid.: 80–1, 134–48; Bouez 1985: 157–8.

6   Quotations from Roy and Roy 1937: 124–5, 157, 224–5; also ibid.: 122–3, 174, 188–9, 195–7, 223, 226; Hari Mohan 1961: 195, 201; Vidyarthi and Upadhyay 1980: 132; Sinha 1984: 34–6. In these areas generally, a basically symmetric prescriptive ideology of affinal alliance may be found in local low castes as well as among the 'tribes' (e.g. the Domb of Koraput; Georg Pfeffer, personal communication).

7   This may indicate reincarnation: perhaps these ascendants will only die if they are ready to be reborn in –2 level descendants, i.e. as the children of the married couple.

8   Quotation from Nakane 1967: 118; also Roy 1936: 381–4; 1938: 130; Gurdon 1914: 78–9, 111, 113; Das Gupta 1984: 94–5, 111; Nag 1965: 24–5; Chattopadhyay 1941: 33–4; Ehrenfels 1955: 314–15; Bhowmik 1971: 140; Hodson 1921b: 126; Natarajan 1977: 21. It will be obvious that I disagree with Arhem, who sees the Khasi system as one of simple asymmetric affinal alliance, without any rule of delay before the renewal of alliances (1988: 264–5). See Parkin 1988c: 57 for a further if partial discussion of Khasi kinship terminology. The above précis of the Khasi alliance system supersedes earlier remarks in Parkin 1986b: 60.

9   Toffin 1986: 169–70; McDougal 1979: 132.

10   Parkin 1987.

References Cited

ABERLE, David F. 1967. A Scale of Alternate Generation Terminology, *Southwestern Journal of Anthropology* 23: 261–78.

ADHIKARI, A.K. 1984. *Society and World View of the Birhor*, Calcutta: Anthropological Survey of India.

ALI, S.A. 1973. *Tribal Demography in Madhya Pradesh*, Bhopal: Jai Bharat Publishing House.

ALLEN, N.J. 1976. Sherpa Kinship Terminology in Diachronic Perspective, *Man* n.s. 11: 569–87.

— 1982. A Dance of Relatives, *Journal of the Anthropological Society of Oxford* 13 (2): 139–46.

— 1985. The Category of the Person: A Reading of Mauss's Last Essay, *in* Michael Carrithers, Steven Collins and Steven Lukes (eds.), *The Category of the Person: Anthropology, Philosophy, History*, Cambridge: Cambridge University Press.

— 1986. Tetradic Theory: An Approach to Kinship, *Journal of the Anthropological Society of Oxford* 17 (2): 87–109.

— 1989a. The Evolution of Kinship Terminologies, *Lingua* 77: 173–85.

— 1989b. Assimilation of Alternate Generations, *Journal of the Anthropological Society of Oxford* 20 (1): 45–55.

ARCHER, W.G. 1974. *The Hill of Flutes*, London: George Allen and Unwin.

ARHEM, Kaj 1988. Into the Realm of the Sacred: An Interpretation of Khasi Funerary Ritual, *in* S. Cederroth, C. Corlin and J. Lindström (eds.), *On the Meaning of Death: Essays on Mortuary Rituals and Eschatological Beliefs*, Uppsala: Acta Universitatis Upsaliensis.

ASHLEY-MONTAGU, M. 1937. *Coming Into Being Among the Australian Aborigines: A Study of the Procreative Beliefs of the Native Tribes of Australia*, London: Routledge.

BAHADUR, K.P. 1977. *Castes, Tribes and Cultures of India, Vol. III: Bengal, Bihar and Orissa*, Delhi: Ess Ess Publications.

BAILEY, F.G. 1959. For a Sociology of India?, *Contributions to Indian Sociology* 3: 88–101.

— 1961. 'Tribe' and 'Caste' in India, *Contributions to Indian Sociology* 5: 7–19.

BAINBRIDGE, B.B. 1907–10. The Saorias of the Rajmahal Hills, *Memoirs of the Asiatic Society of Bengal* 2: 43–84.

BANERJEE, B. 1969. Religious Practices in a Munda Village, *Bulletin of the Cultural Research Institute* 8: 79–86.

BANERJEE, H.N. 1962. Social-Ritual Status of the Kharia in the Background of Manbhum, *Bulletin of the Cultural Research Institute* 1 (2): 16–28.

BANERJEE, S. 1981. *Impact of Industrialisation on the Tribal Population of Jharia-Ranigunge Coal Field Areas*, Calcutta: Anthropological Survey of India.

BARBOUR, P.L. 1921. Buruçaski, a Language of Northern Kashmir, *Journal of the American Oriental Society* 41: 60–72.

BARNES, R.H. 1976. Dispersed Alliance and the Prohibition of Marriage: Reconsideration of McKinley's Explanation of Crow-Omaha Terminologies, *Man* n.s. 11 (3): 384–99.

BASHAM, A.L. 1975. *A Cultural History of India*, Oxford: Clarendon Press.

BASU, A. 1972. Village Sat-Simulia: A Case Study of Social Change of the Munda Community, *Bulletin of the Cultural Research Institute* 9 (3–4): 86–9.

BECK, Clemens 1967. Kharia-Hochzeit in Jharsuguda, *Anthropos* 62 (3–4): 555–8.

BENEDICT, Paul K. 1942. Thai, Kadai, and Indonesian, *American Anthropologist* 44 (4): 576–601.

— 1966–7. Austro-Thai Studies, *Behaviour Science Notes* 1: 227–61 and 2: 203–44, 275–336.

— 1976. Austro-Thai and Austroasiatic, *in* Philip Jenner, L.C. Thompson and Stanley Starosta (eds.), *Austroasiatic Studies*, Honolulu: University of Hawaii Press, Oceanic Linguistics Special Publications, no. 13 (2 vols.), Vol. 1: 1–36.

BHADURI, M.B. 1944. Some Munda Religious Ceremonies and their System of Reckoning Time, *Man in India* 24: 148–53.

BHANDARI, J.S. 1963. Kinship, Marriage and Family among the Korwa of Dudhi, *Eastern Anthropologist* 16 (2): 79–106.

BHATTACHARYA, S. 1954. Studies in the Parengi Language, *Indian Linguistics* 14: 45–63.

— 1956. Field Notes on Nahali, *India Linguistics* 17: 245–58.

— 1957. *Ollari: A Dravidian Speech*, Delhi: Department of Anthropology, Government of India.

— 1966. Some Munda Etymologies, *in* N.H. Zide (ed.), *Studies in Comparative Austroasiatic Linguistics*, The Hague: Mouton.

— 1968. *A Bonda Dictionary*, Poona: Deccan College.

— 1970a. Kinship Terms in the Munda Languages, *Anthropos* 65: 444–65.

— 1970b. The Munda Languages and South-East Asia, *Bulletin of the Indian Institute for Advanced Study* 1970: 23–31.

— 1975. Munda Studies: A New Classification of Munda, *Indo-Iranian Journal* 17 (1–2): 97–101.

BHATTACHARYYA, A. 1953a. The Birjhia of Palamau, *Bulletin of the Department of Anthropology* 2 (1): 1–16.

— 1953b. An Account of the Birhor of Palamau, *Bulletin of the Department of Anthropology* 2 (2): 1–10.

BHOWMIK, K.L. 1971. *Tribal India: A Profile in India Ethnology*, Calcutta: World Press.

BHOWMIK, P.K. 1963. *The Lodhas of West Bengal*, Calcutta: Punthi Pustak.

— and B. CHAUDHURI 1966. Some Aspects of Magico-Religious Beliefs and Practices of the Munda, *Folk-Lore* 7: 100–7.

BHOWMIK, S.K. 1980. Ethno-linguistic Study of the Kharias, *Bulletin of the Cultural Research Institute* 14 (1–2): 52–5.

BISTA, D.B. 1972. *People of Nepal*, Katmandu: Ratna Pustak Bhandar.

BISWAS, P.C. 1935. Primitive Religion, Social Organisation, Law, Government among the Santals, *University of Calcutta Anthropological Papers* n.s. 4: 1–84.
— 1956. *Santals of the Santal Parganas*, Delhi: Bharatiya Adimjati Sevak Sangh.
BLOCH, Maurice, and Jonathan PARRY (eds.) 1982. *Death and the Regeneration of Life*, Cambridge: Cambridge University Press.
BODDING, P.O. 1932, 1934, 1935a, 1935b, 1936. *Santal Dictionary*, Oslo: Norske Videnskaps-Akademi (5 vols.).
BOSE, N.K. 1928. Marriage and Kinship among the Juangs, *Man in India* 8 (4): 233–42.
— 1929. Juang Associations, *Man in India* 9 (1): 47–53.
— 1971. *Tribal Life in India*, Delhi: National Book Trust.
BOSE, R. 1950. Gadbas, *in* A.V. Thakkar (ed.), *Tribes of India, Vol. I*, Delhi: Bharatiya Adimjati Sevak Sangh: 173–5.
BOUEZ, Serge 1975. Parenté et hiérarchie chez les Santal, *L'Homme* 15 (3–4): 109–28.
— 1985. *Réciprocité et hiérarchie: L'Alliance chez les Hos et les Santal de l'Inde*, Paris: Société d'Ethnographie.
BURROW, T., and S. BHATTACHARYA 1962. Gadba Supplement, *Indo-Iranian Journal* 6 (1): 45–51.
BURROWS, L. 1915. *Ho Grammar*, Calcutta: Catholic Orphan Press.

CAMPBELL, A. 1953, 1954. *A Santali-English and English-Santali Dictionary*, Pokhuria: Santal Mission Press (2 vols.).
CARRIN-BOUEZ, Marine 1986. *La fleur et l'os: Symbolisme et rituel chez les Santal*, Paris: Editions de l'EHESS.
CHAKRABORTY, B. 1972. A Comparative Study of Family Types and Couple-Children Ratio among the Santals of Two Different Ecological Areas, *Bulletin of the Cultural Research Institute* 9 (1–2): 103–10.
— 1978. Problems and Prospects of the Semi-Nomadic Birhors of West Bengal, *Bulletin of the Cultural Research Institute* 13 (1–2): 30–9.
— 1979. Understanding a Semi-Nomadic Tribe: The Birhors of West Bengal, *Bulletin of the Cultural Research Institute* 13 (3–4): 5–19.
— 1980. The Birhors of West Bengal and the Rehabilitation Scheme: A Case Study, *Bulletin of the Cultural Research Institute* 14 (3–4): 80–6.
— and S. KUNDU 1980. Some Aspects of the Mahali Social Organization: A Preliminary Appraisal, *Bulletin of the Cultural Research Institute* 14 (3–4): 87–92.
CHANDRA SEKHAR, A. 1964. *Gadabavalasa*, Census of India, Vol. II, part VI (1961), Village Survey Monograph 5.
CHATTERJEE, A.N., and T.C. DAS 1927. The Hos of Seraikella, *University of Calcutta Anthropological Papers* n.s. 1, passim.
CHATTERJEE, B.K. 1931. The Social and Religious Institutions of the Kharias, *Journal of the Asiatic Society of Bengal* n.s. 27 (2): 225–30.
CHATTOPADHYAY, G. 1964. Kinship and Marriage Among the Hos, *Bulletin of the Cultural Research Institute* 3 (2): 13–25.
— and B.C. RAY CHAUDHURI 1958. The Name-Giving Ceremony of the

Hos of Seraikella, *Eastern Anthropologist* 11 (2): 113–27.

CHATTOPADHYAY, K.P. 1941. Khasi Kinship and Social Organization, *University of Calcutta Anthropological Papers* n.s. 6: 1–40.

— 1946. Korku Marriage Customs and Some Changes, *Journal of the Royal Asiatic Society of Bengal*, Letters 12 (2): 43–70.

CHAUDHURI, B. 1966. Life in a Munda Village, *Bulletin of the Cultural Research Institute* 5: 126–32.

CHAUSSIN, Elizabeth 1978. Aspects spatiaux de l'organization sociale des Saora, *L'Homme* 18 (1–2): 167–82.

CHOUDHURY, B. 1963–4. Saora, *Adibasi* 1963–4 (3): 101–6.

CHOUDHURY, N.C. 1977. *Munda Social Structure*, Calcutta: KLM.

CHOUDHURY, U. 1952. Marriage Customs of the Santals, *Bulletin of the Department of Anthropology* 1 (1): 86–116.

COOK, W.A. 1965. *A Descriptive Analysis of Mundari*, Ann Arbor: University Microfilms.

CULSHAW, W.G. 1941. Some Beliefs and Customs Relating to Birth among the Santals, *Journal of the Royal Asiatic Society of Bengal, Letters* 7: 115–27.

— 1949. *Tribal Heritage: A Study of the Santals*, London: Butterworth.

DALTON, E.T. 1872. *Descriptive Ethnology of Bengal*, Calcutta: Superintendent of Government Printing.

DANDA, A. 1962. Cultural Patterns Regulating Laws of Inheritance of the Santals, *Modern Review* 112 (4): 306–10.

— 1971. Production Allocation in Tribal Chhattisgarh, *Journal of the Indian Anthropological Society* 6 (2): 97–105.

DAS, A.K. 1964. *The Koras and some Little-Known Communities of West Bengal*, Calcutta: Government of West Bengal, Bulletin of the Cultural Research Institute Special Series 5.

— 1965. A Systemic Analysis of the Social System of the Munda Community, *Bulletin of the Cultural Research Institute* 4: 9–12.

— 1967. Scientific Analysis of 'Santal' Social System, *Bulletin of the Cultural Research Institute* 6 (1–2): 5–9.

— et al. 1966. *Handbook of Scheduled Castes and Scheduled Tribes of West Bengal*, Calcutta: Government of West Bengal, Bulletin of the Cultural Research Institute Special Series 8.

DAS, G.N. 1956a. A Note on the Hill Bondos of Koraput District, *Vanyajati* 4: 103–12.

DAS, N.C. 1979. Fertility Study of a Juang Village, *Eastern Anthropologist* 32 (3): 185–91.

DAS, R.M. 1962. *Women in Manu and His Seven Commentators*, Varanasi and Arrah: Kanchana Publications.

DAS, Shri N. 1956b. The Birjhia of Palamau and their Adjustments, *Vanyajati* 4 (4): 143–6.

DAS, T. 1931a. The Bhumijas of Seraikella, *University of Calcutta Anthropological Papers* n.s. 2, passim.

— 1931b. The Wild Kharias of Dhalbhum, *University of Calcutta Anthropological Papers* n.s. 3, passim.

DAS, Veena 1977. *Structure and Cognition: Aspects of Hindu Caste and Ritual,* Delhi: Oxford University Press.

— and Jit Singh UBEROI 1971. The Elementary Structure of Caste, *Contributions to Indian Sociology* n.s. 5: 33–43.

DAS GUPTA, D. 1966. A Note on Linguistic Changes in Bhumij and Juang, *Bulletin of the Philological Society of Calcutta,* A.S. Sen Felicitation Volume: 91–8.

DAS GUPTA, P.K. 1984. *Life and Culture of Matrilineal Tribe of Meghalaya,* Delhi: Inter-India Publications.

DAS GUPTA, S.B. 1978. *Birjhia,* Calcutta: K.P. Bagchi.

DASGUPTA, B.K. 1978a. Social Mobility Movements Among the Tribes of Eastern and Central India, *Journal of the Indian Anthropological Society* 13 (1): 11–17.

— 1983. The Ho of Bihar, *Adibasi* 23 (1): 42–5.

DASGUPTA, D. 1978b. *Linguistic Studies,* Calcutta: Anthropological Survey of India.

DATTA, B. 1933. Traces of Totemism in some Tribes and Castes of N.E. India, *Man in India* 13 (2–3): 97–114.

DATTA-MAJUMDAR, N. 1956. *The Santal: A Study in Social Change,* Delhi: Government of India, Department of Anthropology.

DE CANDOLLE, B. 1961. Contributions à l'étude des Nahals (Inde), *Anthropos* 56: 750–88.

DEKA, U., and P. PATTOJOSHI 1975. Genetic Survey of the Gadaba of Orissa, *Man in India* 55 (3): 227–34.

DELIEGE, Robert 1980. Divisions and Hierarchy among the Bhils, *Man in India* 60 (1–2): 38–50.

— 1981. The Bhils or the Tribe as an Image, *Eastern Anthropologist* 34 (2): 117–29.

DEOGAONKAR, S.G. 1986. *The Hill-Korwa,* New Delhi: Concept Publishing Company.

DHAN, R.O. 1961. The Hos of Saranda: An Ethnographic Study, *Bulletin of the Bihar Tribal Research Institute,* 3 (1): 37–105.

DIFFLOTH, Gerard 1974 Austro-Asiatic Languages, *Encyclopaedia Britannica* (15th edn.), Macropaedia: 480–4.

DIXIT, P.K. 1966. *Pipalgota,* Census of India Vol. VIII, part VI (1961), Village Survey Monograph 7.

DONEGAN, Patricia Jane, and David STAMPE 1983. Rhythm and the Holistic Organization of Language Structure, *in* J.F. Richardson, M. Marks and A. Chukerman (eds.), *The Interplay of Phonology, Morphology and Syntax,* Chicago: Chicago Linguistic Circle.

DRIVER, W.H.P. 1892. The Korkus, *Journal of the Asiatic Society of Bengal* 61 (1): 128–32.

DUMONT, Louis 1957. For a Sociology of India, *Contributions to Indian Sociology* 1: 7–22.

— 1959. Review of Verrier Elwin, *Bondo Highlander, Contributions to Indian Sociology* 3: 60–74.

— 1962a. The Conception of Kingship in Ancient India, *Contributions to Indian Sociology* 6: 48–77.

— 1962b. 'Tribe' and 'Caste' in India, *Contributions to Indian Sociology* 6: 120–2.

— 1966a. Descent or Intermarriage? A Relational View of Australian Section Systems, *Southwestern Journal of Anthropology* 22: 231–50.

— 1966b. *Homo Hierarchicus: essai sur le système des castes*, Paris: Gallimard.

— 1966c. Marriage in India, The Present State of the Question III: North India in Relation to South India, *Contributions to Indian Sociology* 9: 90–114.

— 1970. Sur le vocabulaire de parenté kariera, *in* Jean Pouillon and Pierre Maranda (eds.), *Mélanges offerts à Claude Lévi-Strauss à l'occasion de son 60ème anniversaire*, Paris and The Hague: Mouton (2 vols.), Vol. 1: 272–86.

— 1971. On Putative Hierarchy and Some Allergies To It, *Contributions to Indian Sociology* n.s. 5: 58–78.

— 1983. *Affinity as a Value: Marriage Alliance in South India, with Comparative Essays on Australia*, Chicago: The University of Chicago Press.

EDMONSTON-SCOTT, W.J. 1920. The Basque Language: Its Kolarian Origin and Structure, *Bulletin of the School of Oriental Studies* 1 (3): 147–84.

EHRENFELS, U.R. 1955. Three Matrilineal Groups of Assam, *American Anthropologist* 57 (2): 306–21.

ELWIN, Verrier 1939. *The Baiga*, London: John Murray.

— 1940. 'I Married a Gond', *Man in India* 20 (4): 228–55.

— 1942. *The Agaria*, Calcutta: Oxford University Press.

— 1943. *Maria Murder and Suicide*, Bombay: Oxford University Press.

— 1947. *The Muria and their Ghotul*, Bombay: Oxford University Press.

— 1948. Notes on the Juang, *Man in India* 28 (1–2): 1–146.

— 1950. *Bondo Highlander*, Bombay: Oxford University Press.

— 1955. *The Religion of an Indian Tribe*, Bombay: Oxford University Press.

EMENEAU, Murray B. 1954. Linguistic Prehistory of India, *Proceedings of the American Philosophical Society* 98: 282–92.

— 1969. The Non-literary Dravidian Languages, *in* Thomas A. Sebeok (ed.), *Current Trends in Linguistics, Vol. V: South Asia*, Paris and The Hague: Mouton.

ENCYCLOPAEDIA MUNDARICA [*Encyc. Mund.* in text]: see HOFF-MANN, J. 1930 *et seq.*

EXEM, A. van 1978. Haram and Singbonga: The Concept of the Supreme Being According to Munda Mythology, *in* P. Ponette (ed.), *The Munda World: Hoffmann Commemoration Volume*, Ranchi: Catholic Press.

— 1982. *The Religious System of the Munda Tribe*, St. Augustin: Collectanea Instituti Anthropos Vol. 28.

FENG HAN-YI 1937. The Chinese Kinship System, *Harvard Journal of Asiatic Studies* 2: 141ff.

FERNANDEZ, F. 1969. A Critique of Verrier Elwin's Anthropology: Hill Bondo Social Organization and Kinship Analysis, *in* C. Pradhan *et al.* (eds.), *Anthropology and Archaeology*, Bombay: Oxford University Press.

FERREIRA, J.V. 1965. *Totemism in India*, Bombay: Oxford University Press.

FRUZZETTI, Lina M. 1982. *The Gift of a Virgin: Women, Marriage and Ritual in a Bengali Society*, New Brunswick: Rutgers University Press.

FUCHS, Stephen 1966. Clan Organization among the Korkus, *Journal of Asian and African Studies* 1 (3): 213–19.

— 1973. *The Aboriginal Tribes of India*, Delhi etc.: Macmillan.

— 1988. *The Korkus of the Vindhya Hills*, Delhi: Inter-India Publications.

FÜRER-HAIMENDORF, Christoph von 1943a. Avenues to Marriage among the Bondos of Orissa, *Man in India* 23 (2): 168–72.

— 1943b. Megalithic Ritual among the Gadabas and Bondos of Orissa, *Journal of the Royal Asiatic Society of Bengal* 9 (1): 149–78.

— 1945a. The Problem of Megalithic Cultures in Middle India, *Man in India* 25: 73–86.

— 1945b. *The Reddis of Bison Hills* (Vol. II of *The Aboriginal Tribes of Hyderabad*), London: Macmillan.

— 1950. Youth Dormitories and Community Houses in India, *Anthropos* 45: 119–44.

— 1953. The After-life in Indian Tribal Belief [Frazer lecture, 1951], *Journal of the Royal Anthropological Institute* 83: 37–49.

— 1954. Review of Verrier Elwin, *Bondo Highlander*, *Bulletin of the School of Oriental Studies*, 16 (1); 177–8.

— 1956. The Descent Group System of the Raj Gonds, *Bulletin of the School of Oriental and African Studies*, 18 (3): 499–511.

— 1985. *Tribal Populations and Cultures of the Indian Subcontinent*, Leiden and Köln: E.J. Brill.

FÜRER-HAIMENDORF, Elizabeth von 1958, 1964, 1970, 1976. *An Anthropological Bibliography of South Asia*, Paris and The Hague: Mouton.

GAUSDAL, J. 1942. The Khut System of the Santals, *Journal of the Bihar and Orissa Research Society* 28 (4): 431–9.

— 1953. Ancestral and Sacrificial Clans among the Santal, *Journal of the Asiatic Society of Bengal* 19 (1): 1–97.

— 1960. *The Santal Khuts*, Oslo: Instituttet for Sammenlignende Kultur-forskning / H. Aschenhong (W. Nygaard).

GAUTAM, M.K. 1977a. *In Search of Identity: [The] Case of the Santal of Northern India*, Leiden [no publisher given].

— 1977b. The Santalization of the Santal, *in* Kenneth David (ed.), *The New Wind: Changing Identities in South Asia*, The Hague: Mouton.

GHOSH, B.N. 1967. The Ways of Acquiring Mates in Tribal Chotanagpur, *Folk-Lore* 8 (2): 403–10.

GHOSH, H.N. 1916. The Bhumij of Chota-Nagpur, *Journal of the Bihar and Orissa Research Society* 2 (3): 265–82.

GHOSH, R. 1966. Koras of Midnapur, *Man in India* 46 (1): 81–6.

GHURYE, G.S. 1943. *The Aborigines—'So-Called'—And Their Future*, Poona: Gokhale Institute of Politics and Economics.

GODELIER, M. 1973. *Horizons, trajets marxistes en anthropologie*, Paris: Maspéro.

GRIFFITHS, W.G. 1946. *The Kol Tribe of Central India*, Calcutta: Royal

Asiatic Society Monographs, Series 2.

GRIGNARD, F.A. 1909. Oraons and Mundas from the Time of their Settlement in India, *Anthropos* 4: 1–19.

GRIGSON, W.V. 1949. *The Maria Gonds of Bastar*, Oxford: Oxford University Press.

GUHA, U., M.K.A. SIDDIQUI and P.G.R. MATHUR 1970. *The Didayi: A Forgotten Tribe of Orissa*, Calcutta: Anthropological Survey of India.

GUPTA, S.K. 1977. Traditional and Emerging Political Structures, *in* S.C. Dube (ed.), *Tribal Heritage of India, Vol. 1: Ethnicity, Identity and Interaction*, Delhi etc.: Vikas.

GUPTA, S.P. 1964. An Appraisal of the Food Habits and Nutritional State Among the Asur, Korwa, and the Sauria Pahariya of Chota-Nagpur Plateau, *Bulletin of the Bihar Tribal Research Institute* 6 (1): 127–79.

GURDON, P.R.T. 1914. *The Khasis*, London: Macmillan.

HANSDA, P.N. 1983. The Names of the Santals and the Changes, *Man in India* 63: 183–93.

HARI MOHAN 1961. Socio-Economic Organization and Religion among the Hill Kharias of Dhalbhum, *Bulletin of the Bihar Tribal Research Institute* 3 (1): 180–212.

— 1979. The Korwa: A Study in Culture Change, *Bulletin of the Bihar Tribal Research Institute* 21 (1–2): 79–104.

— 1982. Customary Laws of the Korwa Tribe, *Bulletin of the Bihar Tribal Research Institute* 24 (1–2): 39–44.

HEAD, J., and S.L. CRANSTON 1977. *Reincarnation: The Phoenix Fire Mystery*, New York: Julian Press and Crown Publishers.

HEINE-GELDERN, Robert von 1928. Die Megalithen Südostasiens und ihre Bedeutung für die Klärung der Megalithenfrage in Europa and Polynesien, *Anthropos* 23 (1–2): 276–315.

— 1932. Urheimat und früheste Wanderungen der Austronesier, *Anthropos* 27 (3–4): 543–619.

HENLEY, Paul 1982. *The Panare: Tradition and Change on the Amazonian Frontier*, New Haven and London: Yale University Press.

HERMANNS, M. 1966. *Die Religiös-Magische Weltanschauung der Primitivstämme Indiens, Vol. II: Die Bhilala, Korku, Gond, Baiga*, Wiesbaden: Franz Steiner Verlag.

HEVESY, Wilhelm von 1930. Does an 'Austric' Family of Languages Exist?, *Bulletin of the School of Oriental Studies*, 6: 187–200.

HOCART, A.M. 1931. Alternate Generations in Fiji, *Man* 31: 222–4.

HODSON, T.C. 1921a. The Doctrine of Rebirth in Various Areas of India, *Man in India* 1 (2): 1–17.

— 1921b. The Khasi and Garo Marriage Systems Contrasted, *Man in India* 1 (2): 106–27.

HOFFMANN, J. (with A. van EMELEN) 1930 *et seq*. *Encyclopaedia Mundarica [Encyc. Mund.* in text], Patna: Superintendent Government Printing (14–15 vols.).

HRACH, H.G. 1978. From 'Regulated Anarchy' to 'Proto-Nationalism': The Case of the Santals, *in* R.R. Moser and M.K. Gautam (eds.), *Aspects of Tribal Life in South Asia I: Strategy and Survival,* Berne: University of Berne Institute of Ethnology.

HUFFMAN, F.E. 1986. *Bibliography and Index of Mainland Southeast Asian Languages and Linguistics,* New Haven and London: Yale University Press.

HUGH-JONES, Christine 1979. *From the Milk River: Spatial and Temporal Processes in Northwest Amazonia,* Cambridge: Cambridge University Press.

ICKE-SCHWALBE, Lydia 1979. Historical-Ethnological Classification of the Munda and Oraon in Chotanagpur, *Journal of Social Research* 22 (2): 57–70.

— 1983a. Village Studies among Christian and Non-Christian Munda in Chotanagpur, *Journal of Social Research* 26 (1): 1–34.

— 1983b. *Die Munda und Oraon in Chota Nagpur: Geschichte, Wirtschaft und Gesellschaft,* [East] Berlin: Akademie-Verlag.

— 1988. Familienwirtschaft und Clan in bäuerlichen Stammesgesellschaften Indiens, *in* J. Hermann and Jens Köhn (eds.), *Staat und Gesellschaftsformation,* [East] Berlin: Veröff. d. ZIAGA d, Adw., Band 16: 271–5.

INDEN, R.B., and R.W. NICHOLAS 1977. *Kinship in Bengali Culture,* Chicago: University of Chicago Press.

IZIKOWITZ, Karl Gustav n.d. The Gotr Ceremony of the Boro Gadaba, *in* Stanley Diamond (ed.), *Primitive Views of the World,* New York and London: Columbia University Press.

JAIN, R.K. 1958. Features of Kinship in an Asur Village, *Eastern Anthropologist* 12 (1): 25–40.

JAINI, P.S. 1980. Karma and the Problem of Rebirth of Jainism, *in* Wendy O'Flaherty (ed.), *Karma and Rebirth in Classical Indian Tradition,* Berkeley etc.: University of California Press.

JHA, J.C. 1964. *Kol Insurrection in Chota Nagpur,* Calcutta: Thacker Spink.

JORDAN-HORSTMANN, M. 1972a. Review of Sugiyama Koichi, *A Study of Munda Village Life in India, Anthropos* 67: 280–4.

— 1972b. Der dumme Weber: Spotterzählungen bei den Mundas, *Anthropos* 67: 564–85.

KARVÉ, Irawati 1965. *Kinship Organization in India,* Bombay: Asia Publishing House.

— 1968–9. Kinship Organization in India and the Place of the Mundari-speaking People in it, *Adibasi* 1968–9 (1): 1–25.

KOCHAR, V.K. 1963. Terms and Usages among the Santals of Bolpur Area, Birbhum, *Bulletin of the Anthropological Survey of India* 12 (1–2): 47–56.

— 1965. Village Organization among the Santals, *Bulletin of the Bihar Tribal Welfare Research Institute,* 7 (1): 5–22.

— 1970. *Social Organization among the Santal,* Calcutta: Editions Indian.

KOLENDA, Pauline 1978. Sibling-Set Marriage, Collateral-Set Marriage, and Deflected Alliance among Annana Jats of Jaipur District, Rajasthan, *in* Sylvia Vatuk (ed.), *American Studies in the Anthropology of India*, New Delhi: Manohar.

KONOW, Sten 1908. Notes on the Munda Family of Speech in India, *Anthropos* 3: 68–82.

KORN, Francis 1973. *Elementary Structures Reconsidered: Lévi-Strauss on Kinship*, London: Tavistock.

KOSAY, Hamit 1939. Türkische Elemente in den Munda-Sprachen, *Türk Tarih Kurumu Belleten* 3: 107–26.

KUIPER, F.B.J. 1948. Munda and Indonesian, in *Orientalia Neerlandica, a Volume of Oriental Studies*, Leiden: Oostersch Genootschap.

— 1962. *Nahali: A Comparative Study*, Amsterdam: N.V. Noord-Hollandsche Uitgevers Maatschappij.

— 1965. Consonant Variation in Munda, *Lingua* 14: 54–87.

— 1966. The Sources of the Nahali Vocabulary, *in* N.H. Zide (ed.), *Studies in Comparative Austroasiatic Linguistics*, The Hague etc.: Mouton.

KUPER, Adam 1982. Lineage Theory: A Critical Retrospect, *Yearbook of Anthropology* 11: 71–95.

LEACH, Edmund 1945. Jinghpaw Kinship Terminology: An Experiment in Ethnographic Algebra, *Journal of the Royal Anthropological Institute* 75: 59–72.

LEUVA, K.K. 1963. *The Asur: A Study of Primitive Iron Smelters*, Delhi: Bharatiya Adimjati Sevak Sangh.

LÉVI-STRAUSS, Claude 1949. *Les structures élémentaires de la parenté*, Paris: Presses Universitaires de France.

— 1966. The Future of Kinship Studies, *Proceedings of the Royal Anthropological Institute* 1965: 13–22.

LINGUISTIC SURVEY OF INDIA VOL. IV: Munda and Dravidian Languages (1906) [*LSI* in text]. Calcutta: Superintendent of Government Printing.

MCDOUGAL, Charles 1963a. *The Social Structure of the Hill Juang*, Ann Arbor: University Microfilms.

— 1963b. The Social Structure of the Hill Juang: A Précis, *Man in India* 43 (3): 183–91.

— 1964. Juang Categories and Joking Relationships, *Southwestern Journal of Anthropology* 20 (4): 319–45.

— 1979. *The Kulunge Rai: A Study of Kinship and Marriage Exchange*, Kathmandu: Ratna Pustak Bhandar.

MCDOUGALL, John 1977. Agrarian Reform vs. Religious Revitalization: Collective Resistance to Peasantization among the Mundas, Oraons and Santals, 1858–95, *Contributions to Indian Sociology* n.s. 11 (2): 295–327.

MAHAPATRA, A.K. 1980, Forces of Change Among the Tribes of Rural Bengal, with Special Reference to Santals, *Bulletin of the Cultural Research Institute* 14 (3–4): 23–8.

MAHAPATRA, K. 1976. Echo-formation in Gtaq, *in* Philip Jenner, L.C. Thompson and Stanley Starosta (eds.), *Austroasiatic Studies*, Honolulu: University of Hawaii Press, Oceanic Linguistics Special Publications, no. 13 (2 vols.), Vol. 2: 815–31.

MAHAPATRA, S. 1977. Ecological Adaptation to Technology—Ritual Conflict and Leadership Change: The Santal Experience, *in* Kenneth David (ed.), *The New Wind: Changing Identities in South Asia*, The Hague: Mouton.

MAJUMDAR, D.N. 1924. On the Terminology of Relationship of the Hos of Kolhan, *Journal of the Asiatic Society of Bengal* n.s. 20 (5): 199–204.

— 1926. Marriage and Betrothal among the Hos, *Journal of the Asiatic Society of Bengal* n.s. 22: 149–68.

— 1930. Social Organization among the Korwa, *Man in India* 10 (2–3): 104–15.

— 1932. The Cycle of Life among the Korwa, *Man in India* 12 (4): 253–75.

— 1937. *A Tribe in Transition*, Calcutta: Longmans, Green & Co.

— 1939. Tribal Cultures and Acculturation (Presidential Address), *Proceedings of the 26th Indian Science Congress*, Lahore.

— 1944. *The Fortunes of Primitive Tribes*, Lucknow: Universal Publishers.

— 1950. *The Affairs of a Tribe*, Lucknow: Universal Publishers.

— 1961. *Races and Cultures of India*, London: Asia Publishing House (4th edn.).

MALHOTRA, S.P. 1963. Kinship Organization among the Birhors, *Bulletin of the Bihar Tribal Research Institute* 5 (2): 311–24.

MANDELBAUM, David G. 1970. *Society in India*, Berkeley and Los Angeles: University of California Press (2 vols.).

MARTEL, G. 1965. Le culture de riz chez les Santal du Bengale, *Bulletin de l'École Française d'Extrême Orient* 52 (2): 313–58 *et seq.*

— 1979. Les Birhors, chasseurs, collecteurs, nomades du Bihar, *Bulletin de l'École Française d'Extrême Orient* 66: 105–13 *et seq.*

MARTEN, J.T. 1911. *Central Provinces and Berar, Part 1: Report*, Calcutta: Census of India.

MASPERO, H. 1948. Note sur la morphologie du tibéto-burman et munda, *Bulletin de la Société Linguistique de Paris* 44 (1): 155–85.

MAUSS, Marcel 1938. Une catégorie de l'esprit human: la notion de personne, celle de 'moi' [Huxley Memorial Lecture 1938], *Journal of the Royal Anthropological Institute* 68: 263–81.

MAZUMDAR, B.C. 1927. *The Aborigines of the Highlands of Central India*, Calcutta: University of Calcutta.

MEGGITT, M. 1965. *Desert People: A Study of the Walbiri Aborigines of Central Australia*, Chicago: University of Chicago Press.

— 1972. Understanding Australian Aboriginal Society: Kinship Systems or Cultural Categories?, *in* Priscilla Reining (ed.), *Kinship Studies in the Morgan Centennial Year*, Washington: Anthropological Society.

MISHRA, K.C. 1981–2. Aspects of Juang Folklore, *Adibasi* 21: 11–38.

MOHANTY, S.U.C. 1973–4. Bond-Friendship among the Gadaba, *Man in Society* 1: 130–55.

— 1981–2. Kharia, a Picturesque Tribe of Orissa, *Adibasi* 21: 1–10.

MOHANTY, U. 1963–4. Kharia, *Adibasi* 1963–4 (3): 175–8.

MOHAPATRA, P.K. 1963–4. Didayi, *Adibasi* 1963–4 (3): 127–30.

MUKHERJEA, C.L. 1962. *The Santals*, Calcutta: A. Mukherjee.

MUKHERJI, S. 1964. The Santals of the Sunderbans, *Bulletin of the Cultural*

Research Institute 3 (3–4): 67–71.

MUKHOPADHYAY, S. 1975. *The Austrics of India: Their Religion and Tradition,* Calcutta: K.P. Bagchi.

— 1976. *A Profile of Sundarban Tribes,* Calcutta: KLM.

MUNDRI, L.S. 1956. A Munda Birth, *Man in India* 36 (1): 56–72.

MUNRO, A.C.M., and G.V. SITAPATI 1931. The Soras of the Parlakimedi Agency, *Census of India,* Vol. I, part IIIB: 200–4.

NAG, M.K. 1965. Effects of Christianity on a Few Aspects of Khasi Culture, *Bulletin of the Anthropological Survey of India* 14 (1–2): 1–34.

NAKANE, Chie 1967. *Garos and Khasis: A Comparative Study in Matrilineal Systems,* Paris: Mouton.

NATARAJAN, N. 1977. *The Missionary among the Khasis,* Delhi: Sterling Publishers.

NAVLAKHA, S.K. 1959. The Authority Structure among the Bhumij and Bhil: A Study of Historical Causations, *Eastern Anthropologist* 13 (1): 27–40.

NEEDHAM, Rodney 1962. *Structure and Sentiment,* Chicago and London: University of Chicago Press.

— 1967. Terminology and Alliance II: Mapuche, Conclusions, *Sociologus* 17: 39–53.

— 1968. Endeh: Terminology, Alliance, and Analysis, *Bijdragen tot de Taal-, Land- en Volkenkunde* 124 (3): 305–35.

— 1973. Prescription, *Oceania* 43: 166–81.

— 1974. The Evolution of Social Classification: A Commentary on the Warao Case, *Bijdragen tot de Taal-, Land- en Volkenkunde* 130 (1): 16–43.

— 1980a. Diversity, Structure, and Aspect in Manggarai Social Classification, *in* R. Schefold, J.W. Schoorl and J. Tennekes (eds.), *Man, Meaning and History: Essays in Honour of H.G. Schulte Nordholt,* The Hague: Martinus Nijhoff.

— 1980b. Principles and Variations in the Structure of Sumbanese Society, *in* James J. Fox (ed.), *The Flow of Life: Essays on Eastern Indonesia,* Cambridge, Mass., and London: Harvard University Press.

NIGAM, R.C. 1971. *Survey of Kanauri in Himachal Pradesh,* Calcutta: Census of India Monograph 3.

— and D. DASGUPTA 1964. Mundari and the Speech of the Bhumij: A Study in Bilingualism, *Bulletin of the Anthropological Survey of India* 13 (3–4): 163–98.

OBEYESEKERE, Gananath 1968. Theodicy, Sin and Salvation in a Sociology of Buddhism, *in* E.R. Leach (ed.), *Dialectic in Practical Religion,* Cambridge: Cambridge University Press.

— 1980. The Rebirth Eschatology and its Transformations: A Contribution to the Sociology of Early Buddhism, *in* Wendy O'Flaherty (ed.), *Karma and Rebirth in Classical Indian Traditions,* Berkeley etc.: University of California Press.

O'FLAHERTY, Wendy 1980. Karma and Rebirth in the Vedas and Puranas, *in* Wendy O'Flaherty (ed.), *Karma and Rebirth in Classical Indian Tradi-*

tions, Berkeley etc.: University of California Press.

ORANS, Martin 1959. A Tribal People in an Industrial Setting, *in* Martin Singer (ed.), *Traditional India: Structure and Change,* Philadelphia: American Folklore Society Bibliographic and Special Series 10.

— 1965. *The Santal: A Tribe in Search of a Great Tradition,* Detroit: Wayne State University Press.

PANDEY, S. 1966. Santali Elements in Magahi, *Bulletin of the Philological Society of Calcutta,* A.S. Sen Felicitation Volume: 40–2.

PANDYE, S.S. 1962. Tribal People of the Melghat: The Korku, *Indian Geographical Journal* 37: 91–4.

PARKIN, Robert J. 1983. Lévi-Strauss and the Austroasiatics: 'Elementary Structures' under the Microscope, *Journal of the Anthropological Society of Oxford* 14 (1): 79–86.

— 1984. 'Kinship and Marriage in the Austroasiatic-speaking World: A Comparative Analysis', Oxford: D. Phil. thesis.

— 1985. Munda Kinship Terminologies, *Man* 20 (4): 705–21.

— 1986a. Comparative Munda Kinship: A Preliminary Report, *Oxford Studies on India* 1 (1): 59–74.

— 1986b. Prescriptive Alliance in Southeast Asia: The Austroasiatic Evidence, *Sociologus* 36 (1): 52–64.

— 1987. Kin Classification in the Karakorum, *Man* 22 (1): 157–70.

— 1988a. Reincarnation and Alternate Generation Equivalence in Middle India, *Journal of Anthropological Research* 44 (1): 1–20.

— 1988b. Marriage, Behaviour and Generation among the Munda of Eastern India, *Zeitschrift für Ethnologie* 113 (1): 67–85.

— 1988c. Prescription and Transformation in Mon-Khmer Kinship Terminologies, *Sociologus* 38 (1): 55–68.

— 1990. Terminology and Alliance in India: Tribal Systems and the North-South Problem, *Contributions to Indian Sociology* n.s. 24 (1): 61–76.

— 1991. *A Guide to Austroasiatic-Speakers and their Languages,* Honolulu: University of Hawaii Press.

— forthcoming. Sur quelques correspondances et emprunts en termes de parenté austroasiatiques, *Bulletin de l'École Française d'Extrême Orient.*

PARRINDER, G. 1970. *Avatar and Reincarnation,* London: Faber and Faber.

— 1973. *The Indestructible Soul: The Nature of Man and Life after Death in Indian Thought,* London: Geoge Allen & Unwin.

PARRY, Jonathan 1979. *Caste and Kinship in Kangra,* London etc.: Routledge & Kegan Paul.

PATNAIK, N. 1964. Caste Formation among the Juang of Orissa, *Man in India* 44 (1): 22–30.

— 1970. Changing A Community's Culture, *Man in India* 50 (2): 189–96.

PATTANAYAK, D.P. 1968. Some Comments on Parenga Kinship Terms, *Indian Linguistics,* Murray B. Emeneau Festschrift Volume: 250–6.

PETIT, C. 1974. 'La Culture matérielle des Saora', thèse pour le doctorat de 3ème cycle, Université de Paris III.

PFEFFER, Georg 1982a. *Status and Affinity in Middle India,* Wiesbaden: Franz Steiner Verlag.

— 1982b, Tribal Social Organization and 'Hindu' Influence, *Internationales Asienforum* 13 (1–2): 45–54.
— 1983. Generation and Marriage in Middle India: The Evolutionary Potential of 'Restricted Exchange', *Contributions to Indian Sociology* n.s. 17 (1): 87–121.
— 1984a. Santal Totemism, *South Asian Anthropologist* 5 (1): 37–43.
— 1984b. Mittelindische Megalithen als Meritökonomische Katagorien, *Paideuma* 30: 231–40.
— ms. Exchange of Souls: Complementary Agnation in Gadaba Mortuary Rites.

PINNOW, Hans Jürgen 1959. *Versuch einer historischen Lautlehre der Kharia-Sprache*, Wiesbaden: Otto Harrassowitz.
— 1960. Über den Ursprung der voreinander abweichenden Strukturen der Munda-und Khmer-Nikobar Sprachen, *Indo-Iranian Journal* 4 (3–4): 81–103.
— 1963. The Position of the Munda Languages within the Austro-Asiatic Language Family, *in* H.L. Shorto (ed.), *Linguistic Comparison in Southeast Asia and the Pacific*, London: School of Oriental and African Studies.
— 1966. A Comparative Study of the Verb in the Munda Languages, *in* N.H. Zide (ed.), *Studies in Comparative Austroasiatic Linguistics*, The Hague etc.: Mouton.

PONETTE, P. (ed.), 1978. *The Munda World: Hoffmann Commemoration Volume*, Ranchi: Catholic Press.

PRASAD, N. 1961. *Land and People of Tribal Bihar*, Ranchi: Bihar Tribal Research Institute, Government of Bihar.

PRASAD, S. 1962a. Linguistic Affinity of Bhumij Dialect, *Bulletin of the Bihar Tribal Research Institute* 4 (1): 69–75.
— 1962b. A Pilot Survey for the Demographic Study of Asurs, *Bulletin of the Bihar Tribal Research Institute* 4 (2): 103–17.
— 1974. *Where the Three Tribes Meet: A Study in Tribal Interaction*, Allahabad: Indian International Publishers.

PRINCE PETER, H.R.H. 1963. *A Study of Polyandry*, The Hague: Mouton.

PRZYLUSKI, J. 1924. Les Langues Austro-Asiatics, *in* A. Meilet and M. Cohen (eds.), *Les Langues du monde*, Paris: Société Linguistique de Paris.
— 1930. Emprunts anaryens en indo-aryen, *Bulletin de la Société Linguistique de Paris* 30 (2): 196–201.

RADCLIFFE-BROWN, A.R. 1950. Introduction, *in* A.R. Radcliffe-Brown and Daryll Forde (eds.), *African Systems of Kinship and Marriage*, London etc.: Oxford University Press.
— 1953. Dravidian Kinship Terminology, *Man* 53: 112.

RAMADAS, G. 1931. The Gadabas, *Man in India* 11 (2): 160–73.

RAMAMURTI, G.V. 1931. *A Manual of the So:ra (or Savara) Language*, Madras: Government Press.
— 1938. *Sora-English Dictionary*, Madras: Government Press.

RANI, S.K. 1957. Coming of Age Among Munda Girls, *Bulletin of the Department of Anthropology, Bihar University* 1: 71–9.

RAY, G., G. CHATTOPADHYAY and B. BANERJEE 1954. Religious

Beliefs of the Hos, *Man in India* 34: 288–300.

RAY CHOWDHURY, T.C. 1929. The Bhumij of Mayurbhanj (Orissa), *Man in India* (2–3): 95–115.

RISLEY, H.H. 1891. *Tribes and Castes of Bengal*, Calcutta: Bengal Secretariat Press (4 vols.).

RIVIERE, Peter 1984. *Individual and Society in Guiana: A Comparative Study of Amerindian Social Organization*, Cambridge: Cambridge University Press.

RIZBI, B.R. 1977. The Hill Korwa of Surguja, Madhya Pradesh, *in* A.K. Danda (ed.), *Tribal Situation in Northeast Surguja*, Calcutta: Anthropological Survey of India.

ROSE, A.J. 1902. Unlucky and Lucky Children, and Some Birth Superstitions, *Folk Lore* [Britain] 13: 278–80.

ROSNER, V. 1956. The Turis, *March of India* 8 (7): 44–7.

— 1967. Leadership among the Korwa of Jashpur, *in* L.P. Vidyarthi (ed.), *Leadership in India*, London: Asia Publishing House.

ROUT, S.S.P. 1962. Types of Marriage among the Juang of Keonjhar District, Orissa, *Orissa Historical Research Journal* 9 (3): 168–77.

— 1969–70. Handbook on the Juang, *Adibasi* 1969–70 (1–2): 1–97.

ROY, David 1936. Principles of Khasi Culture, *Folk-Lore* 47: 375–93.

— 1938. The Place of the Khasi in the World, *Man in India* 18 (2–3): 122–34.

ROY, Sarat Chandra 1912. *The Mundas and their Country*, Calcutta: City Book Society.

— 1915. *The Oraons of Chota Nagpur*, Ranchi: Man in India.

— 1917. A Note on Totemism among the Asurs, *Journal of the Bihar and Orissa Research Society* 3 (4): 567–71.

— 1925. *The Birhors*, Ranchi: Man in India.

— 1926. Asurs, Ancient and Modern, *Journal of the Bihar and Orissa Research Society* 12 (1): 147–52.

— 1928. *Oraon Religion and Customs*, Ranchi: Man in India.

— 1931. The Effect on the Aborigines of Chotanagpur of their Contact with Western Civilization, *Journal of the Bihar and Orissa Research Society* 17: 358–94.

— 1935a. *The Hill Bhuiyas*, Ranchi: Man in India.

— 1935b. Past Migration of the Kharia Tribe, *Journal of the Bihar and Orissa Research Society* 21 (4): 214–30.

— and R.C. ROY 1937. *The Kharias*, Ranchi: Man in India (2 vols.).

ROY, S.N. 1927. The Savaras of Orissa, *Man in India* 7 (4): 277–336.

ROYCHAUDHURY, P.C. 1961. Bitlaha: A Santhal Ritual, *Quarterly Journal of the Mythic Society* 52 (1): 1–5.

ROYCHOUDHURY, B.K. 1963. The Mahali: A Basket-Making Tribe of West Bengal, *Bulletin of the Cultural Research Institute* 1 (3): 30–5.

— 1964. The Birhors, *Bulletin of the Cultural Research Institute* 3 (1): 19–30.

RUSSELL, R.V. and HIRA LAL 1916. *The Tribes and Castes of the Central Provinces of India*, London: Macmillan (2 vols.).

SACHCHIDANANDA, 1953. The Tribal Village as a Social Unit, *Journal of the Bihar and Orissa Research Society* 39 (2): 185–93.

— 1956. Characteristic Features of the Tribal Village in Bihar, *Journal of Bihar University* 1: 58–60.

— 1957. Social Structure of a Chota-Nagpur Village, *Bulletin of the Department of Anthropology, Bihar University* 1: 1–13.

— 1964. *Cultural Change in Tribal Bihar: Munda and Oraon*, Calcutta: Bookland.

— 1979. *The Changing Munda*, Delhi: Concept Publishing Company.

— 1981. Values, Morality and Ethics among the Munda of Chotanagpur, *in* Adrian C. Mayer (ed.), *Culture and Morality: Essays in Honour of Christoph von Fürer-Haimendorf*, Delhi: Oxford University Press.

SAHA, N.K. 1972. *On Role Analysis: A Study of Inter-Personal Relations among the Santals in a West Bengal Village*, Calcutta: Prantik.

SAHAY, K.N. 1977. Tribal Self-Image and Identity, *in* S.C. Dube (ed.), *Tribal Heritage of India, Vol. 1: Ethnicity, Identity and Interaction*, Delhi etc.: Vikas.

SAHU, L.H. 1942. *Hill Tribes of Jeypore*, Cuttack: Servants of India Society.

— 1943. Bhumiya Marriages, *Man in India* 23: 173–4.

— 1952. The Gadabas of Orissa, *Modern Review* 91: 468–70.

— 1953. The Gadabas, *Vanyajati* 2 (2): 61–3.

SANDHWAR, A.N. 1978. *The Korwa of Palamau: A Study of their Society and Economy*, Vienna: Acta Ethnologica et Linguistica 44, Series Indica 9.

SARKAR, G.N. 1919. Birth and Funeral Ceremonies among the Ho, *Journal of the Bihar and Orissa Research Society* 5: 134–42.

SARKAR, S. 1934, 1935. The Malers of the Rajmahal Hills, *Man in India* 14 (3–4): 248–70 and 15 (4): 251–9.

— 1937. The Social Institutions of the Malpahariyas, *Journal of the Asiatic Society of Bengal, Letters* 3: 25–32.

SATPATHY, G. 1963–4a. Gadaba, *Adibasi* 1963–4 (3): 151–6.

— 1963–4b. Parenga, *Adibasi* 1963–4 (3): 165–6.

SCHMIDT, Pater Wilhelm 1906. Die Mon-Khmer-Völker: ein Bindeglied zwischen den Völkern Zentral-Asiens und Austronesiens, *Archiv für Anthropologie* n.s. 5: 59–109.

— 1935. Die Stellung der Munda-Sprachen, *Bulletin of the School of Oriental Studies* 7: 729–38.

SEBEOK, T.A. 1942. An Examination of the Austro-Asiatic Language Family. *Language* 18 (3): 206–17.

SEDLAR, J.W. 1980. *India and the Greek World: A Study in the Transmission of Culture*, Totowa: Rowman and Littlefield.

SEN, B.K. 1955. Notes on the Birhors, *Man in India* 35 (2): 110–18.

SEN, J. 1965. Ethnographic Notes on the Birhors, *Bulletin of the Anthropological Society of India* 14 (1–2): 45–58.

SENGUPTA, S.K. 1966. A Brief Account of Mahali Marriage Customs, *Folk-Lore* 7 (2): 72–83.

— 1968a. The Structure and Composition of Mahali Families, *Bulletin of the Cultural Research Institute* 7 (1–2): 124–36.

— 1968b. Preferential Systems of Marriage of the Mahalis, *Bulletin of the Cultural Research Institute* 7 (3–4): 62–9.

— 1969. *The Portrait of Mahali Economy in Midnapur*, Calcutta: Editions Indian.

— 1970. *The Social Profile of the Mahalis*, Calcutta: K.P. Mukhopadhyay.

SHAFER, Robert 1954. *Ethnography of Ancient India*, Wiesbaden: Otto Harrassowitz.

SHRIVASTAVA, L.N.R. 1957. Munda Eschatology, *Bulletin of the Department of Anthropology, Bihar University*, 1: 66–70.

SIDDIQUI, M.K.A. 1976. The Didayi Kinship System, *Bulletin of the Anthropological Survey of India* 25: 1–8.

SINGH, B. 1977a. Aspects of Kodaku Culture, *in* A.K. Danda (ed.), *Tribal Situation in Northeast Surguja*, Calcutta: Anthropological Survey of India.

— 1977b. Gathering Economy of Kodaku, *in* A.K. Danda (ed.), *Tribal Situation in Northeast Surguja*, Calcutta: Anthropological Survey of India.

— and A.K. DANDA 1986. *The Kodaku of Surguja*, Calcutta: Anthropological Survey of India.

SINGH, J.P. 1980. Changing Patterns of Tribal Government: The Case of the Santals, *Eastern Anthropologist* 33 (3): 221–30.

— and R.D. SINGH 1976. Santals: A Socio-Economic Study, *Indian Geographical Studies Research Bulletin* 6: 33–9.

SINGH, K.S. 1978. The Munda Land System, *in* P. Ponette (ed.), *The Munda World: Hoffmann Commemoration Volume*, Ranchi Catholic Press.

— 1983. *Birsa Munda and his Movement 1874–1901*, Calcutta: Oxford University Press.

SINGH, V.K. 1972. A Socio-Cultural Study of Gadaba, *Vanyajati* 20 (2): 102–8.

SINHA, D.P. 1958a. Cultural Ecology of the Birhor: A Methodological Illustration, *Journal of Social Research* 1 (1): 86–96.

— 1960. Portrait of a Birhor Chief: Biographical Study in Culture Change, *Journal of Social Research* 3 (1): 57–68.

— 1968. *Culture Change in an Inter-Tribal Market*, London: Asia Publishing House.

— 1984. *The Hill Kharia of Purulia*, Calcutta: Anthropological Survey of India.

SINHA, Surajit 1957. The Media and Nature of Hindu-Bhumij Interactions, *Journal of the Asiatic Society of Bengal, Letters* 23 (1): 23–38.

— 1958b. Changes in the Cycle of Festivals in a Bhumij Village, *Journal of Social Research* 1 (1): 24–9.

— 1962. State Formation and Rajput Myth in Tribal India, *Man in India* 42 (1): 35–80.

— 1966. *Ethnic Groups, Villages and Towns of Pargana Barabhum*, Calcutta: Anthropological Survey of India.

—, J. SEN and S. PANCHBHAI 1969. The Concept of Diku among the Tribes of Chotanagpur, *Man in India* 49 (2): 121–38.

SITAPATI, G.V. 1938–9, 1940–1, 1942–3. The Soras and their Country, *Journal of the Andhra Historical Research Society* 12 (2): 57–76, 12 (3): 157–68, 12 (4): 189–207, 13 (2): 113–36 and 14 (1): 1–16.

— 1948–9. The Interpenetration of the Aryan and the Aboriginal Cultures in India with Special Reference to the Soras, *Quarterly Journal of the*

Mythic Society 39: 29–39.

SOMASUNDARAM, A.M. 1949. A Note on the Gadabas of Koraput District, *Man in India* 29 (1): 36–45.

SOMERS, George E. 1977. *The Dynamics of Santal Traditions in a Peasant Society*, Delhi: Abhinav Publications.

SRIVASTAVA, A.R.N. 1976. On the Methodology of Residence Classification, *Eastern Anthropologist* 29 (3): 287–94.

— 1979. Studies on Culture Change in the Tribes of Bihar, *in* L.P. Vidyarthi and M. Jha (eds.), *Growth and Development of Anthropology in Bihar*, Delhi: Classical Publications.

— and K.K. VERMA 1967. Demographic Aspects of Marriage among the Korwa of Palamau, *Journal of Social Research* 10 (1): 53–63.

SRIVASTAVA, L.R.N., A.A.C. LAL and P. LAL 1971. *Identification of Educational Problems of the Saora of Orissa*, Delhi: National Council of Educational Research and Training.

STAMPE, David 1965, 1966. Abstracts of Recent Work in Munda Linguistics, *International Journal of American Linguistics* 1965: 332–41 and 1966: 74–80, 165–6, 390–7.

STANDING, Hilary 1976. 'Munda Religion and Social Structure', London: School of Oriental and African Studies, Ph.D. thesis.

— 1981. Envy and Equality: Some Aspects of Munda Values, *in* Adrian C. Mayer (ed.), *Culture and Morality: Essays in Honour of Christoph von Fürer-Haimendorf*, Delhi: Oxford University Press.

SUBBA RAO, A.V. 1965. Traces of Culture Change among Kathera Gadabas in Andhra Pradesh, *Journal of Social Research* 8 (2): 63–6.

SUBBARAYAN, V. 1948. *Forgotten Sons of India*, Madras: Government Press.

SUGIYAMA, Koichi 1969. *A Study of the Munda Village Life in India*, Tokyo: Tokai University Press.

SURYANARAYANA, M. 1977. 'Marriage, Family and Kinship of the Saoras of Andhra Pradesh', Waltair: Andhra University, Ph.D. thesis.

SZEMÉRENYI, O. 1978. Studies in the Kinship Terminologies of the Indo-European Languages, *Acta Iranica*, 16: 1–240.

TEDESCO, Paul 1943. Sanskrit *milati* 'To Unite', *Language* 19 (1): 1–18.

— 1945. Sanskrit *munda-* 'Shaven', *Journal of the American Oriental Society* 65: 82–98.

THIEME-BRESLAU, Paul 1939. Indische Wörter and Sitten, *Zeitschrift der Deutschen Morgenländischen Gesellschaft* 93: 105–37.

THUSU, K.N., and M. JHA 1972. Clan and Family among the Ollar-Gadba of Koraput (of Orissa), *Eastern Anthropologist* 25 (2); 161–8.

TIEMANN, Günther 1970. The Four-*Got*-Rule among the Jat of Haryana in Northern India, *Anthropos* 65: 166–77.

TOFFIN, Gérard 1986. Review of Serge Bouez, *Réciprocité et hiérarchie: L'Alliance chez les Hos et les Santal de l'Inde, L'Homme* 26 (3): 168–70.

TOPNO, M. 1955. Funeral Rites of the Mundas on the Ranchi Plateau, *Anthropos* 50: 715–34.

— 1978. Spirits in the Life and Belief of the Mundas, *Sevartham* 1978: 5–26.

TOPNO, S. 1970. The Changing Pattern of Munda Personal Names, *Eastern Anthropologist* 23: 171–8.

TRAUTMANN, Thomas R. 1981. *Dravidian Kinship*, Cambridge: Cambridge University Press.

TRIPATHI, B. 1973. *A Portrait of Population*, Cuttack: Census of India.

TROISI, J. 1976. *The Santals: A Classified and Annotated Bibliography*, Delhi: Manohar.

— 1979 [1978] *Tribal Religion: Religious Beliefs and Practices among the Santals*, Delhi: Manohar.

TROMBETTI, A. 1928. I numerali africani e mundapolinesiani, *in* W. Koppers (ed.), *Festschrift Publication d'Hommage offerte au P.W. Schmidt*, Vienna: Mechitharisten Congregations Buchdruckerei.

TURNER, R.L. 1976. *A Comparative Dictionary of the Indo-Aryan Languages*, London: Oxford University Press.

TURNER, Victor W. 1967. Aspects of Saora Ritual and Shamanism: An Approach to the Data of Ritual, *in* A.L. Epstein (ed.), *The Craft of Social Anthropology*, London: Tavistock.

UXBOND, F.A. 1928. *Munda-Magyar-Maori: An Indian Link Between the Antipodes*, London: Luzac & Co.

van der VEEN, K.W. 1973. Marriage and Hierarchy among the Anavil Brahmans of South Gujarat, *Contributions to Indian Sociology* n.s. 7 (1): 36–52.

VERMA, B.B. 1959. Social Organization and Religion among the Sauria Pahariya of Rajmahal (S.P.), *Bulletin of the Bihar Tribal Research Institute* 1 (1): 67–102.

— 1960. Social Organization and Religion among the Mal Pahariyas and the Kumarbhag of Santhal Parganas, *Bulletin of the Bihar Tribal Research Institute* 2 (2), 1–32.

VIDYARTHI, L.P. 1958. Cultural Types in Tribal Bihar, *Journal of Social Research* 1 (1): 75–85.

— 1960. The Birhor (The Little Nomadic Tribe of India), *in* A.F.K. Wallace (ed.), *Men and Cultures*, Philadelphia: University of Pennsylvania Press: 519–25.

— 1963. *The Maler: A Study in Nature-Man-Spirit Complex of a Hill Tribe in Bihar*, Calcutta, etc.: Bookland.

— 1964. *Cultural Contours of Tribal Bihar*, Calcutta: Punthi Pustak.

— and B.K. RAI 1977. *The Tribal Culture of India*, Delhi: Concept Publishing Co.

— and V.S. UPADHYAY 1980. *The Kharia: Then and Now*, Delhi: Concept Publishing Company.

VITEBSKY, Piers 1979. Field Notes (unpublished).

— 1980. Birth, Entity and Responsibility: The Spirit of the Sun in Sora Cosmology, *L'Homme* 20 (1): 47–71.

— 1982. 'Dialogues with the Dead: The Experience of Mortality and its Discussion among the Sora of Central India', London: School of Oriental and African Studies, Ph.D. thesis.

— forthcoming. The Creation of Metaphor in Sora Ritual through Grammatically Parallel Verse Forms, *in* David Stampe (ed.), *Proceedings of the Second International Congress of Austro-Asiatic Linguistics* (1979), Mysore: Central Institute of Indian Languages.

VOEGELIN, C.F., and A.M. VOEGELIN 1966. Languages of the World: Indo-Pacific Fascicule Eight, *Anthropological Linguistics* 8 (4): 1–64.

WILLIAMS, B.J. 1968. The Birhor of India and Some Comments on Band Organization, *in* R.B. Lee and I. de Vore (eds.), *Man the Hunter*, Chicago: Aldine Publishing Company.

YAMADA, Ryuji 1970. *Cultural Formation of the Mundas*, Tokyo: Tokai University Press.

YEATTS, M.W.M. 1931. Madras, *Census of India*, Vol. XIV, Part 1.

ZIDE, A.R.K. 1976. Nominal Combining Forms in Sora and Gorum, *in* Philip Jenner, L.C. Thompson and Stanley Starosta (eds.), *Austro-Asiatic Studies*, Honolulu: University of Hawaii Press, Oceanic Linguistics Special Publications, no. 13 (2 vols.), Vol. 2: 1259–94.

ZIDE, N.H. 1958. Some Korku Kinship Terms in Proto-Munda, *Bulletin of the Tribal Research Institute, Chhindawara* 1: 9–21.

— 1969. Munda and Non-Munda Austro-Asiatic Languages, *in* T.A. Sebeok (ed.), *Current Trends in Linguistics, Vol. 5: South Asia*, Paris and The Hague: Mouton.

— and David STAMPE 1968. The Position of Kharia-Juang in the Munda Family, *in* B. Krishnamurti (ed.), *Studies in Indian Linguistics (Professor M.B. Emeneau Sastripurti Volume)*, Poona and Annamalainagar: Centres of Advanced Study, Deccan College, Poona University and Annamalai University.

ZIDE, N.H., and A.R.K. ZIDE 1976. Proto-Munda Cultural Vocabulary: Evidence for Early Agriculture, *in* Philip Jenner, L.C. Thompson and S. Starosta (eds.), *Austro-Asiatic Studies*, Honolulu: University of Hawaii Press, Oceanic Linguistics Special Publications, no. 13 (2 vols.), Vol. 2: 1295–1334.

— forthcoming. A Linguistic Analysis of some South Munda Kinship Terms, I *in* Jeremy Davidson (ed.), *Papers in Mon-Khmer Linguistics in Honor of H.L. Shorto*.

Index